CHRISTIAN-MARXIST DIALOGUE
IN EASTERN EUROPE

CHRISTIAN-MARXIST DIALOGUE
IN EASTERN EUROPE

PAUL MOJZES

AUGSBURG Publishing House • Minneapolis

This book is dedicated to those who have risked in order to promote the Christian-Marxist dialogue
and
to Elizabeth, Bernard, and Leonard Mojzes, who have endured dislocations so that this book could be written.

CONTENTS

Foreword

Paul Mojzes, the author of this volume, is a unique person. Therefore this is a unique book. Many works have been written in this century about Christianity and Marxism out of many different experiences and points of view. Detached scholarly discussions of comparative ideas have been matched by passionate descriptions of actual encounters. Christian apologists for Marxist Socialism have fought with embittered refugees from Communist tyranny. Dialogue has been played off against encounter, ideology against life experience. In few realms of discourse has the confusion been so great.

Mojzes' uniqueness consists in the fact that he understands all this and transcends it at the same time. Born to a Protestant minister's family in northeast Yugoslavia, he knew in his school days the problem of Christian survival in an atheist dictatorship. He also learned the power and attractiveness of Marxist ideology. As an emigrant from his country, he has never lost a passionate concern for Christian life and witness in that encounter. Rather, he has overlaid it with a broader and deeper scholarship which remains in continual dialogue with both Christians and Marxists from all the countries of Eastern Europe, to whose languages he has access by extension of his childhood mastery of Serbo-Croatian, Hungarian, Russian, and German. There are few scholars with the linguistic tools he possesses to do the job this book has done. There are even fewer whose passionate concern with the subject matter strengthens the objectivity of their insight rather than distorts it. This is the spirit and these are the tools with which Paul Mojzes goes about his work.

The result of all this is a book which almost no one else could have written. It is a large work with an enormous amount of detail. The whole history of Christian-Marxist dialogue in the Communist dominated countries of Eastern Europe is here portrayed. There is much more of it than most of us had realized. It takes a variety of forms, which the author organizes into a typology, and it is the richness and variety of the dialogue which will most impress the reader. Tens of thousands of people who are actively concerned for Christian-Marxist relations, for the study of Marxism in its various expressions, and for relations with the countries of Eastern Europe, will depend on this book as a continuing source and reference.

CHARLES C. WEST
Princeton Theological Seminary

PREFACE:
THE PERSONAL
STAKES IN
THE DIALOGUE

THE PERSPECTIVE OF THIS WORK

The people of the world are in the grip of two major socio-economic ideas regarding human freedom. One—capitalism—maintains that the optimal freedom is reached by the minimal societal interference. The other—socialism—proclaims that maximal liberty is achieved by decisive social engineering and planning. Both have been able to extend the experience of freedom to many people. Conversely, both have shown a tragic ability to crush many who do not adapt to or who oppose the system. Each has its powerful gravitational pull which gives shape to people's lives. However, they also distort many experiences, including the experience of the light of God, just as space distorts or bends light rays. Neither capitalism nor socialism is absolutely true. As each can extend true liberties, they can be said to be relatively true. Believers in each system see their own experience as the true one; the other seems warped. In concrete circumstances one can be better than the other, given certain individual or group references, but neither can rightly claim the possession of absolute truth.

Christianity has no inherent, constant preference for either capitalism or socialism. Capitalism produces mass economic misery in certain parts of the world, with overabundance in

11

others, and exercises a subtle hold on people in the forms of excessive individualism and consumerism. Socialism helps many people from the lower classes but produces political misery and economic shortages and often leads to totalitarianism. Neither capitalism nor socialism provides a unifying, constant principle around which the lives of persons can be successfully integrated. Just as Einstein's theory of relativity provides for a constant in terms of time and space—the speed of light—so Christianity provides a constant through faith in God. It is interesting that so many religious persons refer to God as "Light." The light of God as experienced in faith provides a dependable yet mysterious (meaning full of potentials) criterion which is the integrating principle of the universe. That criterion can be, indeed must be, applied to both capitalism and socialism in order for either of them to be properly interpreted. Human beings may find their Christian (or Jewish) beliefs providing them with the absolute referent by which they are able to judge their relativistic preference for capitalism or socialism.

The encounter and dialogue between the Christian faith and capitalism has lasted for many years. It still needs to take place, perhaps more honestly and intensely than ever before. The encounter and dialogue between Christians and Marxists is of more recent origin and has not yet moved beyond the fledgling stage. This book is an attempt to define and describe this latter encounter in a locality in which Christianity and socialism coexist most intensively, Eastern Europe. Its purpose, then, is to describe and evaluate the encounter with the conviction that this will help Christians (and perhaps also Marxists, but in other ways) in their task of applying their absolute faith to the relative, but no less real, experience of Marxism.

There is, unfortunately, a thread of truth in the statement that both Communists and Christians seek dialogue more in those countries in which they are out of power than in those in which they are in power. The dialogue in Eastern Europe is altogether too strongly influenced by political considerations. Such considerations have prevented the emergence of dialogue in some countries (e.g., Bulgaria and Rumania), obstructed it (e.g., Yugoslavia) or completely eliminated it (e.g., Czechoslovakia). Despite the sharp limitations experienced by both Marxists and Christians who have engaged in dialogue, the Eastern European experience is still of crucial importance because it is there that both coexist on the same terrain and where the Marxist theory is being put into practice by the state apparatus. While Christian-Marxist relations in the rest of the world are not necessarily determined by the encounter in East Europe, the East European situation cannot be overlooked. Therefore the fortunes of the Christian-Marxist dialogue in Eastern Europe are of consequence not only in the respective Eastern European countries, but also elsewhere, where the Eastern European dialogue is bound to be examined in regard to the integrity displayed by both sides.

It is tempting to underestimate or overestimate the impact and the significance of the Eastern European dialogue. Those who look for fireworks, for newsworthy events, for controversial heroes like the dissenters, for spectacular changes in history, may be tempted to undervalue the dialogue. Its proponents, not having taken hardline positions on either end of the spectrum, tend to find few supporters at home or abroad. A Christian participant in the dialogue may be appreciated neither by other Christians nor by Marxists. The same may be the case with Marxist participants. Those who consider Eastern Europe a stagnating, rigid system and see the dialogue as a ray of hope in an otherwise bleak situation may tend to overrate the impact which the dialogue has upon the general conditions of life in socialist countries. The truth is that the protagonists, on the whole, are very courageous people who have a more comprehensive vision of reality than most of the people in their environment, but, like the prophets of old, they are unappreciated and mostly unsuccessful in their own time. A time may come which will praise them for their foresight. This book was intended as an early and somewhat cautious song of praise to the pioneers and participants in this new mode of encounter between Christians and Marxists.

The intention of this book is to provide a comprehensive narrative of the dialogue in East Europe. The introductory chapter of the book offers the setting and describes the perimeters of this project. Chapter 1 indicates the significance of the dialogue within the greater scope of Christian-Marxist relations. Chapters 2 and 3 will recount the history of the dialogue. The remaining chapters (4-7) will deal with the content of the dialogue. The last chapter contains some of the author's conclusions.

Many people had a direct or indirect part in the making of this book. Those who helped in the stage of collecting data, though crucial, are too numerous to mention. Some of them showed courage and dedication in providing data—a matter of considerable importance when dealing with a politically sensitive topic. After the first draft was written several colleagues kindly responded to my invitation to be critical readers. They offered many useful suggestions which were utilized in the process of completing and revising the manuscript. Dr. Charles West, dean of the Princeton Theological Seminary, was the principal reader; his keen observations and expertise in the field influenced my decisions at several junctures. Professors Dr. Albert Rasker of the University of Leiden in Holland, Dr. Rudolf Weiler of the University of Vienna in Austria, Dr. Lucio Lombardo-Radice of the University of Rome in Italy, Dr. James Will of Garrett-Evangelical Theological Seminary in Evanston, all read the first draft and made useful suggestions. Other colleagues read segments of the manuscript. Dr. Jan Milič Lochman of the University of Basel in Switzerland read the sections pertaining to Czechoslovakia; Dr. Mihailo Marković of Belgrade University and University of Pennsylvania, the segments on Yugoslavia; and Dr. Leslie Laszlo of Concordia University in Montreal, the sections on Hungary; and the Rev. Charles Robertson of Bloomington, Indiana, the sections on Poland.

Others have assisted with the stylistic aspects of the work. Here I need to acknowledge my indebtedness to Barbara Peterson and Rosemarie Pucci.

Despite all this help, the responsibility for positions expressed in the book and errors which may have remained in the text are my own.

PERSONAL INVOLVEMENT IN THE ENCOUNTER

In October 1976, standing on the holy ground of the ruined gas chambers and crematoria in Birkenau (Auschwitz), where my grandparents were destroyed with countless individuals as part of the "final solution" by a totalitarian system, I confronted a maze of confused questions and affirmations. The resolves that "it must never happen again" and that mutual cooperation and dialogue are the ways to overcome the tragedies of a hateful past were mixed with questions regarding the value and meaning of human life and the role of individual and collective responsibility for the direction of human history in the face of such unimaginable evil. Nor was it merely a meditation about the past, because the unspeakable terror of Hitler was matched and possibly surpassed by Stalin. Hundreds of thousands, perhaps millions, languished in camps,

prisons, and other inhuman conditions, committed there by
systems extolling human happiness and common welfare, and
acting in the name of a better future.[1] Even today, perhaps to
a lesser degree, many injustices and atrocities continue in both
socialist and nonsocialist societies. Can a handful of Christians
and Marxists, who sought each other out and are still seeking
to dialogue, change anything?

The thread of these tragic events and of Christianity and
Marxism are interwoven in my life too, so that interest in the
encounter is not merely an academic one. My father, a Methodist preacher, was murdered by a fascist camp guard in 1942
before I was of an age to comprehend the enormity of the crime
and the loss. My mother, a pious Christian, soon took over his
responsibility as an ordained minister. Christian values and
the story of salvation enveloped me throughout my childhood.
In the Yugoslav schools after World War II, I was exposed to
a militant and dogmatic Marxism which was coupled with, in
the first postwar decade, what has been euphemistically called
"administrative measures," against the churches and other
real or imaginary opponents of the regime. In the Novi Sad
High School and at Belgrade University Law School, this was
supplemented by a more rational pedagogic approach. The non-
scientific props of my religious education began to crumble,
and soon I not only accepted Marxism as *the* scientific worldview, but I became an active leader in the local People's Youth
movement, well on my way to joining the Communist Party
of Yugoslavia. My church attendance, at this point due almost
entirely to respect and love for my mother, did not, however,
escape the watchful eyes of the Party. It prevented me from
being acceptable for Party membership.

When a series of surprising events enabled me to study in the
United States, where I later decided to stay, two intellectual
and spiritual processes gradually took place. The courses in
religion, which I took out of curiosity, soon attracted me to my
present vocation. They introduced me to a liberal Protestant
interpretation of Christianity which could accommodate both
my search for a respectable scientific and rational approach to
life and my need for meaning and purpose in life supported by
a system of values that demeans neither the individual nor
society. I was also able to see beyond the apparent consistency
of Marxism as I began to question the presuppositions as well
as to see the disastrous consequences of some of the postulates
of dogmatic Marxism. Nevertheless, I have never become an
anti-Communist because I consider all anti-movements futile.

My Christian worldview brings me into conflict with certain Marxist ideals and realities, no less than it brings me into conflict with certain capitalist ideals and practices or even certain Christian ideals and practices. But I rejected the total acceptance or rejection of any system, even of Christianity, which I embrace as my primary context and highest allegiance.

Subsequently my educational concentration became the history of religions in Eastern Europe. Since 1967 I have been able to make annual trips to Eastern Europe, two of which lasted a semester each. Since 1969 nearly every summer I have taught "Religion in East Europe" and "Christian-Marxist Relations" in Graz, Austria, and in 1972 and 1973 I led faculty summer-seminars in Yugoslavia and Eastern Europe. This has brought me into personal contact with many prominent protagonists of the Christian-Marxist dialogue. These contacts were followed by participation in such conferences as the Korčula Summer School in Yugoslavia; the meeting of the Christian Peace Conference in Siófok, Hungary, and Zagorsk, U.S.S.R.; the Paulus-Gesellschaft Symposium in Florence, Italy; and a meeting in Warsaw on the *Ost-Politik* of the Vatican. A conference on disarmament and European security in Torun, Poland, and a World Conference of Religious Leaders for Peace in Moscow followed. All of this enlarged my understanding of the dynamics of the Christian-Marxist relations which fluctuate from year to year and from country to country. It also convinced me that the Eastern European contribution to such dialogue was not being disseminated throughout Eastern Europe, nor elsewhere. A systematic historical approach to Christian-Marxist dialogue was obviously lacking.

Thus I began collecting East European books and journals, taking notes on lectures, taping conversations, and interviewing participants in the dialogue over a period of seven to eight years. In 1975 I was nominated as an exchange scholar to Yugoslavia by the International Research and Exchanges Board upon an invitation from Zagreb University's Institute for Social Research, Section for the Study of Atheism and Religion, to undertake research on the Yugoslav Marxist study of religion. However, the rejection by the Yugoslav authorities of my nomination altered the research project into a broader area of investigation, of which this book is the final product. That semester was spent primarily in Austria in the guest house of the Paulus-Gesellschaft, making inroads into the vastness of literary materials. The vast diversity of Eastern European conditions, secular as well as ecclesiastical, created difficulties. There is no one today who knows equally well the conditions in all Eastern European countries. Fortunately, the country in which the dialogue has shown the greatest variety, Yugoslavia, is also the country most familiar to me.

My involvement in the Christian-Marxist dialogue was not restricted to Europe. In the drastically different circumstances of the United States, I taught courses on this subject at Rosemont College and Villanova University and delivered lectures elsewhere. As the managing editor of the *Journal of Ecumenical Studies*, I committed myself to theoretical and practical ecumenical dialogue, including the Christian-Marxist dialogue, to which the journal devotes consistent, though not major, attention. Of great meaning also was my involvement in Christians Associated for Relationships with Eastern Europe (CAREE). As chairperson of the Christian-Marxist Encounter Task Force of CAREE I was in touch with many in the United States who share interest in this dialogue. Under my coordination, cooperation between CAREE and the Institute of International Understanding with the Institut für Friedensforschung of the University of Vienna and the International Institute for Peace of Vienna culminated in the first conference in which Marxist and Christian thinkers from East and West Europe met with their counterparts from the U.S. The conference took place at Rosemont College in January 1977. Likewise I took active part in the subsequent symposia in Kishinyov, U.S.S.R., in 1978; Stockholm, Sweden, in 1979; and Detroit in 1980. Lecturing on the Christian-Marxist dialogue in Dubrovnik, Yugoslavia, and directing the first two North American Christian-Marxist dialogues, the first at Rosemont in 1978 and the second in Dayton, Ohio, in 1980 completed the theoretico-practical involvement in this dialogue so far.

The opportunity to write the first draft of this book came during a sabbatical leave granted to me by Rosemont College in the spring of 1979. A concurrent fellowship by the Institute for Ecumenical and Cultural Research at Collegeville, Minnesota, provided the ideal setting and stimulus for long periods of uninterrupted research and writing which provides for more consistency in the narrative. Thanks to that opportunity, the idea behind this book became a reality.

STATEMENT OF PURPOSE

No history of the Christian-Marxist dialogue of any Eastern European country, or of the entire region, has been written.[2]

This makes the present task more difficult but also conversely more necessary. It is my purpose to present a comprehensive, almost encyclopedic account of all dialogues which took place from their inception to the present. Since only very few of the protagonists of the dialogue are known in the West or even known to each other, I will present each person's views in an almost anthological fashion. Being aware of the limitations of this approach and the unavoidable repetitiveness which it brings about, I selected this method nevertheless because I intend to make the present work a repository of data which could serve future historians and analysts of the Eastern European scene. Conditions in Eastern Europe are not favorable for the preservation of ideas or the faithful recording of events concerned with the dialogue. Hence I undertook the task of collection and narration.

When faced with the choice of classifying views and presenting them in a condensed form, or of allowing each dialogue participant to speak for himself or herself, I selected the latter approach. The reason is that my primary purpose was not merely to instruct the reader as to the options available in dialogue but to preserve individual viewpoints, some of which would otherwise vanish. The decision of what is of importance must not be allowed to depend on what is accidentally preserved. I intend this book to preserve as much as can be found on this topic at this juncture and allow readers to draw their own conclusions as to which views merit greater attention.

This does not mean that I shrank from utilizing typologies. Whenever a clear opportunity presented itself, I constructed them in order to facilitate understanding. The reader is asked, however, to pay careful attention to the criteria according to which the typology was drawn rather than to apply extraneous criteria which are not applicable to the main issue of the dialogue.

Dialogue, indeed, is the main issue. The occasional detours into other forms of Christian-Marxist relations were undertaken to render more intelligible the problems of dialogue. I decided to describe, analyze, and evaluate the dialogue in Eastern Europe—nothing more. That is the goal of this study.

LIMITATIONS

In a world which is increasingly interdependent it is tempting to reach for a book designed for one purpose in order to find answers to related questions. To attempt to deal with related questions blurs the focus, however. Therefore it is necessary to define at the outset what this study will not deal with.

This is not a study in church-state relations in Eastern Europe, nor is it an exploration in recent church history or religious policies of the respective governments. It is not a philosophico-theological treatise. Elements of all of these are to be found herein, but the major intent is to undertake a historical survey and analysis of the actual dialogue between Christian and Marxist partners which has taken place either in East Europe or by East European participants. It is primarily a scholarly presentation of the Eastern European contributions to the Christian-Marxist dialogue. But insofar as I have Eastern European roots and maintain an active interest in that area, it is also a concrete contribution to that dialogue, with the hope that this work will be one of the stimuli to continued dialogue. The idea for the book and the early research coincided with "the deep freeze" of Eastern European dialogue, but the later stages of research and writing took place in an atmosphere of slow, uneven "thaw." My hope is to make a humble contribution to reinvigoration of the dialogue, but the social realities are the true determinants of the perimeters of the dialogue.

Research on this topic is subject to certain specific difficulties. Conditions in Eastern Europe are even more unfavorable for the collection of material on the dialogue than they are for the collection of materials on church-state relations. It is impossible to collect evenly relevant material in all Eastern European countries. Conditions vary enormously from country to country and from time to time.

In terms of the socioeconomic structure and Marxist inspiration, Eastern Europe is connected with other countries such as Outer Mongolia, North Korea, Cuba, China, and Vietnam. This book will not deal with them. Eastern European countries have certain affinities to each other which do not exist in respect to the non-Eastern European communist countries. Thus, the generalizations and typologies, which may or may not apply to the non-Eastern European countries, have been designated to apply only to Eastern Europe.

Certain direct and indirect links do exist between the dialogue in Eastern and Western Europe. However, this book shall not deal with the Western European dialogue. Only when obvious direct links or dependencies exist between Eastern and Western European dialogues will they be acknowledged, without, however, exploring the Western European segment of the link. This interrelatedness will be most obvious in the case of the Paulus-Gesellschaft dialogues and the International Peace Symposia to which separate sections in this book have been devoted. However, even in these instances clear attention is given only to Eastern European contributions.

Another limitation stems from the extent of the author's experience in various Eastern European countries. While I have been to all Eastern European countries except Albania, I know the situation in some better than in others. Since monographs on the dialogue in any of these countries do not exist, one has to depend on the existing literature which rarely deals explicitly with the dialogue. This material is not always or easily available. Nor are oral sources equally accessible. Consequently a certain unevenness in the depth of the analysis or the scope of the coverage inevitably and regrettably occurs.

AUTHOR'S WORLDVIEW

While the author's biases will be evident to informed readers, it is nevertheless best to admit to the most relevant ones. My primary identification is Christian (United Methodist). I do not hold to the view that a symbiosis of Christianity and Marxism is possible or desirable. I am not a Marxist, nor am I especially attracted to Marxism. I do believe that Marxism has some useful insights and challenges for Christians. I believe in liberal democracy, political and ideological pluralism (in society as well as in the church), and I believe in welfare obligations of the state. I believe in the social responsibility of the individual and the state, which can ultimately lead to maximizing creative freedom for all individuals in society. Yet I do not regard any social system, capitalist, socialist, or some future system yet to emerge, as able to solve all problems; neither has religion been able to solve all problems, despite its promises. There is a self-evident need for change in society; evolutionary change is preferable to revolutionary in those societies where change is not being obstructed or entirely prevented. Yet revolutionary changes, in the sense of real and thorough change of inhumane conditions into humane conditions, are necessary in all societies. The duty of all Christians is to contribute to such substantial altering of evil conditions.

The dogmatic or "orthodox" Marxist version, prevalent in Eastern Europe, is unacceptable to me. The way Marx's ideas are being used to justify totalitarian, exploitive policies is repulsive. It is not easy to avoid the trap of becoming anti-

Marxist when one witnesses and experiences this form of Marxism. But the formalistic, fundamentalistic, dogmatic, frequently barren and authoritarian expressions of Christianity experienced in the same geographic area could easily make one anti-Jesus or anti-Christian. Such forms of Christianity are also unacceptable to me. Yet I do not support excommunications or judgments made on the basis of the popularity or acceptability of one's views. The criterion of authenticity for identification with Christianity or with Marxism will be based here only on the person's or group's own self-mage. If they sincerely believe themselves to be followers of Jesus or Marx, they will be regarded in this book as Christians or Marxists.

Certain expressions of Marxism and Christianity are preferable from my viewpoint. They need not coincide with my own views, though, like most, I find compatibility with my own views more comfortable. A scholar must make a judgment on the basis of compatibility with the main thrust of the founder. Such evaluations will not be avoided. Personal experience has brought me in contact with undogmatic, creative Christians and Marxists who have ideas which do not lead to mutual rejection. It is these Christian and Marxist views, which often do not fit into the mold and are found irritating to their own establishments, that I find more stimulating and, ultimately, more substantially contributing to human welfare. In this respect, differences are welcome and refreshing. These differences, including differences in worldviews, ideologies, and religious orientations, "make for the fullness and richness of life. We should not merely be mutually tolerant, but we should rejoice over our differences, which supply our life with saving tensions." [3] This should be the motto of the Christian-Marxist dialogue.

Since I am a historian of religion and this book aims to provide the history of the dialogue in Eastern Europe, the reader is entitled to a brief statement on the author's philosophy of history. I see both religious and secular history as an arena where human beings exercise their God-given freedom in relating to one another as they strive to live meaningful lives. In this search for both self-expression and community and in their struggle for physical and spiritual survival, people act out choices which may have a range from dire to happy consequences. God's intervention in this arena is felt through those people who are inspired to do God's will as they best understand it. Good deeds on the part of both believers and non-believers bring humanity closer to the reign of God, to the

doing of God's will. Self-serving and destructive actions partially frustrate God's will for humans, but they do not ultimately defeat God's purpose for the universe. It is my unconditional trust that at the basis of the universe there is a source
of purposiveness, goodness, and other important values—God.
In the context of the Christian-Marxist relations, one could
say that those acts which make Christians and Marxists work
for general human benefit are the will of God; those acts which
cause suffering, loss of human dignity and creativity, and crip-
ple individuals and social groups obstruct God's purpose for
humanity.

A historian's task is to describe, to evaluate, to interpret. I
have tried not to impose my philosophy of history on the descriptive portions of this narrative, but have presented the
facts as objectively as I can without withholding my basic
value judgment that dialogue between Christians and Marxists
is better than attempts to destroy or disregard each other.

Auschwitz, Birkenau, and the other sites of the Holocaust
could still become opportunities for a new, better page in
human history. At the end of the first thirty years after these
horrors came into full view, power and exploitation still prevail in both capitalist and socialist countries, despite many
propagandistic claims to the contrary. Many have seen in the
dialogue the hoped-for shift to a new mode of operation between those who differ. While the dialogue has not yet brought
this transformation, hopefully it will be seen in later historical
perspective "as the modest beginning of a radically dialogical
future—and most genuinely new phenomena in history have
quite modest and unspectacular beginnings." [4]

Notes

1. This is not to equate fascism and communism, for the former is
inherently evil in ways in which communism is not. However, certain
forms of communism have drifted into evil practices which cannot be
condoned in the name of a greater future happiness.
2. There is a brief history of the dialogue in Poland written by Stanisław Kowalczyk. See Chapter 3.
3. Arthur Jores in *Schöpfertum und Freiheit* (Munich: Paulus-Gesellschaft, 1968), p. 15. Transl. by Mojzes.
4. Milan Machovec, *A Marxist Looks at Jesus* (Philadelphia: Fortress
Press, 1976), p. 38. Hereafter abbreviated to *AMLJ*.

1

DIALOGUE IN THE CONTEXT OF CHRISTIAN-MARXIST RELATIONS

Christian-Marxist relations in Eastern Europe comprise a great variety of specific forms and attitudes. They range from violent persecutions to dialogue, with many other possibilities, such as cooperation, coexistence, benign mutual neglect, hostile tensions, and conflict. Dialogue is neither the typical nor the original relationship between Christians and Marxists. It is rather a relatively recent development, which has not yet received endorsement by large numbers in either camp. The process has been illustrated in a book by one of the most important initiators and propagators of the dialogue, the French Marxist Roger Garaudy's *From Anathema to Dialogue.*[1] That title captures the transition that took place for some Christians and Marxists. Most, however, justly or unjustly, are still on the level of anathematizing the other.

THE SIGNIFICANCE OF DEFINING THE DIALOGUE

Dialogue is not taken for granted in Eastern Europe—not between churches and religions, not between various interpretations of Marxism, and not in the relationship of Marxists and Christians. Nor is dialogue merely a matter of methodology of

23

the relationship, although that is basically what it is. If it were merely an accepted methodology, then a great deal more attention would have been given to the content or subject matter of dialogue. Curiously, however, the major concern so far has not been to resolve certain theoretical issues between Christians and Marxists, but to determine whether or not to dialogue. Sharply contested are the definitions of dialogue and its goals, as well as the need for it. Naturally, many arguments for and against dialogue will flounder on the definition of dialogue. Thus the question of the nature and purpose of dialogue is of paramount importance in Eastern European Christian-Marxist relations. Instead of this being merely a clarifying methodological issue, it becomes a crucially substantive one.

Greatly variant attitudes toward dialogue can be discerned. Some say dialogue between such diametrically opposed worldviews is impossible. Others are astonished that attempts are made at dialogue when they assume that hostility is the major characteristic of those relations. Still others, including proponents and former participants of the dialogue, say it is now dead. Some view dialogue as an act of betraying one's own position. Others view it as a more modern vehicle of conversion or at least of achieving goals not possible by confrontation.

From such divergent views it is clear that the respective speakers do not share the same definition of dialogue. In the light of alternatives to dialogue it will become clear why dialogue is the most desirable form of relationship between Christians and Marxists. Thus it will be imperative to obtain the best possible definition and to attempt to put it into practice.

ALTERNATIVES TO DIALOGUE

The history of Christian-Marxist encounters is for the most part the history of alternative forms of relating to each other. Dialogue is a recent addition to these alternatives.

Since this book is dedicated to the dialogue, only scant attention will be given to other forms of encounter. Most of the existing literature on Christian-Marxist relations dwell on those alternative forms of encounter rather than on dialogue.[2] Alternatives vary from country to country and from church to church, as well as from one historical period to another.

Prior to the Communist revolution, Christians either disregarded Communists or feared them. In general they were entirely aloof from them. Sometimes they actively supported persecutions or the outlawing of Communist parties. The Com-

munists in the Soviet Union and Eastern Europe did not actively seek Christian cooperation or support. On the whole they
were very critical of the church, though they welcomed the
cooperation of individual Christians or clergy. After the socialist revolution, they persecuted many believers and attempted
to obliterate the churches. (I do not intend to discuss here to
what degree this was a justified or at least understandable
policy in view of the churches' association with the established
order which the revolution disassembled.) The scope and intensity of the persecutions varied from country to country, ranging from unbridled fury to allowing a variety of activities
within the institutional churches. The most violent period of
persecutions ceased after the Communist parties felt sufficiently safe in their ruling position.

Then the tactic changed. Depending on historical circumstances (including the strength of the churches and the party,
the degree to which a church was compromised during Nazi
occupation, and the political traditions of a church) the Communist Party sought control of the churches or a compromise
with them. Sometimes it deescalated the pressures. At other
times it increased them again. These pressures took both legal
and extralegal forms. At a minimum it included antireligious
propaganda.

Even when Communists sought the active cooperation of
churches for some specific measure, the restrictions on the
freedom of religion were never entirely lifted. The most relaxed
and lenient Communist policies still contained the heavy arm
of totalitarian control. Religious people and churches never
became equal partners in cooperative ventures. To a large degree these policies were not directed exclusively at churches
or religious people but were consonant with the totalitarian
regime into which Eastern European socialism evolved.

The response of the churches varied too. Some reacted with
acquiescence; others fought back and saw no possibility for
any kind of adjustment or *modus vivendi*. Some disregarded
the new social system and continued their activities as best as
they could, holding that all social systems are sinful. For them
one persecution was merely substituted for another. This led
to complete separatism and sectarianism. Still others sought
to cooperate and even to extol the new system, but sought no
theoretical dialogue. Smaller groups even attempted to provide
support of the new order with a modicum of critical approach.
They decided that their involvement should not be marred by
constant opposition but rather by affirmation, except when

their conscience was violated. Then they would refuse to cooperate on that specific issue. The latter alternative was the closest to dialogue and historically evolved into dialogue sooner than other alternatives.[3]

The common weakness in all of these alternatives is that at least one party in the relationship attempted to manipulate the other for its own purposes and it did so primarily on the basis of might. One or the other party was placed into its predicament involuntarily and responded not from a position of freedom and integrity but from a position of coercion and dearth of alternatives.

It is self-evident that not all alternatives are equally desirable. The hierarchical order in which one may arrange these, if one had the choice, would differ, depending on the ultimate aim of the group or person. Those desiring the quick demise of the opponent may shirk from coexistence or cooperation because it would seem that it unnecessarily delays such demise. Those bent on survival may prefer cooperation when they are convinced that annihilation of the opponent is impossible.

What characterizes all these relationships is that the other group or person is not perceived or treated as a full partner. In all of these cases the other is not even seen as fully human; only an alienated, reified concept of the other prevails.

CONDITIONS FOR DIALOGUE

Certain external and internal conditions are necessary in order for dialogue to take place. External conditions are historical circumstances which either create a proper climate for the dialogue or make such dialogue difficult or impossible. Internal conditions, on the other hand, are attitudes of the partners which either prevent the relationship from becoming a dialogue or foster it.

The specific external conditions which provided the proper atmosphere for the emergence of the dialogue in the 1960s will be described later. Here some general remarks will suffice. It is clear that a certain degree of freedom for both parties must exist for a dialogue to take place. One cannot be forced to dialogue, nor can one dialogue with "a knife at one's throat." Conditions of outright persecution preclude dialogue. So do conditions of hostile confrontation and propaganda. On the opposite side of the spectrum, the desire to fully conform to the other, based on a false sense of solidarity or unity, can also forestall dialogue.

The "objective" need for dialogue must also exist. Objective needs are those that are not the needs of one or the other partner, which could be labeled as "subjective." Both partners will experience some conditions to which response by one of them alone will not be sufficient to deal adequately with the situation. Roger Garaudy characterized this "objective need" by saying that the human future cannot be created against the believers or without them, and, correspondingly, it cannot be built against Communists or without them.[4] Such recognition of mutual interdependence is a precondition of dialogue.

Of the internal conditions for dialogue the most important ones are to know one's own views well, to believe that truth is attainable, to have respect for the partner, and to consent to the notion that reality is greater than any one person or group can grasp and interpret.[5]

To know one's own views well means to have convictions and to allow one's partner to have convictions. It is not a helpful situation when one or both parties are required to change the content of their own views in order to make dialogue possible. In the course of dialogue one's own views may change if one becomes convinced that the former view was wrong, but this should not lead to utter relativism. The partners also need to examine whether they are using the same terms or concepts for different realities, because this leads to confusion. Should partners enter the dialogue with the purpose of rethinking their entire conceptual framework, the consequences may be to confuse their partner or to alienate themselves from their own milieu. However, some rethinking may be necessary if one takes the search for truth seriously.

Both partners in dialogue need to acknowledge that there is truth and that they are entering into dialogue for the sake of truth. A more comprehensive and more accurate form of truth is being sought. They must agree that there is an objective validity of values which can be recognized. But truth in this sense is neither looking for an exact middle position nor a superficial syncretism. Complete skepticism of any truth-claim will not help the dialogue, nor will the claim that one must never, under any conditions, depart from one's own stated positions. Both partners need to acknowledge the rules of logical thinking as well.

Respect for the partner means the willingness to trust the partner. The authenticity and sincerity of the partner is presupposed. Respect for the partner demands that the partners listen to one another rather than prejudge or depend on third sources for information. The freedom of other humans must be implicitly or explicitly recognized.

Should any partners dogmatically assert that they possess the entire experiential truth and can interpret it infallibly and unchangeably, no dialogue can take place. Only the admission that something can be learned from a partner can enable us to enter subjectively into dialogue. Both sides must be able to acknowledge this.

RATIONALES AND CAUSES OF DIALOGUE

According to a Yugoslav Roman Catholic sociologist of religion, Jakov Jukić, the reason for the dialogue is that "the world is dualistic (antitheistic and antiatheistic) or even pluralistic, but united in responsibility." [6] This responsibility extends into the past. The world as it is today is the product of all past actions, especially the past actions of Christians. Though Christians built that world, they tend to blame others for the way it is. [7] Since no group can build the future alone, there is the need for consultation on the shape of that future as well as common actions.

One of the giants of the Christian-Marxist dialogue of the 1960s was the Czech Marxist philosopher Milan Machovec. For having been the President of the Human Rights Society in Prague and for his openness toward dialogue and his attempts to reinterpret Marxism along the lines which he felt to be truer to its founder, he was removed from his teaching post at Charles University in Prague after the Soviet intervention in Czechoslovakia. Today he lives in forced obscurity in his own country, though he could have opted to teach abroad. He discerned the following preconditions of the dialogue:

1. The existence of common causes, such as the increasing danger of nuclear warfare, superpower domination, and regression in growth.

2. Comparable causes, namely occurrences in both Christianity and Marxism, such as the disappointment of thinking people in both groups with the "mediocrity, the deadness or the compromises of their own institutions." [8] To this one can add the increasing plurality of views in both movements.

3. Specific causes on each side. These emerge either as a result of strengths or weaknesses of either tradition but lead to a greater openness that tends to question the universal and exclusive claim of salvation. [9] Among these may be such events as the breaking up of monolithic structures, important reorien-

tations (e.g., Vatican II or the Twentieth Congress of the Communist Party of the Soviet Union), recognition that a tactical
approach is not working, or that reality has not changed as
one expected, etc.

Several events occurring in the Christian or Marxist camp
need to be singled out as having been most contributive to the
emergence of the dialogue. They prepared the setting for the
start of dialogue in its specific Eastern European forms.

Firstly, polycentrism emerged in Eastern Europe. With disagreements in strategy and interpretation of Marxism and the
pressure of historical realities, it was necessary for Marxists
to develop a variety of postures, not only toward believers but
toward life in general. Political polycentrism is a well-recog-
nized situation in which one can discern the distinct accents
of pro-Soviet Marxism-Leninism, Yugoslav self-managing socialism, Eurocommunism, Maoism, Albanian and Rumanian
anti-Soviet Marxism-Leninism, humanistic Marxism of Czechoslovakia, and so forth.

Less appreciated is the fact that there are today at least two
very distinct and possibly incompatible types of Marxism
which must not be carelessly identified. Distinction must be
made between dogmatic Marxism and humanistic Marxism.
Vast difference between them exists in regard to almost all
matters. This distinction is painfully, though reluctantly, recognized by many Marxists. An increasing number of Marxists
today accept this cleavage. One of the leading Italian Marxist
thinkers, Lucio Lombardo-Radice, stated that he has recently
come to the radical conclusion that Marxism is not one movement but two, one being Marxism-Leninism, i.e., the dogmatic
form of Marxism often called *diamat*,[10] and the other, praxis
or humanistic Marxism.[11]

To simplify the issues, a brief working distinction between
the two can be made. *Diamat* can be described as the rigid acceptance of a certain body of Marxist teachings as interpreted
by Lenin and the official leadership of a respective Communist
party. The praxis or humanistic Marxism flexibly applies certain insights of Marx as a methodology of dealing critically
with present-day problems. This distinction will be crucial in
the chapter dealing with the history of the dialogue because
these two groups of Marxism take different attitudes toward
dialogue. The latter are generally more willing to engage in
dialogue, though examples of the former in dialogue with
Christians are not altogether lacking.

Secondly, the death of Stalin, de-Stalinization, and the Twentieth Congress of the Soviet Communist Party occurred. As long as the Stalinist aberration prevailed over communism no dialogue could take place. Nikita Khrushchev's policies toward religion were not enlightened. In fact, they resulted in more pressure upon the churches in the U.S.S.R. than in the immediate postwar Stalinist period. Yet Khrushchev's open criticism of the cult of Stalin provided the opportunity for the "thaw" which affected all areas of Eastern European life, including the intellectual facets. In this more liberal atmosphere, Marxist thinkers even of the dogmatic bent, but especially of the humanistic orientation, could develop new ideas and express new concerns which would turn out to be more congenial to the Christians. Christians responded more favorably to this new atmosphere and to this new thought than they did to former Stalinistic views and practices.

Thirdly, the Cold War subsided. The resumption of human and intellectual contacts between Eastern and Western Europe, which were always cherished, was made possible again. The first international meetings between Christians and Marxists in Western Europe, in which some Eastern Europeans participated, as will be described in the section on the Paulus-Gesellschaft, would not have been possible without this occurrence. Nor would the limited dissemination of ideas regarding the dialogue have been possible if the Cold War conditions had continued to prevail.

Fourthly, *aggiornamento* and renewal took place not only in the Roman Catholic Church but in most churches. Pope John XXIII and the Second Vatican Council were symbolical of what was taking place in many Christian churches. While a great deal of anticommunism abounded in the churches of both East and West, the leadership of the World Council of Churches and certain Eastern European church leaders continuously advocated a different stance toward communism than toward fascism. They suggested that communism not be demonized and favored a nuanced attitude toward various forms of Marxism.[12] Marxists noted that among Christians there were those who did not harbor invariably hostile attitudes toward them. But a clearer major symbol was needed for what was already happening on a small scale. This took place when the most intransigent and implacable of the churches in respect to communism got a new leader and attempted to renew itself through a council. John XXIII received general acclamation as a humane, caring, and loving person—even by Communists. His posture toward communism, as well as the council's, was different when compared to his predecessors'. He favored dialogue with those who differed—not excommunication or anathematizing. The Roman Catholic Church was coming to terms with the modern world. The Communists knew that if the Roman Catholic Church can come to terms with it, so can the other churches. With a new spirit abounding, a new mutual relationship, called dialogue, could take place.

Fifthly, explicit statements concerning religion and churches, different from previous condemnations, were made by such Marxist leaders as Palmiro Toggliati and Roger Garaudy. Toggliati's speech at the Italian Communist Party Congress at Bergamo in 1963 and his so-called "Yalta Testament" were the first ones in which the head of a Communist Party unambiguously asserted that religion is not to be viewed as an obstacle to progressive politics and that Communists ought to seek avidly Christian cooperation. This was a far cry from former condemnations, though, of course, it did not convince everyone, not even all Communists, that communism has changed its views toward religions.

Taken individually none of these preconditions would have been sufficient to make dialogue possible. However, taken jointly, when these did in fact occur in the late 1950s and early 1960s, they convinced many Christians and Marxists that the time was right for seeking new alternatives for mutual relating. Add to these preconditions a variety of common concerns, such as those provided by Machovec above, and it becomes clear why this new approach was embraced by some leading members on both sides.

MOTIVES AND PURPOSES OF DIALOGUE

The question of the purpose of the dialogue will reemerge in Chapter 5 in the context of defining the dialogue. Here we shall merely single out a few explicit statements of purpose. The best known contemporary Hungarian Marxist philosopher from Budapest, József Lukács, a longtime participant in dialogues at home and abroad, suggested that the purpose of the dialogue is to deal theoretically with certain problems which emerge from the struggles of everyday life. This theoretical discussion should encourage more effective common action. Otherwise the dialogue may degenerate into "mere quibblings or wasteful academic discussions." [13]

The Yugoslav Marxist sociologist Oleg Mandić from Zagreb suggested that the purpose of the dialogue is to help the majority of the world who live in poverty, misery, and hunger. This vast majority of people belongs to some religious organization.[14] Although this is a long process, he suggested that humane people will struggle for improvement through dialogue.

It is obvious that dialogue needs a goal. Purposeless dialogue is hard to envision. The basic question is whether it has a worthy purpose. Under specific historical conditions different purposes may emerge as praiseworthy. The following purposes can be listed: 1) attempts to better grasp the truth, 2) the achievement of greater justice, human freedom, brotherhood or sisterhood, and 3) action for the welfare of all or part of humanity.[15] The purpose of the dialogue should never be to endanger another group, e.g., Muslims, Jews, existentialists, or dissidents. Only a method such as dialogue, which is infused with humility, openness, selflessness, friendship, care, respect, and responsibility (which can all be subsumed under the term *love*), when carried out in conjunction with the search for truth can yield results consonant with the intended goal.[16]

In the East German context, however, the dialogue is often seen in much more restricted terms. It is to serve the purposes of the "antiimperialist struggle." [17] This is meant in an international context. In East Germany, Martin Robbe says:

> Marxists and Christians were in all matters and at all levels of societal life together without discussing their worldviews. Therefore it would be totally misleading and a step backward to bring their mutual relationship to the formula of "dialogue." A "dialogue" may help Marxists and Christians to work together in the struggle against imperialism. In the G.D.R., however, we are much farther along and have greater tasks to fulfill: they work together and carry a joint responsibility in shaping of the developed system of socialism.[18]

Most of those who have participated in the dialogue will find the above an unreasonable restriction of the dialogue. They would include in their list the purposes of getting to know the other, of enriching and completing their own vision, of fighting the dogmatists in their own institutions, of humanizing the world by changing it, and, finally, of making it possible to engage in useful joint actions.[19]

Finally, one must not forget the political motives or purposes of the dialogue. This may be to gain a greater measure of religious or political freedom, to obtain political support for specific measures, especially those unpopular and not easily achievable without the support of the other, and so forth. Sometimes such purposes are not primary and often they are part of the "hidden agenda." When the political motive emerges as the primary purpose of dialogue, the chances are that no real dialogue will take place or that it will soon deteriorate. The political pressures in the context of Christian-Marxist relations play a great role. The fate of the dialogue often depends on oscillating political contingencies.[20]

A PROVISIONAL DEFINITION OF DIALOGUE

A comprehensive discussion of definitions or descriptions of dialogue will be found in Chapter 5. In order to make the chapters on the history of the dialogue (Chapters 3 and 4) intelligible, the following working definition of dialogue is proposed: Dialogue is a way by which persons or groups of different persuasion respectfully and responsibly relate to one another in order to bring about mutual enrichment without removing essential differences between them. Dialogue is both a verbal and attitudinal mutual approach which includes listening, sharing ideas, and working together despite the continued existence of real differences and tensions. Dialogue is a conscious process in which partners seek to give and take without recourse to force or intimidation. Mere cooperation for practical purposes, in which ideological or religious views are of no concern to the partners, is not dialogue. Dialogue comprises both theory and practice. Dialogue is an effort to surmount limits imposed by present social relations. It goes beyond mere influence by another view, even if that influence drastically alters or profoundly shapes one's own world view. Unless two distinct groups or persons—one Christian, the other Marxist, are *consciously* involved as distinct protagonists in the give and take of theory and practice, something other than dialogue is taking place. Being aware of partnership in a joint enterprise is of crucial importance for the definition of dialogue.

Notes

1. New York: Random House, 1968.
2. Among the better books in English are Karl Barth and Johannes Hamel, *How to Serve God in a Marxist Land* (New York: Association Press, 1959); Trevor Beeson, *Discretion and Valour: Religious Conditions in Russia and Eastern Europe* (Glasgow: Collins, 1974); John Bennett, *Christianity and Communism Today* (New York: Association Press, 1960); J. Hutchinson Cockburn, *Religious Freedom in Eastern Europe* (Richmond, Va.: John Knox Press, 1958); Robert Conquest, *Religion in the USSR* (New York: Frederick A. Praeger, Inc., 1968); Martin C. D'Arcy, *Communism and Christianity* (New York: Devon-Adair Co., 1957); Vladimir Gsovsky, *Church and State Behind the Iron Curtain* (New York: Frederick A. Praeger, 1955); Ernest Johnson,

A Vital Encounter: Christianity and Communism (New York: Abingdon Press, 1962); Ralph L. Roy, *Communism and the Churches* (New York: Harcourt, Brace and Co., 1960); Gerhard Simon, *Church, State and Opposition in the U.S.S.R.* (Los Angeles: University of California Press, 1974); Robert Tobias, *Communist-Christian Encounter in East Europe* (Indianapolis: School of Religion Press, 1956); Charles West, *Communism and the Theologians* (London: SCM Press, 1958). In addition there are many books dealing with specific countries, e.g. Ludvik Nemec, *Church and State in Czechoslovakia* (New York: Vantage Press, 1955), or Michael Bourdeaux, *Faith on Trial in Russia* (New York: Harper & Row, 1971), or Stella Alexander, *Church and State in Yugoslavia since 1945* (Cambridge: Cambridge University Press, 1979), as well as many articles.

3. It would lead to too much digression to identify here the specific countries or churches. Critical involvement was practiced most clearly by the Church of the Czech Brethren, and when the attempt at "socialism with a human face" emerged in Czechoslovakia, it soon led to dialogue.

4. Garaudy, pp. 31-32.

5. The first three items are analyzed by Manfred Spieker, *Neomarxismus und Christentum: Zur Problematick des Dialogs* (Munich, Paderborn,Vienna: Verlag Ferdinand Schöningh, 1974), pp. 221-230.

6. Jakov Jukić, *Religija u modernom industrijskom društvu* (Split: Crkva u Svijetu, 1973), p. 7. Jukić is the pseudonym for a prominent Yugoslav sociologist who does not wish to endanger his teaching career by admitting officially to his Roman Catholicism. Transl. by Mojzes.

7. *Ibid.*, pp. 8-9.

8. Machovec, *AMLJ*, p. 19.

9. *Ibid.*

10. *Diamat* is a Soviet coinage of "dialectical materialism" as a science of natural and social developments.

11. Lombardo-Radice's letter to Mojzes, Gianella (Orbetello), Italy, August 25, 1979.

12. Ans. J. van der Bent, *Christians and Communists: An Ecumenical Perspective* (Geneva: World Council of Churches, 1980), *passim.*

13. József Lukács, "Cooperation and Dialogue," in *Varieties of Christian-Marxist Dialogue*, ed. by Paul Mojzes (Philadelphia: Ecumenical Press, 1978), p. 100. (Hereafter *Varieties.*) Originally appeared as a chapter entitled "Dialogue" in Lukács book *Affirmative to Man* [Hungarian title not available] (Budapest: Magvető, 1973).

14. Oleg Mandić in "Discussion" in *Christliche und marxistische Zukunft* (Munich: Paulus-Gesellschaft, n.d.), p. 201.

15. Spieker, p. 228.

16. *Ibid.*

17. Martin Robbe, "Ideologische Aspekte des antiimperialistischen Bundnisses von Marxisten und Christen," in *Deutsche Zeitschrift für Philosophie*, Vol. 19, No. 2 (1971), pp. 179 f. Cited in Spieker, p. 243, f.n. 264.

18. *Ibid.* Transl. by Mojzes.

19. Spieker, pp. 236-240. The relevance of utilizing Spieker's views is that he took serious account of the views of a number of East European thinkers, such as Hromádka, Machovec, G. Lukács, Vogeler, Kołakowski, Schaff, etc.

20. Paul Mojzes, "Politics and the Christian-Marxist Dialogue," in *Journal of Ecumenical Studies*, Vol. 8, No. 1 (1971), pp. 90-94.

2

HISTORY OF THE DIALOGUE (Part 1)

GENERAL CONSIDERATIONS

Many factors stand in the way of an evenhanded historical presentation of the course of the dialogue in Eastern Europe. Unevenness of the existence and availability of sources, different patterns of relating to one another, different political and religious traditions, linguistic obstacles, all stand in the way of access to data to write a definitive history of the dialogue. Nevertheless the aim here is to present as comprehensive a history of the dialogue in Eastern Europe from its inception to the present as possible at this stage. This task will be done on a country-by-country basis, accompanied by a history of the dialogues by the Paulus-Gesellschaft and of the International Peace Symposia, which gathered Christians and Marxists from many countries.

The inception of the dialogue in Eastern Europe is tied fairly closely in a chronological and organized manner to the beginning of the dialogue in Western Europe. There are those who maintain that the dialogue between Christians and Marxists in general "goes back to the very beginning of the Marxist tradition." [1] That is an assertion which has not been documented. If this assertion considers the development of religious socialism as dialogue, it is incorrect. Religious socialism is an autonomous development, though it drew some inspiration from Marx and the Marxists. Inspiration and indebtedness, as was stated earlier, do not constitute dialogue. A few claims have been made that the dialogue started with Lenin and the Russian Orthodox Church in practical matters in 1920 and lasted till 1928 when Stalin decided to liquidate religion.[2] Others trace the beginning of dialogue to the 1930s in France and Italy, when Communist officials invited Roman Catholics to cooperate in light of the increasing threat of fascism and some left-wing Catholics tentatively responded to this "policy of the outstretched hand." [3] Manfred Spieker argued persuasively that the French Communist and Catholic initiatives of the 1930s cannot be taken as the beginning of the dialogue.[4] Certain writings and attitudes of such Marxists as Antonio Gramsci, Palmiro Togliatti, Maurice Thorez, and perhaps even Lenin can be seen as generating a more positive climate for the emergence of dialogue. On the Christian side, Nicholas Berdyaev, Sergej Bulgakov,[5] Hewlett Johnson, Teilhard de Chardin, Francois Mauriac, Emmanuel Mounier, and other French intellectuals, including those gathered around *Terre Nouvelle,* contributed to a more sympathetic understanding of Marxism.

None of those approaches, however, can be considered dialogue as described provisionally in the previous chapter. The actual dialogue began in the 1960s, or at the earliest the 1950s.[6] The preconditions of its commencement were the death of Stalin (1953), the Twentieth Congress of the Communist Party of the Soviet Union (1956), polycentrism among Communist parties, emergence of humanistic Marxism, improved international relations in light of the gradual cessation of the Cold War, the pontificate of John XXIII, the Second Vatican Council, Protestant reluctance of absolute condemnation of communism, and participation of Eastern European churches in the World Council of Churches. These were all factors preparing the ground for dialogue.

The confluence of these various developments changed the political and intellectual atmosphere in Eastern Europe. The immediate postrevolutionary zeal of Marxists had waned, and a more moderate, stable course was undertaken. The Marxist governments realized that religion could not be suppressed in one or two generations, and tacit admissions had to be made that religion would survive in the foreseeable future. Correspondingly, the churches stopped expecting a quick demise of socialist regimes and grudgingly accepted their existence within the context of socialism as a more or less permanent factor in their lives. The climate had changed so much that theologians spoke appreciatively of Marx, Lenin, and their heritage, and Marxists expressed appreciation for Jesus, early Christianity, and, with more difficulty, the contemporary role of Christianity.[7] Coexistence had brought about limited appreciation, which, in turn, opened the gates for dialogue.

To what degree is the Eastern European dialogue indebted to the Western European dialogue? No easy formula can be given. In the years prior to the commencement of the dialogue, Eastern European thinkers, despite their traditional links to Western intellectual life, were forced to wrestle with the problem by themselves since they had found themselves in an unprecedented situation not shared by Western thinkers. But as the Cold War relaxed and the traditional ties were resumed, mutual exploration of experiences and ideas again became possible. The Polish Roman Catholic intellectuals looked for inspiration to the French Catholic intellectuals, who took the Marxist heritage seriously. The Czechoslovak Christian and Marxist thinkers were inspired by Western European, particularly German, participants in the Paulus-Gesellschaft dialogues and eagerly sought both direct contact and discussion of issues raised by thinkers like Rahner, Metz, Bloch, and Garaudy. In turn the speeches and writings of Hromádka, Machovec, Průcha, Gardavský, Lochman, and others were eagerly digested and responded to by Western dialogue partners. To a lesser degree this is evident among the Hungarian and Yugoslav thinkers, though the reciprocal influence upon the West is not as prominent as in the Czech case. To this day the developments of Catholic-Communist relations in Italy are carefully being observed, especially in Yugoslavia, where the protagonists of the dialogue would benefit from a harmonious resolution of Christian-Marxist tensions in Italy, while the opponents of the dialogue would justify their hard-line position if that relationship deteriorated. Thus it is unquestionable that the views of Toggliati, Lombardo-Radice, Girardi, Bloch, Rahner, Garaudy, and others provided a definite challenge and impact on Eastern European thinkers. A careful analysis of that impact will not be attempted here.

Of greater significance for the history of the Eastern European dialogue is the inner dynamic within each country under consideration. There is a frequent temptation to generalize the experience of one country and conclude that the same developments are valid in all others. Many Western thinkers tend to take the case of Czechoslovakia, or to a lesser extent East Germany or Poland, as the representative case which provides them the opportunity to generalize. But the proper avenue for approaching the history of the dialogue is very different.

The first step should be the understanding of the inner dynamic of the general developments of each Eastern European country.[8] One must understand the differences between Eastern European countries in their application of Marxist ideas to their own concrete historical circumstances. Then one can more readily appreciate, for instance, the post-1956 climate in Hungary with the government of János Kádár attempting to introduce "goulash-Communism," and the resulting benefits to Christian-Marxist relations. Or one can see that the Yugoslavian concept of self-governing socialism undoubtedly creates a very particular climate in which Christian-Marxist relations flourish with much local variation. The historical power of Roman Catholicism in Poland provides a clue to the development of the dialogue there, just as understanding of the experiences of the people of Czechoslovakia sheds light on the monumental effort by such thinkers as Machovec, Kalivoda, Gardavský, and others, who are simultaneously the products and producers of the magnificent "effort to buy and to rebuy socialism in freedom and with freedom."[9] Understanding the recent past of Germany and the general East German concern over its relationships with West Germany, as well as its ties to the Soviet Union, places one in the position to understand relations between Christians and Marxists in that country.

Knowledge of the specific circumstances in each country contributes the best clue for understanding the retardation or progress of dialogue in that place.

TYPOLOGY

Rather than choosing an arbitrary order of presenting the history of the dialogue, a typology is suggested here, according to which the dialogues, in various countries as well as the international ones, can form clusters. This provides an easier overview and an understanding of existing alternatives, some of which may be preferable to others. The typology is not a listing of logical possibilities, but of existing realities. The criteria for the typology is *the stance toward dialogue.* Other criteria are possible but they might be more suitable to church-state relations, Christian attitudes toward society, or Marxist political use of churches, none of which is pertinent to our major concern. Since this book deals with dialogue, it is suitable that the attitudes toward dialogue and the mode of its practice be the guiding criterion for the typology.

The problem with using a typology is that it may tend to obscure the real and significant differences which exist from country to country. Many casual, though intelligent, observers are unaware of these differences and tend to lump all Eastern European countries together. The typology might do a disservice if it were to reinforce such views. Nor should one expect clear-cut demarcations between the clusters. Only prevalent attitudes have been taken into consideration in the classification. In individual cases there are encounters which could fall into a category other than the prevalent pattern.

Using, then, the stance toward the dialogue as the criterion for the typology, the following six types are proposed:

TYPES OF DIALOGUE

Type 1: Total absence of dialogue, annihilation of churches by the Communist government:
   Albania

Type 2: Avoidance of dialogue, coexistence and political accommodation leading to limited cooperation:
   U.S.S.R.
   Bulgaria
   Rumania

Type 3: Practical dialogue despite official disclaimers:
   East Germany

Type 4: Carefully managed dialogue in order to facilitate cooperation, recognition of each other's strength:
   Hungary
   Poland
   International Peace Symposia

Type 5: Critical involvement in dialogue, pluralism of expectations and attitudes:
   Czechoslovakia
   Yugoslavia
   Paulus-Gesellschaft International Congresses

Type 6: Dialogical engagement in freedom, unprivileged position of either partner
   Some dialogues of the future?

As will become evident, these types apply only during a limited historical period. Nearly all countries of Eastern Europe went through the phase characterized as Type 1 and Type 2.

Here they are classified according to their most noted pattern, even if that pattern was of limited duration (e.g., Czechoslovakia was in Type 5 only between 1964 and 1968), or that only a minority practices the approach (e.g., Yugoslavia).

We will follow the sequence dictated by the typology rather than chronological order, which is more common in historical presentations. It should therefore be pointed out that the dialogues in Poland, and Czechoslovakia, and by the Paulus-Gesellschaft, were the first ones to take place. A reader attempting to understand the dynamics which brought about the first dialogues may wish to turn to those sections first.

TYPE 1: Total Absence of Dialogue: Annihilation of Churches by the Communist Government

AREA WIDE

Following the pattern established in the Soviet Union in 1917, all of the Eastern European governments established a "postrevolutionary" policy of obliteration of churches (or severe restrictions) and antireligious propaganda. For Christians, it involved a desperate struggle for survival and generally little willingness to accommodate themselves to the new regimes. Practically no one thought of cooperation, except for a handful of clergy who were either sympathetic to the regime or opportunistic, and some Marxists who wanted to use them to infiltrate the churches. The thought of dialogue never occurred. Every Eastern European country, except perhaps Poland and East Germany, went through this phase for a shorter or longer period (usually several years) only to decide that it was not a workable long-range policy. Only Albania made it a permanent policy.

ALBANIA

Official sources in Albania stated in 1967 that no single religious institution continued to exist, thereby making a claim to be the first totally atheist country in the world.[10] While it is impossible to investigate whether private religiosity continues to be nurtured in the hearts of individual Albanians, all reports by Albanian authorities and outside observers confirm that Albania has obliterated its churches and mosques. Since 1945 the Albanian Communist Party leadership never wavered in its goal to destroy religion. There has never been even the most remote inclination toward dialogue inside this most isolationist country in Europe, nor has any Albanian ever attended any of the international dialogues. In respect to the dialogue, to use medical language, there has never been any cardiac or brain wave in evidence.

TYPE 2: Avoidance of Dialogue: Coexistence and Political Accommodation Leading to Limited Cooperation

In three Eastern European countries dialogue is not popular and has not been practiced. Communism and Christianity have come to coexist, sometimes working out the sort of accommodation which led to tolerance, and, in a few instances, to more or less cordial cooperation. These countries are the Soviet Union, Bulgaria, and Rumania. Christian-Marxist relations vary in each of these countries but they share in common their avoidance of engaging in dialogue. In Rumania the churches are showing a greater vitality, and correspondingly there is more official talk of the cooperation of Christians with the state than in those countries where the state has limited political need for the churches.

U.S.S.R.

With the exception of a few recent instances of willingness by Marxists and Christians from the Soviet Union to take part in some international dialogues, the attitude of both Soviet Marxists and Christians toward the dialogue is totally negative. We have already dismissed the idea that dialogue took place in the Soviet Union from 1920-1928.[11] Neither has it ever taken place since then. Howard Parsons, philosopher at the University of Bridgeport, who is generally sympathetic to the Soviet Union, reports interviewing Nikolai Alexander Sergei-yevich, representative of the Committee on Religious Affairs in Novosibirsk. Asked, "Is there dialogue between Marxists and Christians?" Sergeiyevich replied, "No—there are no dialogues and no disputes. There is an atmosphere of discussion and of attentiveness to religion. Discussion sometimes calls forth insults toward believers."[12]

How can there be dialogue, when, for instance, Ilyichov, leader of the propaganda section of the Communist Party, said that liquidation of religion is the *sine qua non* of building socialism?[13] The Soviet Marxist view still typically holds that "religion, as before, is the enemy of truth and reason, and it will stay like this as long as it exists."[14] Even attempts by some Russian Orthodox theologians to be supportive of the Communist government is not appreciated, but scorned.[15]

The church leaders, Russian Orthodox and others, similarly reject the notion of dialogue. Some cooperation may take place on a concrete issue, like defense of the country or peace, but philosophically and theologically there is nothing that the two have to say to one another.[16]

This attitude is substantiated by many people who know the situation in the Soviet Union. The West German Protestant theologian Wieland Zademach, for instance, wrote:

> Everyone who knows Soviet conditions will naturally state that even in Russia there are many willing to begin the dialogue. Mostly among the intellectuals, but also in the wider circles of young people, there is a great inner preparedness for dialogue with other world-views, especially with the religious and Christianity. However, due to the dogmatic course which is ideologically pursued by the official Party now as it has been before, these opportunities for dialogue cannot find an expression in literary form, in publications.[17]

With Christians from abroad the matter is slightly different. Sometimes private dialogue may be had with a progressive Marxist philosopher.[18] On rare occasions a group of Marxist philosophers meet with a group of visiting theologians and engage in open discussion. But these encounters can be more adequately described as chances to inquire about one another, to ask questions and receive answers of an informational nature. Albert Rasker, a Protestant theologian from Leyden, the Netherlands, for instance, reported taking a group of his students to Leningrad and Moscow in 1969 and 1971, where they engaged in such discussion both with philosophy students and literary figures. Professor Charles West of Princeton Theological Seminary reported encounters of a visiting delegation of the National Council of Churches of Christ in the U.S.A. with Soviet Marxists in 1962 and 1974. He noted the difference in the temper of the two meetings. In 1962 there was a somewhat standoffish attitude, but it was clear that some of the members of the Soviet group, for instance, the scholar Yuri Levada, were studying Western religious phenomena with great interest. The 1974 encounter proved to be more open to exploring the constructive aspects of Christian-Marxist relationships. There seemed to be a willingness to admit that Christianity did not face a quick demise and that the present situation called for a modification of their antireligious line. The chance for more informal meetings during the reception following the formal session showed that individual Soviet scholars were quite interested in a give and take with Christians.[19]

The documents of the Moscow International Consultation of Communist and Workers' Parties in 1969 stated that in some countries a united effort of Marxists and of the wider democratic masses of Catholics and believers of other religions is very much needed and that this is a way toward profound social change.[20] But this does not apply to the Soviet Union. However, since that time, cautiously and only in a few carefully selected settings, Soviet Marxists and Christians have participated in international dialogues on peace. Those dialogues will be described later. At this point it suffices to evaluate this participation.

The Soviet participants in these dialogues are mostly highly placed scholars and ecclesiastical leaders. Generally the Russian Orthodox Church is represented by one person, while the Marxist side has four to six members in the delegation. They tend to explain their party or church position intelligently and straightforwardly. Neither side tries to dominate the meetings, but occasionally the Marxists do engage in some surreptitious tactical moves. These mostly consist of a "hidden agenda" of trying to have the entire membership of a symposium support the most recent Soviet foreign policy position in respect to detente or peaceful coexistence. Their formal presentations rarely take into account the contributions of the partner, beyond perhaps a few quotations used in a "proof-text" manner. They speak and they listen. They defend their positions when under attack, but they are never self-critical. They show no independence from their official positions, though they may well represent the more flexible positions within their party or church.

Professor Nikolai Kowalski of the Institute of the International Working-Class Movement of the U.S.S.R. Academy of Sciences in Moscow is one of the most prominent scholars from the Soviet Union to take part in these symposia and one of the moving spirits of this enterprise. He stated that these dialogues are "in accord with the spirit of the times, namely, the desire of the Christians and Marxists to better understand each other, to compare their views and to take account of the position of the other side [sic]." [21] Kowalski saw common concern regarding human destiny in the face of the catastrophic nuclear threat as the main motivating force of this dialogue. On this issue, he believed, the two came closest to one another, as both movements can be seen as champions of peace.[22] Issues of social progress are also of common concern, though the two differ in regard to "the ultimate objectives of that progress." [23] Kowalski expressed the often heard caution that such dialogues must not become occasions for "ideological capitulation" or renouncing of one's position, but rather they are discussions on matters of common concern while firmly adhering to one's own ideas and positions.[24] At this point Kowalski stated his disapproval of the dialogues of the 1960s, conducted by the Paulus-Gesellschaft, without explicitly naming that organization, saying that they collapsed exactly because the protagonists failed to adhere to their "fundamental ideological foundations." [25]

> The current dialogue has quite a few enemies. They would like to prevent any rapprochement, moreover cooperation between the Christians and the Marxists. Their favourite argument alleges that for the Communists the dialogue is merely a "tactical manoeuvre." [26]

He concluded that the dialogue is spreading worldwide despite differences in the Marxist and Christian appraisal of religion, which must not come in the way of their joining forces in the struggle for a better future. For Kowalski, the dialogue is both "important and urgent." [27]

Documents like this are primarily for foreign consumption, though segments of it may well appear in the Soviet mass media. Published materials on the dialogues, however, are not entirely lacking.[28] The tendency of the Soviet press is to describe these meetings as conferences of scholars of different ideological orientations rather than to give them the label of Christian-Marxist dialogues.

The ostensible basis for the present Soviet involvement in dialogue is the platform of the Moscow Congress of the World Peace Council of 1974, where the mechanism proposed for the purpose of advancing peace was a wide, constructive, and democratic dialogue in which viewpoints could be exchanged without pressuring or imposing one's own ideological or political views on others.[29] This platform was preceded by the International Consultation of Communist and Workers' Parties in Moscow in 1969 and more explicitly confirmed at the meeting in East Berlin in 1976, which provided legitimation for the Soviet participants in these dialogues.

The Soviets have become convinced that cooperation for the purpose of achieving peace, which until recently has been restricted only to like-minded fellow-travelers, does not bring the desired ends. They have now become interested in broadening this base, especially as they realize that many people, including the masses of believers, genuinely seek peace. The only mechanism which would enable such cooperation is dialogue, but dialogue under fairly stringent guidelines, lest it shake up their own internal governing structures.

A number of scholars in the Soviet Union have turned their attention to the study of the impact of religion upon social life and to the writings of Western and Third World theologians. Here they found, perhaps to their surprise, that not all religious people uncritically support their own power structure and the *status quo,* and that many, indeed, are eager to advance the cause of peace. Nikolai Kowalski pointed out that believers are motivated by their religious doctrines and their faith in the work for peace.[30] He suggested that the form in which this struggle for peace takes place varies in socialist and capitalist countries. In socialist countries the believers see their task as supporting the progress of their socialist homeland and the victory of peace. In capitalist countries, on the other hand, the faithful struggle against monopolism and take concrete measures against imperialist aggression.[31] While Kowalski believes that religious people show evidence of the increasing influence which has been exerted upon them by the revolutionary workers' movement, he does admit that religion in itself can generate the impulse to work for peace. One suspects that this kind of statement may run afoul of the more dogmatic Marxists in the Soviet Union, who are unwilling to make even the slightest concessions to religion. Kowalski concluded his article by singling out the International Peace Symposia as "examples of a principled ideological discussion . . . between Christians and Marxists."[32]

While the Soviets select a prominent Marxist academician to head their delegation to the peace symposia and to deliver the main paper—people such as Yuri Zamoshkin, Oleg Bykov, Alexander Galkin, Mihail Mtschedlov, and Kowalski—one should not neglect the importance of the director of the International Institute for Peace in Vienna, who is a Russian citizen. His ability and support determines the success of the symposia to a large degree. From 1971 to 1977 this role was conducted with eminent success by the able, sincere, and friendly Vladimir Bruskov, who genuinely believed in the dialogue and cooperation between Christians and Marxists. After Bruskov's retirement this position was filled by the equally affable Lev Burnyashev. Bruskov considered the main purpose of these symposia to be "seeking for ways and meth-

ods of resolving problems of social development under conditions of peaceful coexistence." [33] The goal of these efforts
would be

> to afford to all nations free and independent development under
> their own freely chosen social system; to free people from the
> burdens of armament and to transfer military expenditures to
> provide for the satisfaction of social needs; to create humane
> conditions for work and life.[34]

In the International Peace Symposia the main Marxist position paper was always delivered by a Soviet Marxist. An investigation of those papers shows that they make no reference
to Christian views. The papers deal with war and peace primarily from a socioeconomic and political view and show great
awareness of the U.S.-Soviet antagonism. Cooperation against
aggression and imperialism across ideological lines is being
urged, but no call is being made specifically to Christians,
domestically or internationally. Indeed in this respect they are
monologues addressed, as it were, accidentally to Christians.
They could just as well be addressing Social Democrats or
Buddhists.

In these dialogues the Russian Christians also support the
official Soviet position, though they tend to do so less asser-
tively and often restrict themselves to some innocuous statement on the contribution of their church to world peace. Their
statements also tend to be vague, not directed to anyone in
particular. The relationship between Marxists and Christians
in the Soviet Union is seen by them as good and as following
constitutionally guaranteed guidelines. Here the statements
coincide with the expressed views of Soviet Marxists. Mutual
dialogue is unnecessary, they maintain, since matters have
been developing in cooperation and freedom. While the statements regarding their mutual relations should be taken with
more than a "grain of salt," apparently neither side experiences the need for dialogue.

The exception to this generalization is Archpriest Vitaliy
Borovoy. This dynamic theologian, representative of the Moscow Patriarchate to the World Council of Churches in Geneva,
untiring traveler, vigorous protagonist of Russian Orthodoxy,
called with passion and consummate skill upon the Marxists,
specifically the Soviet Marxists present at the Symposium in
Saltsjöbaden, Sweden, June 1979, to dialogue with Christians,
not only abroad but with the Russian Orthodox Christians in
the Soviet Union. According to him the Soviet Union's achievements are not only Marxist achievements but also Christian

achievements, since Christians, who are more numerous than Marxists in the U.S.S.R., have selflessly contributed to the country's progress. Admitting that some Christians have acted in a reactionary way, he challenged the view that the Russian Orthodox Church is reactionary and called for frequent and open dialogues in the Soviet Union on matters of mutual concern.[35]

Voices like Borovoy's are rarely heard. It is questionable to what extent his call to dialogue in the Soviet Union will even be transmitted to those who make decisions about such matters in this highly centralized society, much less whether it will be heeded. But the call has been made—and made ably. Perhaps if he persists, and if there are others in the churches like him who will raise their voices calling for dialogue, the largest country in the world may yet experience something new, namely the willingness on the part of its dominant Marxist group to engage other groups in the country in dialogue, rather than in propaganda and pressure.

BULGARIA

Relations between Christians and Marxists in Bulgaria resemble very much the relations in the Soviet Union, not only because the Soviet Union is currently Bulgaria's conscious model, but because historically the two countries have had good relations.

The view of Patriarch Kiril of the Bulgarian Orthodox Church sums up the general view regarding dialogue:

> Our dialogue is carried on every day through work and love of our country. Every day we work together for the good of our country. To many persons abroad who have asked me, either provocatively or out of curiosity, whether there is a sincere closeness and cooperation between believers and non-believers in Bulgaria, I have replied in conformity with the reality: "In a family there can be both believing and non-believing members, but they love each other because they are bound together by blood. Our national family is like that. In it there are both non-believers and believers, but all work together for the well-being of our country. This is called creative dialogue which rather significantly differs from the verbal one." [36]

After having gone through a period of very intense persecution of Christians from 1948 to the middle 1950s, the Communists of Bulgaria succeeded in "domesticating" (pacifying) the churches. Officially the churches are cooperative in exchange for the rather narrowly construed "privilege" of freedom to worship.

A certain amount of dialogue takes place between Christians and Marxists in the universities, but none of this is allowed to find its way into print and the Central Committee of the Bulgarian Communist Party still organizes courses on atheism for antireligious lectures.[37]

Very rarely have Bulgarian Marxists or Christians attended the international dialogues. When there, they kept a low profile, generally by restricting themselves to delivering a text prepared in advance supporting whatever is high on the agenda of Soviet foreign policy, showing here again that Bulgaria is the Soviet Union's most dependable satellite.

RUMANIA

The Communist Party of Rumania seems to have more need for the cooperation of Christians, particularly the Rumanian Orthodox Church, than its Soviet and Bulgarian counterparts. Until the 1960s Rumania was a docile Soviet satellite, but since then has carried out a maverick foreign policy aiming at greater national independence. Since it still maintains a very strict authoritarian rule at home, it needs to rally the support of the population along the lines of Rumanian nationalism. The Rumanian Orthodox Church can help splendidly both in respect to the international situation as well as in making the Rumanian majority clearly dominant over the numerous minorities for greater internal cohesion.

The churches in Rumania seem to enjoy a relative prosperity as long as they do not venture outside the restricted confines designated for them.[38] Yet the Rumanian Orthodox Church is too strong a social force to be entirely bypassed in the process of governing the country. Even President Nicolae Ceaucescu's immediate family are practicing Christians. Hence the government is seeking at least tacit cooperation, which it is receiving because a relatively independent Rumania is more to the church's liking than one totally reliant upon the Soviet Union. The churches in Rumania enjoy a distinctly more favorable status than the churches in the Soviet Union.

Within the country no formal, and to our knowledge no informal, Christian-Marxist dialogue has taken place. Rumanian representatives do not frequently attend the International Peace Symposia. When they do, they are more interested in making distinctions between Rumanian and Soviet attitudes toward disarmament (only thinly veiling their distrust of the Soviet positions) than to engage in dialogue with Christians. Only one person, Ileana Marculescu, one of the few liberal

Marxist philosophers in Rumania, attended the Paulus-Gesell-schaft Congress at Marianske Lazňe and read a paper at the World Council of Churches consultation on Christianity and Marxism in Geneva in 1968.[39] In April of 1969 in Paris Marculescu wrote an essay devoted to the memory of the recently deceased Joseph Hromádka, saying that "he has always been at the side of those who suffer, because similar in this respect to the best intellectuals of his country and elsewhere, he has played a losing game, without however losing hope in the future unity of justice and reason in humanity." [40] In the essay she attempted to distinguish between faith and conviction and faith and ideology. Though her definition of faith is unclear, one can conclude that conviction and ideology are different, though they may have touching points and that therefore they are not necessarily mutually exclusive. Her few explicit mentions of the Christian-Marxist dialogue make it evident that she favors this type of encounter. There is no evidence, however, that there are others in Rumania eager to pursue it.

TYPE 3: The Practice of Dialogue Despite Official Disclaimers

EAST GERMANY

This form of the encounter is practiced in only one country, East Germany. East Germany, or as it is officially called, the German Democratic Republic, is the only predominantly Protestant land under Communist control.[41] Bypassing reasons for the phenomenon, let us note that East German Marxists are highly ideologized. "They tend to be more 'Marxists' than Moscow," is a frequent remark.[42] One can discern a similar enthusiasm for ideology and the defense of Soviet positions or those of the Socialist Unity Party of the G.D.R. by some of the Christians who endorse unconditional cooperation with Marxists. Yet the possibility of both cooperation and of sharp conflict is not paralleled in any other Eastern European country.[43] This stems from the fact that on one side there are many Christians in the G.D.R. who have serious reservations about developments in their country and are proceeding cautiously and defensively in their relations with the government and the Marxists. On the other side there is a very vocal group of Christians who have come to wholeheartedly endorse unreserved cooperation with Marxists within the socialist framework. Sandwiched in between are those who are wrestling with the meaning of Christian existence within a socialist country and have come to reject both the escapist and uncritical collaborationist attitude.[44] "Critical solidarity" is the most apt description of the stance of this middle group.

The main clues for understanding the situation in East Germany are to be found in the perplexing situation in which both Marxists and Christians found themselves in post-World War II Germany. Nazism had wrought havoc with the German soul, and the country lay in ruins, defeated by its former victims. Guilt feelings about the past and concern about the future, which seemed totally out of their own control, characterized the immediate postwar period. The need to rebuild from ruins and take care of the fundamental necessities of life made it impossible to give serious thought to questions of ideological or theological speculation. Into leadership positions in the government and the churches came mostly those who had resisted Nazism. Communists, Christians, and others had been incarcerated in concentration camps together.

East Germany was the Soviet occupational zone in which the Soviet authorities quickly moved to impose Communist patterns, though the hope for a reunited Germany was still ostensibly held until the late 1950s, when it became apparent that German unification would not take place in the near future. The precarious situation tended to force East German Marxists into full reliance upon Moscow. Ideologically East Germany's Marxists do not deviate from the orthodox Marxist-Leninist lines, but they do have to make allowances in applying them to a country with strong Christian traditions. A coalition of socialist and communist parties brought about the formation of the Socialist Unity Party (hereafter S.E.D., its formal German abbreviation). A few other parties, including the Christian Democratic Union (hereafter C.D.U.) were allowed to participate in the political life of the country, and still do so. Thus a place was made for formal Christian participation in political life. In the beginning the C.D.U. thought of itself as an independent political party, but it soon became evident that its leadership recognized its own role as following the leadership of the S.E.D., which claimed to know the only correct course for the country by applying the principles of scientific socialism. The C.D.U. has negotiated with the S.E.D. on family law, education, and other items but the party, on the whole, shows no inclination to strike out on its own. Even outside the scope of the C.D.U. some Christians acknowledge the leading role of the S.E.D. and perceive it as God's will[45] The National Front, in which the five political parties interact on local, regional, or state level, is a place where some political activity by Christians takes place, but usually the churches and Christians have to seek alternate ways in which to interact with society. Although the pressures on the churches in East Germany were akin to those in other socialist societies, the Christians tended to make a more pronounced impact on society than they did in many other socialist countries because of the vitality of the churches.

The Christian-Marxist encounter in East Germany can be periodized in the following manner:

1945-1948: Soviet Zone authorities and East German Marxists were very careful in their handling of Christians. They cooperated on rebuilding the country but on the whole no significant interaction took place.[46]

1949-1957: The East German state applied traditional Marxist-Leninist pressures against the churches, and the churches reacted by engaging in *Kirchenkampf,* i.e. a struggle against atheism and state restrictions. External and internal emigration took place. Many Christians fled to the West. Others who did not flee resisted the measures of the state with all available means short of warfare. Some Christians did, however, participate in the strikes and armed resistance in the brief revolt of 1953.

1958-1963: Slow adjustment to a changed situation took place.[47] German unity was now beyond reach. It finally resulted in the separation of the Evangelical Churches of East and West Germany, which had remained as a symbol of German unity. The church started searching for ways of serving in the G.D.R. and gradually started to accept that their existence would be in the context of a socialist society.

1963 to the present. With the advent of detente, the processes of the previous period accelerated. Since church-state relations in the G.D.R. depend to a great deal on the status of the relationship between the two Germanies, whenever the tensions between the two are lessened, the Marxists are less threatened by the idea that the church may be betraying them to their West German rival. The Christians in this period tended to develop creative adaptations not merely to living in a socialist country but to actively, yet critically, cooperating in developing their homeland. The postwar problems were now left behind; the churches, particularly the Federated Evangelical Churches, the largest Protestant body, were organizationally strong and could express themselves clearly on government policies and society. No longer was it a *Volkskirche* which fought the Communists the way it was unable to fight the Nazis, but it became a church in the *diaspora* that was learning how to witness for Christ under circumstances of few, if any, privileges in a society which was more hostile than indifferent toward Christians. Thus Christians tried to adjust to Marxism. In the earlier stages this adjustment consisted of only addressing the Marxists when the Marxists failed to uphold some cherished liberties. At this stage Christians were also willing to listen. Many, however, became aware of the danger of symbiosis, surrender, or antagonism as forms of encounter with Marxism. They prefer a church *in* socialism rather than a church *for* socialism, a church *of* socialism, a church *against* socialism, or a church *alongside* socialism.

One might assume that the form of encounter which the most creative segment of Christians choose is dialogue with Marxists. *De facto* this is probably the case, but there is still an almost total unwillingness to use this term in literature or in public.[48] Likewise the East German Marxists avoid the term. This careful avoidance of the word *dialogue* establishes a need for a separate typology for East Germany, although the situation is not so drastically different from the one in Poland and Hungary, where the word is being cautiously, but openly, used. One suspects that the basic reason for reluctance in using the word itself is the great dependence of East Germany on the Soviet Union, and, since the Soviets do not favor the usage of the word in Christian-Marxist relations, the East German Marxists, who have not distinguished themselves by any sense of identity apart from Soviet Marxist-Leninism, feel they dare not encourage its use at home. It is probably a calculated judgment on the part of East German Marxist leadership that in their quest to obtain cooperation, preferably uncritical cooperation, they stand to lose more in an open dialogue than by making only those concessions which cannot be avoided. Those Christians who most enthusiastically conform to this policy (and there are such fellow-travelers among East German Christians who, perhaps because of opportunism or because of guilt feelings for Christian complicity with Nazis are now bending backwards to show how "progressive" they are) are often rewarded with high government positions, generally higher than in other Eastern European countries.

Thus Christians and Marxists who are part of the establishment generally concur that the ideological differences between Christianity and Marxism should neither be increased nor decreased, nor should such differences be openly discussed because "ideological co-existence is strictly rejected." [49] So, while in matters of ideology no dialogue takes place, in social problems there is an ongoing dialogue. [50] Often Christians voice their disagreements with specific official policies. This was the case with military training in schools, alternate civil service instead of induction in the army, higher education for Christian young people, second-class-citizen status for Christians, and so forth. No group of Christians, with perhaps the exception of Poland, has so consistently raised critical questions in regard to government policies as have the East Germans. Yet, still, those encounters have not been labeled by the partners as dialogue.

Perhaps hesitance to use the term dialogue occurs because the small minority of Christians who are for uncritical cooperation have been more vocal and influential than their number warrants. Among them the most outstanding are Otto Nuschke, Gerald Götting, Emil Fuchs, Gerhard Bassarak, Adolf Niggemeier, Otto Fuchs, Hubertus Guske, and others. This group justifies their rejection of the dialogue by saying that dialogue between Christians and Marxists, especially as it has been carried out by the Paulus-Gesellschaft, has as its aim the weakening of the unity and solidarity of socialist countries. This is a trick of the capitalist world, which chooses this weapon as a desperate measure to slow down the demise of capitalism. Socialism is peace. Peace is the greatest priority of our time. Hence a dedicated Christian must not do anything that goes against the interest of the established socialist states, which are the objective tool in the hand of the working class. Christians and Marxists have different worldviews. Nothing can be done to reconcile these views. But Marxists are the working class leaders. Progressive Christians have the high calling of assisting them in their task of creating a new society. A Christian must not be neutral in respect to socialism, but distinctly partisan, in favor of socialism. [51] Any dissent or disagreement is simply a new form of counter-revolution, the latest form of which is the propaganda drive for religious liberty. [52] Even representatives of this group who have participated in the International Peace Symposia fastidiously avoid the use of the word dialogue. [53]

The government allows Christian political activity in favor of socialism. Individual Christians are allowed to cooperate politically within the various organizations of which they are members, urging a policy of alliance with Marxists, but they are not admitted into membership in the Socialist Unity Party.

The churches are not allowed to have their own political concepts.[54] Accordingly each person must make two separate judgments: religious and political. The religious choice is for or against the church. The political choice is for or against capitalism or socialism. Socialism gives the appearance of being against the church, say Christians in favor of uncritical cooperation, but in actuality it is in conformity with Christian principles. With capitalism the reverse is true.[55] Thus, according to Christians who are sympathetic to socialism, the choice is simple: if one is against capitalism, the cause of most of the world's evils, then one must choose to work actively for socialism.[56] There is no third alternative.

> The government is ready to accept the Church's cooperation and to welcome its declarations of solidarity with the socialist state, but it cannot agree that the church has a critical role vis à vis society or that the Christian faith has anything to offer which has not already been provided by the insights of Marxism. In these circumstances it is unrealistic to expect very much in the way of creative Christian-Marxist dialogue—at least not in public.[57]

Some Christians favoring the East German form of socialism declared that the relationship between Christians and Marxists is "close and confident . . . determined by mutual respect and cooperation." [58] They reject both the choice between Christianity and Marxism, and attempts at syncretism. Many common aims are pointed out, especially similarities in motives for social engagement. Solidarity in one's place of employment and work for the happiness of the neighborhood in a community of cooperation and brotherhood and sisterhood is what binds Marxists and Christians.[59] In practice, by identifying with each other in social involvement, the traditional differences between Christianity and Marxism have been relegated to a secondary plane, according to those willing to cooperate.

Walter Ulbricht, former East German head of State, declared in a speech to selected theologians:

> . . . socialists, communists, and Christians—regardless of their different ideologies—belong together and simply must work together to shape life and society, and to secure peace on this earth. A Christian who takes his humanist and social ideals seriously, who has freed himself of prejudices and the burden of a dead past, should in fact not be able to do otherwise than unite with socialism. And I believe we should always welcome Christians on all state and social levels and treat them with respect and friendship.[60]

But there is another group of Christians who do not wish to cooperate with the Marxists. In their opinion the experience of church complicity with Nazism ought not to be repeated in the case of Communism, which many see as another form of totalitarianism, though not necessarily as odious as the Nazi type. They too maintain that there can be no dialogue between Christians and Marxists.

A group of Catholic priests, for instance, stipulated in a working paper the minimal conditions for dialogue: freedom of opinion, acknowledgment of partnership, and the concrete stipulation of goals for common endeavor, despite the retention of irreconcilable differences. However, they cited the lack of such conditions and compared the "dialogue" to the partnership of a lamb with a wolf. Since the wolf aims to eat the lamb, there is nothing to discuss. Attempts at dialogue would be like the attempt of the lamb to howl like a wolf as its contribution to the dialogue.[61] In 1956 the Catholic Bishop of Meissen, Dr. Otto Spulbeck, stated, "We live in a house, the foundations of which we did not build, the fundamental principles of which we consider false." [62]

Such resistance to cooperation and a staunch opposition to Communism was generally typical of an earlier era and was particularly well symbolized by the Lutheran Bishop Otto Dibelius of Berlin. While few care to copy Dibelius' style, there are many Christians who do not trust the Marxists, just as there are East German Marxists who are equally distrustful of Christians.

From the perspective of the *de facto* dialogue, the most important group is a third group of Christians, who are seeking to work out a mode of Christian existence which will accept joyously its task of witnessing for Christ while supporting many Marxist programs designed to strengthen peace, justice, and equality in the land and in the world. In this diverse group the most prominent representatives are Johannes Hamel, Heino Falcke, Heinrich Gruber, Carl Ordnung, Elizabeth Adler, and Günther Jacobs. Many of the formal statements of the Federation of Evangelical Churches and other churches can likewise be included in this group. The problem facing them has been well stated, in an anonymous essay:

> . . . while we believe that practicing love means keeping up your relationship with someone, we do not mean by this that you have to join in or approve of everything that person does. This provides the fundamental problem that faces the church in the Eastern European social order. How can we give practical

shape to the ideal of remaining in contact with the other side, while not simply joining in everything they do? [63]

People like Falcke and Hamel sought a new orientation in theology and church life, an orientation which sees Communism from the perspective of the affirmation of the gospel and yet maintains the independence and freedom to protest and say no when the affirmation of certain policies becomes impossible. This new orientation has come to affirm that Christians cannot reject the state because it is built on a worldview different from Christian expectations.[64] The church can neither be an underground movement, nor can the state be disobeyed because it is not a "Christian state." In the past Christian opposition to the state in East Germany was so vigorous that the state perceived Christians as hostile to all of its measures. The church witnessed courageously but did not love fervently enough the atheists and Marxists, according to the protagonists of this group.[65] The church lives in the state and should be loyal to the state but it must, ultimately, rest on the apostolic injunction to obey God rather than the state.

One of the first protagonists of conversations between Christians and Marxists was Heinrich Gruber, the representative of the Evangelical Church in Germany with the East German government until 1958. In a letter to J. Hromádka of Czechoslovakia in December 1955, he wrote that it should be possible to have conversations in which the partner is not automatically considered as not being able to be right.[66] He noted that many Christian people in East Germany expect that the political situation will change, while Marxists think the church will wither. He maintained that the Marxists wanted to force the church to face up to the new situation of living in a socialist society. Conversations are now both possible and necessary. Gruber wanted to build bridges between Christians and Marxists rather than be a partisan. In a 1965 meeting of the World Council of Churches in Stockholm, Gruber again urged cooperation between Christians and Marxists and criticized both sides for their weaknesses and reluctance. Marxists should stop considering the Christian faith as superstition, and Christians should not confuse the Confessing Church with bigotry.[67] But Gruber's attempts to bring about *detente* between Christians and Marxists were rejected at that time both by Bishop Dibelius and other church leaders and by the government which retired him from his post, despite his frequent endorsement of general government policies, because he critized the government on its church policies.[68]

Johannes Hamel, former student pastor at the University of Halle and, since 1955 teaching practical theology at the seminary in Naumburg, is probably the best known representative of the new orientation in the West. Hamel's correspondence with Karl Barth received wide attention in the late 1950s.[69] Hamel paid for his popularity and courage by imprisonment and harassment in his own country while sometimes being accused of being "too soft on Communism" in the West. Yet he consistently maintained the need to be neither a fellow traveler to Communism nor a fellow traveler to anti-Communism. His conviction was that the gospel must be proclaimed in the Marxist countries and that the Marxists, like the empires of old, though persecuting the believers, can be tools in God's hands. He, and others, counseled Christians not to flee from East Germany, but he simultaneously requested the government to alleviate problems leading to the flight.[70]

Hamel's major attention was directed to the Christians themselves, to aid them in understanding their new position and their opportunities for serving God and human beings in the new society. The most deadly threat was not the alien society in which Christians found themselves but the failure to see this form of existence as the ground for obedience to God.[71] Christians must acknowledge the good that comes out of Marxist rulers and systems, be grateful for it, and assist in increasing that good.[72]

However, Hamel also addressed himself to the issue of dialogue. By his question as to whether or not there might be a dialogue in East Germany, he implicitly negated the claims that there already is an ongoing dialogue and implicitly denied the claim that dialogue is not necessary because East Germany is on a supposedly higher level of harmonious cooperation. Hamel asserted that the churches were starting to prepare for this dialogue in the 1970s. For the previous 20 years the churches had accepted and respected the new society, occasionally criticizing some of its weaknesses.[73] Now the churches are not questioning whether property should be socialized, but they are asking whether many of the problems in the country can be solved in a better way. Nor do the churches question the leading role of the S.E.D. But they are wondering what should be the limits of power of such leadership and how such power should be concretely exercised.

The first expression of the church's willingness to dialogue was a letter by seven out of the eight leaders of the Federation of Evangelical Churches, written March 1968, about the new

constitution of the G.D.R. They urged that socialism ought to
lead to righteousness by means of legality and by some means
of control of the government's actions.[74] The question now is
whether the S.E.D. Party will see such dialogue as possible
and useful.

Hamel wondered whether the new generation of Christians
and Marxists might be more ready for such dialogue. The new
generation is in overall sympathy with the new regime, but
they want socialism to be actualized more effectively. Thus
dialogue between the young should not be impossible unless
the Party and the cooperationists impose an obligation for
unquestioned support, such as has been mandated as a gradu-
ation requirement for all future clergy by the theological
school of Humbolt University in Berlin. Here the future clergy
was requested to use all religious means in support of socialism
as defined by the officialdom. Such documents, stated **Hamel,**
would be a block to the development of the dialogue.[75]

A third representative of the "critical solidarity" group is
Heino Falcke. According to Falcke, Christ frees the Christians
to be in East Germany for others, not for themselves.[76] He
developed the theological basis for encounter with society by
suggesting that to be for others means to cross barriers between people as a means of implementing the love of Christ.
It also means to feel solidarity with the suffering in the world,
including those within socialism, who suffer, search for meaning, are alienated from themselves, and face the problem of
death.[77] Christians have learned from socialism that freedom
includes liberation from hunger, discrimination, exploitation,
and war. In addition, it means to develop others for the creative fantasy called love.

Yet Christians in East Germany, according to Falcke, need
no "specifically G.D.R. theology" as some have suggested, placing it next to the gospel.[78] Nor should Christians simply take
over socialist analyses and, uncritically, translate them into
theological jargon. Christians must try to understand the
given situation by listening to the word of Christ. They
should not merely *understand* the world but seek to *change* it,
stated Falcke in an obvious application to Christianity of
Marx's catchy phrase regarding the task of philosophy.

Falcke stated that in East Germany many think that Christians ought to allow themselves to be led by Marxist social
teachings. They are in favor of a retreat of religion into the
private sphere while socialism controls the public life, hence
retiring the Christian faith from public life.[79] Christians,

however, cannot allow this, because Christ works everywhere, especially in society, bringing freedom and a sense of direction. Lutherans had talked theologically about the "two kingdoms" (the domains of God and of Caesar), but *in life* they must not retreat to this division, according to Falcke. Christians must not falsify the gospel by agreeing to become the religion of alienation. Instead they must be freeing agents for humanity. Even the socialist society is under the rule of the liberating Christ.[80]

Christian self-understanding and the understanding of the Christian's role in society can be derived neither from the Marxists nor from the anti-Communists, stated Falcke. Christians cannot give a simple "yes" or "no" to their society. Neither opposition in principle nor unquestioned cooperation can be the Christian posture. *Critical cooperation,* encouraged by faith, is the proper pattern. Socialism seeks to free humanity from all alienation and servility. The cross and the resurrection make a Christian critical, not about this goal, but about the exaggerated hopes of achieving this task. Yet the same liberating Christ makes it necessary to support socialist efforts. Thus a Christian can fight injustice and unfreedom in every society, including socialist societies. The Christian is also free to work together with Marxists for justice in the common life. A Christian needs to help in those areas where socialist society has disappointed and where its goals are unclear. Christians believe in a socialism which is capable of improvement.[81]

In conclusion Falcke expressed hope that greater freedom of discussion would be granted in East Germany so that those who think *differently* would not always be accused of thinking *falsely*. The S.E.D. could become more authoritative if it became the author of liberty, and this would help people assume responsibility. Cooperation by all groups in society should be accepted. More freedom of information ought to be granted so that people can make informed decisions. The churches, on the other hand, should assist individuals to work more responsibly in the East German society.

I have found no evidence which would suggest readiness on the part of the Marxist authorities to accept these initiatives for dialogue. Nor have those Marxist thinkers who are not intimately linked with the establishment stepped into the openings for dialogue created by Gruber, Hamel, Falcke, and the like.

Ruth Zander, an East German Christian, offered an analysis of the reasons for the lack of ideological dialogue. On the

Christian side the reasons for the absence of dialogue are these: 1) Christians have difficulty in entering into dialogue with an ideology which makes absolutist claims; 2) they often mistakenly expect conditions in which there will be no atheistic or ideological pressures in society; 3) many are frustrated that the church ceased to be established; 4) Christians quickly see difficulties in socialist daily practice but do not see their own failings; and 5) many of the church members, particularly the older ones, expect that socialism will disappear in due time.[82]

On the Marxist side she pointed out the following reasons for holding back: 1) they subscribe to the notion of no ideological coexistence; 2) Christianity is identified by them with class-society, and they think that dialogue might then indirectly support class society; 3) they do not wish to concede independent strength to Christianity; power is to be vested only in the S.E.D.; 4) initiatives for dialogue by the church are interpreted by them as propaganda; 5) criticism is to be directed only toward those who are nonsocialists; socialism is to be exempt from criticism; and 6) they still adhere to a criticism of religion which follows along nineteenth-century over-simplifications.[83]

Ruth Zander's observations seem to be remarkably on target. She provided an explicit confirmation that the relationship between Christians and Marxists is devoid of dialogue. She also provided some of the reasons for this state of affairs. She emphatically confirmed, however, that important encounters, meetings, and cooperation of individual Marxists and Christians in daily tasks, do take place. And so do encounters of high level representatives of the S.E.D. and church leaders, some of which were described earlier.

The first such meeting took place on February 9, 1961, between Walter Ulbricht, then the leader of the East German government, and a delegation of theologians, church leaders, and laypeople led by Dr. Emil Fuchs. The title given to this meeting was "Christians and Marxists Are Connected Through Common Ideals and Goals." Even more important was the second meeting on March 6, 1978, between Erich Honecker, Ulbricht's successor, with Bishop Albrecht Schönherr, president of the church leadership, at the head of a Christian delegation; here it was declared that the church wants to be the church not *against* but *in* socialism. The latter meeting had a great significance for the social and diaconal work of the churches, which has been appreciated by the East German government. (East Germany is the exception to the general rule in Eastern Europe that social work by the churches is strongly discouraged or even prohibited.) Yet these meetings cannot be labeled as public dialogue because too many earmarks of a true dialogue are lacking. But the high-level meetings between government and church authorities do serve the purpose of building confidence and regulating relations, which provides a healthier atmosphere in which Christian-Marxist relations can take place.

The ambivalence in relations between Christians and Marxists still persists.[84] In the event of some major internal shifts in East Germany, or on account of the changing vicissitudes of the international scene, the relationship between Christians and Marxists could undergo changes which may yet prove to be among the most fruitful in all of Eastern Europe. Potentially East Germany is the most likely candidate to change to Type 4. The conditions for such dialogue do exist, though the government itself does not favor it, seeing little reason why it should retreat from its position of as little discussion as possible, a position which seems to offer security. As long as the reliance upon the Soviet Union by East German Marxists is complete, little is to be expected from the Marxists. The high educational level of both Marxists and Christians is conducive to dialogue. And so is the diversity which exists within the churches. The three groups in East German Christianity —those who do not wish to cooperate, those who practice "critical solidarity," and those who offer uncritical, unqualified support to the Marxists—agree, at this point, on rejecting the formal dialogue. But the group practicing "critical solidarity" has already initiated a *de facto* dialogue. A change in the world political situation (e.g. the impact of the Polish situation in the 1980s) or a substantial strengthening of the "critical solidarity" group could bring about a formal, even exciting dialogue. The churches in East Germany have undergone the most intense critical examination of themselves and their relationship to the socialist state. One may expect that this arduous task will pay off if conditions for formal dialogue should emerge.

Notes

1. Harvey Cox, "The Christian-Marxist Dialogue: What Next," in *Marxism and Christianity*, ed. by Herbert Aptheker (New York: Humanities Press, 1968), p. 15.

2. Tomo Vereš, *Filozofsko-teološki dijalog s Marxom* (Zagreb: Filozovsko-teološki institut Družbe Isusove, 1973), p. 163.

3. The term is credited to Maurice Thores, then General Secretary of the Communist Party of France. Among those who trace the dialogue to the thirties are Kevin Devlin, "The Catholic-Communist Dialogue," in *Problems of Communism* (Washington), Vol. 15, No. 3 (May-June 1966), pp. 32-34, and Vereš, p. 164.

4. Spieker, pp. 230-231.

5. Sergej N. Bulgakov, *Sozialismus im Christentum?* (Göttingen: Vandenhoeck & Ruprecht, 1977).

6. Mojzes, "The Current Status of the Christian-Marxist Dialogue and Suggested Guidelines for Conducting the Dialogue," in *Varieties*, pp. 3-5.

7. Machovec, *AMLJ*, p. 18. On pp. 19 and 217-218 Machovec cites theologians like Hromádka, Helmut Gollwitzer, Karl Rahner, Georges Casalis, Jürgen Moltmann, Giulio Girardi, Albert Rasker, John C. Bennett, Wolf-Dieter Marsch, Johann Metz, and Marxists like Ernst Bloch, Archibald Robertson, Erich Fromm, Roger Garaudy, Branko Bošnjak, Cesare Luporini, Lucio Lombardo-Radice, Konrad Farner, and Vitězslav Gardavský. We should certainly add Machovec to that list, as well as Robert Havemann and József Lukács on the Marxist side, and Charles West and Jan Lochman on the Christian side.

8. These conditions cannot be described in this volume. Prior acquaintance with the history, especially recent history of each country or the area would be helpful for a better grasp of the issue treated in this book. Writings by Zbigniew Brzezinski, Hugh Seton-Watson, Andrew Gyorgy, Robert Lee Wolff, Adam Ulam, and others could be helpful.

9. Lombardo-Radice's letter to author, Gianella (Orbetello), Italy, August 24, 1979.

10. Peter Prifti, "Albania—Towards an Atheist Society," in *Religion and Atheism in the U.S.S.R. and Eastern Europe*, ed. by. Bohdan Bociurkiw and John Strong (Toronto: University of Toronto Press, 1975), p. 388.

11. Asserted by Vereš, p. 163. Contrary evidence is overwhelming. It should suffice to refer to Robert Tobias, *Communist-Christian Encounter in East Europe* (Indianapolis: School of Religion Press, 1956), pp. 9-118.

12. Parsons, *Christianity in the Soviet Union* (New York: AIMS, 1972), p. 40.

13. Andrija Krešić, *Kraljevstvo božje i komunizam* (Belgrade: Institut za madjunarodni radnički pokret, 1975), p. 28.

14. V. I. Garadža and A. D. Suhov, "Predgovor," in *Nauka i teologija u XX veku.* S Ruskog preveli B. Savić i M. Ignjatović, (Belgrade: Gradina, 1973), p. 5. Transl. by Mojzes.

15. I. G. Ivanov, "Savremena teološka interpretacija religiozne slike sveta," in *ibid.*, p. 133.

16. The author has heard the late Metropolitan Nikodim of Leningrad and Archbishop Vladimir of Tula and Beleev make such statements.

17. Wieland Zademach, *Marxistischer Atheismus und die biblische Botschaft von der Rechtfertigung des Gottlosen* (Düsseldorf: Patmos Verlag, 1973), p. 75. Transl. by Mojzes.

18. Interview with Silvin Eiletz, S.J., November 29, 1979, at Mondsee, Austria.

19. Information from letter of Rasker to author, Oegstgeest, Holland, August 10, 1979, and West to author, Princeton, August 8, 1979.

20. Elisabeth Leska, "Die Dokumentation L. N. Mitrochins über den Dialog der Marxisten und Christen," (unpublished mimeographed semi-

nar paper submitted at the Catholic Theological Faculty, University of Vienna, Winter 1975/76).

21. Kowalski, "The Marxists' Approach to a Dialogue with the Christians," photocopied statement prepared for a press conference at Saltsjöbaden, Sweden, June 1979, numbered 1ML0/0 14297, p. 1.

22. *Ibid.*, p. 2.

23. *Ibid.*

24. *Ibid.*

25. *Ibid.*

26. *Ibid.*

27. *Ibid.*

28. E. g. D. Atamali and Yu. Denisov, "Razoruzheniye: Mneniye Marksistov i Hristian," *Mirovaya Ekonomika i Mezhdunarodniye Otnosheniya* (Moscow), No. 12 (1978), pp. 111-113.

29. Oleg S. Harhardin, "Principi i formi sotrudnichestva mirolyubivoy obshchestvenosti," in *Obshchestvenost' i problemy voiny i mira*, (Moscow: "Mezhdunarodniye Otnosheniya," 1978), p. 80.

30. Nikolai A. Kowalski, "Religioznyie sily v dvizhenyii za mir," in *Obshchestvenost' i problemy voiny i mira*, p. 251.

31. *Ibid.*

32. *Ibid.*, p. 262. Transl. by Mojzes.

33. Vladimir S. Bruskov, "Mezhdunarodnii institut mira v Vene," in *Obshchestvenost' i problemy voiny i mira*, p. 402. Transl. by Mojzes.

34. *Ibid.*

35. This was the gist of his frequent remarks as remembered by this author.

36. From *Slaviani* (March, 1969), pp. 18-19, quoted in Marin Pundeff, "Church-State Relations in Bulgaria Under Communism," in *Religion and Atheism in the U.S.S.R. and Eastern Europe*, p. 342.

37. Trevor Beeson, *Discretion and Valour* (Glasgow: Collins—Fontana Books, 1974), p. 298. Beeson's book is the most reliable single volume on the position of Christians in Eastern Europe.

38. There have been cases of overt persecution even in recent years, especially for such groups as Baptists who may not adhere to the numerous restrictions.

39. Her paper "Dogmatism and Integrity" was published in *The Christian-Marxist Dialogue*, Paul Oestreicher (ed.), (New York: Macmillan Co., 1969), pp. 204-211. This paper does not deal explicitly with the dialogue but advocates flexibility and integrity rather than dogmatism in Marxist thought.

40. Marculescu, "Faith and Conviction," in *Communio Viatorum* (Prague), Vol. 12, No. 3 (Fall 1969), p. 107.

41. Predominantly Lutheran, organized into three Lutheran "territorial churches" and into five Federated Evangelical Churches (which contain also Calvinistic congregations). Eight percent of the population is Roman Catholic. About one percent belongs to the "free churches" (Methodist, Baptist, etc.).

42. Interview with Rudolf Weiler, December 12, 1975, in Vienna.

43. Beeson, p. 170.

44. Bé Ruys, "Vorwort" in *Stimmen aus der Kirche in der DDR*, ed. by Bé Ruys (Zurich: EVZ-Verlag, 1967), p. 8.

45. E.g. Bruno Schottstädt of the Gossner Mission, Berlin, G.D.R., at the "Symposium on Anabaptist and East European Expressions of Marxism," Elkhart, Indiana, November 24, 1980.

46. Sam Dahlgren, *Das Verhältnis von Staat und Kirche in der DDR* (Uppsala: CWK Gleerups Förlag, 1972), pp. 14ff.

47. "Votum des Theologisches Ausschusses der Evangelischen Kirche der Union, beschlossen am 17, Juli 1973," in *Zum politischen Auftrag der christlichen Gemeinde* (Barmen II), (Gütersloh: Verlaghaus Gerd Mohn, 1975), p. 13.

48. Ruth Zander, "Dem Marxismus begegnen," in *Denkpause im Dialog,* ed. by Michael Mildenberger (Frankfurt A/M: Verlag Otto Lembeck, 1978), p. 39.

49. Johannes Huhn, "Die Existenz der Christen im Socialismus, insbesondere in der D.D.R.," in *Internationale Dialog Zeitschrift,* Vol. 7, No. 4 (1974), p. 344. Transl. by Mojzes.

50. Bruno Schottstädt, "Dialogue Between Christians and Marxists in My Country Today" (photocopied theses), January 23, 1980.

51. Gerhard Bassarak, "Konvergenztheorie in der Theologie?" in *Christen und Revolution: Konvergenz und Theologie* (Köln: Paul-Rugestein, 1971), p. 15. Peter Weiss, "Parteihnahme für den Sozialismus," in *Blick in Unsere Presse* (Berlin), 1975, pp. 35-36. Gerald Götting, "Bewahrung im Dienst am Nächsten und am Frieden," in *Blick in Unsere Presse,* 1977, pp. 31-39. Helmut Fritzsche, "Zur Zukunft der Kirche," in *ibid.,* pp. 56-58.

52. Herbert Trebs, "Wider den Geist der Lüge," in *ibid.,* p. 54.

53. Adolf Niggemeier, "Friedliche Koexistenz und Friedenserziehung," in *ibid.,* pp. 40-46.

54. Huhn, p. 344.

55. *Ibid.,* p. 345.

56. Bassarak, pp. 15-17.

57. Beeson, p. 186.

58. Adolf Niggemeier, "Christian and Marxist Cooperation in the G.D.R.," in *Varieties,* p. 109.

59. Gerald Götting, *Christliche Mitverantwortung in Sozialismus* (Berlin: Union Verlag, 1965), p. 110 cited in Krešić, p. 118.

60. Quoted in George H. Brand, "The Status of Religion in the German Democratic Republic," in *Religion and Atheism in the U.S.S.R. and Eastern Europe,* p. 268.

61. Wolfgang Knauft, "Die katholische Kirche in der DDR 1954-1976," in *Stimmen der Zeit* (Freiburg), Vol. 102, No. 2 (February 1977), p. 99.

62. *Ibid.* Transl. by Mojzes.

63. Elizabeth Adler (ed.), *Here for a Reason: Christian Voices in a Communist State,* transl. by Leslie Seifert (New York: The Macmillan Company, 1964), p. 110.

64. Adler, p. 41. Cited from "An Interpretation of the Barmen II Thesis for the Church in the D.D.R."

65. *Ibid.,* p. 47.

66. Dahlgren, p. 131.

67. *Ibid.,* p. 133.

68. *Ibid.,* p. 135.

69. Karl Barth and Johannes Hamel, *How to Serve God in a Marxist Land* (New York: Association Press, 1959).

70. Hamel, "Wahrnehmung gesellschaftlicher Verantwortung durch die evangelischen Kirchen in Deutschland—ein Rückblick," in Alfred Burgsmüller (ed.), *Zur politischen Auftrag der christlichen Gemeinde (Barmen II),* (Gütersloh: Verlagshaus Gerd Mohn, 1974), p. 28.

71. *Ibid.,* pp. 28-29.

72. Barth and Hamel, p. 120.

73. Hamel, "Wahrnehmung . . . ," p. 30.

74. *Ibid.*, p. 31.

75. *Ibid.*, pp. 32-33.

76. Falcke, "Christus befreit—darum Kirche für andere," in *Zum politischen Auftrag der christlichen Gemeinde (Barmen II)*, p. 217.

77. *Ibid.*, p. 219.

78. *Ibid.*, p. 224.

79. *Ibid.*, p. 225.

80. *Ibid.*, p. 226.

81. *Ibid.*, p. 227.

82. Zander, pp. 39-41.

83. *Ibid.*, p. 42.

84. Wolfgang J. Koschnik, "Church and State in East Germany," *Church and State*, Vol. 30, No. 1 (January 1977), p. 14.

3

HISTORY OF THE DIALOGUE (Part 2)

TYPE 4: Carefully Managed Dialogue in Order to Facilitate Cooperation: Recognition of Each Other's Strength

This type of dialogue is characterized by caution in order to improve relations and cooperation between Marxists and Christians. This is usually done not out of conviction that dialogue is desirable in and of itself but out of necessity. Each side recognizes that under present circumstances it cannot achieve its aims without taking the other side seriously. Since neither is willing to collaborate blindly, the dialogue is seen as a vehicle which can clarify mute points and facilitate cooperation. Hungary and Poland are two nations which, somewhat differently, utilize this method. Currently they share the reputation of being the most liberal nations inside the Soviet bloc (which does not include Yugoslavia). The Peace Symposia are international in make-up and differ significantly in regard to the manner in which the dialogue takes place. But the criterion used to determine the typology shows that they belong more to this group than to Type 5.

HUNGARY

There is a distinct difference in the manner in which the majority Catholic Church (about 70 percent of the population), and the Protestant churches, primarily the Hungarian Reformed and the Lutheran (about 20 and 5 percent of the population respectively) relate to the Marxist state. In the initial period after the Communist takeover the leadership of the Roman Catholic Church strenuously opposed the changes introduced by the government. This conflict was symbolized by the stance of József Cardinal Mindszenty. While the initial stage of the conflict was marked by outspoken opposition to the new regime and political trials against the clergy, it soon changed to a quiet resistance and lower profile. Only since 1971 have the relations between the Roman Catholic Church and the state improved.

In the Reformed and Lutheran churches a sharp split occurred between opponents of and sympathizers with the new order. With not so gentle government intervention, the sympathizers of the regime quickly seized the top ecclesiastical positions and led the Protestant church leadership into a posture of overt cooperation with the government. The leader of this movement was the theologian Albert Bereczky, later bishop of the Hungarian Reformed Church. He played an analogous role to Hromádka, whose fame he never reached, but whose reputation for controversy he shared. Though suspected by many, he appears to have been a man of integrity who acted out of sincere convictions. This was not the case of all of his colleagues, in particular of János Péter, who sometimes sinisterly wrought havoc in the churches serving Caesar more than God. During the 1956 revolt many of the cooperators were forced by their constituency to resign only to be reinstated by government pressure after the revolt was crushed. This leadership (consisting mainly of bishops Albert Bereczky, János Péter, Tibor Bartha, and much later Károly Tóth on the Reformed side, and Lutheran bishops Lajos Vetö and Zoltán Káldy) developed lines of close cooperation with little or no critical ingredient in their approach.[1]

A sharp struggle between church and state dragged on from 1947 to 1955. The churches resisted the ever-increasing restrictions which were being imposed by the state which, even by the admission of its own spokesperson, used excessively harsh methods in the struggle which they labeled as "class struggle."[2] This process included the crassest sorts of interference in the internal life of the church, such as trials of church leaders like the Lutheran Bishop Lajos Ordás, József Cardinal Mindszenty, and others, and terror of various sorts, some of which came to a gradual end only during the process of de-Stalinization.

During the Hungarian revolt of 1956 a brief period of no restrictions ensued. Many of the churches used this time to get rid of the unwanted changes. With the crushing of the revolt by means of Soviet troop interventions, the imposed government of János Kádár tightened the reigns and reimposed both the restrictions and most of the ousted leaders. But somewhat surprisingly, the government of János Kádár was able to gradually ease the restrictions. The Hungarian churches felt it to be to their advantage to support the process of liberalization, which gradually brought about the "normalization" of relations between a government that saw the advantage of cooperation and churches which learned to live with some restrictions.

It was this atmosphere of gradual relaxation which prevailed in Hungary when the Christian-Marxist dialogue started outside of it. As the situation in Hungary stabilized, the government allowed some Hungarians to involve themselves in this dialogue by attending the Paulus-Gesellschaft congresses. One of these was the Catholic theologian, András Szennay from Budapest, who started contributing important articles on the nature of dialogue and its role for the church after Vatican II.[3] Of all the Hungarian writers he presented by far the finest theoretical understanding of the meaning of dialogue, which, according to him, included also dialogue on ideological or philosophical issues. In this respect, however, he has few followers in Hungary, as most Hungarian participants in the dialogue tend to prefer the discussion of practical issues.

The Hungarian Marxists were eager to make it clear that improvement of relations between church and state was not to be confused with ideological relativism. Already after the conclusion of the 1964 agreement between the Vatican and Hungary a Marxist author wrote:

> . . . from the conclusion of the agreement, of course, it does not follow that we would approve if one should confuse the good relations between the believing builders of socialism with the peaceful coexistence of religion and Marxism, with the dissolution of their ideological antagonism. On the contrary: exactly in order that the Catholic masses could participate with growing activity in the constructive work which aims also at assuring their welfare, it is necessary to debate their views: to help their further development in the direction of socialism. To help them also combat the religious limitations of their ideas.[4]

On the Marxist side, after a protracted struggle between the dogmatic Marxists and liberal Marxists and with the aid of suitable political developments in the later years of the Kádár regime, the liberal view gained ascendancy. The most open of the Marxist scholars was the philosopher József Lukács of the Eötvös Lorand University of Budapest. Since the 1960s he had shown a keen interest in dialogue with Christians. He disagreed with the suggestions made by András Szennay, that the common task of Marxists and Christians is joint acquisition of intellectual truths as they explore the questions of meaning of life, right and wrong, and other theoretical questions.[5] Instead he agreed with Professor István Király that in regard to those questions only polemics can take place. However, the proper aim of the dialogue is to seek ways to improve the cooperation between Christians and Marxists. In order to facilitate this cooperation, which started before the emergence of the dialogue, theoretical discussion may be undertaken, leading ultimately to better understanding and improved cooperation.[6] Accordingly,

> . . . dialogue has been transformed into practice, but this practice needs discussion again, or it needs a particular type of dialogue. Based on agreement on the most decisive questions, tolerant and consistent dialogue has been and is always demanded.[7]

Lukács then explained that the agreement has to be on building a socialist society. This dialogue is needed for the sake of the "objective interest of the people, and the interest of humankind." [8]

Here lies the clue to the fundamental characteristic of all dialogues of this type. It stems from the Marxist discovery that in some instances they cannot go it alone. Hence they are willing to make pragmatic arrangements, including dialogue, if this is required to bring the arrangement about. But the dialogue is to be carried out carefully with only official representatives of the Communist Party and with no theoretical departures from "orthodox" Marxism. Some concessions may be made to Christians on account of the dialogue, but they are rarely invited to join in shaping the destiny of the country, and then only in times of crisis. Only if Christians are "progressive" (do not question the ultimate aims of Marxists), are they welcome to dialogue. Changes in basic postures are not expected.

A Marxist, of course, will never expect from Christianity that it would become revolutionary, even though today there are millions of Christians who become revolutionaries due to the dictates of their conscience. But if Christians become better acquainted with Marxist aims (and Marxists, too, should get acquainted more deeply with Christianity), they will very often find some moral or social statements which, they might think, Christians themselves could have asserted *mutatis mutandis.*[9]

Lukács optimistically expected that Christians will find much in Marxism or socialism which they could approve of or embrace and thereby the two would advance human progress.

A confirmation of Lukács' attitudes, which are held in high esteem in government circles, came in an article by György Aczél, deputy prime minister and member of the Political Committee of the Hungarian Worker's Party. This article was of great political significance for the religious situation in Hungary not only because of its highly placed source but also because of its conciliatory tone.

Aczél stated that dialogue "has a clarifying and fruitful effect on the socialist national unity" and that it is the best approach to differences and ideological problems.[10] The international situation brings about the obligation to cooperate across ideological, political, and economic lines of difference. In the churches the progressive churchmen gained an upper hand. For a while "sectarian distrust, dogmatism, and the personality cult [reference to the rule of Mátyás Rákosi and Stalinism] tended to confuse within the party the political struggle against reactionaries with the ideological struggle against religion." [11] The "counter-revolution" of 1956 brought a great strain in mutual relations but it subsequently became possible to unite the people. Hungarian unity is thus "dialectical unity in diversity where ideological hegemony is held by Marxism-Leninism." [12] The church people in Hungary know that Marxist goals would not only benefit people in Hungary but that they are harmonious with their own faith.

For a Marxist, dialogue is not only a way to understand one another better but a way to disseminate Marxist scientific ideology outside the party.[13] Ideological indifference cannot be tolerated. Clear ideological commitment makes the dialogue more honest. Ideological differences do not preclude cooperation. Cooperation can take place in 1) working places where many Christians work for socialism, 2) church-state relations through dialogue of officials, and 3) in respect to ideas, where despite differences there may be common assent to concrete

notions such as "thou shalt not steal or kill." The two may
come closer to one another in search of higher moral goals.[14]

The policy of the Kádár government is a paraphrase of the
Gospels: "Who is not against Marxists is with them." [15] Marxists realize that they will coexist with Christians for a long
time. The contemporary world requires both to respond to the
burning questions of the day.

> The ideological confrontation hinders the practical union of
> communists and Christianity only if in the meantime they lose
> sight of the great, common historical goals which are deter-
> mined by the current national and international social relations
> under the shadow of the danger of thermonuclear war.[16]

One should assume that the reply to Aczél was the result of
considerable deliberation. It was penned by the Roman Catholic Bishop of Pécs, József Cserháti. He observed, and by repeating Aczél's words underscored these elements in Aczél's
article, that the churches were invited to share responsibility
for the cultural and material progress of the Hungarian people in order to achieve national unity and national rapprochement.[17] For Catholics, too, the central issues are human beings,
the future, and the new society. He found that Aczél proposed
a new start, a searching together for "possibilities, conditions,
and real purposes of the solutions offered." [18] He noted that
the Hungarian Marxists and Christians share as values the
happiness of the Hungarian people: "the church, maintaining
its own way of seeing the world, wishes to contribute the
deliberate cooperation of the faithful in the service of the
common good under socialism." [19]

In the opinion of Cserháti the 1960s dialogues in the West
aimed to talk others into concessions and therefore failed.
The real purpose of the dialogue is to bring about ideological
interaction between two unmeltable ideologies in order to contribute toward general human progress. He noted that Aczél
invited more than loyalty and service of community by Christians, asking them to endorse the Marxist-Leninist analysis of
political, economic, and cultural matters, urging Christians to
incorporate these into their own views. Cserháti seemed to be
stopping short of accepting this demand. He was pleased by
some of the positive things Aczél pointed out in the religious
history of Hungary, but said,

> . . . we have to describe such an evaluation as very useful, al-
> though we do not consider it satisfactory because it does not
> refer to essential requirements like recognition of the value of

religion and acceptance of its community-creating moral effects.[20]

Cserháti then listed Christian demands in dialogue: 1) the domination of Marxists in society should not be based on power hunger but only for the sake of human well-being. 2) administrative interferences, which still take place, should be removed; 3) Marxists should stop treating Christians as second-class citizens; 4) freedom of religious instruction should be provided; this is still a problem; 5) the needs and rights of the people, personal dignity, and personal freedom of conscience should be respected; 6) pluralism and wider democracy is demanded; and, 7) the independent, intrinsic value of individuals and groups should be respected.[21]

It should be pointed out that Bishop Cserháti has written very ably and persuasively in the journal *Vigilia* on the need for dialogue already in 1975.[22] In these articles Cserháti emphatically acknowledged the achievements of Hungarian socialism and praised the Marxists for their good work. But he also aimed to show that the Hungarian Catholic Church has consistently served the people. In these articles he was critical of the failures of the church and maintained that the church has gone through important changes in abandoning its feudalistic character and becoming a servant church. He maintained that serving the needs of Hungary is identical with being a good Christian. The bishop seems to show no critical distance between nation and Christianity. Yet it should be simultaneously admitted that along with praises for Marxist achievements in Hungary he was concerned about the suffering of the people due to the Marxist excesses committed in the name of progress. His main intention seems to be the establishment of the church as a partner rather than an obstacle in the growth and development of present-day Hungary as a pluralistic society built by both Marxists and Christians.

Cserháti's well-publicized views apparently brought no overt reaction from Marxists. Perhaps the absence of comments means a tacit recognition of the integrity of Cserháti's position. It may not be as pleasant, but it probably commands more respect even by opponents than the position of those Christian leaders who, for the sake of privileges for their churches, will eschew any public criticism of their society, vying with the most obedient *aparatchiks* (bureaucrats) in expressions of loyalty which stress unanimity. In the exchange between Aczél and Cserháti there may be the seeds of a more open, critical dialogical relationship than generally practiced at this stage.

Much will still need to be done to convince the partner of sincerity, a task difficult but possible in present-day Hungary.

The state visit of János Kádár to Pope Paul VI in the spring of 1977 was interpreted both by authorities and by church leaders as a sign that dialogue is possible even on the highest level. Imre Miklós, president of the Council for Religious Affairs, stated both his dedication to dialogue, domestic and international, and his approval of the particular style of dialogue promoted by József Lukács.[23] This is a hopeful sign for the future because Lukács is a humane, thoughtful, agreeable, cooperative, and sensitive individual. Should his influence remain strong, the dialogue in Hungary may increasingly become open and critical.

POLAND

Conditions of the Christian-Marxist dialogue in Poland are so unique that the study of them is likely to produce, as it has produced for this writer, some surprising results. At the very outset one is confronted with contradictory claims about the existence of the dialogue. Some Poles maintain that there is no dialogue in their country but only mutual accommodations, saying that neither Marxists nor Christians are fascinated by theory but are mostly interested in practical solutions to daily problems.[24] Others maintain that Poland is the sole Eastern European country where genuine dialogue is being practiced.[25] While the claim that it is the only real dialogue in a socialist country is not well founded, the unavoidable conclusion is that, indeed, a great deal of genuine dialogue is taking place. Not only is it taking place, but Poland provides the earliest instance of Christian-Marxist dialogue in the world! This comes as a surprise because heretofore my conclusions, as well as other researchers, have pointed to Italy, France, Czechoslovakia, and the Paulus-Gesellschaft dialogues as the earliest instances, dating back to 1964.[26] It is now obvious that the dialogue started in Poland as early as 1956, but certainly by 1962 it reached a developed form. However, the Poles did not announce these dialogues with great fanfare to the international community, and thus their pioneering efforts were known largely only to themselves. This may well be the place, then, to draw attention to this distinctive quality of quiet pioneering in a difficult endeavor. Poland provides for the world not merely an interesting encounter, the experience of which now influences world Christianity through the election of the Polish Karol Cardinal Woytiła as Pope John Paul II, but also the single longest sustained experience of dialogue. While the example of the Polish dialogue may not shine brilliantly in the sky, its light is like that of a reliable and persistent orientation star which is increasingly being noticed by the world community.

What are some of the peculiarities of the Polish situation which produced an early and lasting dialogue? The most prominent feature is the role of Catholicism in the national life of Poland throughout the millenium of the existence of the Polish state. The Roman Catholic Church has a phenomenal influence which permeates so many aspects of Polish life that Polish Marxists have had to take the Catholic power seriously from the very outset of their rule. Not surprisingly, some Marxists have remarked jokingly that Poland is, in fact, a kingdom in which Stefan Cardinal Wyszyński is the king. This influence of the primate of the Catholic church is not merely personal or symbolic opposition to a form of government which many Catholic Poles do not cherish, but it has historical roots. From the early days of the Polish kingdom it was the practice for the primate of the church to be the *interrex* during an *interregnum*. This right to be the viceroy when Poland had no king was the traditional basis from which the head of the church addressed the people and the government in matters of great national importance with well-founded authority and confidence. The historical experience of Poland was that the Roman Catholic Church stood faithfully by the people through all times of crisis. Thus Polish patriotism became closely identified with Catholicism. Through its age-long struggle with Orthodox Russia and Protestant Prussia, Catholicism became a pronounced national trait. This loyalty of the church to the nation and vice versa persisted into the most recent times. The Polish Marxists, upon coming to power in 1948, were unable to accuse the churches of collaborating with the Nazis during World War II, for the opposite was in evidence since thousands of priests died in concentration camps and in resistance activities. During that period there were many instances of cooperation between Christians and Marxists in their common struggle against the Nazis.

The power of the Catholic church is so great that, although separation of church and state is constitutionally affirmed and largely accepted, in reality no clear-cut separation exists. This church exerts such influence that even many communists are under its sway.[27] Communism is viewed by many Poles as a socioeconomic system rather than a philosophical interpretation of the world, and consequently not many are interested in theoretical questions. Many members of the Polish United Workers' Party are believers, and the majority of these are open practitioners as well. No wonder, then, that there is no statement in the Polish United Workers' Party statutes requiring members of the party to be atheists or materialists. It would have restricted the growth of the party. For many such people, it is a "schizophrenic existence," bringing together their private religious belief and their socioeconomic life imbued with Marxist inspiration.

Another important characteristic of Polish Catholicism is its scope and nature. Catholicism in Poland is a mass phenomenon. So many Poles are Catholic (about 90 percent) that being Polish and being Catholic are almost synonymous. Polish Catholicism does not only have large numbers, it is also comprehensive, in the manner religion used to be in the Middle Ages. It touches all strata of the population. It touches many aspects of individual and communal life, and it does so effortlessly and unself-consciously. Watching Polish Catholic religiosity leads the outside observer to compare it with pre-Enlightenment Christianity, as deeply rooted among people as life itself.

All these factors tend to affect Christian-Marxist relationships. The periodization of these relationships, as in other Eastern European countries, depends heavily on the political events which largely determine those relations.[28] Four distinct stages of the dialogue are discernible:

1. Polemical discussions (1944-1948)
2. Absence of dialogue; minimal coexistence (1949-1956)
3. Spontaneous and mass dialogue (1956)
4. Constructive dialogue (1957—present) [29]

The fourth stage itself is longer than the previous three and is not uniform. This might suggest the need to divide it, but the nature of the changes during this stage are not qualitative but quantitative. They are oscillations in the degree of intensity in which the constructive dialogue is taking place. The dialogue has become livelier since about 1970.

A survey of events in the four stages with emphasis on the latter two stages follows.

1. The period from 1944 to 1948 was the period of a coalition government of the non-Marxist and Marxist parties. During this time polemics between Christians and Marxists took place mostly in the press. Carrying out the polemics were primarily the leading Roman Catholic periodical, *Tygodnik Powszechny* from Krakow, and Marxist periodicals *Odrodzenie*

and *Kuźnica*. Jan Piwowarczyk, editor of *Tygodnik Powzsech-ny*, initiated the discussion with a series of articles on Marxist philosophy, sociology, and ethics.[30] Stefan Żołkiewski replied in *Odrodzenie*, and Adam Schaff did so in *Kuźnica*. Piwowar-czyk took on Schaff to carry on the discussion which was po-lemical but calm and factual.[31] Marxism and Christianity were seen as mutually exclusive philosophies.

Another round of discussion took place when Marxists Jan Koff, Adam Ważyk, and Artur Sandauer labeled Christianity "fideism," charging that it takes no social responsibility. This was challenged by Jerzy Turowicz, then editor of *Tygodnik Powzsechny*, who proclaimed a Christian personalism and, in turn, denied the possibility of Marxist humanism. Then in 1948 the Rev. Kazimierz Kłosak wrote a book, *Materializm dialektyczny* [*Dialectical Materialism*]. A methodological cri-tique of Kłosak's book was written by the Marxist philosopher Lezsek Kołakowski.

These are examples of what transpired during the period when there was still a free exchange of ideas. The negative aspect of this polemic was that neither side noticed much that was positive in the other's views. Even when common elements were detected, they were criticized. The positive aspect of the polemics was that the ideological contradictions were clearly noticed, that an analysis of each other's view was being under-taken, and that each side defended its own view.[32] One should add that during this time a battle took place between Marxists and their political opponents in which the churches could have gotten deeply enmeshed, but church leaders wisely avoided involvement, thus preparing the ground for a reconciling, pastoral role in the national life. The opportunity for engag-ing in genuine dialogue during this stage of relationship was missed.

2. From 1949 to 1956 no dialogue took place. A very trou-bled political period ensued after the Marxist takeover, a period which was characterized by Stalinist repression. It found Christians struggling for their rights and for their exis-tence. Many Christians did not agree with the political changes in the country. It was a period of attempted subjugation of the churches and their struggle for survival, though the Polish bishops concluded an unprecedented agreement with the gov-ernment in 1950 without the Vatican's blessing. Under those conditions dialogue was unthinkable.

3. In 1956, during the anti-Stalinistic Polish uprising and the introduction of the liberal Polish regime of Władisław

Gomułka, several spontaneous dialogues took place. Students in the department of philosophy at Warsaw University, as well as at the Catholic University of Lublin, organized spontaneous dialogues. In January the two faculties organized a scholarly session about the social function of philosophy and, in April, another one on the notion of matter. They also compared Marxist and Christian humanism, and while they gave recognition to each other's humanism, they saw no common goals or ways and perceived opposition to one another.[33] There were also debates among writers in *Tygodnik Powszechny* and the Marxist *Po Prostu* and *Argumenty* in 1957 about Christian-Marxist cooperation, tolerance, and the role of religion and humanism.[34] They displayed misunderstanding and animosity, yet recognized the necessity of such contacts.

The lively and spontaneous dialogues, many of which took place between 1956 and 1958, were described by Kowalczyk as chaotic, hasty, superficial, and unproductive of concrete results, but their psychosocial effect was dramatic. It showed that the situation during the Stalinist period need not be normative for Christian-Marxist relations and that dialogue is possible.

4. The stage from 1957 to the present has been labeled *constructive dialogue*. Several contributing factors brought about this stage. On the Christian side it was the prudent ecclesiastical position over against the state. This stand was led by the Roman Catholic hierarchy and by the Polish Ecumenical Council, representing the Orthodox and Protestant churches, as well as by Roman Catholic lay groups, Znak, Pax, and the Christian Social Association.[35]

The formal founding of Znak dates to 1956, but its roots go back to the group of Catholic intellectuals gathered around the periodical *Znak* and the weekly *Tygodnik Powzsechny* in Krakow. They are dedicated to church renewal. While the Catholic hierarchy does not embrace Znak enthusiastically on account of the hierarchy's concern with presenting a united front toward the world, which internal criticism by Znak members tends to weaken, there is an oscillating relationship between Znak and the hierarchy. The Znak group, which since 1956 has five parliamentary deputies in the *Sejm* [Parliament], tends to present to the government both a supportive and a critical stance. Among the organized Catholic lay groups, the Znak circle is the most independent of the government line. While socialism in Poland is accepted as a *fait accompli,* some members are critical of the form in which socialism operates and have expressed their views publicly. Thus, for instance, the

Znak deputy, Stanisław Stomma, lost his position in the *Sejm* because he first abstained and then did not support the new Polish Constitution of 1978. Znak is now split over this and similar issues into two separate groups.[36]

The Pax Association was founded around the weekly *Dziś i Jutro* and the daily *Słowo Powszechne* in 1945. It too has five deputies in the *Sejm*. Its orientation is pro government, while its relationships with the hierarchy are so poor that the hierarchy forbade the priests to be involved with Pax. Pax espouses the sort of socialism that is being promoted at any given time by the government and differs from the Marxists only in metaphysics. Many suspect strong governmental influences in Pax's program and activities.[37] But in recent years Pax seems to be striking a more independent stance and basing its position on the social teachings of the church, and the variety of views which characterize its members has come more visibly to the surface. They tend to support the Solidarity Workers' Movement, as do the Znak groups.

The Christian Social Association was founded in 1957 by people splitting off from Pax who desired a more balanced attitude toward the government. They have two members in the *Sejm* and publish a series of journals, among which are *Za i Przeciw, Novum, Hejnał Mariacki* and the *Information Bulletin* (in English, French, and German). They accept socialism in Poland as the *de facto* system without showing excessive enthusiasm.[38] They attempt to nurture a good relationship with the hierarchy, which does not react enthusiastically.

All of these groups tend to gather many of the prominent Catholic intelligentsia and provide for them a forum of expression both through their active press and through clubs, where likely discussion takes place on a variety of topics. This is in addition to the limited political activity allowed to these associations. This gives an arena for channeling the energies of some Catholic intellectuals. One should remember that these political and intellectual activities always take place within the constraints of government-tolerated activities. Their press and publication, like all publications in Poland, were carefully censored and self-censored.[39] Sometimes the more outspoken and independent articles written by the editors are not allowed to appear in their own journals but have to be published clandestinely by the *samizdat* or published abroad and smuggled in.

Another significant factor is the existence of strong Christian educational institutions, the Catholic University of Lublin and the several theological academies. The faculty and students in these institutions have been able to maintain the kind of intellectual activity which keeps the Christian option attractive and to provide well-educated leaders for the dialogue.

On the Marxist side, contributing to the emergence of dialogue were two prominent philosophers who did not involve themselves directly in the dialogue, but contributed to opening new vistas in Marxist philosophy. They were Adam Schaff and his former student Lezsek Kołakowski. Schaff, a philosopher at Warsaw University, became interested in the young Marx's understanding of the human being and of freedom. This culminated in his book *Marxism and the Human Individual.*[40] He had been considered in the 1950s and 1960s the most significant party theoretician. His new views found a very receptive audience, although these views were increasingly dangerous from the perspective of the party bureaucracy. He had already shown interest in a practical Christian-Marxist dialogue when, in the name of the Institute of Philosophy and Sociology of the Polish Academy of Sciences, he initiated with Catholic scholars a joint project on the History of Medieval Philosophy, tapping the monastic library resources. This met with a good deal of mistrust on part of both the Party and the monasteries, but they worked out a unique cooperation in which over 15,000 manuscripts were read, catalogued, and described with no conflicts between two groups of scholars.[41] With Schaff's involvement in the Paulus-Gesellschaft's meeting in Cologne, 1964,[42] and his philosophical emphasis on human freedom of each individual as the core of Marxism, as well as for political reasons, he was eventually dismissed from Central Committee membership, but was never expelled from the party. He still enjoys a reputation as a great international scholar, but has become marginalized in terms of political influence.

Lezsek Kołakowski placed a similar emphasis on the exploration of freedom. More than Schaff, he studied religious phenomena, pointing out how sometimes dissenting or even "heretical" views made their way into the established churches. Undoubtedly his own unorthodox views and his criticisms of Stalinism became the rallying point of many young Marxist intellectuals. This increasingly brought him into conflict with the Party. In 1966 he was expelled from the Party. Two years later he lost his teaching position and was forced to move to the West.[43] Kołakowski's studies of Marxist humanism and the alienation and transcendence of reason continue to exert some influence, though (except in dissident circles) this has been diminished since his departure from Poland.[44]

Discussions took a more organized form in 1960 and by 1962 reached a form which can be recognized as the inception of the kind of sophisticated encounter that can be described as the dialogical stage of the encounter. Some articles showing openness toward this possibility were published in 1960 in *Znak* and the Marxist periodical *Argumenty*. Students from several universities organized a philosophical discussion at Zakopane in September 1960, which, while not labeled a Christian-Marxist dialogue, nevertheless had representatives of both present and interacting with each other.[45]

In 1962 the dialogue started in earnest, apparently preceding the impulses toward dialogue manifested at the Second Vatican Council, impulses which are often credited by Catholics as giving them the inspiration to enter the dialogue. The dialogue was started by Tadeusz Mazowiecki, editor of the influential Catholic monthly *Więź*. He first wrote "Kredowe kolo" ("Chalk Circle") and "Perspektywy dialogu" ("Prospects for Dialogue").[46] He urged that it is necessary to go beyond mere tolerance in order to see the strengths and weakness of the other and to engage in constant interaction. He maintained that Catholicism is too integral to Poland to be "ghettoized" and neglected. The dialogue should not be mere propaganda and apologetics. Marxists should notice the progress which Christianity has been making in recent years. Mazowiecki asked whether Marxists should not take advantage of the opportunity to dialogue with those who stand for progress.

The reply came in *Argumenty* from Tadeusz Mrówczyński, who urged Marxists to respond to a qualitatively improved Catholicism. The entire system of thought should be engaged in dialogue rather than merely a few fragments thereof. More restrained replies came from the pens of Janina Zakrzewska and Paweł Beylin, who thought that issues of worldview ought not to be included in such dialogue. To this, Mazowiecki replied that issues of worldview are essential if one is to reach intelligent solutions on other matters.[47] It should be noted that these articles dealt with the method of dialogue rather than a specific subject matter, which seems to be the first step in all dialogues. Since dialogue is a novel approach, it is imperative that some understanding be reached as to what is meant by this new method of encountering the other. The Polish practice of 1962 showed that certain groups among Catholics and Marxists were willing to embrace this new way of dealing with each other, though the theory of the dialogue had not yet been appropriated by either of their worldwide constituencies.

An international confirmation that the dialogue was taking place came in 1962 when Jacek Woźniakowski of the Znak circle spoke at a meeting on atheism held in Paris, informing those present about dialogue in Poland.[48]

During the following year the dialogue was continued. Janusz Zabłocki, who had become editor of *Więź*, carried out a dialogue with the Marxist professor of philosophy Tadeusz Jaroszewski, who was destined to rise to high positions within the Polish United Workers' Party and the government. Zabłocki discussed the personalistic philosophy of the French Catholic thinker Emmanuel Mounier, showing how it opens new vistas for Catholic engagement in changing the world and how Catholics are able to embrace some non-Catholic thinking. He suggested that Polish Catholicism is at a crossroads. In his reply entitled "Propozycja dialogu" ("A Proposal for Dialogue"), Jaroszewski stated that Mounier's views form an interesting challenge to Marxists.[49] At this point, Jaroszewski advised against ideological dialogue, a view which he was to change later, but proposed practical social issues.

Practical social issues did become the subject of meetings on cooperation between believers and nonbelievers in 1964, as the Polish Catholics picked up some of the Vatican II themes on relationships between believers and nonbelievers. But by 1965 more theoretical issues started emerging. Thus a discussion about the French Jesuit theologian, Teilhard de Chardin, took place between some representatives of the Pax organization (M. Tazbir, M. Roztworowski, M. Wrzeszcz, and Z. Czajkowski) and the Marxists (T. Mrówczyński, W. Mysłek, T. Jaroszewski, and J. Ladosz). Their papers were published in book form in 1970, entitled *Dialog i współdzialnie (Dialogue and Cooperation)*.[50] The writers emphasized ideological and political cooperation, but not doctrinal dialogue.

In 1967 several Poles traveled to Marianske Lazňe, Czechoslovakia, in order to participate in the International Christian-Marxist dialogue.[51] This was reported in some of the Polish press.[52] But there is no evidence that this international symposium gave the direct impulse to domestic Polish dialogue that it did in Czechoslovakia and Yugoslavia.

By 1967 dialogue had become so well domesticated in Poland that it assumed wider proportions from that year onward.[53] The Marxist journal *Zeszyty Argumentów* devoted a number of articles to discussing Christian theologians. Jan Guranowski explored the thought of the revolutionary Italian Salesian priest Giulio Girardi, while Tadeusz Płuźański analyzed the thought of the French Jesuit Jean Yves Calvez, whose thesis that both atheism and religion are difficult to verify empirically was challenged by Płużański. Articles by several foreign Marxists were also included in the publishing schedule: those of Inga Kuchanova (U.S.S.R.), rejecting ideological compromise as well as monolithism but advocating dialogue; Luciano Gruppi (Italy), advocating common approaches on the basis of shared values; and György Lukács (Hungary), advocating dialogue in the name of effective understanding and action.[54] A radio program on the prospects of dialogue in which Guranowski and Jaroszewski participated was also printed in *Zeszyty Argumentów.*[55]

Stefan Moysa, S.J., a professor of theology at the Jesuit Seminary in Warsaw, stated in 1968 that dialogue is a positive development in the life of the Polish people and that dialogue reflected the theological renewal of the church. In the journal of the Warsaw Catholic Theological Academy, *Collectanea Theologica,* he wrote on the significance of dialogue.[56]

In an article with a self-evident title "Komunism—katolycism—dialog" in the Marxist journal *Człowiek i Światopoglad,* Wojciech Pomykało pointed out that conditions for a dialogue between Communists and Catholics existed since the days of their cooperation in World War II. In 1970 this journal devoted a number of articles to this theme. Jan Guranowski's "Antynomie i perspektywy dialogu" expressed preference for the dialogue as a way of coming to understanding one another with a view to cooperation over dialogue as a mere discussion and exchange of ideas. He also suggested many themes for dialogue.[57] Płużański then compared Teilhard de Chardin's philosophy of the human being to that of Marx and investigated the Christian response to disputes in the contemporary world.[58] Besides noticing the fundamental differences which do exist between Marx and Teilhard, Płużański discussed those tendencies that are similar. Then in *Studia Filozoficzne* Płużański compared the meaning of life according to Marxism, existentialism, and Christianity and showed that between Marxism and Christianity there are similarities, as, for instance, in the notion of loving one's neighbor.[59]

The collected essays of one Christian and one Marxist writer appeared in book form in 1970. Tadeusz Mazowiecki published a work mostly devoted to the methodology of dialogue, entitled *Rozdroża i Wartości (Crossroads and Values),* Tadeusz Jaroszewski's book was entitled *Osobowość i wspólnota (Personality and Community).* His work is a philosophical investigation of human beings and community according to Marxism, structuralism, existentialism, and Christian personalism. Both books received good reviews. Many of the reviewers expressed agreement with the authors. It is evident that a shift had taken place, a shift from the purely methodological questions to analysis and evaluation of the role of human beings, i.e., issues of philosophical anthropology. Janusz Zabłocki's collection of essays written between 1949 and 1970 was published in 1971 in book form entitled *Na polskim skrzyżowaniu dróg (At the Polish Crossroads)*. Considerable sections of this work were devoted to various aspects of dialogue.

A Catholic priest, Stanisław Kowalczyk, wrote articles on issues of personality and community for *Collectanea Theologica*, entitled "The Social Character of Man as a Basis for Christian-Marxist Dialogue," published in 1971, and one in 1972 entitled "The Marxist and Christian Concept of Freedom." In these articles Kowalczyk pointed out the convergent segments in the two systems of thought. On freedom, he noted that while Marxism and Christianity have different notions of axiological freedom, both recognize freedom and ascribe humans a right to it. However, they differ sharply in their ontology of freedom, though recently there have been some instances of more convergent analyses.[60]

Józef Majka, the rector of the Catholic Seminary in Wrocław, organized a scholarly symposium on the contemporary philosophy of human beings at which two papers relevant to the dialogue were delivered. One was by Kowalczyk, on Marxist anthropology, and the other by the Marxist Jan Szewczyk also described Marxist anthropology.[61] These papers from the symposium were published in 1973 in book form as *Współczesna filozofia człowieka (Contemporary Philosophy of Human Beings)*.

A landmark event took place in January of 1972 when Janusz Kuczyński, the editor of *Studia Filozoficzne*, organized a Christian-Marxist dialogue on "Philosophy and Peace." At this dialogue Mieczysław Gogacz, professor of the Warsaw Catholic Theological Academy, stated that the philosophy of the human being is the basis for any philosophy of peace. Zabłocki explored the significance of the recent papal documents *Pacem in terris* and *Populorum progressio* for an understanding of peace. The inherent relationship of peace with the defense of human beings and their value was likewise pointed out by the Marxist authors Jaroszewski, Władysław Stróżewski, Marian Dobrosielski, and Tadeusz Tomaszewski.[62]

In 1972 Jaroszewski and Zabłocki contributed to the *Internazionale Dialog Zeitschrift* tandem articles that provided a description of dialogue in Poland.[63] Both authors characterized the change in relationships from one of confrontation and animosity to one in which coexistence and collaboration are possible and desirable. Different forms of cooperation and dialogue, ranging from dialogue between average Catholics and average Marxists within the Front of National Unity, to contacts between the party chiefs and the hierarchy or between scholars of the two movements were reported. As he did in other writings, Jaroszewski pointed out that new values can be created in dialogue, and that the dialogue has a good future in a land where there is a unique meeting of Catholicism with Marxism under socialist conditions. Zabłocki saw the possibility of complete normalization of church-state relationships and stated that the mutual relations of Marxists and Christians cannot be determined in a power struggle. Catholicism has shown remarkable adaptability to new situations and is showing signs of renewed vigor. Zabłocki stated that the time has come when relationships between Catholics and Marxists do not have to be conducted by the church hierarchy, but that it is also time to cease assuming that those Catholics who are involved in the dialogue are in conflict with church authorities.

A similar tandem of articles was published in 1973 by *Chrześcijanin w Świecie*, and translated into English *(The Christian in the World)*, French, and German versions of that journal in 1974. The articles were Kowalczyk's "The Christian-Marxist Dialogue in Poland Till the Present," and Jaroszewski's "Confrontation, Dialogue, and Collaboration."

Kowalczyk raised the question, Can Marxists and Christians have a fruitful dialogue despite their opposing ideologies? He wondered whether there is a sufficient openness and dynamism in both views which could lead to mutual enrichment through dialogue. In both camps there are still many who favor a dogmatic approach, but living ideologies develop and this gives hope. In Christianity, besides certain absolute truths of faith, there is also a certain pluralism in respect to the changing elements. Christianity is a universal and open religion. Nature and the supernatural are part of one reality, hence eschatology does not stand in the way of the Christian's involvement in this life. Marxists, on the other hand, also have more than one interpretation of their classics. The time of dogmatism is over, and a time of wider exploration, especially in interpreting the nature of the human individual, has arrived. Evolution in the thought of these two systems brought about a situation where the partners do not seek to defeat one another doctrinally but seek the larger truth and mutual enrichment. Truth and the good know no borders. Thus dialogue in Poland is both a fact and a chance. It is a fact because it has been achieved, though not easily. As chance it relies on hope that cooperation can create common human and national values, the wish to get nearer to each other, and the effort, patience, and good will of both sides.[64]

Jaroszewski raised the question as to whether Marxists, trying to build socialism in a predominantly Catholic country, are going to run into opposition or can count on Christian cooperation. He thought that the humanistic Marxist aims would evoke a positive response among Christians, not because of constraint, but because of the conviction that these are true values.[65] The only method of gaining Christian acceptance of socialist ideology is dialogue, though philosophical confrontation is desirable. No pressure or discrimination should be applied. The Catholic church has often played a significant role in Polish national aspirations. After some unfortunate clashes in the early postwar years a series of cooperative efforts have been undertaken, 1) in everyday life, 2) with lay Catholic organizations (Pax, the Christian Social Association, and Znak) 3) between church and state authorities, and 4) between Catholic and state academic institutions.[66]

Relations between the government and the Vatican are being normalized, according to Jaroszewski. The specific earmark of the Polish dialogue is that, unlike dialogues in Western Europe, it has not been restricted to philosophical questions but includes often heated debates on questions of economic development, cultural, scientific, and political issues, not only with supportive Catholics but also with hesitant Catholics.[67] Questions of peace, social justice, participation of citizens in public decisions, and other related issues have also been subject to dialogue. Marxists have come to appreciate the significance of some Catholic thinkers such as Mounier and Teilhard for the development of humanistic culture.

> This is where I can see solid grounds for a Catholic-Marxist meeting—a sphere of discussing *par excellence* philosophical questions, linked with a vision of man, society, with an assessment of modern civilization and culture, but at the same time a sphere which serves to strengthen an ideological cooperation between Catholics and Marxists, . . . There also exists the problem of joint moral responsibility for the world. There is the problem of justifying our historical options. . . .

A philosophical dialogue viewed from this angle is no longer in opposition to a social one, and they are now firmly linked up.[68]

The dialogue in Poland and other socialist countries could go much further than the dialogue in capitalist countries if Christians and Marxists seek to cooperate on the variety of moral and economic questions facing them jointly, e.g., how to humanize the scientific and technological revolution, how to improve socialist relations, how to popularize culture, how to improve economic performance, and so forth.

> Finally, I wish to emphasize that there are tremendous cognitive and social values that can be derived from dialogue. The leading of a dialogue provides an opportunity to discover new values and questions which in the situation of isolation would have passed unnoticed, an opportunity to undertake, by both sides from their own cognitive viewpoints, all those essential problems of man and modern culture that have so far been perceived by only one side.[69]

Jaroszewski concluded by saying that ideological confrontation on worldviews continues but that Marxists now realize that among Christians there are many who are in favor of progressive tendencies. One can no longer maintain, as it was thought in the past, that a religious orientation directly causes a reactionary social posture.[70] Instead of applying pressure upon religious people, Marxists will now want to win them over to a concrete program of action and, in the future, even to their worldview. In the meantime they have concluded that cooperation between people of different worldviews, based on dignity and respect for all and the right of each person to the expression of his or her own philosophic views, is the aim of Marxists.[71]

If Kowalczyk's and Jaroszewski's statements are reflections of reality rather than tactical moves by individuals, then dialogue in Poland has achieved, at this point, an enviable sophistication reaching beyond tolerance to mutual respect and cross-fertilization.

In December 1973, Janusz Zabłocki, a "Znak" deputy, spoke in the *Sejm*, saying that Christians and other religious people of Poland and other countries seek an answer to the basic questions as to whether the postrevolutionary state will honor the rights of the churches and of religion as well as the civil rights of the believers, as the Communists promised when they sought power.[72] He stressed that the answer to such questions is not yet clear, as many of the processes are still ongoing.

The Catholic Center for Social Studies and Documentation translated the book *From "Syllabus" to Dialogue* by the French Catholic J. Francois Six.[73] This book contained many of the official and semiofficial documents of the Roman Catholic Church on dialogue. Rev. Majka, who wrote the preface, suggested ways in which these ideas can be appropriated for the Polish situation.

Since many Vatican II documents dealt with the question of Catholic dialogue with atheism, Marxist atheism became the subject matter for study by Polish Catholics. Kowalczyk explored the issue of atheism in terms of its being rooted in the Marxist classics.[74] In addition, two special issues of *Ateneum Kapłańskie*, edited by Bishop Kazimierz Majdánski, were devoted to the issue of dialogue with nonbelievers. In them, nine priests and a number of other scholars wrote not merely about theism and unbelief in general, but about religion and Marxism in particular with such topics as "Dialogue: Giving and Accepting Testimony" by Bohdan Cywiński and "The Problem of Religion as Seen by Marxist Classics and Contemporary Marxists" by Kowalczyk.[75]

From 1973 onward *Studia Filozoficzne*, under the editorship of the Marxist Janusz Kuczyński, as well as its English language version, *Dialectics and Humanism*, took up the question of the Marxist-Christian dialogue as part of its editorial policy and published from that time on, with remarkable regularity, articles by both Christian and Marxist scholars dealing with philosophical issues affecting their relationship. Kuczyński himself, who wrote frequently on the subject, started the series with an article entitled "The Marxist-Christian Dialogue." [76] Kuczyński claimed that dialogue in Poland is both more advanced and more creative than in capitalist countries. He provided a good deal of historical information about the dialogue, but it was not as well organized and thorough as that of Kowalczyk. It is clear that not all Christian contributions were acceptable to him. He cited the work of Bohdan Cywiński, *Rodowody niepokornych* (Genealogies of the Unsubmissive), as a book not serving the dialogue nor characterizing its era because it combined various political trends and even combined opposite ideologies into models of conformism and nonconformism.[77] According to Kuczyński, opposition in Poland has nothing to offer, and the church should avoid alliances with those in political opposition. That is the prerequisite for and main premise of the dialogue.[78] One may assume that Cywiński touched a few tender Marxist sensibilities. No dissident is welcomed by them. Political anti-Communism is not seen as an acceptable option. On the other hand, Kuczyński cited approvingly the views of Zabłocki on giving the state the priority in shaping progress, while the church would become increasingly an ally of the state.[79] Kuczyński believed that "at least a preliminary form of commitment to socialism is today the reason of Christianity as an institution and, perhaps even the chance [for success] of Catholicism in Poland." [80] From the perspective of Catholicism, dialogue is a means of seeking understanding with the socialist world, but for Marxism, stated Kuczyński, "dialogue is a consequence of overcoming open class antagonism, or modifying it so as to create a new historical, cultural, and political situation." [81]

Kuczyński distinguished three stages of the dialogue: 1) preliminary and political dialogue, 2) humanist dialogue and 3) the dialogue of truth.

1. During the preliminary or political stage, the objective of the dialogue is cooperation on such issues as peace, justice, and disarmament, because these are held in common by both partners. Dialogue can start when the church departs from defending the capitalist world and moves to a more democratic stance. Under conditions of political struggle there can be no dialogue, and Kuczyński did not favor, correctly so, using the word dialogue to describe prior historical forms of positive relations between Christians and Marxists.[82] Christians engage in dialogue out of political weakness and religious strength so that they can draw on their partners' political strength. The motivation of the Marxists is different. They are coming from positions of strength and with the historical certainty that their cause will prevail. In dialogue they are inviting Christians to share in creating a new world.[83] The tensions in the dialogue are based only on differences in worldviews, not on political and class antagonisms, which must be settled before dialogue takes place.

2. The humanist dialogue is a higher stage. Its subject is the human being. It can take place only in a socialist society between partners who espouse socialist views. It takes place in an environment in which there is no political diversity, one free from notions of political democracy. In it various kinds of socialists are united in promoting human interest, including struggling against capitalism.[84] Zabłocki's view of *homocentrism* could have emerged in Catholic thought, according to Kuczyński, only in a socialist environment. Christians can, perhaps, combine motivation with socialist motivation for the ad-

vance of humanity. This will be a pluralism of nonantagonistic values. Pluralism as an ideological model will, however, be abolished.

3. The highest stage is the dialogue of truth which is a purely scientific pursuit of truth free of all interests, class determinants, and vestiges of the past. Fully disinterested cognition will lead to a complete unity of ideals and of culture in society.[85] It is apparent that this stage is one of the future. At this stage, dialogue is not based on pluralism. The word diadogue here may not connote the same notion as it does today, as there will be "a basic homogenity of the socio-cultural world," "a total order in the human world." [86]

No Polish Christian responded to these ideas formally, but, to their credit, the editors of *Dialectics and Humanism* printed a sharp critique of Kuczyński's views from a Christian perspective by a Canadian professor, Albert Shalom, with, of course, a reply by Kuczyński.[87]

Zabłocki presented his views of the developing Christian-Marxist relations on the thirtieth anniversary of that coexistence.[88] He pointed to the sweeping changes that took place in Poland during that period and traced how these changes affected the church. The main point of his interest was how the sociopolitical events affected Polish Roman Catholic social teachings and work. For that purpose he divided the thirty-year period into five periods determined primarily by crucial events in church-state relations. According to him, fundamental changes in Catholic social thinking occurred only from the fourth period onward, namely since 1956. For the dialogue with Marxists the crucial period of engagement begins with the fourth stage, the postconciliar time from 1962 onward when Polish Roman Catholics started in earnest to apply Vatican II insights to the domestic situation.[89] Catholics living in countries of Marxist-Leninist orientation have become politically mature, are able to read "the signs of the times," and work on social development even with nonbelievers. With such statements Zabłocki placed himself among the number of those Christians who would fit the mold of Kuczyński's second stage, though Zabłocki stated that Marxists need to give a satisfactory answer as to whether there is a place for Christian cooperation, not only in the first stages after the take-over, but also in the process of the further building of a communist society.[90]

Mutual relationships and questions on the methodology of the dialogue were not the only ones raised in the Polish context. Christian reactions to technological progress, technology

and its future role were surveyed by Marxists Janina Jaku-
bowska and Tadeusz Płuźański in "From *Sacrum Imperium*
to the *Technopolis* of the Future."[91] They maintained that
Christianity had to repudiate many of its traditional views in
order to save itself from extinction.

Then a classic Christian theologian was scrutinized—St.
Thomas Aquinas. This was done by means of a Christian inter-
pretation by Andrew A. Woźnicki of the University of San
Francisco and a Marxist response paper by Józef Borgosz.[92]
The discussion centered on the Thomistic notion of unity and
plurality or diversity of a community of beings.

As if the above were insufficient evidence that the dialogue
in Poland is not merely on the level of practical issues which
occasionally need theoretical consideration, but sometimes deal
with primarily philosophical issues, another dialogue took place
on Catholic mediocentrism.[93] Mediocentrism is defined as that
attitude toward history which "either postulates an assessment
of the past implying a recognition of the Middle Ages as
the most excellent epoch in history, or ascribes a universal
timeless quality to certain theories and values created in the
medieval times."[94] Andrzej Kasia disputed this mediocentric
historical view from a Marxist perspective. The editorial board
of *Studia Filozoficzne*, which had originally published Kasia's
article, organized a symposium on January 9, 1971, with Catholic participants Mieczysław Gogacz, Andrzej Grzegorszyk, T.
Żeleźnik, H. Bednarek, and J. Lichański, and Marxists Zdisław
Kuksewicz, Kasia, Kuczyński, S. Sarnowski, and Borgosz.[95]

Some new and some old themes were raised in 1978 and
1979. The Christian Wiesław Mysłek and Marxist Józef Wołkowski addressed themselves to the importance of work for human beings, i.e. the philosophy of work.[96] The discussion, while
interesting from a theoretical perspective, has great significance in the Polish situation because in instances of low labor
productivity and considerable labor unrest, the highest church
authorities have assisted the beleaguered government by making an appeal to the workers and farmers to go back to work
and to apply themselves to raise productivity. This issue is
among the core concerns of the workers' strikes in 1980.

The questions of methodology were not, however, exhausted. In addition to an article by Mieczysław Rakowski, which
will be reported on below in the context of a public dialogue in
the pages of the foremost Polish daily, *Polityka*, Kuczyński's
article, "Marxism, Lay Culture, Christianity," showed the ma-
turing of Kuczyński's approach toward Christians.[97] The paper

was a speech delivered at the Third National Meeting of the Society for Propagation of Lay Culture in November 1977. No Association of Atheists was ever formed in Poland as it was in the Soviet Union, but this society comes closest to gathering those who are against religious influences in Poland.

Kuczyński, whose views became predominant in this society, pointed out how his own thinking on Christianity had changed. He now advocated an enlightened, tolerant, dialogical approach toward Christianity. He admitted to having thought that Christianity could not be a form of humanism, but he had changed his mind because of Catholic developments under socialism in Poland, as well as because of Vatican II and the developments which took place in theology.[98] "Something great, something of a historical importance, occurs in the [*sic.*] Christianity of our time." [99]

Kuczyński showed the kind of appreciation and acknowledgment of the positive influences of religion upon society and the explicit seeking of cooperation that has not been seen elsewhere in Eastern Europe. He passionately urged his colleagues, particularly those more dedicated to the task of the atheization and secularization of Poland, to adopt a constructive and appreciative approach to religion. When one adds to this Kuczyński's almost rhapsodic praise on the election of Karol Woytiła to the papacy, which will be reported below, he illustrated what changes can take place in a person under the impact of dialogue if conditions in society are supportive.

Józef Borgosz wrote still another article, in which he stated that the chief aim of the dialogue is to resolve the practical and theoretical problems of today.[100] Huge numbers of people are involved in these dialogues, mostly in search of peace and disarmament. The dialogue is being carried out from well-established, often mutually exclusive, bases and orientations. The essential novelty of the dialogue for the church is that cold war tactics have been abandoned for this new approach. But in addition to being a method of conversation and cooperation, dialogue also involves doctrinal confrontation and controversy.[101] Theoretical and practical dialogue cannot be artificially separated, as the dialogue for peace illustrates. The Marxist notion of the unity of theory and practice should be helpful here to the partners in dialogue. Theoretical dialogue alone is limited and futile, leading only to philosophical confrontation based on traditional differences, which tends to obstruct cooperation.[102] Of significance to Borgosz is that Christians have always gotten actively involved in carrying out progressive revolutions, such as the October Revolution and other Eastern European socialist revolutions.[103] The reason for successful cooperation is that Marxists are capable of setting aside theoretical differences in order to bring about cooperation. Dialogue is thus initiated by revolutionary praxis and not by doctrinal discussion.

The historical characteristics of every nation, according to Borgosz, make dialogue peculiar to each national situation, hence the historical and gradualistic approach to dialogue by Marxists on a world view scale. A hierarchy of tasks needs to be established in each specific situation. At the top of the list should be promotion of *detènte,* and gradual, but complete, universal disarmament. Peace is the supreme value and greatest obligation to which all differences must be subjugated.[104] Theoretically the church has been for peace, but the practical ways of building peace are complex and require grappling with the issue. It is not enough for the hierarchy to be in favor of peace. Many Christians in nonsocialist countries are subject to class differentiation, and this may determine their attitude toward peace. Only Christians in socialist countries, who are no longer divided into antagonistic classes, unequivocally favor peace. After starting a general dialogue for peace, it is important to move to concrete disarmament talks. The second most important issue for dialogue is the question of social justice.[105] Then follow other practical problems, such as consumerism. At the end of the list of priorities is the dialogue about ontological principles, which are antithetical and tend to lead to a controversy of worldviews.[106]

V. I. Garadja explored the attempts of modern Catholic theology, in particular its representative, Karl Rahner, to come to grips with the modern world by way of reinterpreting transcendentalism and history and attempting to harmonize the two.[107] He thought that this harmonization had been accomplished only by expressing disenchantments with present revolutionary achievements. Only from the perspective of implied philosophical evaluation can one surmise that the author is a Marxist, for nowhere does he find it necessary to resort to explicit references to Marxism, which is indicative of his having reached a level of scholarly sophistication that makes it possible to explore a subject matter without the overwhelming need to explicitly "grind one's own ax."

The same issue contains S. Kowalczyk's "On the History of the Christian-Marxist Dialogue in Poland," which, as has been previously acknowledged, contributed a great deal of concrete information and interpretative material to this book.

The untiring Kuczyński again appeared with an article entitled "The Sense of Existence: Creativity and Community." [108] He diagnosed the problems of existence as the passage of time, separation, solitude, isolation, helplessness, and the routine of daily life. The liberal mass culture of today cannot offer real solutions but only escapism from the problems of human existence. Christianity and Marxism are allies in the attempt to save human lives from contemporary mass culture and to transform people so that they can find meaning in life.[109] Creating and cocreating various values brings meaning to life. Kuczyński saw the issue of meaning in life as one of the most significant of today.

The election of the Archbishop of Krakow to the papacy was an event that gladdened the heart of almost every Pole, regardless of ideological orientation. This elation can be clearly discerned in Kuczyński's "To Elevate the World—The Potential of John Paul the Second's Pontificate." [110] This is no reserved assessment; few more enthusiastic appraisals of the chances of Karol Woytiła's papacy could be found elsewhere, except those written by Polish Catholic writers. Kuczyński saw this as the beginning of a new stage of greater universalism, a recognition for Poland's cultural values created over centuries and a recognition by the Catholic Church of the importance of socialism for future human progress. The election of John Paul II signified to Kuczyński that the Roman Catholic Church had decisively turned the corner, which it started to do with John XXIII and Paul VI, in selecting a man for the papacy who has the skill, experience, and understanding of the workers' movement. This man personifies the unique Polish experience of Catholic and Marxist coexistence. He holds progressive views on social issues and conservative views on religion. The whole world now looks with expectation to the contribution of Poland's experience.[111] Cooperation can be expected from him in endeavors for peace, social justice, and active participation of Christians in building socialism. Kuczyński expected that "the best form of Polish experiences will radiate the whole world over, multiplying values in the world of ours." [112] After itemizing some of the past achievements and future challenges of the dialogue between Christians and Marxists, Kuczyński wondered whether Christianity would become a truly uniting power and expressed the conviction that it can do so only if the present generation of Christians and Marxists do not dissipate the enormous energies which can be unleashed in "the dialectics of the social cooperation between opposing philosophies." [113]

This appreciative Marxist appraisal of one of the outstanding sons of the Polish Roman Catholic Church and the top man in the Vatican is by no means typical of the general Polish Marxist attitude toward the leadership of the Catholic Church. The contrary is the case if one is to take the overall picture. Thus a shift took place among the Marxists. Likewise the Church's response to Marxism slowly shifted from opposition, distrust, and fear to caution, limited support, and initiatives to dialogue.

The Roman Catholic Church in Poland is a vigorous organization with an active clerical and lay constituency. It deemed itself, even prior to World War II, as apolitical but responding to social needs of the people. Its bishops and clergy considered themselves as pastors of a people in whose name they seek to defend the humanitarian, moral, and religious values.[114] Only the hierarchy is regarded as representing truly the interest of the entire Catholic community. The church has direct contacts with the government, although direct meetings of the head of the church and the head of the state happen rarely. The bishops, particularly the late Stefan Wyszyński, the primate of the church, address the people and, often indirectly, the government, in the form of pastoral letters which address themselves boldly, though diplomatically, to those social issues which are of great concern to the church and its members. These pastoral letters frequently tend to be critical of certain practices of the government: censorship of the press, the right of labor to protest and demonstrate, obstacles in the religious education of young people, and problems affecting the family. But at times of national crises, as in 1956, 1970, 1976, and 1980, the hierarchy, especially Wyszyński, played a forceful role. In 1956 there was a perceived threat of Soviet intervention unless the Gomułka government was supported. At that time the hierarchy felt that the calamity would be greater if Poland was militarily taken over by the Soviets. In 1970-71 when Władysław Gomułka was toppled during labor unrest and Edward Gierek took over, and in the riots of 1976 when the Soviet invasion did not loom so large, the primary consideration of the church was the restoration of social order. In 1980 when Soviet invasion became the paramount concern, the church again pleaded for restraint in order to preserve national independence. The church had become quite self-conscious of its social responsibilities. While the church asked its members to work more conscientiously, to respect the law, and to endure shortages in consumer goods, it simultaneously defended the workers and said quite plainly that the workers' grievances were justified and that government policies provoking the unrest and especially its repression were unjustified and illegitimate.[115] In defending Polish national existence and people's welfare the church is loyal but offers constructive criticism, which, of course, is not always welcomed by the government, but which reflects the depth and the integrity of the church's concern.

Pope John Paul II comes out of this context. When he offered criticism of certain forms of "liberation theology" in Latin America at CELAM III in Puebla, Mexico, January 1979, he reflected the accumulated wisdom of the Polish Roman Catholic Church. That wisdom shows that undue politicization of the clergy tends to boomerang and that partisanship in not only divisive but impairs the spiritual services to the entire church membership. One should be thoroughly familiar with Marxism, as he is. One can support those concrete programs of Marxism which benefit the people, as many lay people and clergy are doing in Poland. But one should not become a flag carrier of Marxist interpretations and revolutionary movements. The church is on the side of the people, particularly the poor and oppressed people. But its social analysis is not a Marxist social analysis, and its weapons for change are not Marxist weapons. The realities of the Polish road to socialism, with its advantages and disadvantages, will probably color at least the early years of John Paul II's pontificate. Those in Western Europe and Latin American countries eager for a synthesis between Marxism and Christianity are not likely to find an ally in John Paul II. Caution, prudence, and a certain flexibility based on strength are likely to be the qualities transmitted by the experience of the Polish Catholic Church to the worldwide Roman Catholic community, and to the ecumenical church. This interpretation of the role of the church was well expressed by Kazimierz Morawski, leader of the Christian Social Association:

> We wish the Church to remain the Church, and the religion not to be shield for any political movements, irrespective of their tint. Exploitation of religion for political purposes was always harmful first of all for the Church itself, for its supernatural mission of ministry.[116]

Formal relations between the state and the church are handled gingerly, but willingness to cooperate is asserted at the highest levels. Edward Gierek, former First Secretary of the United Worker's Party, stated in 1976:

> I believe there is a broad field for fruitful cooperation of the Church and the State in the implementation of important national goals. I repeat this once again—I was and am for such cooperation and I see in this cooperation big sense. This is, by the way, not only my personal view, such is also the stand of the Political Bureau of the Central Committee of our party and the stand of the supreme authorities of our state.[117]

Similar sentiments were expressed by Edward Gierek in his visit to Pope Paul VI, December 1, 1977, a visit which served the purpose of further normalization of relations.[118] This took place shortly after Gierek had a meeting with Cardinal Wyszyński on October 29, 1977. The Primate of Poland expressed his position:

> The Church in Poland does not tend to fight with the system or the state. The Church defends the purity of evangelical teaching, freedom in exercising its own duties, equality of citizens in the area of world outlooks and religion and of basic human rights. The Church defends its freedom to carry out the duties of the service to work spiritual salvation of the people, make them useful in the home community on the earth. So, if we expect anything, it is above all wider margin of freedom for the Church. Certainly we shall not misuse it against the Nation or against the State.[119]

He added, "At last something is changing in our country though perhaps not in fundamental, doctrinal ways, not in world outlook, not as we would wish it."[120] He stressed that the church does not seek power, does not seek to be "a state within a state," but it recognizes that there are links between the economic and political life and Christian morality, and to these the church must address itself.

In a letter to Kazimierz Kakol, minister of religious affairs, Wyszynski reproached Kakol for stating that the church is involved in antistate activity. Rather it is the state that exceeded the legitimate field of political activity by attempting to include all aspects of life in its domain and by distorting the history of Poland. People have the right to defend their own rights from governmental intrusion. In addition, the church should be compensated for some of the wrongs perpetrated against it during the Stalinist period.[121]

Whether or not such exchanges are to be considered a dialogue is a debatable question. Professor Andrzej Zuberbier, a priest, in an interview given to *Więź*, expressed his own reservations on this point.

As far as the dialogue with atheism is concerned, and many Christians in the West are expecting us to go into it. I think that there are no proper conditions for such a dialogue in this country. If there comes to a confrontation between believers and nonbelievers it is rather polemics and not dialogue.[122]

A homily by Cardinal Wyszyński on January 6, 1978, at St. John's Cathedral in Warsaw, did spell out his program for the development of church-state relations in the spirit of dialogue. This was published in *Tygodnik Powszechny*.[123] Wyszyński declared the church's willingness to participate actively in all areas of the nation's life and gave positive overall evaluation of the socialist government pledging support for the "preservation of our national, social, professional, economic, and religious sovereignty." [124]

The homily, coupled with the above-mentioned high-level visits of Gierek to Wyszyński and Paul VI, provoked a response by a member of the Central Committee of the Polish United Workers' Party, Mieczysław Rakowski, who is also editor of the daily *Politkya*.[125] Rakowski stated that after coming to power, the Polish "radical left wing" wanted to establish good relationships and dialogue with the Vatican, but the representatives of the Vatican did not accept this offer. Many church people were actively antisocialist.[126] On the Marxist side the policy of dialogue and cooperation were undermined by sectarians [meaning Stalinists] who carried out repressive measures against the churches. Rakowski complained that Christians sometimes want to leave the impression that the church never did anything wrong. The Vatican and the Roman Catholic Church started gradually to change and to share many concerns about the world, such as détente, peace, and social plagues, for instance, alcoholism, drugs, hunger, and brutality. In the spirit of reconciliation the popes met with leaders of many socialist countries. These exchanges created a more favorable mutual interpretation. These changed relations, however, "do not signify relinquishing by either side of its ideological canons." [127]

The wider world gives encouragement to dialogue in Poland, according to Rakowski. Meetings between Gierek and Wyszyński are dialogues in which a sharing of respective viewpoints takes place, aimed at cooperation and a lessening of conflict and tension. But sometimes the church asks for too much. One needs to distinguish between rightful aspirations for an increasing place for the church and one which would impose the church's view upon those who do not share it.[128] For Rakowski the central concern for the dialogue is the material improvement in the living standard and in the spiritual values of the Polish tradition, its sociocultural heritage. Communism brought about a drastic improvement of life in Poland and solved many problems. Even for the Catholic Church the situation for more effective work is possible under socialism because so many problems which demean people have been solved.[129] Socialism solved some problems which even the church was against. It also liberated the church from ties with conservative forces. Socialism is not without some problems, but these can be solved, stated Rakowski.

Christian responses in *Polityka* were invited. They came from Zabłocki, "In the Interest of Dialogue and Cooperation"; Wojciech Ketrzynski, of the Christian Social Association, "A Dialogue for Cooperation"; and Janusz Bilak, "Most Important Is Direction," [130] At least one Christian response, by the chaplain Ludwig Wisniewski, O.P., was not accepted by *Polityka.*

Zabłocki congratulated *Polityka* for bringing the dialogue into the daily press where the masses of people could read it, but took Rakowski to task for certain deformations and over-simplifications. He took issue with the statement that it was the church which rejected the invitation of the party to dialogue in the immediate poswar era, and suggested that the blame is to be found at least as much in other factors. He blamed Rakowski for certain caricatures of Catholicism as an other-worldly, individualistic, status quo-supportive, caritative faith. He reminded Rakowski that it was the Polish episcopate which on April 4, 1950, was the first ever in history to have signed an agreement with a communist government in the midst of the cold war and the Vatican's negative stance against communism. He agreed that the dialogue does not mean ideological "ceasefire":

> For, the same as the Marxist Party cannot drop its ideological struggle, Catholicism cannot likewise renounce its apostolic work which is an essential part of its mission. The crux of the problem lies elsewhere, namely in the kind of measures used by each side in that ideological rivalry, in what degree it is the matter of arguments and persuasion and not of administrative pressure. . . . a lay state is the state which is not religious but not anti-religious either. It is a state in which religion is not official ideology but neither is atheism; a state which allows every citizen the freedom of choosing philosophy of life and preserves neutrality on the matter; does not let its administra-

tive apparatus to be engaged on either side. Only a thus understood lay state—especially in a country with such overwhelming majority of believers as Poland—can be a truly all-national
state.[131]

Wojciech Ketrzynski attempted to point out that the church's
mission throughout history is not the same as that of political
and revolutionary movements. Hence the religious attitude is
going to be different from the Marxist. The question is how to
carry out this discussion of different attitudes without impair-
ing national unity. This can be done if confrontation does not
take primitive, fanatic forms, and the principle of toleration
is applied at all levels of the dialogue.[132]

Jerzy Turowicz, editor of *Tygodnik Powzsechny*, attempted
to contribute to this dialogue by writing an article, "Dialogue,
Pluralism, and Unity," for his own paper, but it was banned
by the censor. It was finally published in the Polish *samizdat*,
Spotkania, and eventually translated into English.[133] Turowicz
stated that various declarations by government and church
leaders do not amount yet to a changed situation in which a
true dialogue between Christians and Marxists could flounrish.
Actual changes in society leading to the recognition of genuine
ideological pluralism and to greater freedom are needed before
the current ideological conflict could be transformed into genuine cooperation and dialogue. Turowicz did not deny progress
in many areas, yet he maintained that there are still political
pressures and limitations for the church and a reluctance to
recognize the rightful activities of the church, which include
care for the welfare of the people and of society.[134] "Catholics
as Catholics have no access to the 'official' structures and cultural centres controlled by the State." [135] Catholic publications
are severely restricted by limiting the supply of paper and by
censorship.

> The advocates of socialism often appeal to us not to divide so-
> ciety into believers and unbelievers. . . . [T]his division is made
> not by us, the believers, but by the discriminatory system,
> which often treats believers as second class citizens.[136]

Only true democratization of society and acceptance of pluralism based on true equality will bring about an effective diadogue between church and state, between Christians and
Marxists, leading to genuine national unity.

Did the papal visit to Poland in June 1979 contribute to a
more effective, genuine dialogue? A qualified yes can be given,
taking into account that the visit is too recent to be evaluated
properly. The visit certainly made an enormous impact upon

the population. While a few restrictions were imposed, on the whole the government behaved correctly and gave the Pope a proper welcome. The government emphasized the religious nature of the visit but did organize a number of meetings between John Paul II and various government officials. The Pope was both prudent and courageous in his triumphant tour of the country. In regard to Marxism, he stated in his address to priests at the Shrine of the Holy Virgin in Czestochowa that they should pursue the dialogue between church and state, but to be "aware of our diametrically opposed concepts of the world" ascertaining that "fundamental human rights and the free activity of the Church be respected." [137]

John Paul II seeks "true dialogue" concerning the "*de facto* application of religious liberty which is guaranteed in all Eastern European constitutions yet so often restricted in practice." [138] The papal visit was used for such purposes even the day prior to the Pope's arrival, when, at a meeting between Gierek and Wyszyński, a greater harmony and "new impulses for cooperation" between church and state were sought.[139] Undoubtedly religious liberty and other liberties are *prerequisite* for fruitful interaction, just as they are the *result* of improved interaction.

What was indeed obvious is that Polish Marxists no longer deny either to others or to themselves that the masses of their country are religious. This does not necessarily mean that the people are antisocialist. They may very well be accepting socialism for one reason or another, but the enthusiastic applause for the Pope does mean that they are at least against the state's affording privileges to atheism and restricting the rights of the church and of individual believers. It would be surprising if that message were lost on both the government and the hierarchy. In time this cognition is likely to affect the dialogue between the leaders of church and party.

Thus far little attention has been given to the dialogue among dissidents which in the opinion of some may be the major open dialogue going on in Poland today.[140] This dialogue, since it has no access to the official press, takes place in *samizdats*, or in writings published abroad and smuggled into Poland, and through teaching in the "flying university." The main Marxist in the opposition movement interested in an open dialogue with Christians is Adam Michnick, who published *Kosciol, lewica, dialog (The Church, the Left, Dialogue)*.[141] Michnik's book deals with church-state relations and the role of the church in Polish society, subjects generally avoided by official Marxist publications until recently. But he is interested in religion, religious persons, and religious institutions in modern society. He criticized leftists, even those who were not Stalinists themselves, for contributing to Stalinist tactics against religion by their failure to recognize the human values inherent in religion and the humane role played by the church in society.[142] The discussion sparked by this book is seen by some as the first truly open dialogue since it is carried out by publications which bypass the censor.[143]

The scope and influence of this dialogue is even more difficult to measure than the impact of the papal trip. Nor is it possible to make a judgment as to which aspect of the dialogue, the intellectual,[144] the leadership, the dissenting, or the dialogue of the daily interaction of average Christian or Communist citizens is in the long run the most beneficial for human welfare. All of them are needed.

One may conclude from the above that dialogue in Poland has made significant strides. Surprisingly it did not make an international impact, as did the one in Czechoslovakia or the Paulus-Gesellschaft. Perhaps the reason is that it did not produce well-known theoreticians, as have some other countries, as no significant reappraisals of either Marxism or Christianity took place. But it produced honest, or at least fairly honest, exchanges about differences and similarities. The dialogue in Poland is based on the power which both partners have over against each other and their awareness of that strength. Of importance also is the duration of that dialogue. Depending which features of dialogue we use as criteria, we might say that the encounters of 1956, if they be judged dialogical, can be seen as historically the earliest dialogues. But certainly by 1962 there had been a considerable published give-and-take which was definitely dialogical. The single most important reason for the early advent of the dialogue is that there was a ready-made vehicle for its communication: the existence of a strong Christian, especially Catholic, press, which was not the case in other Eastern European countries, where the Christian press had been reduced to minor house organs.

While the experiences of the Polish dialogue have not made a significant international impact until recently, one may expect that this situation will change substantially with the election of John Paul II. This will take place both by his own application of Polish experiences to the international encounter of Christianity with Marxism, and through the limelight in which his office stands and the inevitable attention that is being given to his background, thus leading to current and future explorations of the Polish experiences. It will be a pleasant surprise for many to find that there is a great deal of substance to be found in that experience.

What the impact of the workers' strikes of 1980 and 1981 with their secular and religious demands, the topping of the Gierek government and its replacement by the Stanisław Kania and Wojciech Jaruczelski governments, the threat of a Soviet invasion, the church's advocacy of moderation, and the death of Cardinal Wyszyński in 1981 will mean for the dialogue is totally uncertain.[145] The dialogue in Poland is indeed at its most important crossroads. It might be halted as drastically as it was in Czechoslovakia and revert to Type 2. It might continue under the present precarious circumstances with caution and occasional outbursts of courageous innovation. Or it might result in the kind of pluralism and creativity that marks Type 5 or even Type 6. Many people around the world, Marxists and Christians alike, look toward Poland with concern, anxiety, excitement, and hope. Henryk Sienkiewicz, a nineteenth-century romantic novelist, once wrote the book, *Quo Vadis?* Today we may ask, *Quo Vadis Polonia?*

INTERNATIONAL PEACE SYMPOSIA

The International Peace Symposia were organized by the Institut für Friedensforschung (hereafter called Institute for Peace Research) of the University of Vienna, Austria, and the International Institute for Peace, also of Vienna. These two institutes continue to be the main driving force of the symposia, although other cosponsors have joined them in preparing and carrying out the symposia. The main idea governing this endeavor is that Christians and Marxists need to work for peace and to share with one another the inspiration which they find for this effort in their own traditions. These dialogues are to be carried out carefully, diplomatically, and by responsible representatives of the mainstream of the Christian and Marxist movements. Neither would look only for those partners who are most sympathetic to one another, but, recognizing unbridgeable differences in ideology, they would inform each other of their views and search for ways to work jointly for peace.

The Institute for Peace Research was founded in 1967 under the leadership of Professors Rudolf Weiler and Karl Hormann. The former, a priest who is teaching ethics and social ethics at the University of Vienna, became the main driving force of the peace symposia and is, undoubtedly, its most important personality. Originally the Institute was sponsored only by the Catholic Theological Faculty of the University of Vienna, but several years afterwards the entire University of Vienna became its sponsor. Still the Institute tends to maintain its unofficial character as a Roman Catholic peace institute.

The other major partner in the Peace Symposia is the International Institute for Peace in Vienna. It is an organization consisting formally of institutional and individual members from East and West for the purpose of organizing peace research and conferences aiming at promoting peace. Actually it is more substantially supported by the socialist countries, in particular by the Soviet Union. Its first executive director was Vladimir Bruskov, who ably directed the work of this institute for eight years until he was replaced in 1977 by Lev Burnyashev, who was executive director until 1981. Both men are Soviet Marxist journalists and scholars. Bruskov's dedication and ability inspired great trust in dialogue partners. Weiler and he ably presided over a series of symposia between Christians and Marxists from 1971 to 1977. Burnyashev likewise learned what it takes to bring together very diverse people to discuss issues relating to peace.

The basic procedure in organizing the symposia is that the International Institute for Peace invites the Eastern European participants, and the Institute for Peace Research the Western Europeans. The majority from Eastern Europe are Marxists, with some Christians among the participants, and vice versa for Western Europe. Informal consultation takes place in order to suggest possible participants, without, however, ultimately threatening the privilege of each institute to decide on its own constituency at the symposia. On the basis of a good working relationship between the institutes, the theme, the main speakers, the place and time are worked out to be acceptable to all concerned. In order to stimulate the dialogue, a basic agreement was reached that most of those invited would be academicians, that the number of those invited would be small enough so that each person would have a chance to speak more than once and participants could get to know each other. It was also agreed that the program of the symposia would not be too demanding so as not to stand in the way of socializing and getting to know one another as human beings. The latter provision has become a significant earmark of the symposia, placing value on the informal contacts among participants which often enable an open and sincere exchange of opinions far beyond the one that takes place at the formal sessions.

At the earlier formal sessions, two major papers relating to the main topic were presented, generally one by a Soviet Marxist and one by a West European Christian. Likewise, one or two respondents were selected to start the discussion. Later others could present prepared speeches, but the emphasis was on a more spontaneous discussion. At later symposia, when the North American contingent was added, this structure was slightly amended to allow for an active autonomous participation of members from that group. All participants were encouraged to submit papers prepared in advance or their actual remarks at the symposia for later publications.[146]

The first Peace Symposium took place in Vienna in November 1971. This was at the time when many, having witnessed the suspension of the Paulus-Gesellschaft international dialogues, were proclaiming that the dialogue itself was dead. The nature of these dialogues would, to be sure, be quite different from the dialogues of the 1960s, but a different style and approach made possible a dialogue between a group of Christians and Marxists who were somewhat more official and perhaps somewhat more conventional, but thereby more representative. The theme was "The Problem of International Peace and of Peaceful Co-existence."[147] Weiler's counterpart in delivering the other main paper was Nikolai Kowalski of the Institute for the International Workers' Movement in Moscow, a first-class intellectual who was to become the most authoritative academic supporter of these symposia. Kowalski's address was entitled, "Some Aspects of the Problem of Peaceful Coexistence and European Security."[148] The other Eastern European participants in the dialogue were Alexei Belyakov, Bruskov, Dimitri Yermolyenko, M. Krutogolov, and Nikolai Polyanov from the Soviet Union, and Jerzy Wiatr from Poland. The sole Christian from Eastern Europe was Imre Timko from Hungary, dean of the Catholic Theological Academy in Budapest, who later became a bishop.[149]

The second symposium was held in Moscow, September 10-17, 1973, with the theme "Ways and Means for the Resolution of Problems of Social Development from the Perspective of Different Worldviews." The main speakers were again Kowalski and Weiler. Respondents were Mihály Simai, Marxist economist from Budapest, and Gustav Wetter from the Vatican. Of the 38 in attendance, 20 were from Eastern Europe (plus six observers from the U.S.S.R.). Kowalski's address was entitled "Contemporary Sociopolitical Problems and World Peace," while Simai presented a paper, "Coexistence, Convergence or Peaceful Competition." [150] Eastern Europeans who participated in the discussion were Mihail Andreyev, Elena Blinova, Grigoriy Morozov (Marxists), and Archbishop Vladimir [151] from the U.S.S.R.; Sergiu Tamas (Marxist) from Rumania; Herbert Bertsch and Heinrich Esrin (Marxists) and Hans Moritz (Christian) from East Germany; Jósef Wojcik (Christian) from Poland; Felix Vašečka (Marxist) from Czechoslovakia; and Marko Matić (Christian) from Yugoslavia. In comparison to the first symposium, which simply explored the possibilities of cooperation within the context of European security, the second meeting was already able to make some advances in terms of both the complexity and comprehensiveness of issues discussed.[152] A joint press release by the two institutes declared:

> There was agreement that differences in worldview can be resolved without recourse to force with the help of dialogue. Without endangering the convictions as to their being correct, people of different worldviews are able, through dialogue and other exchanges and contacts, to cooperate in various spheres. Among those specifically discussed were environmental protection, the Third World and problems of developing nations (struggle against hunger and racism), culture and education, full employment and the humanization of labor, youth and family, and the protection of health.[153]

A series of more informal dialogues took place in Vienna when the Institute for Peace Research invited Jan G. Vogeler, a Marxist philosopher from Lomonosov University in Moscow, as guest professor during the academic year 1973-74. While he tended to be the central figure, since the sessions were organized in his honor, there were other Marxists occasionally present, e.g. Adam Schaff, Vladimir Bruskov, and Walter Hollitscher (an Austrian Marxist teaching in East Germany). Similar guest lectures, seminars, and conversations took place in Vienna when Soviet philosophers and economists came to visit at various times.

The Third Peace Symposium with the topic "Worldview and Peace" took place from November 1-3, 1974, in Henndorf near Salzburg, Austria. The main Marxist paper was delivered by Yuri Zamoshkin of the Institute for the U.S.A. and Canada in Moscow, entitled "Ideology and Peace." Participating in the discussion from Eastern Europe were Kowalski, U.S.S.R.;

József Lukács (Marxist) and Károly Pröhle (Christian) from Hungary; Václav Výsohlid (Marxist) from Czechoslovakia; and Bertsch from East Germany.[154]

At the Fourth Symposium in Tutzing near Munich, West Germany, held November 17-20, 1975, the theme was "Peaceful Coexistence and Social Progress." The Soviet paper was delivered by Alexander Galkin, entitled "Détente and Social Progress." Participating in the discussion were some from Eastern Europe who made earlier appearances, namely Bertsch, Lukács, Kowalski, and Moritz, as well as Ion Livescu (Marxist) from Rumania and Michal Dobroczynski (Marxist) from Poland.

Beginning with the Fifth Symposium, North Americans were added in substantial number and started cosponsoring these events. Under the aegis of the Institute for International Understanding and the leadership of Paul Mojzes, the fifth symposium took place at Rosemont (near Philadelphia), Pennsylvania, U.S.A., January 10-13, 1977, with the theme "Peaceful Coexistence and the Education of Youth." [155] The main papers were presented by Professors Charles West of Princeton Theological Seminary and Zamoshkin of Moscow. Along with Zamoshkin the most influential Eastern European was Lukács. Both contributed to the high level of the scholarly discussion, which soon dissipated the fears of the Eastern Europeans that they would be subjected to vile attack in the land of their main adversary. The other Eastern European participants were Archbishop Vladimir of Dimitrov (Christian), Bruskov, Vladimir Kultygin, Victor Linnik, Lev Mitrokhin, and Sergey Plehanov (Marxists) from the U.S.S.R.; and Adolf Niggemeier (Christian) and Max Schmidt (Marxist) from East Germany. So well pleased were they with the atmosphere of cordiality and patient though critical exchange that they decided to host the sixth symposium again on their territory.

The Sixth Symposium took place in Kishinyov, Moldavia, U.S.S.R., April 24-27, 1978, with the theme "Disarmament Problems from Different Ideological Viewpoints." The main papers were presented by Weiler and Oleg Bykōv, Institute of World Economics and International Relations, Moscow. The Eastern European participation was numerically higher than at other meetings. From Bulgaria came Antony Hubanchev (Christian) and Todor Stoychev (Marxist). From Czechoslovakia Václav Medek (Christian) and Bohumir Janoušek (Marxist) came. The G.D.R. was represented by Bertsch and two Christians, Hubertus Guske and Hans Heinrich Jenssen. Imre Várkonyi (Christian) and Ervin Réti (Marxist) represented Hungary. From Poland came Zbigniew Lesiewski (Christian), while from Romania came Nicolae Moraru (Marxist). Bishop Yonofam of Kishinyov was the Christian from the Soviet Union; the others were Marxists Andreyev, Galkin, Kowalski, Lev Semeyko, Grigoriy Lokshin, Alexey Khomenko, Boris Melnik, and Pyotr Krucheniuk, as well as Belyakov and Burnyashev from the International Institute for Peace in Vienna.[156]

The Seventh Symposium took place in Saltsjöbaden near Stockholm, Sweden, June 10-16, 1979, with the theme "Peaceful Coexistence from the Perspective of Different Worldviews." The Soviet paper on the topic was delivered by Mihail Mtschedlov of Moscow. From the Soviet Union were also Kowalski, Burnyashev, Sergei Gribkov (Marxists) and Vitaliy Borovoy (Christian). Borovoy made an unusually strong impact as one of the most independent and passionate Christian voices from Eastern Europe to speak at these Peace Symposia in the spirit of dialogue with Marxists of his own society. He received little direct response from them. Other participants from Eastern Europe were Tadeusz Mýslik (Christian) from Poland, Neculai Mancaş (Marxist) from Romania, Cinoldr and Výsohlid from Czechoslovakia, and Bertsch and Jenssen from East Germany.

The Eighth Symposium took place in Detroit, Michigan, September 21-26, 1980, with the theme "The Responsibility to Safeguard Peace Regardless of Ideological Differences." The Western paper was delivered by Professor Max Mark of Wayne State University (the first Jewish analysis at these symposia) and one by Vice-Admiral John Lee. The Marxist position paper, entitled "The Marxist Concept of Ideology, Ethics, and Foreign Policy in the Early Eighties," was written by Yuri Zamoshkin and Vladimir Gantman. It was read by its main writer Zamoshkin, a veteran of these symposia. The paper is of interest for its emphasis on "universal humanitarian values" regardless of ideologies, its defense of treaty obligations [natural in the aftermath of the Soviet intervention in Afghanistan] and support of peaceful coexistence. Ethical issues within Marxism and in dialogue were stressed. The writers tried to underscore that nuclear war would also destroy the deposit of the Christian heritage on which Marxists erected their own social values.

The other Soviet Marxist participants were Burnyashev,

Yuri Denisenko, and Yuri Denisov. The other Eastern Euro-
peans who took part in the symposium were Archbishop Nico-
lae Corneanu (Rumania), Adam Jozefowicz (Marxist from
Poland), Bertsch and Wolfgang Ganthus (Marxists from East
Germany), and the Marxist Gyula Gyovai and Catholic priest
Béla Bacsoka (Hungary).

The Detroit symposium reinforced the importance of these
meetings in times of great international tension resulting from
the events in Afghanistan, Iran, and Poland. It was decided
to hold the 1981 symposium in Madrid, Spain.

Several noteworthy characteristics of these dialogues need
to be stressed in order to explain their longevity and effectiveness. Among the positive characteristics are the following:

1. The low profile of these symposia is consonant with their
scholarly character. Little publicity and the absence of joint
resolutions characterize these symposia.

2. The semiofficial nature of the meetings is of value. In
attendance are generally people recognized as moderate representatives of their party or church. While each institute follows different procedures in drawing up the list of participants, the procedures are suited to the context in which the
participants live.

3. The careful preparations and the continued contacts
after the symposia provide a continuity of endeavor.

4. Some of the participants are those who have already
been to an earlier symposium, while others are new, giving both
continuity and change to the meetings.

5. The tactfulness and flexibility exercised by the participants, and especially the consummate diplomatic skill of Weiler, keep these symposia evolving but within the confines of
what is possible and comfortable for the Eastern Europeans.

6. The high level and competence of the Soviet participants
is noteworthy. The Soviets make up the bulk of the Eastern
European delegation and are their unchallenged and ostensible, though not their official, leaders. They have not attempted to dominate the meetings. Their views are expressed clearly, thoughtfully, and moderately, generally more so than those
of some of the other Eastern Europeans, who seem to be more
anxious to press upon the others the official Eastern European
line.

7. There is an avoidance of destabilizing the internal situation in both Eastern and Western Europe. No attempt is made
to weaken the system of the other.[157]

8. They provide opportunities for informal probing beyond

the official limits, yet are under the umbrella of official recognition, which is of particular importance to Eastern Europeans. This satisfies those who have the need for restrictive ground rules for the dialogue.

On the negative side one may mention the following characteristics:

1. The impression is that there are sometimes parallel monologues, rather than a dialogue, taking place. Many participants, particularly the Marxists, almost never place their own position into question but repeat the values and achievements of their side.[158] Generally very little self-criticism has been expressed.

2. Some participants attend these meetings without sufficient prior preparation. Some Eastern Europeans receive very little advance notification, and a few are totally unacquainted with the ongoing process. This ignorance of purpose, history, and process leads to attempts to read statements prepared in advance, often on a topic nearly unrelated to the theme of the symposium. Much time is lost on these lengthy statements and on attempts on part of the moderators to curtail this practice.

3. The false impression is created that Marxism and Christianity can be represented and the cause of peace served only by official, "orthodox" members. For example, the Marxists who are not pro-Soviet have made few appearances. This is advantageous to the notion of a Marxist or even general Eastern European unity which is nonexistent in reality. The Yugoslav, Albanian, Chinese, or other Marxist views seem not to be welcome.

4. The brief communique which is issued in the name of the sponsoring institutes (not the participants) seems to have a disproportionately great importance for the Soviet sponsors. Their eagerness that the communique declare support for the official Soviet position of the moment seems to overshadow their interest in the dialogue itself. This was particularly noticeable at the Kishinyov and Slatsjöbaden symposia.[159]

On the balance these symposia are very worthwhile. They are a recognition by Marxists that world peace cannot be promoted without Christians and a similar recognition by Christians that they must engage in dialogue with Marxists, despite the frequent lack of trust. The greatest value of the symposia is, most likely, their role in trust building. Without greater mutual understanding there can be no trust. Without trust there can be no peace. Mutual admiration of each other's worldview is definitely not the *leitmotif* of these symposia; respect for each other's strength and enduring presence and role in world affairs is. Most important, however, is better mutual understanding, which functions on a different level for each partner, but which is of significance because of their proximity to the official political decision-makers. Some of them are likely to assist in the making of decisions not only in respect to peace, but in Eastern countries in respect to their policies toward churches, and in Western countries in assessing the partners' interest in peace beyond the level of pure propaganda.

TYPE 5: Critical Involvement in Dialogue Resulting in Theoretical Innovations: Pluralism of Expectations and Attitudes

The main distinguishing marks of this stance toward dialogue is that, at least for short periods of time or for a smaller group of participants, it is possible to engage in a critical and self-critical exchange out of which can emerge some theoretical and practical changes. No great pressure is exercised to obtain a unity of attitudes and expectations in respect to each other. This dialogue presupposes a modicum of freedom for individuals within both groups. But this is not the main distinguishing mark because it also characterizes the previous type, particularly in the case of Poland and the International Peace Symposia. In distinction to Type 4, the awareness of power relationships plays a lesser role.

Its main distinguishing feature is that individual participants in the dialogue do not see themselves as mouthpieces of an officially promulgated Marxist or Christian orthodoxy but as creative thinkers deeply rooted within their respective traditions who turn creatively toward the questions affecting their mutual relationship and who are not reluctant to acknowledge the possibility of being enriched by the partner. This dialogue may at times turn antiestablishment and/or be rejected by the establishments of their respective constituency.

Exploration of issues beyond the conventional level and an imagination for future prospects is more pronounced in this type than in the other. There is a greater degree of giving of one's self, acknowledging the risk that the process of dialogue may bring an unsettling quality to the relationship. Such dialogue in its inception is usually not calculated but is the spontaneous outgrowth of historical circumstances. But being subject to the enthusiasm of the spontaneity, it tends to be less resistant to pressures, attacks, and changing circumstances.

It was this form of dialogue which became synonymous with dialogue in general by many casual observers. A greater number of ground rules for an "ideal" dialogue tend to be observed in this type of encounter than in the others. Its distinct weakness, or perhaps strength, depending on one's perspective, is that it tends to be attacked and rejected by the establishment. Protagonists of this dialogue are regarded either as pioneers of an era of greater freedom in dialogue, or as traitors to the "orthodox" version of their cause.

Dialogues in Czechoslovakia and Yugoslavia, as well as the international congresses of the Paulus-Gesellschaft, can be classified into this division. The dialogue in Poland and the Peace Symposia sometimes, in some of its personalities, assume many characteristics of this type.

CZECHOSLOVAKIA

The dialogue in Czechoslovakia was meteoric. The almost imperceptibly tiny spark of its inception burst into brilliant radiance only to vanish suddenly as it burned out in a hostile environment.

The earliest anticipations of the dialogue can be traced to Christian initiatives in the early 1930s in a series of discussions and lectures on Marxism and Christianity at the Academic Y.M.C.A. in Prague under the leadership of the later famous theologian Joseph Hromádka.[160] The Czechoslovak Communist Party, however, showed no interest in these initiatives, and hence no dialogue took place. During World War II practical cooperation between Christians and Marxists occurred with the anti-Nazi struggle. But, in the period between 1945 and 1948, when such cooperation could have been translated into dialogue under relative freedom and democracy, it did not take place. After the Communist *coup d'etat* of February 1948, an extremely severe Communist repression set in, which aimed at obliterating all real and potential opposition to communism.

One would expect that all churches would have recoiled as the majority Roman Catholic Church did. But with the return of Joseph Hromádka from the United States in 1947, the Evangelical Church of the Czech Brethren, the largest and most influential Protestant church, had a leader who would take a different stance toward communism. This controversial, yet very able theologian, had an attitude toward communism that was more than conciliatory, though it should be stressed that his attitude was based more on pastoral concerns than on his philosophy of history.[161] Out of his experiences and his studies of Marxism, Hromádka had become convinced that communism was the wave of the future which would build a more humane society on the heap of the bankrupt, liberal bourgeois society.[162] Thus, he believed, it was the task of the Christians to unhesitatingly support the new socialist order as it fundamentally reflects much of the social impetus of the church of Christ. Had Christians been able to create a better social system, they might be justified in criticizing the new social order. But this had not been the case. They must therefore now endorse and work for this new social order which is rooted in the gospel and is God's act in history.[163] After saying a wholehearted "yes" to the Marxist communist endeavors, it might be possible later for Christians to exert greater influence upon that order and, ultimately, to lead humanity beyond the point to which communism is capable of. As Charles West aptly stated it:

> We are left with the image of a train which is on the right track, moving with proper speed and power, but which stops before the last station. Christianity is needed, on the political level, to complete the revolution which Communism has begun.[164]

Hromádka's voice was primarily turned toward Christians both in the East and the West, stimulating a dialogue and debate—the latter more frequently—about the proper Christian response to crisis and to communism. At the first session of the World Council of Churches in Amsterdam, 1948, Hromádka delivered, in that vein, a speech opposing the attempt of the U.S. Secretary of State, John Foster Dulles, a prominent Christian layman, to involve the churches in an anti-Communist crusade. He continued the effort to block this oversimplified Christian anti-Communism and a decade later, he wrote:

> We who live within the orbit of socialistic experiments have been distressed by a continuous effort on the part of many Western Christians to discourage us, to warn us and to predict our eventual defeat and frustration. We very well know that the most difficult spiritual struggle is still ahead of us. But we also know that we have to carry it on the plane of socialism, and to resist any temptation of going back and of associating ourselves with the traditional Christian civilization. On the ground of socialism we must gradually establish all the prerequisites and institutions, safeguarding, socially and politically, human dignity and freedom. We know about the sinfulness and corruption of man. We know that no social and politi-

cal order can bring about salvation and perfect freedom of humanity. We very well know that the most adequate social organization, legal and political structure, are in a position to provide nothing more than a framework for the real, genuine human life in love, compassion, truth and hope. But we know that we are responsible also for this framework and that the framework which is, in our countries, under construction has all the promise of history. It all depends on our burning faith, devoted service, compassion for the people we live with, and on the courage of our hope whether or not we can speak, not of the future of the decadent Christian civilization, but of the certainty that the same Lord of history manifested in Jesus Christ will on the ruins of all temples and sanctuaries establish a communion of His followers. Even under quite different historical conditions.[165]

While Hromádka was capable of unstinting praise for both the theory and practice of communism, it would be unjust not to mention his willingness to be critical of communism. Primarily this meant a helpful and positive criticism aimed at helping the communists to avoid the excesses of which every revolution is capable.[166] This would include making concrete appeals on behalf of people who were somehow victimized in the process. But it also meant disagreement with communists about theory, which, he conceded, "may be wrong in many ways." [167] He went on to itemize this:

Its philosophy of history, its view of man, its revolutionary strategy and political tactics may have been rough and ready; but they were only means employed by the communists, in order to help man and human society and to further the progress of mankind.[168]

On the whole, Hromádka tended to see problems in communism as possible aberrations of individuals; the mainstream was heading in the right direction. Therefore the Christians are justified in saying many "yeses" lest they be compromised as automatic opponents. This support may make it possible for the Christians to utter courageously the absolute "no" should the occasion for it arise.[169]

Leaving aside the various positive and negative consequences of Hromádka's emphatic endorsement of communism, the fact that Czechoslovak communists, despite lingering distrust, could depend on support of the leadership of the Protestant churches would, in the long run, foster the emergence of dialogue. Hromádka's long-standing willingness to dialogue with people of other orientations helped his colleagues in the Church of the Czech Brethren and other Protestants, upon whom he had a great influence, be ready for dialogue when the opportunity arose.

Hromádka had accepted Thomas Masaryk's maxim that "democracy is discussion." [170] He appealed to people to be tolerant toward other worldviews in personal encounters. The partner was to be interpreted from the best vantage point, respected, and truly listened to. Christians, in particular, ought to follow this approach. The partners' humanity provides the common base for dialogue. The "Christian" human being and the "Marxist" human being can meet "not as representatives of ideological systems but as human beings with their hearts and minds, sorrows and sins, desires and aspirations." [171] As the content for dialogue, in addition to concrete problems of the contemporary situation, he suggested the ultimate principles and norms which form the common basis of both groups. The partners would bring it to their own motivation in search of peace, reconciliation, and justice.[172]

Hromádka thus became a trailblazer of the dialogue, with a theology which extolled the virtues of socialism, and thereby made himself increasingly palatable to those thoughtful Marxists who followed his publications, especially such works as *The Gospel for Atheists,* published in Czechoslovakia in 1958. By 1964 Hromádka had become fully aware of the needs and possibilities of an explicit dialogue with Marxists and addressed himself directly and at length to these questions in the book *Pole je tento svět* [*The Field Is This World*], published on the occasion of his seventy-fifth birthday.[173]

After giving a theological justification of the relationship of the gospel to the world and advocating intra-Christian dialogue on those issues, he called for a dialogue between Christians and "the builders of the new orders," particularly the Marxist-Leninists.[174] He started out by clarifying that for Christians the atheism of Marxists is not of essence but a historical by-product of workers' liberation. "Socialist atheism is not *primarily* and *essentially* a revolt against God, but a struggle for man in all his personal needs and in his social relationships as well." [175] It is human beings that matter to both Christians and Marxists. The question, What is a human being? is the subject for dialogue *par excellence.* The partners in dialogue must not approach this question from rigidly ideological viewpoints. Each needs to start the quest with self-criticism and self-examination and must not seek the abandonment of goals and plans by the partner, but be involved in the passionate pursuit of human emancipation.

We long for the number of these genuine and enthusiastic builders of new orders among men to be as great as possible, and for their enthusiasm, conviction and self-sacrifice to have an attraction, especially for the young people and adolescents. Yes, it is important that the believing Christian descend to the depths of his faith in order to comprehend the people of this type who are around him, in order to feel the beat of their hearts, the zeal of their thoughts, and the purity of their humanity. And we also long for these people, so mistrustful of everything that hints of religion and the church, not to be deceived by superficial or petrified phenomena and to reflect on the work of those who, in the name of their God, led by the prophets and the Gospel, have intervened in history, aroused the conscience of men, had revolutionay effect (even if not by political means) on the structure and orders of social life.[176]

Hromádka summarized his proposition as follows:

... a dialogue between a confessor of the Gospel and a Communist . . . can be fruitful only if each descends to the depths of *his own* faith or *his own* convictions and if each thoroughly thinks through *his own* fundamental thesis, the basis for *his own* thinking and practical life. *It is not a question of seeking compromises or mutual adaptations.* In other words, *it should not be a synthesis.* . . . Any attempts to seek premature agreements and mutual adjustments must lead to a confusion of ideas, moral uncertainty and practical ineffectiveness.[177]

The Christian can bring to the dialogue the great biblical insights about the glory and misery of human beings, pointing to those values that are enduring as well as those faults in human beings that plague people under all social orders. The Marxists can teach Christians about the need for radical changes in human society based on the knowledge of social laws. The full impact of this dialogue can be expected to take place in the future more so than in the present.

Today's Marxist (Leninist) ideology is a militant weapon and for a long time will retain its impact. In a period of struggles and fights for the very existence of the new society, this ideology must not be diluted or deprived of its power. But after the new society has consolidated, in a period of normal tasks and relationships . . . the old formulas and doctrines will not suffice . . . this movement of dialectical and historical thinking about the visible, material world that will some time encounter the reality of the witness of the Gospel, the reality that cannot be passed over and ignored, and which will have to be faced positively.[178]

The time for this positive encounter with the gospel was nearer than Hromádka could have anticipated. Some Marxists had started wrestling with these questions even before Hromádka wrote those lines. With the stepped-up pace of relaxation, the dialogue came surprisingly quickly, proving that these processes are thwarted only by the heavy hand of bureaucratic or military intervention.

Already in 1957, during the dark times of repression, Milan Machovec, professor of philosophy at Charles University in Prague, published a short version of his book *Smysl lidského života* [*The Meaning of Human Life*].[179] Those were inauspicious times for the publication of such a book. In 1965 it appeared in print in a more complete version with an added last chapter entitled, "Dialogue," which proved to give the most significant Marxist theoretical exposition of the need for dialogue. Though the French Marxist Roger Garaudy's *From Anathema to Dialogue* (1964) has been considered the Marxist breakthrough in favor of dialogue, Machovec's theoretical contribution is not lesser than Garaudy's. With his theoretical endorsement of dialogue, Machovec was just beginning a very prolific writing career on dialogue with Christians, which, to do it justice, would require a separate volume. Machovec is one of the giants of the world wide Christian-Marxist dialogue and perhaps its most seminal thinker.

Machovec considered dialogue to be the highest possible form of interpersonal and intergroup relationships. It consists of dialogue with others, with oneself, and even with "not-myself" (confronting death as the negation of self). He considered it the means of creating the most heightened awareness, which, for a Marxist, should play the same elevated place as prayer does for believers. Prayer is communication with God, who is actually the alienated self; dialogue is the authentic communication. However, people of the twentieth century are ill-prepared for dialogue because of oversimplification, overorganization, and the antagonisms between social systems.[180] Yet despite many obstacles to it, the dialogue plays an absolutely essential, central role in our being human. All of the inner abilities of the partners, not just their cognition, is involved in dialogue.

Four conditions must exist to have dialogue:

1. Participants must have courage to open up and expose not only their strengths but also their weaknesses.[181]

2. Each participant must share all that she or he knows, regardless whether the partner is a friend or foe. Tactical

shrewdness betrays not only the partner but also oneself as
it denies one's own conviction to have views which are of some
consequence to the partner.[182]

3. The reason for dialogue is the concern for the concrete,
human interest of the partner. It is not sufficient to hold humane theories. The concrete behavior toward the partner as
a true human being, as a sister or brother, is the actual criterion of humanity. Otherwise, not only is the partner reduced
to an object, but the self becomes a lonely figure among
objects.[183]

4. Only personal engagement assures success to dialogue.
The art of modern life should be the willingness to take the
risks for one's self and the other, rather than retreat to safety
at the first danger signal.[184]

The use of force negates dialogue (potential use is even
more threatening than actual). So does the tendency to develop
hierarchies, because it is hard to be honest with those on whom
one depends. Differences and irritations must exist for the dialogue to evoke true involvement. "Dialogue, in so far as it is a
true dialogue, meaning to take hold of things 'at their roots,'
has as its goal only the truth and the interests of the entire
human society." [185] "Without dialogue one of the basic Communist goals could not be carried out: the wholesome and harmonious development of the human personality." [186]

In 1965 a German edition of a previous Czech publication
appeared under the title *Marxismus und dialektische Theologie: Barth, Bonhoeffer, und Hromádka,* in which Machovec
stressed the importance of the Marxist encounter with living
forms of religiosity. Then he turned his attention to theories
of convergence in "Hoffnungen und Befürchtungen der An-
näherung." [187] He remarked that convergence already takes
place in our common consumer society in which people are
more interested in things than in other people. A new ethics
should be sought, a new consciousness of transcendence, in
order to overcome this spiritual crisis. Since this is what
Christendom has attempted to do over the period of many
centuries, it would be well if people listened to the likes of
Augustine and Kierkegaard in order to more successfully
grapple with the issues.

Hromádka and his colleagues finally elicited Marxist publications which differed from the former primitive propaganda
by being open and engaging. Machovec's work, which is not
only, nor perhaps primarily, a response to the Christian openness, became an epoch-making breakthrough in the Marxist

study of Christianity, in Marxist attempts to come to grips with the most developed forms of religion.[188] His own intellectual productivity is one of the main reasons for the brightness of the meteoric phase of the dialogue. However, he humbly refrained from claiming to be of significance. Instead he singled out the following specific Czechoslovak conditions which aided in the emergence of the dialogue: 1) the Czechoslovak self-identity as a West-East people who can serve as a bridge between different groups, 2) a people who started the first reformation in Europe and were still reform minded, and 3) a people who took seriously Masaryk's statement that "democracy is discussion," as well as that human beings are their own environment.[189]

Among the practical roots of the dialogue Machovec saw the willingness of many Christians to involve themselves in the traumatic and revolutionary movements, even at the cost of their lives, and work together with Marxists; at the same time, Christians realized that Marxists equally suffered in defense of their country. Theoretically the roots of the dialogue can be traced to the Marxist recognition of the Christian "Good Samaritan Principle," ultimately following Jesus in respecting persons not for their opinions but for their actions on behalf of others. Christians, on the other hand, recognized that the basic feature of Marxism is not its atheism, but its profound humanism. After the Marxist take-over, it became obvious to thinking Marxists that creating a "new human being" was not nearly as easy as had been imagined.[190] New economic relations did not automatically change many negative forms of human behavior and Marxists began to understand better Christian failures to implement changes in society according to their own best insights. Some Marxists started granting the possibility that Christians may have gained valuable experience during two thousand years of social involvement. An inner need for dialogue emerged within Marxism. Since the experience showed that organizing a new society was much more difficult and complex than initially anticipated, Marxism "needed to understand itself differently, reflect on things differently than before, must work out its theories and concepts in a much more complex way than before." [191]

Machovec did not restrict his work to book writing. In the early 1960s he offered a seminar on "Marxist Criticism and History of Religion" at the Charles University, which by 1964 became a "dialogue seminar." At considerable risk to his career he invited Western and Czechoslovakian Christians as speakers. In addition to some prominent Western theologians who visited Prague and were invited to deliver a lecture at the seminar, the following native Christians also participated: J. Hromádka, J. Souček, J. Lochman, J. Smolik, M. Opočenský, Z. Trtik, J. Němec, Anežka Ebertová, Večerka, and Haban. The Marxist participants, in addition to Machovec, were Zbyněk Fišer, Jiří Čvekl, and Vladimir Sadek.[192] These seminars became a practicing ground for dialogues as well as sources for authentic information about Christianity, untainted by dogmatic approaches.

Milan Opočenský, one of the participants in these dialogues, urged Christians to make their contributions to society boldly, not to wait or ask for Marxist permissions. He noted that the "manifold alienations of modern man has not yet been overcome by the socialist structure of society." [193] He pointed out how the international relaxation of tensions introduced the era of dialogue and how it would be erroneous to regard the socialist countries of Eastern Europe as a monolithic bloc, since each respective country has different spiritual and national traditions. The Czechoslovakian Christians wish to be first-class citizens who, on the basis of their understanding of the gospel, "see some realities more clearly and deeply and we feel that we are obliged to put this understanding into the life of our society." [194] Though "theoretically the socialist structures of society create better prerequisites for a full development of human life," there are still many personal and social evils.[195] Christians need to enter the dialogue, calling to attention their insights which could serve as correctives. However, they must not shy away from justified Marxist criticism of Christianity. The Christian commitment to service in the manner of Jesus Christ has already found response in Marxist theory and practice.[196]

In addition to Machovec, the philosophers Vitězslav Gardavský, Milan Průcha, Robert Kalivoda, and Jaroslav Krejči, and sociologists Erika Kadlecová and Jaroslav Hranička were among those Czechoslovak Marxists who were attempting to rethink Marxism with special reference to their encounter with Christianity. Gardavský, a professor of philosophy at the Military Academy at Brno, Moravia, was one who made the greatest public impact when he published a series of essays on Christianity in the *Literárni Noviny* (Prague) in 1966 and 1967. These essays were later published under the title *God Is Not Quite Dead*.[197] Gardavský challenged the common Marxist presupposition that faith is absurd and atheism is self-evident by proposing that at times it may be more absurd not to believe in God than to believe. Instead of rejecting the great figures of the Judeo-Christian tradition, Gardavský aimed to appropriate them for the Marxist as part of a heritage with which each person ought to be familiar. Thus he explored, appreciatively, the figures of Jacob, Jesus, Augustine, Thomas Aquinas, and Pascal. Then he proceeded to examine Christianity and atheism in an open, fair manner, not content to leave the clichés unexamined. He found that both Christianity and communism share the most fundamental value of love for human beings. He felt that this and other values of Christianity need to be analyzed and soaked up by Marxism, which will "no longer feel the need to steer well clear of it." [198]

Gardavský's book received an enthusiastic reception marking him as perhaps the most influential Marxist contributor to the dialogue at home.[199] Soon he elicited interest outside of Czechoslovakia, though abroad Machovec's influence was greater.

Further contribution to the dialogue was made by the Section for the Theory and Sociology of Religion of the Czechoslovak Academy of Sciences, under the leadership of Erika Kadlecová and her coworkers, Jaroslav Hranička and Ladislav Prokupek. They hosted in Prague the second colloquium of Marxist Sociologists of Religion, on December 6-9, 1966.[200] Present were Marxist researchers of religion from all Eastern European countries except Rumania and Albania. Many papers on the nature of religiosity, secularization, and atheism were read. The sociological approach to this field was in its infancy among Marxist scholars. One of the most significant features of the colloquim was that those present tackled the question of dialogue. While they maintained that conditions in each country dictated the specific approach to dialogue, they were unanimous in endorsing its necessity.[201]

With this kind of international support, as well as the steadily liberalizing tendencies in their own society, the same Section of the Czechoslovak Academy of Sciences hosted and cosponsored with the Paulus-Gesellschaft the only international Christian-Marxist Congress which took place in a socialist country.[202] The dialogue took place in Marianske Lazňe (Marienbad), April 27-30, 1967.

The precondition, a certain maturity and readiness on the part of both partners, has been reached, noted Hromádka.[203] Human beings still experience great needs and suffering, often caused by both Christians and Marxists. The coresponsibility for the past problems and for the future needs of human beings necessitates that both draw together the very best in their traditions, overcome distrust and the caricatures of the past, and engage in dialogue. Hromádka expressed his belief that the conflicts between Christianity and Marxism are removable misunderstandings rather than unbridgable contradictions. Faith and Marxist ideology are not on the same level. Therefore they do not collide irreconcilably, nor can they be synthesized.[204] Dialogues ought to be carefully prepared, both personally and societally, because the dialogue should be an attempt to reach the innermost levels of human experience and aspiration.

Hromádka was right about the possible far-reaching consequences of the dialogue, especially when applied to the Congress at Marianske Lazně. Its impact on later Czechoslovak events cannot be easily evaluated. Some have praised it or condemned it for being the immediate cause of the "Prague Spring" of 1968.[205] It would be gross reductionism to see the causes or even the immediate cause of the "Prague Spring" in this process, causing greater democratization of socialism. But it undoubtedly served as a visible symbol of the profound changes which were taking place in Czechoslovakia. These changes increased with surprising speed and, eventually, led to tragedy. Czechoslovakia might have been ready for such dialogue, but the Soviet Union and certain of its allies were not. For all the differences between socialist countries, there is still a systemic connection between them. When taken in this broader context, the larger socialist community of nations was not yet ready for the dialogue as carried out at Marianske Lazně.

The Congress itself was not a model of good organization in terms of the agenda. The Czechoslovak hosts provided good meeting conditions, but the actual program was organized by the Paulus-Gesellschaft. As at previous meetings, the program was overcrowded. Too little time was left for discussions.[206] The theme was "Creativity and Freedom," but speakers addressed themselves to diverse issues. Discussion often went in disparate directions. Of the 220 participants, many were reduced to mere listeners. Focus was hard to achieve.

Yet these weaknesses were vastly overshadowed by its strengths. The fact that about 170 people, mostly theologians and clergy, came from the West and freely participated in the discussions had an electrifying effect not only on the meeting but also on public opinion. Most of the papers presented were truly pioneering efforts which surpassed the fondest hope for openness and creativity. Indeed, creativity and freedom were much in evidence as practiced by the participants. It was the theme of their speeches. Writers from socialist and nonsocialist countries cross-fertilized each other's thinking, learning much from one another.

Only a cursory survey of the Czechoslovakian contributions will be made here.[207]

Milan Průcha, one of Czechoslovakia's outstanding Marxist philosophers, delivered a paper "On Being Human." Instead of following the customary Marxist approach to human beings, Průcha based his analysis on the classical philosophical approach to the notion of being, relating it to the question of the final aim of human beings. The concept of being, he felt, should not be too quickly resolved either by Marxist or Christian concepts.[208] He attempted to work out a Marxist notion of transcendence, which would go beyond the Christian notion of transcendence by being free "from its religious trammels." [209]

Robert Kalivoda presented a paper entitled "Christianity in the Process of Human Emancipation." In it he maintained that Marx's phrase,"the opiate of the people," could not be regarded as the basis of the Marxian attitude toward religion. Christianity did not merely support the existing social system, but had originally, and throughout history, played a progressive role by opposing injustice. Those Christians who were presently opposing social progress (antisocialists or anticommunists) are, in fact, opposed to the basic values and ideals of Christianity.[210]

Gardavský pointed out that the common heritage of both Marxism and Christianity can be found in the myths of antiquity and the biblical myths. Some contemporary Christian problems stem from having interpreted the biblical myths from the perspective of antiquity, though many contemporary theologians are trying to dissolve the synthesis. Marxists come into the temptation of accepting only the classical concept of freedom, which consists in learning the order of nature. This view has to be also enriched with the biblical view that freedom consists in the act of creativity and self-creation.[211]

Machovec's paper was entitled "Christians and Marxists in Common Quest for the Meaning of Life." He maintained that the question of meaning of life remained even for those who rejected religion as a mystification. The absence of formal religion often made people susceptible to pseudo-religion of idolatrous forms of transcendence: worshiping the state, the party, the future, or a leading personality. The worship of God at least serves as a means of rejecting lesser than ultimate loyalties. Atheism, in its true form, is also a rejection of false divinities.[212]

The success of the dialogue at Marianske Lazně can also be ascribed to the very able hostess, Dr. Erika Kadlecová. She was able to diffuse some of the "time-bombs" to which she referred in her report on the Congress.[213] With her diplomatic but sincere handling of the sometimes probing questions and indictments of the religious policies of the Czechoslovakian state, she was able to forestall what could have become very tense confrontations. An acknowledgement of her understanding of and empathy for the churches was her subsequent appointment as Director of the State Office for Religion in the Alexander Dubček government. In that post she actually worked for the demise of that department, hoping to give more freedom to the churches. She was unable to implement this because after the Soviet invasion she was replaced again by her predecessor, Karel Hrúza, who was much more willing to supervise and constrain religious activities. But during her tenure in that office many people described that period as a time of almost total freedom for the churches.[214] Naturally dialogue flourished!

Just how many dialogues took place during the "Prague Spring," and how many people participated, is impossible to establish. The number is probably in the thousands.[215] The one that was regarded as the first public meeting, of the "show dialogue" kind, was held in Prague on April 29, 1968. On the Marxist side the dialogue partners on the panel were Jiří Čvekl, Vitézslav Gardavský, František Kavka, Jaroslav Krejči, and Lubomir Nový. On the Christian side, Joseph Hromádka, Jan Lochman, J. B. Souček, Ladislav Hejdánek, and Zdenek Trtik were the Protestant participants. Peter Haban, Jiří Němec, and Vladimir Rudolf were the Roman Catholic participants. Machovec presided over the meeting.[216] The format of the meeting, at which the leading roles were played by Hromádka and Machovec, arranged that questions from the audience were submitted in writing and then answered by those to whom they were directed or who were best equipped to handle them. The attendance estimates varied from 1200 to 3000.[217] Large numbers of students participated in what became "a very open and spirited dialogue." [218]

Christians, including the leaders of the churches, supported Dubček's efforts toward democratization, not merely because they stood to gain an advantage but because they were convinced that it meant a unique renewal within the socialist movement.[219] This was clearly expressed also at the Third Assembly of the Christian Peace Conference, which took place in Prague in April, 1968. Cooperation and dialogue grew almost daily.

One of the many intentions of the invasion of the Warsaw Pact troops on August 21, 1968, was to halt the dialogue. Paradoxically it brought, at least for the moment, the most fervent cooperation between Christians and Marxists:

> The dialogue between Christians and Marxists actually won through the events of August 21. That tragic week brought about such a cooperation of the Church with the Party! The churches prayed, prayed for Dubcek, as he was held captive in Moscow. And if the dialogue between Christians and Marxists ten years ago engaged only a handful of theologians and philosophers, when a year ago the number grew into hundreds of thousands, now the situation in Czechoslovakia is such, that no Communist in Czechoslovakia can see in a Christian merely an enemy. Hence this became such a great school of dialogue that all of humanity could win through it.[220]

In fact, formal public dialogues were effectively terminated by the invading forces and the puppet government of Gustaf Husák. The churches were, and indeed, still are packed, but Christians became again second-class citizens. Marxists lost the bid for moral renewal which had spurred them to action in the previous few years. Their model had been to become leaders of the people, leaders who, like Christians, would lead in acts of service. Many of them had been glad that they did not need or get the aid of the police and that their actions were the result of their convictions rather than career seeking or employment as agents of the Party.[221]

But gradually many of the liberties which had been won in the past decade were eroded. Czechoslovakia became again a land of repression and fear. The process of erosion was gradual but increased every year since 1968. There were many acts of courage by both Christians and Marxists who spoke out on behalf of the vision they jointly forged. But these people of courage were removed from positions of influence, repudiated, attacked, and reduced to "non-person" status. While in the first weeks after the occupation the foreign troops were not able to find even a dozen collaborators, in due time the opportunism of some people came to the fore. The Moscow-directed attacks against dialogue were aired not only from government controlled media but were supported even by some church leaders.[222] There is good reason to believe that Gardavský's death in 1978, shortly after a bout of interrogation, is certainly attributable to police brutality. Machovec and others all lost their teaching posts. For a while Machovec supported himself by playing organ in a Catholic Church. In 1979 he was barred even from that activity. In Czechoslovakia no one dares to mention him in print, even in historical references.

Inside of Czechoslovakia, aside from the close ties which were forged earlier and which are likely to remain vividly in the memory of people and could forcefully reappear at the first opportune moment, formal dialogue came to a complete halt in terms of public exchanges, reverting to Type 2. We shall have to wait for a time of greater liberties to find out whether the personal dialogues continue. Most probably they do.

However, Czechoslovakian Christians and Marxists continued, at least for a period of several years, to participate in dialogue abroad, and, even more significantly, to have their works published abroad. A formidable amount of articles and books were created in the late 1960s and early 1970s, many of which must have been begun before August 1968, reflecting an optimism about the dialogue, to which more somber, cautious notes were added as the dialogue in Europe lost its impetus.

Machovec regarded this endeavor as a new stage in the dialogue, better suitable for the 1970s. It consisted in a transformation from "show discussions" to theoretical studies of concrete subjects on Christianity by Marxists and vice versa.[223] Some of these books were still published in Czechoslovakia before the total silencing of their authors. They still hailed the dialogue as Marxism's most important approach to the world.[224] It is significant that those Christians and Marxists who were most prominent in the dialogue while it was popular persevered even under very inclement conditions. By this time a camaraderie had developed between the Czechoslovak Marxists and Christian proponents of the dialogue, a camaraderie which Machovec dared to label as "brotherhood." [225] This was vividly symbolized by the trip of a team of four Czechoslovakians through the United States in 1969, where they engaged in fraternal dialogue at the invitation of the United Presbyterian Church. The team consisted of V. Gardavský and Julius Tomin (Marxists) and Lubomír Mirejovský and Dan Drapel (Christians).[226] Another example was the dialogue between

Albert Rasker of the University of Leiden, a Dutch Protestant theologian, and Machovec at the Beienroder Konvent, West Germany, October 9, 1968.

Jaroslav Krejči, professor at the Pedagogical School of Ostrava, wrote a series of articles in which he carefully inveighed against the monological approach to life, pointing out its dangers, and argued for an enlightened form of atheism which would decisively abandon the misuses of atheism from the previous period of Marxist practice. He eloquently analyzed and promoted the dialogical approach.[227]

Machovec not only discerned that the second stage of dialogue, the dialogue of the 1970s, consisted of writing serious monographs, but vigorously contributed to it. His primary search consisted in looking for the meaning of Jesus Christ's person and message. His interest in the meaning of life, displayed vigorously in the 1960s, would naturally lead him to investigate the person and message of the one whom Christians claimed was imbuing meaning to their lives. *A Marxist Looks at Jesus*, which was never published in Czechoslovakia but appeared first in Germany, is undoubtedly the most profound, thoughtful, and sympathetic study of Jesus by a Marxist.[228] In it he showed not only command of the most significant Christian scholarship in the field, but cast off the customary Marxist prejudices and interpretations of Jesus. One of the most human truths Machovec found was the necessity of "taking up the cross," suffering injustice rather than contributing to it, by those (including Marxists) who care about honesty and truth.[229] Thus he sought to grasp the biblical ideals as lived by Jesus and to adapt them to the modern age, saying that the Marxist must absorb and build on everything that is best in the human heritage. It is unlikely that a Christian would not gain some profoundly new understanding of Jesus by reading this book.

Similarly appreciative and thought-provoking was Machovec's essay "The Case of Jesus' and Marxist Self-Reflection." [230] Likewise Machovec continued his interest in exploring the relationship of atheism to the problem of God.[231]

Evidence of change in Gardavský's post-1968 thinking is sporadic and comes mostly from his unpublished work, "The Angel on the Tip of the Sword," but it is already discernible in the published work, *Hope out of Skepsis*.[232] While in his earlier work he took Jacob, the self-made man, as his model, toward the end of his life Gardavský became attracted to the "suffering prophet," Jeremiah.[233] For Gardavský, Jeremiah was the radical "outsider," one who does not easily belong to any group, one whose views appear insane because he tries to rob the rich and powerful of their sense of security and the powerless of their insecurity. Life consists not only of hopefulness but also hopelessness; the good must be taken with the bad, not with some sort of nostalgic sadness, but with realistic acceptance that in some situations one does not act out of hope but out of hopelessness.[234] This transition in Gardavský's thought was no doubt the result of his intense personal suffering, which eventually led to death a day after release from one of many frequent police interrogations. The year was 1978—a decade after the Soviets dashed the hope that Czechs and Slovaks might create a humanistic form of socialism.

Among Christians too there were those whose eagerness for dialogue could find outlet only in the West. Most notable among them is Jan Lochman, former professor of theology at the Comenius Evangelical Theological School, who accepted an invitation to teach at the Theological School of the University of Basel, Switzerland. He had done much to inform Western readers about the achievements and problems of the dialogue in Czechoslovakia during his year as visiting professor at Union Theological Seminary in New York. As a result of this, his book *Church in a Marxist Society* appeared.[235] In it he developed his thesis that the dialogue is and should be mostly "a mutual interpellation." [236] During the "Prague Spring" he was indeed an ardent practitioner of this mutual interpellation as he sought to interpret and support the democratic socialism of the time and place it in the context of the general Christian tradition, the Hussite reform movement, and the more immediate sources of Czechoslovakian independence and democratic aspirations.[237] He called on the churches to participate in full solidarity in the process of democratizing their society. He mentioned the many cases of former deformations of socialism which caused problems, unfair restrictions, and suffering not only for Christians but for all Czechoslovakians. He therefore endorsed democratic socialism as a renewal of society and called for a renewal in the churches, because the church is for the world. Christian values begin to be treasured again, even by many secularized people. This must not be used egoistically by the churches. The gospel of Jesus is to be declared not only for the believers but also for the unbelievers, including the atheists. Atheism must be demythologized. Christians must free themselves from considering atheists as demons, and must not encounter them primarily on an ideological level, but in the spirit of solidarity and proexistence, i.e. living for others.[238]

Lochman then moved to the exploration of the Marxist critique of religion [239] and then to the study of Marx.[240] In *Encountering Marx* Lochman strove for a proper theological orientation toward Marxism in the aftermath of the disappointments of 1968. Lochman, encountering the uncritical acceptance of Marxism by many Western European students in the early 1970s, said "no" to the question as to whether a Christian can also be a Marxist, but maintained that many Marxist insights can be incorporated critically into a theologian's undertaking. The writings of the "young Marx" are most promising for the Christian who seeks to encounter Marxist thought on the nature of human beings. Particularly useful are Marx's concepts of alienation, the diabolical role of money, and the striving to become fully human. The element of hope and the quest for the future are common ties of Marxism and Christianity. Marxist insights on hope and the future can serve as correctives to Christian one-sidedness. The reverse is equally true.

In conclusion it can be said that the dialogue in Czechoslovakia was, and in its own dimmed, suppressed present version, still is, a mutual engagement carried out in the spirit of constructive criticism. Departures from the preconceived, dogmatic, demonizing notions of the past were frequent. The theoretical innovation, as well as certain forms of practical coexistence of the protagonists of the dialogue, can be instructional for those outside of Czechoslovakia. It could also serve as a departure point should conditions favorable to the dialogue emerge again in Czechoslovakia. For the time being those prospects are very bleak. It remains the destiny of the protagonists of the dialogue to suffer together.

YUGOSLAVIA

The patterns of the encounter between Marxists and Christians in Yugoslavia range from hostility to dialogue. Starting with conflict and confrontation in practice and theory, there gradually emerged cautious but constructive cooperation, as well as critical involvement in dialogue. Four stages may be discerned in the development of Christian-Marxist relations in Yugoslavia:

1. All-out conflict (up to 1953) [241]
2. Deescalation (1953-1962)
3. Suspension of hostilities and peace feelers (1962-1967)

4. Constructive rapprochement and dialogue (1967-)[242]
Within the fourth stage it is possible to delineate two sub-stages:
   a. Unhampered dialogue (1967-1972)
   b. Communist Party constraints upon dialogue (1972-)
A few general statements ought to be made at the outset.

The first is that post-World War II events are intelligible only in the light of what transpired during the war. The policy of the Communist Party of Yugoslavia, which was in a leadership position during the war of liberation, was not to alienate the large masses of peasants, who were overwhelmingly religious. Therefore no atheist propaganda was permitted, and Partisan units were encouraged to accept priests and allow them to perform religious services.[243] Some priests who were sympathizers of the Communist Party before the war reached high political positions. But the vast bulk of church leadership was not only strenuously anti-Partisan but often collaborated with the enemy. Particularly implicated was the Roman Catholic Church in its dealings with the Independent State of Croatia and its leader Ante Pavelić. The Serbian Orthodox Church had its close ties to Draža Mihajlović, leader of the Serbian royalist forces. The bitterness of the Marxists because of these dealings, which they considered traitorous activity against the Yugoslav people, was very great. The drastic changes in attitude toward the churches which took place in 1945, when the Communist Party came into power, can be explained, at least in part, by these wartime activities, for which the churches never publicly admitted regret.

The second is that the dialogue was initiated more clearly by some Marxist scholars than by theologians. In view of the fact that the Communist Party of Yugoslavia (since 1958 renamed the League of Communists of Yugoslavia) was very much in control, this Marxist initiative is psychologically to be expected.

Thirdly, the largest Christian church, the Orthodox Church (now consisting of the Serbian Orthodox and Macedonian Orthodox Churches with a combined adherence of more than 40 percent of the population) and the Protestant churches, which are almost negligible in terms of membership (less than one percent of the population) showed practically no interest in theoretical dialogue with Marxists.[244] For all practical purposes, the Christian-Marxist dialogue in Yugoslavia is a Roman Catholic-Marxist dialogue. This means that, with few exceptions, the partners on both sides stem predominantly from Croatia and Slovenia.

Fourthly, the factor of close national identification with religion (Croats and Slovenes are Catholics,[245] while Serbians, Macedonians, and Montenegrins are Orthodox) is a stumbling block for the dialogue. From this perspective the Communist Party dialogue with Roman Catholics is often perceived as a possible encouragement particularly to Croatian nationalism. Nationalism has been an explosive issue in Yugoslav internal policies.

Fifthly, there were some societal factors, distinct from the rest of Eastern European conditions, which prepared the ground for the Yugoslav specificity of the dialogue. The first of those conditions was Yugoslavia's breakaway from the Soviet bloc in 1948, resulting not only in a consistently non-aligned, peaceful coexistence policy, but also in searching for a communist model different from that of the Soviet Union and its allies. Such a distinct model was discovered by 1953 to consist in self-management of all enterprises, resulting in considerable decentralization of society. The relatively greater influence of people on the local level, which tended to break down the dogmatism of approaches to various issues, became the second condition beneficial to dialogue. The reassessment of the nature of "the leading role" of Communists in society, which brought about the reorganization of the party in 1958, signaled a relaxation in the party's dominance over many societal affairs, religion included. That was another contributing factor to the emergence of the dialogue.

Sixthly, there was the emergence of a group of independent Marxist thinkers, well-trained in both Marxist and non-Marxist literature, who set out boldly to redefine the meaning and role of Marxist thought in the context of a socialist society in the second half of the twentieth century.[246] After an initially hard combat, this group of thinkers (of which the Praxis circle was the most self-conscious trend setter) prevailed over the dogmatist approach and set a lasting, though precariously oscillating, tone to the Yugoslav Marxist intellectual and cultural atmosphere. Yugoslavia prides itself as being the country most authentically true to the revolutionary inspirations of the classics of Marxism and most creative in its application of its principles. Their thinkers have greater latitude than other Eastern Europeans. Yet dogmatism has not been completely eradicated, as a Marxist critic clearly indicates:

The issue is dogmatism from which this society did not ever, except in declarations, truly break away. Let us not forget that our society . . . settled accounts with Stalinists in a Stalinistic manner. Let us not forget that even the greatest anti-dogmatists can be exceptionally dogmatic in their anti-dogmatism. The live tissue of dogmatism in this society blocks creative movement, threatening human liberties and existence, speaking in the name of the proletariat but not from its positions, uses self-management as a screen for the defense of its own positions and not as a true perspective on human beings. This [dogmatic] tissue is still not threatened. This tissue must be destroyed, sacrificing all myths which we have and which we are creating.[247]

The fact that such criticism is published in Yugoslavia is indicative of both the liberties and the limitations to liberties which are vacillating in an uneasy equilibrium. Each development in the country may increase or decrease the dose of liberty. In this context the Christian-Marxist dialogue is the result of liberalization trends in society and, conversely, has an impact upon liberalization.

Seventhly, a certain parallelism is in evidence in the development of both the society and the church, especially in respect to the notion of authority. The Yugoslav Marxists proposed the recreation of authority in society along the lines of self-management. The Second Vatican Council had endorsed the idea of collegiality in the church and society. These two notions proved to be enormously dynamic and released many creative strivings within Marxism and Christianity. These creative rumblings caused many more people to endorse dialogue than under the previously more centralized forms of authority. This particular configuration of self-management and collegiality may well have been the most unique feature of the Yugoslav version of the dialogue.

Eighthly, the absence of any substantial democratic traditions and the complex and often tense relations among various nationalities and their traditional associations with different, often stridently antagonistic, religions makes dialogue a difficult, precarious task. The vast majority of Yugoslavs, even among the educated, are historically, psychologically, and educationally not ready for dialogue. Dialogue has never been an option in their life. Many find it still impossible to understand that people with differences can engage in any other relationship but conflict. This heritage is difficult to overcome, but it may change gradually over a longer period of time.

The origins of the Christian-Marxist dialogue can be traced to the Marxist scholarly study of religion, in itself a novelty at the time.

Two very important books on religion were published by Marxist scholars, indicating a significant departure from conventional Marxist views propagated earlier. One was by a philosopher from the University of Zagreb, Branko Bošnjak, *Filozofija i kršćanstvo*,[248] and the other by a sociologist from the University of Sarajevo, Esad Ćimić, *Socijalističko društvo i religija*.[249] Both of these were reexaminations of the Marxist view on religion, attempting to go back to the primary sources and giving a more complete contextual analysis of Marx's, Engles', and Lenin's views, with a criticism of later oversimplifications and corruptions of these views. Both appraised religion, or specifically Christianity, as alienation, a human projection, and essentially undesirable. Both books reflect a very limited insight into the nature of religion but do come up with some observations that are startling when viewed in context of the environment.

Bošnjak, distinguished for being the first Yugoslav Marxist philosopher to show professional interest in religion, presented what he considered to be a rational criticism of an irrational worldview and identified philosophy (*the* philosophy!) with the former, and religion and theology with the latter. He seriously doubted the historicity of Jesus and attempted to prove the folly of belief in God. A wide variety of philosophical and theological concepts were handled, with attempts made to indicate their untruthfulness and shortcomings. Bošnjak's own Marxist view is strongly influenced by an existentialist outlook on the tragic predicament of humanity.[250] Considerable attention was given to the summary of views on religion as found in the Marxist classics.[251]

Of particular interest is Bošnjak's conclusion that religion can survive in all social systems because it cannot be reduced to the sociopolitical-economic relations. "Every religion by virtue of its essence transcends reality and aims toward that which is the 'eschaton,' i.e., the last things. Therefore no social system can be a barrier for religion. Therefore the withering of religion is not so simple. In Marxist philosophy the phenomenon of religion is considered much simpler than it is in fact." [252] It is not the truth of religion that determines its duration, but the will of those who wish to exempt themselves from natural processes in the hope of life eternal.[253] Thus the key to religion's permanent endurance is the human desire to overcome death and find purpose in a life full of suffering—attempting to find meaning in a situation where there is none.[254]

Esad Ćimić approached religion from a sociological angle.[255] He too surveyed the theory and practice of Marxism's ideas about religion, giving particular emphasis to religion as a specific form of alienation.[256] He considered the process of self-management as the most effective method of overcoming alienation and felt that when a person has overcome alienation he or she will have no more need for religion. Instead of using force, Marxist society ought to eliminate people's sense of dependence. Since religion is a form of false feeling of dependence, there will be less reason to resort to it. While maintaining the position that socialist society is overcoming religion, he conceded that socialist society continues to create conditions of alienation and threats to the individual, which become new sources of religion.[257] Mere knowledge of the sources of the threat to humans does not eliminate religion; religion will thus continue to be a phenomenon for a long time.

The books by Bošnjak and Ćimić were destined to be the steppingstones for the more serious mutual interest of Marxists and Christians after 1967. In the summer of 1966, Bošnjak had invited the foremost Vatican Marxologist, Gustav Wetter, S.J., to the Korčula Summer School, organized by the Praxis circle of which Bošnjak is a member. The Catholic theologian, Mijo Škvorc of Zagreb, later auxiliary bishop, accompanied Wetter. Bošnjak and Škvorc met and agreed to arrange a public dialogue.[258] The dialogue took place at the student center in Zagreb on March 28, 1967, thus becoming historically the first Eastern European public dialogue. About 2500 people attended, overcrowding the hall. There was a great deal of excitement and partisan spirit.[259] The theme of the dialogue was Bošnjak's above-mentioned book, but the exchange between the two highly qualified, polite, and mutually critical men can still be described more aptly as a "boxing match." Each time one of them scored a debating point, the half of the audience which was sympathetic to him cheered! Not an ideal dialogue, to be sure, but an evidence of the openness of Yugoslav society at that time.[260]

For a few Yugoslav Marxists and Christians the participation in the Paulus-Gesellschaft congresses, particularly at Marianske Lazně, Czechoslovakia were experiences of more open, tolerant dialogues.[261] While attending dialogues abroad, the Yugoslav participants met with each other and encouraged one another to commence more serious interaction at home. No consensus developed on the manner of the interaction; some were more truly dialogical in their orientation than others.

A rather devastating, lengthy book review of Bošnjak's *Filozofija i kršćanstvo* was written by the Slovene Catholic philosopher, Janez Janžekovič.[262] Janžekovič pointed to the numerous examples of misinformation, historical inaccuracies, and the faulty logic of Bošnjak and even chided him for not being a Marxist whom Marx would recognize.[263] Janžekovič also criticized Bošnjak's narrow understanding of dialogue, saying that Lucio Lombardo-Radice and Roger Garaudy, as well as some Marxists from Slovenia (who remain unnamed), had gone much further in their encounter with Christians. Janžekovič himself left much to be desired, for he made no attempt to find anything in Bošnjak that could be regarded as positive. In a later work Bošnjak correctly challenged Janžekovič's premise that the Communist parties decide what is Marxism and the Catholic Church decides what is Christian doctrine.[264]

A collection of essays by Marxists on the subject of religion, *Religija i društvo*, contained some divergent Marxist understandings of the dialogue with Christians. Bošnjak did not consider dialogue a wasteful exercise because he did not consider religion a moribund social illusion, but declared that in the field of ideas dialogue can only mean a clear exposition of one's own ideas without seeking the defeat of the partner.[265] All ideas need to be discussed, particularly areas of practical concern, and the most important specific gain from dialogue is that all are given freedom of expression and may point to the errors in their partners' positions.[266] The meaning of dialogue in a world in which various conceptions of reality coexist is that there just might be an area of agreement.

One of the essayists, Oleg Mandić, who represents a narrower Marxist approach toward the dialogue and the Christian contribution to society, provided a short history of dialogues, emphasizing the role of Vatican II, the dialogue between Catholics and Marxists, and the various meetings sponsored by the Paulus-Gesellschaft. Mandić felt that Christians and Marxists have different reasons for engaging in the dialogue. Marxists can prove to the opinionated West that Marxists need not be dogmatic and close-minded, thus improving the Marxist reputation abroad and showing that common positions on some subjects can be found.[267] For Catholics the reason for dialogue is that their adherents in socialist countries may participate as equal partners in the quest for progress.[268]

Ante Fiamengo suggested that dialogue is a suitable method to solve conflicts between Marxists and Christians and to deal with common problems, and that it needs to be carried on within the Catholic Church, within workers' parties, and between Christians and Marxists.[269] Theoretically the two are diametrically opposed, and Marxists must not abandon their materialist and atheist positions or any of their theoretical foundations. Nor do Marxists expect Christians to change their minds. But life is too complex to allow division into two hostile camps; rather it demands coexistence and cooperation. Life transcends the contradictions of materialist-idealist and atheist-theist.[270] Marxists and Christians both need to work on humanizing people, something that is in the tradition of both movements. The increasingly complex relations between theory and practice pose the question of allowing people with religious convictions to become Party members. Fiamengo advocated that the Socialist Alliance of the Working People of Yugoslavia be the broader association in which atheists and believers are united in membership but that the League of Communists remain closed to religious people.[271]

Esad Ćimić considered the dialogue as a necessity for Christians in contemporary society and a sensible approach for Marxists in their effort to build socialism. He maintained that the most important dialogue is between believers and nonbelievers in the process of self-management rather than between the leaders of the church and state.[272] It is imperative in a socialist country that the religious communities accept rather than fight the process of socialization. He also suggested maintaining a clear distinction between church and state relations and the attitude of the League of Communists toward religion.[273]

The most reasoned, unbiased, and appreciative Marxist voice endorsing dialogue with Christians was that of Zdenko Roter, a sociologist at the University of Ljubljana. Roter is a compassionate, intelligent, courageous man of great integrity. He is dedicated to the democratization of society and devoted his journalistic and scholarly talents to providing a greater scope of liberties. His writings are not polemical in nature; they seek to enlighten and inform. He suggested that both politics and religion are forms of alienation that need to be overcome if humans are to find themselves. He criticized efforts by the government to subvert religious organizations for its own purposes, for using discriminatory and devaluating practices against them, and for attempting symbiotic union between church and state. Emancipation of political processes from the influence of religion should also mean the emancipation of religion from political pressures and manipulations. It is foolish to assume base motives and limited intelligence in believers. The Marxist criticism of religion should primarily be a criticism of society and the radical change of social relations rather than criticism of religion itself.[274] Roter presented ten theses on the necessity and desirability of dialogue based on his conviction that Christianity and Marxism have the same tradition, the same problem, that they each have emphases which could enrich the other, that they share a world which is in danger of manifold self-destruction unless the two cooperate for the good of humanity.[275] He subscribed to the notion that the future will permanently remain pluralistic and that Marxism does not seek a monopoly of thought and of patterns of government and social organization. The two, Christianity and Marxism, being so influential, have a common responsibility for the happiness and wholeness of all people.

In his work Roter relied not only on an earlier Marxist theoretical work on religion by Vuko Pavičević,[276] a sociologist from Belgrade University (who died a few years ago), but also on two Slovene Catholics, Janez Janžekovič,[277] and Vekoslav Grmič,[278] who addressed themselves to the question of the church's position in a socialist society.

The Roman Catholic response to these Marxist initiatives was vigorous. The Slovenian and Croatian Catholics undertook to follow different paths.

In Slovenia, where the Catholic Church has received the greatest liberties, perhaps due to the generally high level of democracy in that republic, the Catholics have shown remarkable collective vitality and constitute a significant factor in public life. There were suggestions that Catholics ought to have their own theater, TV and radio programs, and that clergy should participate actively in political life. In one of the villages a priest was reportedly elected to a local government position by popular vote. Thus, Slovenian Catholics demanded full equality in public life and sought to dialogue with Marxists regarding the direction Slovenian society should take.

Those Croatian Catholics who pioneered in the dialogue felt that such a path had too many pitfalls and that it smacked of neoclericalism. They suggested the need for grassroots dia-

logue—a dialogue in which problems are worked out coopera-
tively at the level on which they occur, rather than referring
them to Party or ecclesiastical superiors for solutions from
above, as was done until now. There is risk in this. Many
theoretical possibilities are yet to be realized, their realization
hinging on the successful solution of political, national, and
other problems.[279] The efforts of the group of "liberal" or
"progressive" Catholics who are promoting the dialogue are
resented and opposed by "conservatives," some of whom are
members of the hierarchy, who doubt the possibility and wisdom of serious dialogical overtures and are more comfortable
in their isolationism.[280] In addition, the Christians as a unit
are still under frequent attack by the daily press for alleged
hypocrisy in pursuing *aggiornamento.*

A lively inner dialogue on the forms and destiny of the dialogue with Marxists took place among its Roman Catholic
proponents. Most active were the faculty of the Theological
School and people associated with the center Kršćanska Sadašnjost in Zagreb, as well as a group from Split gathered
around the journal *Crkva u svijetu.*

Liberal Catholic professors Vjekoslav Bajsić, Tomislav
Šagi-Bunić, and Josip Turčinović (the so-called Zagreb circle),
repeatedly attempted to suggest ways in which contemporary
Christians should participate as responsible members of their
society. Theirs was the hard task of convincing both Christians
and Marxists that dialogue is not merely a tactical ploy intended to enable Christians to obtain privileges not available earlier. Many Communists still suspect that the churches wish to
enter the political arena in a big way, and many Christians
frankly see it as an opportunity to rehabilitate their reputa-
tions and perhaps restore the "good old days." Thus Bajsić and
Šagi-Bunić found it necessary not only to promote dialogue
but to explain it as a method of approach toward all those who
were prospective partners.[281] Bajsić, therefore, in a lecture to
a group of Marxists, justified dialogue as being more than the
expedient of the moment, that it was the proper philosophical
approach toward others who are not the same as we.[282]

Some may not regard such statements as earthshaking, but
they are extremely important when one realizes that they
come from the perspective of a church that once claimed absolute truth and that they were directed to Marxists who were
equally insistent on the infallibility of their approach. A rela-
tivization of these claims is neither easy nor insignificant.

Šagi-Bunić and Bajsić did not advocate a renewed political

role for the official church. They rejected the identity of Roman Catholic interest with Croatian national interest, which is tempting both in view of the past and in view of more contemporary sociopolitical frustrations. The church was not asked to change society or model it according to its own precepts. It should not stand in the way of those changes which mean betterment for those people with whom the church was so closely associated.[283] The church and individual Christians do have some political influence and must not avoid its exercise. There is no theological reason why Christians should not actively involve themselves in building a socialist society. Even priests may need to participate actively in the political process, but on a temporary basis only, in order to encourage lay people to do so regularly. They stressed that in a number of places Marxists have formally invited Christians to join more actively in the political process and that now it was up to individual Christians to do as their conscience dictated.

In the fall of 1968 and spring of 1969, an interesting series of responses to the problem of the role of believers as members of a self-managing society were published in the pages of *Svesci* by Antun Ivanov, I. Ivković, and Jure Juras.[284] Ivanov maintained that socialism would become world wide and that the contemporary attitudes of the church toward it, especially in Yugoslavia, would determine whether the church of the future would be in the catacombs or out in the open. He believed that the two former enemies would be able to find a common path through dialogue. The church needed, formally, to instruct believers to take a constructive place in socialist development, to clarify its position toward the new society, to adapt its organizational patterns to the new situation, to study the impact of self-management upon the believers, to investigate the adaptation of moral principles to a self-managing society, and then to issue appropriate instruction to the faithful. Socialism was the most exciting of all social systems, but it lacked spirituality, which could be provided by Christianity.

One might have expected responses expressing dissatisfaction with Ivanov's position as too radical, and surely there must have been many who were shocked by such a provocative advocacy of harmonizing Marxist socialism and Christianity, but not so the response of Ivković and Juras! Both were proponents of the idea of the full participation of believers in the self-managing processes, but both suggested that Ivanov had been treating believers as immature persons who still needed the official church to tell them how to manage themselves and society. Ivković warned of the danger of identifying the church as a defender of specific values and principles. He also warned against placing, on the same level, a person's faith and his or her participation in social processes. The faithful and the nonbelievers are left to the same resources; neither God nor the church can help one to be a better self-manager. Faith determines the meaning of one's life but is not a means whereby one achieves specific goals, such as political citizenship.

Juras found many faults with Ivanov's theses. He suggested that no system, not even the socialist, deserves unreserved adulation, because experience indicates the wisdom of a greater relativism than is evident in Ivanov's position. The role of self-managers should be determined by self-managers alone, and not by the church. Socialism is not devoid of spirituality; if it were, it certainly could not claim to be the best of all systems. Only when the spiritual dimension permeates human relations in the form of freedom and creativity and when the rule of religion or philosophy is ended will self-management become a true reality. The church is not asked to contribute moral principles for this society in the name of something or someone absolute.

Thus Juras suggested a complete and radical depolitization of the "believer." Instead of believers being self-managers, he suggested that self-managers are self-managers (i.e., people are citizens) and some self-managers happen to be believers. Yugoslav society needed to be a-theist, rather than either theist or antitheist. Juras was aware that he and Ivanov were not diametrically opposed but felt that Ivanov had been too paternalistic and absolutizing. Instead, Juras advocated a pluralistic society in which Christianity and Marxism might be natural allies against cultural nihilism and those forms of rationalism that claim to be totally able to save humanity.

A Slovene Marxist sociologist, Marko Kerševan, who is increasingly coming to prominence and has not been attacked by the establishment for his views, attempted a different approach to religious phenomena in the late 1960s. According to him, religion possesses a certain autonomy rather than being merely the reflection of socioeconomic circumstances.[285] The structure of religion is determined basically by the reciprocal relationship between human beings and mystery in five ways: 1) the experience of mystery and how the mystery is represented; 2) "the image of the world" by which human activity and the religious experience are linked; 3) religious practices, particularly liturgy and morality, which institu-

tionalize the relationship to the mystery; 4) the religious
community, i.e. the church, which is formed by those who par-
take in religious practices; and 5) the policy and ideology of
the church in its relationship to the world or specifically the
state.[286] Contrary to Bošnjak, Kerševan claimed that death
and suffering are not the central cause or theme of religion.
Religion stipulates "another world," which affirms the freedom and unalienable uniqueness of personhood, contrary to the
realities of this world. However, this world is also accepted
either in its capitalist or socialist form, in both of which work
is seen by Christians as the source of creativity and development.[287] The "other world" often screens the realities of this
world for religious people. But it can also be, as it is increasingly today, a ground for critiquing this-worldly realities. The
prevalent Marxist approach to religion is faulty because it
oriented itself only by generalized notions about religion, without giving enough attention to scholarly research on the concrete forms of religiosity. This is particularly needed in Yugoslavia, which in its national and religious makeup is very
heterogeneous. Atheism should also undergo the same objective
sociological analysis as religion.[288]

Christians picked up the humanistic Marxist view that
Marxism is not a closed system of thought but a revolutionary
theory for bringing about necessary structural changes. Edo
Marinković, a Christian, considered Marxism primarily an
inspiration and explored the question as to whether alienation
is constitutive or reducible, suggesting that the basis of alienation cannot be found in the economic sphere alone.[289] Utilizing primarily the writings of contemporary French Marxist
authors (Lefebvre, Althusser, and Alexos), Marinković pointed to some deficiencies in Marx's own concepts and concluded
that Marxism as a system, despite its institutionalization, is
less dynamic than Marxism as an inspiration, in which the
inspiration or methodology dialectically overcomes Marxism
as a system. Marx's method must be applied to Marxism.[290]

By 1969 the dialogue was in "high gear." It stayed so until
1972. The number of both Marxist and Christian studies of
each other proliferated significantly. Šagi-Bunić˘ and Bajsić
vigorously elaborated the methodology of dialogue and promoted its use as the most suitable way of interpersonal dealing in a pluralistic society.[291] With its new postconciliar self-
image the church should work out a new manner in which to
relate to nonbelievers.[292] Bajsić took upon himself to report
and analyze in the Christian press, which had only recently

been permitted a freer activity, the many contemporary writings by domestic Marxists on the theme of religion. He noted with satisfaction that most Marxist authors moved from a confused emotive reaction toward religion to a rational, concrete approach. They have come to realize that faith is not identical with clericalism, that the establishment of atheism by the state is no better than the establishment of religion, that religious people are not necessarily antisocialist, and that they have, in any case, shown their loyalty and willingness to involve themselves constructively in building the society.

An internal dialogue had commenced within Marxism on the correct approach to religion, and Bajsić advocated a similar internal dialogue among Christians in their response to Marxism, despite the continued precariousness of the relationship.[293] Both among Marxists and Catholics there are people who have been traumatized in their mutual relations. Among them are many who are either uninterested or opposed to dialogue, and each bad move tends to have reciprocal, often exaggerated, bad consequences. Marxist accusation that the churches opposed socialism does not take into account the psychological moment for Christians. Historically Marxists have identified socialism with atheism. Since theism is central to Christianity, it would be absurd to expect Christians to join an atheist campaign. Even Marxists are starting to realize that the aggressive promotion of atheism is an unaffordable luxury. After all, the state is the state of believers and nonbelievers and therefore should truly be atheist rather than antitheist.[294] Christians ought not to be brought into the undesirable situation of thinking that their contribution to socialism is adversely affecting their church and religion. The mythologizing of history by both Christians and Marxists is dangerous. Both interpret history as a struggle between the "powers of light" with the "powers of darkness," with the inevitable identification of the other side with "darkness."

Bajsić was particularly pleased to see the emergence of the new methodological approaches to religion, particularly the one developed by Kerševan. The crux of the older Marxist method was that religion is a negative phenomenon and the study of its origin will bring about the scientific discrediting of it. It was not realized that this approach tended to perpetuate the negative expressions of religion. Instead of comparing old religious formulas with contemporary science, it would be much more correct to undertake an objective study of *new* religious forms which are the product of new social relations.[295]

Indeed, it has become obvious that almost all Yugoslav Marxist research on religion in the years since 1970 has become more unprejudicial, less biased. They have concentrated either on the empirical study of concrete local religious phenomena, or have attempted to familiarize themselves with the monumental changes in theological and other intellectual and practical endeavors of contemporary Christianity.

The Belgrade sociologist Vuko Pavičević published *Sociologija religije*,[296] and Esad Ćimić, the sociologist from Sarajevo, published *Drama ateizacije*.[297] Pavičević advocated the abandonment of antitheism by the state. In his earlier writings, Ćimić had already effectively maintained that "administrative measures" (physical and legal persecution of religion) are not an authentic Marxian posture. In his new book he sought to assess the impact, often very negative, of the pressures for atheism, especially as they were carried out by the educational system under express instructions from the Communist Party. Important in his approach was his contention that he was "speaking neither for nor against religion but about religion." [298] Ćimić undertook a systematic criticism of the "dogmatic negation" of religion. He also perceived that both the religiosity and the atheism of the new generation that grew up in socialism was "more multidimentional, less stereotyped and spiritually richer." [299]

> Religion is the first question of our infancy and the last question of our old age. After becoming aware of one's personality and after facing up to the so called last questions (perhaps they will one day become the *first* questions for all or almost all people!) religion appears to the human being as one of the intellectual possibilities, as one of the solutions to complex riddles of thought. And religion is the last question of old age because the need for religious consolation increases with the awareness of the approaching of the last accord—death.[300]

Ćimić thus saw the roots of religion in the psychological structure of the personality in its growth toward complete humanization and in the contradictions of contemporary society which cause alienation. Religion is both a sign of that alienation and an attempt, under specific circumstances, to surmount it. The elimination of alienation, and thereby of religion, can take place only in a society in which individuals do not live only for themselves and are free of dictates by superiors. These conditions have not yet been achieved in contemporary socialism, which then continues to produce religiosity, though some of that religiosity is clad in "atheist" clothes. Such "administrative atheism" is a sign of the inhumanity and creative impoverishment of such atheists. The League of Communists of Yugoslavia and the educational system would commit a mistake in propagating atheism as a separate domain of its activity. True atheism consists in actions to rectify conditions which cause alienation, rather than to accord a privileged or inferior treatment to religion.[301]

Mladen Stanković, a little-known Marxist from Zagreb, saw the roots of religion in the attempt to cope with incomplete and imperfect human nature. This is reflected especially in the limitation regarding the meaning of life, as well as in the experience of loneliness.[302] He concluded that the question of one's religiosity or irreligiosity is secondary. The question of one's humanity or inhumanity is primary. This primary criterion of humanity ought to be applied to religion and the church when one makes concrete judgment about their place in the world.

Needless to say, these writings produced a lively discussion in Yugoslav society. It took place in print, in formal public discussions, and, of course, in widespread informal discussions among individuals.[303]

A public library in Belgrade organized two open discussions, one about the book of Pavićević, the other of Ćimić. Both of them took place in 1971. Considerable public interest and attendance were aroused by the two meetings.[304] At the first panel discussion the participants were, in addition to Pavićević, Žarko Vidović (Marxist, Belgrade), Ćimić and Lazar Milin (Serbian Orthodox, Belgrade), and at the second, in addition to Ćimić, the above-mentioned Milin and Pavićević, then Šagi-Bunić (Roman Catholic, Zagreb), and Fuad Muhić (Marxist, Sarajevo).[305]

Even more remarkable was the meeting of the Eleventh Congress of the International Conference of Sociology of Religion which took place September 20-23, 1971, in Opatija. The hosts were the Institute for Social Research of the University of Zagreb and the Center for Conciliar Research "Kršćanska Sadašnjost," Zagreb. Of the more than 200 participants, (including five from Poland), over 80 were from Yugoslavia.[306] Marxists Štefica Bahtijarević, Roter, Ćimić, Kerševan, Srdjan Vrcan, and Vitomir Unković delivered papers, while Marko Oršolić, a Franciscan friar, also delivered a paper. The meeting provided lively and constructive discussion.

Christian-Marxist dialogue became a theme for the media and for scholarly lectures.[307] Professor Srdjan Vrcan invited the Archbishop of Split, the scholarly Dr. Frane Franić, to deliver a lecture on theology and revolution in November, 1970, at the Seminar for Political and Sociological Research at the Law School in Split.[308] This invitation was later reciprocated, and Vrcan lectured at the High Theological School in Split in March, 1971. Similar exchanges took place in Zagreb. Bošnjak lectured abroad to Christian groups (e.g., in West Germany),[309] as well as at the Catholic Theological Seminary about Marxist humanism. Even more frequently he invited Christian scholars to lecture at the Section for the Study of Religion and Atheism of the Institute for Social Research of Zagreb University.[310] That same institute trained about 80 people, some of whom were Christians, and exposed them to a scholarly methodology in the study of religion.

By now the people who had originated the dialogue moved to much more sophisticated and sympathetic positions, while a number of new protagonists of the dialogue made an appearance.

Bošnjak decided the attributes "Marxist" and "Christian" when applied to humanism are nonessential and suggested that the future might bring an anthropocentric order, in which neither Christian nor Marxist designations would be of great, if any, importance.[311] He considered neither religion nor ideology to be essential, but merely a human symptom. The general impression remains, however, that his criticism of all religion is based on criticism of a particular dogmatic type of religion. But his personal openness and willingness to interact is sincere and contagious. He is much more open and sympathetic to religion in personal contacts than he is in his writings.

Ćimić also contributed new ideas, suggesting that the absence of a dialogue in Yugoslavia occurred because there was, until recently, neither authentic Marxism nor authentic Christianity, and that some dynamic loss of identity for both partners is a condition for the establishment of bridges for permanent, mutual, humanistic correction.[312] At the 1971 Conference of the Yugoslav Association of Sociologists at Dubrovnik, Ćimić admitted that the sometimes violent efforts to eliminate religion seemed like attempts to institute an aggressive secular religion, but that a new consciousness and thinking about religion were developing.[313] Atheism, instead of being progressive, may simply be the purest form of a vacuum. The elimination of classical religion did not every-where bring victory to the humanistic and spiritual concerns and dimensions by which earlier forms of humanism and spirituality were replaced. A religion may be a mode of humanization and may serve a progressive role. In our era of individualism and loneliness, religion may activate affirmations of collective norms and values. Administrative liquidation of religion leaves people unprepared for functioning in contemporary society and may create spiritual bankruptcy. In environments of meager material and spiritual resources, the main concern may become what you have rather than who you are. Urbanized society only increases human loneliness. Mass culture, science, and philosophy simply cannot replace religion. The masses may understand some basic tenets of Darwinism, but modern science and philosophy are so complex that they are beyond mass consumption. Since religion is a world-wide mass movement, it often appears as competitor to science. But it continues to be the living, existential, nonexact, empirical "philosophy" available to the average person. Out of religion will perhaps emerge a more acceptable, humane atheism.

Another contributor to the Marxist study of religion and a marked protagonist of the dialogue was the professor of sociology from Split, Srdjan Vrcan, and his assistant, Boris Vušković. Vrcan collected valuable sociological data on the religiosity of young people in Zagreb and Split. He contended that in a socialist society religiosity has its "downs" but also its "ups" and that Marxists need to reinvestigate and reject many views which they have formerly held as self-evident. He suggested it is possible that contemporary Marxists may well need to discover not only what Marx really said about religion, as distinct from what Marxist orthodoxy attributes to him, but also that it may be necessary to consider Marx's notions on religion as the symptom of that human alienation which he desired to eliminate.[314]

The impetus of the dialogue was so great that it led a few people to declare that they are both Christian and Marxist, for which they were attacked by both sides.[315] Even some of the reluctant Serbian Orthodox were pulled into the dialogue. In addition to the above-mentioned participation of the Orthodox theologian Milin in the panel discussion in Belgrade, the Orthodox journal *Teološki pogledi*, informed its readers about the dialogue abroad.[316] However, no subsequent Orthodox interest in this dialogue was manifested.

The general reluctance and reservations about the dialogue by the Serbian Orthodox and the Protestants were shared by some Catholic writers. Thus, for instance, Jordan Kuničić, O.P., warned against too great expectations from dialogue and the danger from "dialogism." [317] He compared Catholic, radical Protestant, and Marxist views of the future and found that they agree that humans are beings capable of projecting into the future, that the future is a normative value with respect to the present, that hope gives the impetus to people in their efforts to achieve a happier future, and that this very hope reflects somehow the limitations and misery of the present moment. But Kuničić regarded these similarities as merely analogous, i.e., quite superficial, because there were more differences than agreements. Nevertheless even such limited dialogue is useful, concluded Kuničić.

The protagonists of the dialogue were not free from criticism and harassment even at the period of maximal liberalization. They sometimes had to defend their record of achievement and to prove their good faith.[318] But few expected the tremendous pressures which would very soon be applied, curtailing almost all public manifestations of the dialogue. The difficulties did not stem from the dialogue itself, but emerged from the contextual situation of the dialogue.

In 1971, amidst the heightened liberalization of Yugoslav society, many incidents of social unrest came into being.[319] Some of them had a decidedly nationalistic character, particularly among the Croatians. Street demonstrations took place. Some nationalistic terrorists infiltrated from abroad, performing sabotage and terrorism. The president of Yugoslavia and chief of the League of Communists, Josip Broz-Tito, who had allowed this transformation of Yugoslavia but had not been its enthusiastic initiator, decided that the processes of liberalization had gone too far. He stepped in decisively in December 1971. A massive purge in the ranks of the League of Communists took place, in several stages, which had enormous repercussions in the government and the society. As many "political and ideological sins" as possible were being lumped together against those who went farthest in the process of liberalization. Many leading individuals, including some who figured prominently in the dialogue, were criticized; some were suspended or expelled from the party; and, in a few instances, they lost their positions. A few left the party, thus demonstrating their disagreement with the reversal of trends.

The dialogue was attacked within the party as a contributive factor to the rise of nationalism. There has always been an apprehension among Communists, justifiable to a degree, of the stepped-up political involvement of the Catholic Church, especially in Croatia. The recovery and strengthening of the church was seen as tied to the rise of Croatian nationalism, and ultimately separatism. Since dialogue seemed to be an increased recognition of the church by Communists, it was feared that this could be interpreted as a support of nationalism, which is one of the greatest dangers for the territorial integrity of the Yugoslav state and is capable of fostering the much-feared Soviet intervention if internal confusion escalates to the point of armed conflict. It may be argued that strengthening of the church and Croatian nationalism are related to each other, but there is no evidence that the protagonists of the dialogue sought to bring about chauvinistic tendencies.

Hardly a single Marxist partner was spared intense pressures, though the dialogue itself was not singled out by authorities for attack. In order to survive the purge, some had to keep "low," others had to recant, still others to choose different fields of scholarly interest. The result was that for the next several years Marxist dialogue partners would not engage in public dialogue. However, many continued discreetly to keep contacts with their Christian friends or to deliver an occasional lecture to visitors from abroad on the dialogue. And, most importantly, they continued to write. It is encouraging that despite the official discouragement of the dialogue, many works have been published since 1972, though the vocabulary had to be adjusted for the changed situation.[320]

The Christian partners fared comparatively better than the Marxists. While some "pot shots" were taken at the church, no drastic measures were taken against Christians. Hence Christian partners mostly took a "wait and see" attitude, saying that they continued to be interested in dialogue and were ready to resume it whenever and wherever the circumstances became suitable.

Such a stance was difficult for both partners. Memories of former repression were still vivid. While physical measures against those displeasing the government were generally things of the past, many Marxists privately shared stories of psychological pressures, ostracism by former colleagues, interrogation by the secret police, removal from positions of responsibility, and attack on their job security. Christians were

less threatened, because generally they held less significant
positions in society. For many Christians the pressure came
from within the church, because many influential Christians
who opposed the dialogue saw in the events of 1971 and 1972,
a justification for their reluctance.

Many of the published contributions which appeared shortly after 1972 were the product of work accomplished during
the earlier high-water mark of dialogue. This is certainly the
case of *Putovi dijaloga* by Archbishop Franić, which is a collection of earlier publications. It is significant that his publications on the dialogue were included in the book, showing
that he still regarded the dialogue important despite low-
ered expectations.[321] His hopes for continued broadening of
intellectual and other contacts in the absence of force had
sharply diminished. No more did he hope to see the day of
reconciliation in his lifetime. He came to the conclusion that
the League of Communists simply does not regard dialogue
with Christians as a necessity, as they can rule the country
without it. Communists theoretically elevate human beings
and seek to be humanists, but in practice a human being is
often repressed if she or he does not conform. Much of Communist credibility with the people is lost when the Communists themselves assume bourgeoise life-styles. The path of
dialogue will be long and hard.[322] This is not to say that this
prelate, well-read in Marxism, abandoned his views that theology and socialism are compatible or that Thomas Aquinas'
notion of just wars may be used to defend the justice of a
revolution. From the outset he rejected the notion of a compromise between the Christian religion and atheism.[323] The
church has come to recognize that it must find ways of agreement with the socialist society, but the question is the manner
of agreement. He also believed that the social dimension of a
person can neither be fully realized in the too individualistic
liberal capitalism nor in the overly collectivistic society, but
only in a free communitarian society (Christian socialism)
based on Christian respect for human dignity.[324] Self-management (the socialization of the means of production) is closer to
the concepts of the gospel than the etatization (central bureaucratic control by the state apparatus).[325] The inspiration of
Marxism upon some forms of theology, particularly the "theology of hope" and the "theology of liberation," give some very
useful insights. But there are also some serious deviations in
these theologies, especially in the form of politicization of faith
and an immanentist eschatology.[326] Christians ought to recog-

nize things of value in Marxism, and vice versa. If both live and work for the people, perhaps some day, despite difficulties, they will be able to find significant areas of agreement.[327] The coming of that "some day" has been considerably retarded by the imposition of restrictions since 1972 according to Franić.

The doctoral dissertation of the Dominican friar Tomo Vereš, professor of theology at the Dominican Schools of Theology in Dubrovnik and Zagreb, was published under the title *Filozofsko-teološki dijalog s Marksom*.[328] In it he undertook to examine the unity of thought and praxis in Karl Marx, his concept of alienation and the overcoming of alienation, and the significance of dialogue. He entered into a critical conversation with Marx, highlighting those aspects of Marx's thought which he found to be true and rejecting or modifying others. Dialogue is a historical necessity, according to Vereš, because society has become pluralistic.[329] Marx's central theme of transforming ideas into reality can be taken by Christians as a starting point for dialogue, though on the whole there are more differences than similarities. In an alienated society people are evaluated by their possessions rather than by who they are. The new society has the potential of freeing people from the overlordship of economic, social, political, and ideological forces. It is directed to the future as the time of genuine existence. But the future cannot be dogmatically anticipated. Christians come into the encounter with the warning that Marxism underestimates the unavoidable and irreducible gap between thought and practice and between intentions and realizations. The initial task of the dialogue is to remove the apparent antithetical stances of the two partners. Among them is the supposed incompatibility between Marxist atheism and Christian theism. However, Marxist atheism denies a different God, presumably the abstract God of the philosophers, not the God revealed to Christians. The concepts of the future are also not incompatible, because both stipulate hope and revolutionary change of the present world. Vereš concluded by saying that Yugoslavia could become an oasis of Christian-Marxist dialogue.[330]

Another doctoral dissertation by a Christian was published as a book, not in Yugoslavia but in Italy, and in Latin. It was the work of the Franciscan friar, Jakov R. Romić, entitled *De dialogo inter marxistas et christianos*.[331] In it Romić carefully explored the thinking of Marx, Engels, and Lenin, seeking for points of contact in the dialogue. He concluded that two major factors stand in the way of dialogue. The first is

the vision of a monolithic future which excludes the possibility
of the survival of Christianity. The other is the practical barriers erected against Christian participation in social change
under socialism. Romić maintained that only when Marxists
make some changes in these postures, as was temporarily
glimpsed in the dialogues of the Paulus-Gesellschaft, could a
real dialogue take place. The founders of Marxism did not
choose dialogue, nor do dogmatic Marxists. The question is
whether the contemporary creative Marxists will be able to
make sufficient allowances in their theories and practice to
facilitate the much-needed yet difficult dialogue which is the
precondition for coexistence in freedom.[332]

A priest of a younger generation, Drago Šimundža, editor
of the journal *Crkva u svijetu* in Split, devoted considerable
efforts to the propagation of renewal in the Catholic Church.
He was also concerned with improved Christian-Marxist relations. He pointed out that despite important differences there
are many ties between Christianity and Marxism which make
it possible for Christians and Marxists to live together humanely.[333] While in the past the emphasis was placed on competition between the two, in the present one can expect them
gradually to narrow the gap and to reappraise each other's
contribution. In practice there are already many people who
have reconciled for themselves the main values of Christianity and Marxism. If one were to remove the vestiges of animosity, though not the differences, it could be expected that
Christians could fully appreciate the work of Marxists for
equality, solidarity, and social justice, while the Christian
message would not be regarded by Marxists as impoverishing, but as enriching humankind.[334] The future may yet more
effectively bring about a common approach in which "the
ideological-totalitarian frame will 'shatter' in front of humane
tendencies of history and of humanitarianism." [335] In Šimundža's opinion life has already gone far beyond theoretical expectations. It is now important to prevent conservative Christian
tendencies and vulgar Marxist interpretations from prevailing
as they would spread distrust and fear in the partners and
lead to repression and conflict. Marxists ought to realize that
Christianity in the twentieth century is stronger than ever
because it has rejected triumphalist aspirations and is now
expressing concerns for peace, love, and human welfare.
Christianity is not an enemy of social change. In some countries Christians are, in fact, the most dedicated socialists.[336]
Šimundža did not naively expect all things to work out for

the good by and of themselves. He was painfully aware of the problems which face a Christian living in socialist society but was ultimately hopeful that relations in the future would be good.[337]

Marxist authors also did not let up in their publishing activities. First to come was Roter's *Cerkev in sodobni svet*.[338] In addition to some introductory work on the sociological classification of religiosity, the main part of the book consisted of a description and analysis of Roman Catholic reactions to socialism, communism, Marxism, and atheism. The author provided a historical survey and classification of the entire range of attitudes, from viewing Marxism as an intrinsic evil to postconciliar willingness to enter into dialogue. The author preferred the latter attitude. He wrote the book in order to show Marxist and other readers that Catholic views are flexible. The thoroughness and objectivity of the author are most impressive. Christians can find only marginal, but no essential, objections to this kind of scholarly work. Roter followed up this book with another one entitled, *Katoliška cerkev in država v Jugoslaviji*.[339] In it Roter tackled the potentially explosive issues of the relations between the state and the Catholic Church in the period from 1945 to 1973. The earlier years of the postwar period, which were especially fraught with excesses, are handled gingerly.[340] It is helpful that Roter placed these issues in the context of broader theoretical, sociological observations about the types of religion which, while not original, are likely to be new for Yugoslav readers. It was Roter's conviction that the period of conflict was over at about 1960 and that since then a period of compromise has come into being. The book explored the context of the dialogue without ever mentioning the word.[341]

Much of Bošnjak's activity on the dialogue was transferred abroad. He attended a number of symposia and conferences, where it became obvious that his views concerning religion were evolving. No more did he deny the historicity of Jesus. Now he tried to compare the forms of thought emanating from Jesus and from Marx.[342] Eschatology remains, according to him, the main feature of religion, as human mortality is the main cause of religion. According to Bošnjak, Jesus introduced the revolutionary idea of the equality of all humans before God. Since there was no social power behind that idea to implement it, Jesus was forced to form an ethics of suffering in this world and of salvation in the next world. The purpose of life was found by Jesus in postulating eternity. In contrast to

Jesus, Marx developed his form of thought as the logic of atheism. Out of the negation of God follows the conclusion that all hope must be lodged in humanity. To the question of meaning in life, the Marxist must answer, "There is none." Human hope must be entirely lodged in the sphere of worldly reality. There is no way of reconciling the contradiction between Jesus and Marx. Fortunately the issue of belief in God is only a content of human thought, not an essential feature of human existence. Consequently, by emphasizing problems of this world, Christians and Marxists can find ample ground for joint endeavor.[343] Bošnjak continued to maintain that the problem of religion cannot be relegated to the inter-relationship of economic and social circumstances. These circumstances are of great importance, since it has been demonstrated that adverse socioeconomic circumstances can form religion or pseudo-religion even in socialism, in the form of Stalinism or other cults of personality.[344] For socialism the fundamental task was to accomplish the separation of church and state in order to break religion's hold over society. Although religion is legally relegated to the sphere of private belief, it continues to have social ramifications stemming from the Christian sense of mission.[345]

About half of his book, *Čovjek na raskršću*, Ćimić devoted to essays on religion.[346] In the essays Ćimić continued to explore the relationship of atheism and religion, finding that under the specific conditions of Yugoslav society religion can frequently be not only the carrier of negative, conservative, and traditional characteristics but also the initiator of positive social involvement at a time when other social forces are in retreat on account of bad experiences.[347] Atheism, under these same Yugoslav conditions, can often become the religion of the negation of religion, i.e. an "atheist religion." [348] Similarly, there is not only ecclesiastical clericalism, but also a party or atheist clericalism. Clericalism is the attempt by a group of people to mediate power by ruling over others. Bureaucracy, with its opposite correlate of political indifference on the part of the masses, is a type of unconscious atheist clericalism.[349] Mediating power is not bad in itself; mediating it in an alienating way is. Should religion and other human endeavors (such as art, science, and philosophy) cease being contributive factors to alienation, they could have a bright future.[350] Only freedom provides the proper condition to surpass the dilemma between religion and atheism. In any case, criticism against religion as religion is merely a theoretical battle and must not become a Marxist preoccupation.

Kerševan continued to pay attention to religion, primarily from the perspective of communist strategy toward religion. Although he still tried to clarify the types of Marxist theory of religion, he maintained that the various theories cannot serve as the basis of Marxist strategy toward religion.[351] Basing his views on an interpretation of Marx and of Lenin, he suggested that the proper strategy toward religion is to evaluate it as to location, time, and influence in terms of the concrete role of religion in class struggle.[352] If it helps win the class struggle, Communists should cooperate with religious people; if it would obstruct the class struggle, Communists will need to oppose them. This judgment needs to be constantly revised. Marxism as a theory of social change has primacy over Marxism as a worldview. Lenin may have made theoretical errors in his view of religion, but he was correct in turning the communist strategy to the primacy of the goals of class struggle.[353]

Christian writers have followed with great interest the development of Marxist attitudes toward religion, and Kerševan's approach, in particular, has received earlier review and praise by Christians because it does not seem to be burdened with the conventional Marxist prejudices.[354] Tone Stres published an article, which is part of a comprehensive study intended for publication as a book, in which he traced Kerševan's methodology to a creative use of the writings of the French Marxist, Luis Althusser.[355] His conclusion was that Kerševan's analyses of religion have great relevance to a Christian understanding of religion, and he judged this to be the best Yugoslav scholarly model for the study of religion. Kerševan's use of Althusser comes as somewhat of a surprise, since Althusser is not known for being a protagonist of dialogue with Christians in France. Althusser considered many of the Marxist humanists as revisionists, and unlike them, believed that the mature Marx radically broke ties with humanism and became scientific but antihumanist.[356] Kerševan did not yet produce a book on this subject, but only a number of essays in which he did not clearly state the degree of his indebtedness to Althusser. What is evident thus far is that he agreed with Althusser that socialism is a science while humanism is an ideology. Religion, too, is to be classified as an ideology. Out of these Althusserian premises, applied to the Yugoslav situation, Kerševan concluded that religion, like other ideolo-

gies, needs to be judged primarily in terms of its contribution
to the victory of the proletariat in the class struggle. Thus
religion is not *a priori* judged by Erševan as good or bad for
socialism. Christian thinkers in Yugoslavia seem to feel that
this kind of Marxist approach to religion is the most unbiased
one and consequently preferable. The dependence on Althusser
may be an explanation as to why Erševan, almost uniquely
among Yugoslav Marxists, has not been attacked by the establishment and is able to place his scholarly material in the journals closest to the government. It is not clear whether for this
reason or for others Erševan has not participated in any of
the person-to-person public dialogues. His role in the dialogue,
unlike that of Althusser, is seen by the protagonists of the
dialogue as beneficial.

The question of the Marxist attitude toward religion was,
of course, not nearly as marginal a matter as some of the dogmatic Marxist theoreticians wanted to make out. This was
proved by the census of 1953, the last one in which Yugoslavs were asked to designate their religious affiliation, at
which time only 12.6 per cent declared themselves atheists.[357]
Subsequent sociological research done by Ćimić, Erševan,
Bahtijarević, and Vrcan confirmed that religion indeed played
a strong, only slightly weakening, role in Yugoslavia. Vrcan
noted that religion was more pervasive in some socialist countries than it was in some nonsocialist countries. Only a very
small group of people had completely cut their ties to religion.
The overwhelming majority had very explicit connections with
religion. The single most important factor that had a negative
impact on the degree of church affiliation was education. The
less educated were more tied to the churches, while the more
educated tended to drift away.[358] Farmers and industrial
workers were among the most religious population, going
against the conventional Marxist claim that the workers are
the first to abandon their church affiliation.[359]

Andrija Krešić, a Marxist philosopher who taught at the
Universities of Sarajevo and Belgrade, had not been noted
for making religion an important subject matter of his scholarly work. With the book *Kraljevsto božje i komunizam*, however, he emerged as potentially one of the most interesting
Marxist philosophers from a Christian's perspective.[360] The
first part of the book has a similar approach to Roter's study
of the Roman Catholic Church in contemporary society. Here
Krešić attempted to summarize the views of various modern
theologians, mostly Catholic and Protestant, toward theological

renewal and, more pointedly, toward communism. He discerned a trend from anticommunism to procommunism, with all shades in between. His descriptions of the most relevant theological points are, on the whole, expertly done, though he did show a tendency to compound the views of theologians as if they were necessarily building one on another. Needless to say, he considered the more radical theologians, rather than the conservative or liberal theologians, as the most promising from a Marxist viewpoint. From a Christian viewpoint it is interesting to see Krešić's genuine understanding of theological concerns such as God's being, the trinity, Christian love, the problem of sin and evil, human creation, and so forth. The most relevant parallels between Marxism and Christianity, according to Krešić, are the question of proexistence, as related to love and property. In primitive Christianity, Krešić, like some Marxists before him, saw the Christian attempt to overcome selfishness and create a truly loving, equal society. This could not succeed because there was only a communism of distribution but not a communism of production. Christian love therefore quickly deteriorated into mere charity. Christian warnings of the dangers of "mammon" and Marx's analysis of the fetishism of money have much in common.

Krešić warned against notions of mere coexistence among Christians and Marxists:

> Ecclesiastical Christianity engaged in a crusade against Marxism and Communism until it came to feel, in more recent times, that it will slowly vanish if it does not adapt to the contemporary world which has Communism as one of its component parts. That was the policy of anti-Communism which has now been replaced by the policy of co-existence with Communism. Political (party and state) Communism replied in the same manner, the policy of the war being followed later by the policy of co-existence. Each side in co-existence retains its ideology with the hope of a proselytized end of the other side, because each side conceives of the future of the world as its own world with no opponents. Thus co-existence is a tactic, but the strategy is still some sort of quiet contra-existence.[361]

Krešić saw the way out from this dangerous delusion through an attitude of mutual proexistence, a dialogical support of each other's existence. For him communism "means the establishment of the community of free individuals which has no purpose or existence apart from free individuals." [362] It makes no difference whether these individuals come "under the sign of the cross or under the sign of the hammer and sickle." [363]

The dialogue has not been entirely relegated to the printed page. Somewhat on the margins of Yugoslav public life have been a series of courses on the "Future of Religion," organized each April since 1977 within the scope of the Inter-University Centre for Post-Graduate Studies in Dubrovnik. The codirectors of these courses were Rudolf Siebert of the University of Michigan in Kalamazoo and Bošnjak (in 1977) and Vrcan (subsequent years). While the courses were attended almost entirely by persons from outside Yugoslavia, among the lecturers were practitioners of the Christian-Marxist dialogue—in addition to the directors, Ruben Alvez (Brazil), Paul Mojzes (U.S.), Trutz Rendtorff (W. Germany), and others—who contributed to the awareness of the ongoing dialogue. To this, one ought to add the participation of the Yugoslavs, Bošnjak, Bajsić, and Romić, at the Paulus-Gesellschaft symposium in Florence in 1975.[364]

Since travel is completely free to Yugoslavs, it is probable that their participation in future international Christian-Marxist dialogues is very likely, provided the organizers of these meetings use effective means to convince individual dialogue partners or their institutions of the benefits of each conference. The nonaligned position of their country has tended to work adversely on such participation, because they often get left out by Marxist sponsors, while Christian sponsors also fall too frequently into the trap of regarding as Marxists only those who are Soviet-oriented or part of the more recently fashionable Eurocommunist group.

Inside Yugoslavia top party leadership is still reluctant to permit formal dialogue in the country. The initiatives of Cardinal König of Vienna; G. Wetter, S.J., from the Vatican; and Bajsić with Vladimir Bakarić, one of the leading Yugoslav politicians, did not succeed.[365] Even those writing about mutual relations had to be careful and tended to write unclearly so that the text can be interpreted in more than one way.[366] In matters of constitution and law there are no great, outstanding problems for Christians. In practice, especially at lower levels such as local govenment and educational institutions, there are still obstructions and difficulties despite attempts on the part of the churches to adjust fully to their existence in socialist Yugoslavia, with no aspirations to return to former "idyllic" times.[367]

In conclusion, one can say that the Yugoslav dialogue had an astonishingly broad base among intellectuals, and that it enjoys considerable longevity. This can be partially ascribed

to the absence of external political pressures upon the dialogue
(criticism of Yugoslav Marxist views on religion by Soviet
writers is generally dismissed with amusement). Yet the dialogue is still dependent on the internal political situation. It
was politics which enabled it to come into being, politics which
placed sharp limits upon it, and it will be politics that may
allow it to flourish again. The potential public reemergence of
the dialogue will have to wait for further development under
Tito's successors.[368]

A new sensibility to questions of ethical, moral, and religious nature has been created among Marxists, who are now
more ready to enter the dialogue. Christians realize that their
level of religious liberty vastly exceeds that being experienced
elsewhere in Eastern Europe (except in Poland) and in Yugoslavia's own past. Hence they have come to terms with their
existence within socialism. Many of the younger clergy and
lay people, who now make up a significant proportion of the
clergy and laity, have been raised under socialism and do not
carry entrenched antisocialist prejudices. They are willing to
accept the fundamental socioeconomic and political system,
though they, like most Yugoslavs, hope and work for modifications and improvements in it. The interest in dialogue is
apparent from the attendance at those public meetings which
did take place, but it is artificially kept low by the authorities'
disinclination to permit such meetings. Hence dialogue did not
develop the rich dimensions which it could have without those
limitations.

It is agreed by nearly all participants in the dialogue that
there are no lasting theoretical obstacles to it. Only political
circumstances and historical encumbrances hinder the dialogue. The dedogmatization of theology and of Marxist theory
has largely taken place among thinkers. Whether this affected
the others is debatable. The leadership in the state and the
churches does not consist of thinkers. Some in both bureau-
cracies are downright suspicious of thinkers, as their theories
tend to erode centralistic notions of authority. This is why
they used their power to bring about a contraction of the dialogue.[369] Dialogue tends to change mutual relations and thus
disturb the status quo, threatening the privileges of those on
top. But it appears that gradually, over the years, a sufficient number of social mechanisms (e.g., self-management,
the local forums of the Socialist Alliance of Working People,
laws, the church press, international agreements, Yugoslavia's
self-image as the freest socialist nation, etc.) have been estab-

lished by which, through protracted struggle, forces favorable
to a genuine dialogue have a chance to assert themselves, allowing the precarious dialogue to take a firm hold as the main
means of Christian-Marxist interaction.

PAULUS-GESELLSCHAFT INTERNATIONAL CONGRESSES

The founder and main driving force of the Paulus-Gesellschaft is Dr. Erich Kellner, a West German Catholic priest
and theologian. In 1956 he founded the Paulus-Gesellschaft,
a society which aimed to bring together scientists and theologians to discuss the place of the Christian faith in the scientific age, when it seemed that an ever increasing number of
intellectuals were alienated from the churches.[370] Christianity
could survive and become universal again if the church would
acknowledge the universal application of the sciences and
restate its own original insights regarding the human condition.[371] The name of the association was derived from St.
Paul's successful interpretation of the Jewish message of
Jesus to the Gentiles. Kellner's view was that such ability had
to be mustered again by Christians in order to salvage the
bankruptcy of historical Christendom and communicate the
eternal verities of the mystery of the humanity of God. The
principle of dialogue was to be used from the beginning, demonstrating that partners in the discussion may lead one another to the truth.

By 1964 about twelve sessions between philosophers, natural scientists, and theologians had taken place, and the theme
was seen as more or less exhausted.[372] But impetus had been
gained and a following in both West Germany and Austria
was obtained. After some consulting, Kellner ventured into a
new orientation by conceiving of a dialogue between Christians and Marxists in the presence of, in Kellner's view, the
"objective" empirical scientists. In the spring of 1964 a symposium was held in Munich with the theme, "Human Being:
Spirit and Matter." [373] Only one Marxist was present, Ernst
Bloch, formerly of East Germany but by then an immigrant
to West Germany and a professor of philosophy at Tübingen,
highly respected for his creative application of Marxism.

That same year the first East European was to enter the
scene. In the fall of 1964 the Paulus-Gesellschaft organized
another conference, in Cologne, "Christianity and Marxism
Today." [374] Among the more than 100 participants, Adam
Schaff of Warsaw, Poland, was the only Marxist and only

East European present.[375] However, Schaff's presence was very important because at that point he was not merely the most important Polish Marxist philosopher but was also a member of the Central Committee of the United Workers' Party. Schaff's presence (which almost turned into absence, as it was hard for him to receive permission to attend) was a bonus to later Marxist participation, though soon thereafter Schaff became marginalized in Polish Marxist circles with his expulsion from the Central Committee in 1968 due to his propagation of ideas not in step with the more hardline doctrinaire Marxists. At Cologne, however, he surprised many Christians with his flexible stand. He himself was astonished by some Christian positions (e.g., Rahner's and Metz's) which he deemed so far-out that he considered them radical departures from the traditional realm of Christianity, as indeed they are from the standpoint of Polish Roman Catholicism.[376]

From April 29 to May 2, 1965, the Paulus-Gesellschaft held the international congress in Salzburg, Austria, with the theme "Christian and Marxist Future." [377] With the assistance of Schaff, such international Marxist figures as Roger Garaudy and Lucio Lombardo-Radice came. The only East German ever to preregister for the meeting, the Marxist Robert Havemann, was not allowed by the G.D.R. government to attend, but he succeeded in sending his paper "Kommunismus —Utopie und Wirklichkeit," which was sharply critical of many communist practices. Several other East Europeans, however, did participate in the congress. Asari Polikarov, a philosopher from Sofia, was the Bulgarian participant.[378] Two Hungarian Christians, Ferenz Gál and Vid Michelics, from Budapest, were present, and so were three Yugoslav Marxist thinkers, sociologist Oleg Mandić from Zagreb University, sociologist Vuko Pavičević from Belgrade University,[379] and philosopher Branko Bošnjak from Zagreb University.[380] The total number of participants probably ranged between 250 and 300.[381]

By now the meetings of the Paulus-Gesellschaft became notorious. The news media of West Germany and Austria found the sensational elements, and before too long the wire services spread the exciting news that Christians and Marxists were able to talk to each other and find some elements of agreement. Christians were capable of saying complimentary things about Marxists, and Marxists were sometimes as self-critical as Christians. The momentum thus gained was spontaneous, and not much time was lost before the next congress took place at Herrenchiemsee, West Germany, in 1966, with the theme, "Christian Humanity and Marxist Humanism." [382] The number of East Europeans increased. Bošnjak,[383] Mandić, Pavičević, Polikarov, and Michelics were repeats. In addition, from Yugoslavia came Ante Fiamengo,[384] a Marxist sociologist from Zagreb; Robert Bacsvary, also Marxist from Zagreb; and Anton Hočevar, a Christian from Belgrade. From Hungary came the increasingly important Marxist philosopher, József Lukács,[385] who can be described as one of the most devoted participants in international dialogues; József Szigeti, a Marxist; [386] and the Christians András Szennay and Béla Saad. From Czechoslovakia came a small but very prominent group consisting of Hromádka, Kadlecová, and Průcha.[387] Průcha was gaining the reputation of a critical, creative Marxist thinker who dared to venture into new areas of philosophic concern, a reputation he justified at Herrenchiemsee by developing the humanistic stand in Marxist thought concerning the question of meaning. By now the Eastern European participation had become so substantial, the reputation of the dialogues so well-known, while "socialism with a human face" in Czechoslovakia advanced so rapidly, that the next step was truly a momentous event in the history of Eastern European involvement in dialogue.

The Czechoslovak Academy of Sciences undertook cosponsorship of the next Congress with the Paulus-Gesellschaft, for the first and only time on Eastern European soil. In 1967 the Congress took place in the resort town, Marinske Lazňe (better known in the West as Marienbad), Czechoslovakia. The theme was "Creativity and Freedom." [388] While the number of Christian participants still exceeded that of Marxists, the Congress attracted the largest number of Marxists ever to attend a dialogue with Christians.[389] From Czechoslovakia came the largest contingent of both Marxists and Christians: Marxists—Beluška Bendlová, Josef Buček, Jiří Čvekl, Jiří Černý, Jan Fojtik, Gardavský, Hranička, Kadlecová, Kalivoda, Bohúmil Kvašnicka, Miloš Kaláb, Machovec, Josef Macek, Lubomir Nový, Průcha, Ladislav Prokupek, Jan Sindelár, Julius Štrinka, and Ladislav Tondl; and Christians—Luděk Brož, Vladimír Benda, Anežka Ebertová, Peter Haban, Hromádka, Lochman, Jan Merell, Jan Michalko, Josef Souček, Antonín Stehlik, Zdeněk Trtik, and Josef Uhrin. From Hungary came Christians—Ferenz Gál, Michelics, Lázslo Pákozdy, Béla Saad, and Szennay; and Marxists—József Lukács, Gyula

Munkácsi, György Ronay, and József Szigeti. From Poland Marxists—Jan Guranowski, Witold Jankowski; and Christians —Janusz Makowski, and Jerzy Turowicz. A Marxist philosopher, Ileana Marculescu, attended from Romania, as did the Marxist Deian Pavlov from Bulgaria. From Yugoslavia came Christians—Bajsić, Stanko Cajnkar, and Šagi-Bunić; and Marxists—Fiamengo, Zlatko Frid, and Mandić.[390] Otto Fuchs, a Christian from Berlin, came from East Germany.

Of those attending, the theoretically most significant were Hromádka and Machovec.[391] Both Christians and Marxists at Marianske Lazňe abandoned stereotyped positions. Christian participants spoke on the tasks of faith in this world, while Marxists, paradoxically, showed interest in transcendence.[392] Christians were no longer seen as notorious idealists, and Marxists were not regarded as mechanistic materialists. As these walls crumbled, the participants realized that, while they were not united by common answers, they were united by the common concern for the course of history and the social role of human beings.[393]

Soon after the meeting at Marianske Lazňe, Czechoslovakia experienced the "Prague Spring" of 1968, an attempt to reform socialism along humanistic lines. This was thwarted by the Soviet invasion of August 1968. Nearly all the Czechoslovakian humanistic Marxists lost their jobs and were rejected by their party. Christian theologians also came under severe pressure unless they condemned the dialogue. Out of solidarity with the suffering Marxist partners and the Czech and Slovak nations, the Paulus-Gesellschaft decided to suspend these dialogues indefinitely, but not before a Youth Congress, which had already been convened, took place in the fall of 1968, in Bonn. Practically no data is available on that Congress except that a number of young Czechoslovaks were still allowed to attend before the border was sealed. A number of Yugoslavs were also there.[394] This meeting was not really a Christian-Marxist dialogue but a meeting of young communists from Eastern Europe with the new left of Western Europe. The meeting was abruptly terminated by Kellner when it was disrupted by the disorderly behavior of some uninvited Western leftists.[395]

With the cessation of the Paulus-Gesellschaft dialogues came appraisals on the reason for their supposed failure. Some Western analysts and participants considered it the "death of dialogue."[396] Some attacked the Paulus-Gesellschaft initiatives as ideological subversion.[397] Others thought that Christians and Marxists could politically cooperate but could not have an ideological coexistence.[398] Still others said that the problem was that the Christians and Marxists who attended the dialogues formed a sort of "joint theology" and could not withstand the disagreement of other Christians and Marxists who thought them to be ineffective agents of social change.[399]

The actual causes of the cessation of the dialogue of the 1960s were the following: 1) decisive action against the dialogue by Marxist dogmatists who feared, rightfully, that the dialogue might portend far-reaching changes in the East European *status quo;* 2) reluctance on the part of ecclesiastical leaders to venture into an uncharted territory that could precipitate confusion; 3) exaggerated expectations on the part of the participants and the general public that the dialogue would make some drastic changes and realignments; 4) the overly spontaneous nature of the dialogue—lack of careful organizational backing and diplomacy; 5) absence of other institutions willing to sponsor international dialogues; 6) strong feeling of solidarity with persecuted dialogue participants; and, perhaps most importantly, 7) Soviet military crackdown and the accompanying uncertainty as to its further military and political implications, thereby bringing about a great deal of caution, insecurity, and suspension of further activity.

The surfacing of "Eurocommunism" in the southern European countries, especially in Italy, provided a new opportunity for the resumption of dialogues by the Paulus-Gesellschaft. In October 1975 it organized, in cooperation with the Teilhard de Chardin Society, a symposium in Florence, Italy. Only three Yugoslavs attended, Bošnjak, Bajsić, and Romić. The first two were on panels reacting to some major papers, but on the whole they did not play an important role as the discussion primarily revolved on the viability of the Marxist-Catholic cooperation in Italy.

In September 1977 the Paulus-Gesellschaft organized a Congress, again in Salzburg, which was to be cosponsored by the Italian Communist Party. However, shortly before the congress, the Party denied its support. The theme was "Toward a Socialist, Democratic, Christian, and Humanist Europe." [400] The theme was almost calculated to alienate Eastern European Marxists. Too little effort was made to woo the East Europeans. Only Lukács of Hungary attended.

The main preparatory paper for the Salzburg meeting was written by the West German political scientist Udo Bernbach.[401] Bernbach approvingly summarized those contributions of the earlier Paulus-Gesellschaft symposia which favored self-criticism, bold reformulation of both Marxism and Christianity, freedom, greater democratization, convergence between Marxism and Christianity, and concern for the well-being of people. It was an accurate summary of the emphases, one which could well be used as a launching pad for further dialogue by Eurocommunists and humanistic Marxists with open-minded Christians, but not one which could be accepted by the official Eastern European Marxist and Christian circles. Bernbach also offered a program of socialist democracy which might be suitable and attractive to Western Europeans and perhaps even many Eastern Europeans who are not in positions of influence, but a program which could not be accepted by the Marxist establishment of Eastern Europe without their simultaneous acceptance of the dismantlement of their own system and their consequent loss of power. By using a position paper of this type as the basis for discussion in Salzburg and by the formulation of the general topic on the future of Europe, a topic which would be socially-minded, democratic (in the traditional Western European sense of the word), humanist, *and* Christian, the Paulus-Gesellschaft had, perhaps unwittingly, precluded serious Eastern European participation in the dialogue. Eastern Europeans ceased to be a significant element in the Paulus-Gesellschaft concerns, which shifted increasingly toward Eurocommunism.

On the occasion of the sixteenth World Congress of Philosophy in Düsseldorf, West Germany, the Paulus-Gesellschaft cosponsored with the American Society for the Philosophical Study of Marxism a one-day symposium on "Marxist Philosophy and Christian Values Today." The meeting took place on August 30, 1978, with about 30 people present.[402] The participants were mostly westerners (e.g. Giulio Girardi, Kellner, John Sommerville, Howard Parsons, Shingo Shibata, Bernbach, and Rasker). Pyotr Fedoseev, the second president of the Soviet Academy of Sciences and a Marxist philosopher, also addressed the meeting, declaring that Soviet philosophers see much value in dialogue and that they are resolved to participate intensively in dialogue with Christians and representatives of other religions. Kellner perceives this as a significant shift in perspective by the Paulus-Gesellschaft, but there is, as yet, no evidence at all that Eastern Europeans have been or can be wooed back to Paulus-Gesellschaft activities.

The Paulus-Gesellschaft dialogues are undoubtedly the most significant and most frequent international conversations between Christians and Marxists. Their pioneering work brought together some of the most notable Catholic and Protestant theologians as well as important Marxist thinkers. The people attracted to the 1960s conferences tended to be among the more creative and critical thinkers. The papers read at the symposia were often ground-breaking efforts. A good deal of spontaneity and enthusiasm was generated, especially in the dialogues of the 1960s. New ideas filled people with excitement, knowing that they were witnessing a genuinely new chapter in Christian-Marxist relations. The presence of the empirical scientists (mostly Western Europeans) was a helpful dimension, though the assumption that they are ideologically neutral was unwarranted. The papers delivered at the congresses provide a repository of insights which may prove of benefit for future ventures. They showed that theologians were capable of avoiding the temptation toward subjectivism and individualism and could think about the societal and historical dimensions of humans, while Marxist thinkers could give assent to the unique and unrepeatable value of human beings. They both showed they could be self-critical as well as critical of the other. They could admit that they could learn from each other and that both still needed to keep growing in order to more beneficially serve humanity.[403]

The weaknesses of the Paulus-Gesellschaft dialogues are also evident. They were unwieldy because of the large numbers in attendance. Too many papers were read. Many participants wanted to speak but not necessarily to listen. The time alotted for the discussion was hardly sufficient for the give-and-take of dialogue. Rather it resembled the discussion of any typical academic meeting. Much too little attention was given to organizational aspects. They were happenings rather than organized meetings. The Paulus-Gesellschaft could profit from able managerial assistance.

One of the crucial weaknesses lay in its organizational structure. On paper it has a structure; in life it is an organization gravitating around the inspiration and leadership of the founder, Erich Kellner. He is a man of high ideals and many ideas. His concern, intensity, and enthusiasm are evident. Through his initiative, some of the finest thinkers rallied around him and attended the meetings, for which he provided the basic framework and funding. He is appealing because he earnestly seeks to serve high ideals at a time of much social change. Yet, at times it seems that his concentration on lofty ideals prevents him from being in touch with the more mundane

realities of life. It is surprising that his philosophy of dialogue has not hindered dialogue more than it has, because he
tends to load the dialogue with emphatic, almost dogmatic,
assertions which are not necessarily widely shared. Equally
suspicious of the Vatican and Moscow, he nurtures the hope of
a convergence between Christianity (especially Catholicism)
and Marxism which would provide more moral and political
leadership than Western democracy is capable of.[404] According to Kellner, capitalist democracy bestows too much freedom
with no concomitant moral restraints. People cannot handle
this. Should Christian moral values be coupled with Marxist
collectivist concerns and pressures, a new society, both socialist and Christian, could emerge. This would truly enhance
human happiness.[405]

Most participants in dialogue are unaware of these personal
expectations of Kellner, and many, if not most, would probably
reject them. However, these "hidden agendas" of the central
figure in the dialogues are bound to create negative aftereffects.
While the major reason for the slack in the dialogue should be
ascribed to social conditions prevailing in Europe in the 1970s,
some blame must be placed on the subjective factors of the
too-centralized leadership of the Paulus-Gesellschaft. An organization which is not imbued with the participatory principle can hardly expect to provide leadership in an endeavor
that calls for plurality of initiatives.

The paucity of other groups in Europe willing to sponsor
dialogues along similar lines makes the Paulus-Gesellschaft
still indispensable. An internal reform could transform it into
a more effective catalyst for dialogue. Still, even with its
shortcomings, the overall evaluation of the Paulus-Gesellschaft
and its leader Kellner must be very positive. The Congresses
of the Paulus-Gesellschaft, particularly those of the 1960s, can
be regarded as the high-water mark of the Christian-Marxist
dialogue.

TYPE 6: Dialogical Engagement in Freedom: Unprivileged Position of Either Partner

This type of dialogue presupposes such forms of political
and economic democracy which would make it possible for
participants to engage in dialogue with no obstruction or ille-
gal pressures. Neither of the partners would have an inherent
advantage because a powerful state or a politically powerful
church endorsed the views of one partner and placed undue

pressures on the other. This does not mean the absence of politically powerful or even leading groups, but it does mean the absence of special privileges or of monopoly in determining social processes. A pluralistic democratic order either of the socialist or nonsocialist type (e.g., a mixed economy) is envisaged here.

Is such a human condition possible and realistic? Is it not a naive, utopian vision which cannot come about in Eastern Europe? Does it not run counter to existing conditions?

Conditions do not exist today in East Europe—nor in the West, for that matter—for such a society. In that respect this type would appear to be unrealistic, defying the existing order. Yet many Marxist and Christian protagonists of the dialogue have expressed an ardent hope for the emergence of such conditions. At a minimum, this notion is a criterion of excellence or a desirable model which serves both as a judgment and a hope. It serves as a judgment upon the existing encounter by being a measure of excellence. It nurtures the hope for better conditions under which desired improvements would take place. Both Christians and Marxists have used similar devices in the past to stimulate change.

In respect to the dialogue many of the outstanding protagonists have advocated dialogical engagement in freedom and without privileges. Many have expressed their longing for no administrative governmental or ecclesiastical interferences. They believe that this type of dialogue is possible. It is hard, of course, to envisage the exact scenario, the set of circumstances, which would bring about dialogue in freedom. But it would be erroneous to suppose that such developments are impossible. Human aspirations for equal opportunity for creative input in weaving the common social fabric have had a powerful attraction until now. Occasionally humanity takes a step closer to its expectations. The shape of human societies is significantly determined by the aspirations of individuals and groups. This aspiration for dialogue in equality and freedom is therefore not a naive mental construct but a reasonable proposal by those who gaze beyond the present horizon into a more humane future in which ethical and dialogical means of encounter will be the rule rather than the exception.

Under conditions of freedom (here are meant all the human rights, products of both the bourgeois and proletarian revolutions) in the economic, social, intellectual, cultural, and political sphere, Christianity and Marxism could interact with considerable creative tension. The process surmounting these tensions could produce solutions promoting general human prosperity, welfare, and happiness. Is it not a prospect worthy of Christian and Marxist aspirations?

Notes

1. For a good short survey of these events see Beeson, pp. 227-254.
2. Imre Miklós, "Relations of a New Type," in *IDOC Bulletin* (Rome) (No. 7, New Series, July 1977), pp. 3-6.
3. Szennay's idea about the dialogue can be found in Chapter 4.
4. Leslie Laszlo, "Towards Normalisation of Church-State Relations," in *Religion and Atheism in the U.S.S.R. and Eastern Europe*, p. 302. Quoted from *Világosság* (Budapest), Vol. 6 (Oct. 1964), pp. 14-15.
5. András Szennay, *Hidden Deity* (Budapest: Saint Stephen Society, 1969), p. 307, as cited by József Lukács, "Cooperation and Dialogue," in *Varieties*, pp. 104-105.
6. Lukács, pp. 100, 105.
7. *Ibid.*, p. 100.
8. *Ibid.*, p. 104.
9. *Ibid.*, p. 106.
10. Aczél, "The Socialist State and the Churches in Hungary," in *The New Hungarian Quarterly*, Vol. 18, No. 66 (Summer, 1977), p. 49. Translated from an article appearing in *Világosság* (Budapest), October 1976.
11. *Ibid.*, p. 54.
12. *Ibid.*, p. 55.
13. *Ibid.*, p. 57.
14. *Ibid.*, pp. 60-61.
15. *Ibid.*, p. 57.
16. *Ibid.*, p. 62.
17. Cserháti, "Open Gates," in *The New Hungarian Quarterly*, Vol. 18, No. 67 (Autumn, 1977), pp. 48-49. Transl. from an article originally in *Vigilia* (Budapest), No. 3 (1977).
18. *Ibid.*, p. 49. It is not clear whether the vagueness is intended or is the author's style.
19. *Ibid.*, p. 51.
20. *Ibid.*, p. 59.
21. *Ibid.*, pp. 56-57.
22. Cserháti, "Dreissig Jahre entwicklung der Kirchenanschaung in Ungarn," transl. from Hungarian into German by Mátyás Esterházy from *Vigilia*, No. 4 (1975), mimeographed, and "Der Dialog der Kirche in Ungarn" (translator's name not provided), from *Vigilia*, November, 1975 (photocopied).
23. Interview with Imre Miklós in Budapest, June 11, 1977.
24. Interview with Jan Zaborowski, October 4, 1975, Warsaw.
25. Interview with Adam Schaff, December 13, 1975, Vienna.
26. Mojzes, *Varieties*, pp. 4-5.
27. Interview with Schaff, Dec. 13, 1975.
28. Mojzes, "Politics and the Christian-Marxist Dialogue," in *Journal of Ecumenical Studies*, Vol. 8, No. 1 (Winter 1971), pp. 90-94.
29. Periodization adopted from Stanisław Kowalczyk, "Der bisherige christlich-marxistische Dialog in Polen," in *Der Christ in der Welt* (Warsaw), No. 2 (1974), pp. 13-14, and Kowalczyk, "On the History of the Christian-Marxist Dialogue in Poland," in *Dialectics and Humanism*

(Warsaw), Vol. 5, No. 3 (Summer 1975), pp. 163-181. For alternate but vaguer periodization see Janusz Zabłocki, "Dreissig Jahre der polnischen Zusammentreffens," in *Der Christ in der Welt*, No. 2 (1974), pp. 6-11, and Janusz Kuczyński, "The Christian-Marxist Dialogue," in *Dialectics and Humanism*, Vol. 1, No. 2 (Spring 1974), pp. 117-132. (*Dialectics and Humanism* hereafter abbreviated *D & H*).

30. Kowalczyk, "On the History of the Christian-Marxist Dialogue in Poland," p. 163. (Hereafter abbreviated as "OHCMDP.") This work is the only history of the dialogue taking place in a given Eastern European country and proved of great help for this work. I gratefully acknowledge my indebtedness and dependence on Kowalczyk for the historical narration of the history of the Polish dialogue up to 1975.

31. *Ibid.*, pp. 164-165.

32. Kowalczyk, "Der bisherige christlich-marxistischer Dialog in Polen," p. 13.

33. *Ibid.*

34. Kowalczyk, "OHCMDP," p. 167.

35. It is outside the scope of this study to describe the orientation, structure, and internal development of these three groups, but a brief description is being provided. There is a sizable bibliography on the Znak and Pax groups. On Znak see for instance S. S. Miller, "The 'Znak' Group: 'Priests' or 'Jesters'? (1956-1970)" in *The Polish Review*, Vol. 21, No. 4 (Winter 1976), pp. 69-84. Adam Bromke, "Catholic Social Thought in Communist Poland," in *Problems of Communism*, Vol. 24, No. 4 (July-August 1975), pp. 67-72. On Pax, see Adam Bromke, "From Falange to Pax," in *Survey*, No. 39 (1961). Jacek Majchrowski, "The Origin and Early Activities of the Pax Movement in Poland," in *East European Quarterly*, Vol. 12, No. 4 (Winter 1978), pp. 385-397. Not much has been written on the Christian Social Association.

36. *Poland: Church Facing Socialism* (Rome: IDOC International, 1979), p. 113.

37. Beeson, pp. 158-159.

38. Remarks on the Christian Social Association are based on personal observations of this author.

39. For specific information see *Czarna ksiega cenzury PRL* (London: ANEKS, 1977). Censorship in all Eastern European countries means that only a limited spectrum of tolerated opinion reaches the public through official publications. Many views are thus not publicized.

40. *Markzism a jednostka ludska* (Warsaw, 1965).

41. Interview with Schaff, December 15, 1975.

42. See below, section on "Paulus-Gesellschaft International Congresses."

43. Later works show that Kołakowski turned into a critic of Marxism. He has also become religious "from a historical and sociological viewpoint." Based on interview of Kołakowski by James Stillman, January 1972, Oxford, England, as described in Stillman's unpublished paper on Kołakowski.

44. For a good sample of Kołakowski's views from that period see Kołakowski, *Toward a Marxist Humanism: Essays on the Left Today*, transl. by Jane Zielonko Peel (New York: Grove Press, 1968), particularly the essay "The Priest and the Jester."

45. Kowalczyk, "OHCMDP," p. 167.

46. *Więź*, Nos. 6 and 10 respectively (1962), pp. 7-16 and 7f.

47. Kowalczyk, "OHCMDP," p. 168.

48. Woźniakowski, "La dialogue en Pologne," in *L'Atheisme du monde; reveil des chrétiens?* (Paris, 1963), pp. 211-213.

49. *Więź*, No. 3 (1963), according to Kowalczyk, "OHCMDP," p. 169.

50. Kowalczyk, "OHCMDP," p. 170.

51. See section below on "Paulus-Gesellschaft International Congresses."

52. Janusz Makowski, "Sympozjum w Mariańskich Lazńiach," *Za i przeciw*, Vol. 11, No. 21 (530), (May 21, 1967), p. 2.

53. Józef Majka, "Dialog z Niewierzacymy" in *Encyklopedia Katolicka*, Vol. 3 (Lublin: Katolicki Uniwersytet Lubelski, 1979), p. 1284.

54. Kowalczyk, "OHCMDP," p. 172.

55. *Ibid.*, p. 171.

56. Moysa, "Znaczenie dialogu z ateizmem marksistowskim we współczesnej odnowie teologicznej," in *Collectanea Theologica*, No. 4 (1968), pp. 187-189.

57. *Człowiek i Światopoglad*, No. 1 (1970), pp. 98-104.

58. Płużański, "Człowiek w perspektywie Teilharda i Marksa," *Człowick i Światopoglad*, No. 3 (1970), pp. 76-86, and "Chrześcijanstwo i spory współczesnego świata," *Miesiecznik Literacki*, No. 12 (1970), pp. 106-112.

59. Kowalczyk, "OHCMDP," p. 174.

60. *Ibid.*, pp. 175-176.

61. *Ibid.*, p. 176.

62. *Ibid.*, p. 177. Four of those papers, by Zabłocki, Jaroszewski, Andrzej Grzegorczyk and Kuczyński were published in the first issue of *Dialectics and Humanism*, Vol., No. 1 (Winter 1979).

63. Jaroszewski, "Polnische Perspektiven," and Zabłocki, "Von der Konfrontation zum dauerhaften Zusammenleben und zur Zusammenarbeit," *IDZ*, Vol. 5, No. 3 (1972), pp. 259-265 and 265-268 respectively.

64. Kowalczyk, "Der bisherige Christlich-Marxistischer Dialog in Polen," pp. 16-17.

65. Jaroszewski, "Confrontation, Dialogue, and Cooperation," from excerpts reprinted in *Church Within Socialism*, p. 186.

66. *Ibid.*, pp. 187-188.

67. *Ibid.*, p. 188.

68. *Ibid.*, p. 189.

69. *Ibid.*, p. 190.

70. Here Jaroszewski seems to be borrowing or at least reflecting the conclusions Palmiro Toggliati reached in March of 1963 at Bergamo that the church ceased to be *instrumentum regni* of the ruling classes. This was pointed out by Lucio Lombardo-Radice in a letter to the author, August 8, 1979.

71. *Ibid.*, pp. 191-192.

72. Zabłocki, "Dreissig Jahre des polnischen Zusammentreffens," in *Der Christ in der Welt*, No. 2 (1974), p. 2.

73. Six, *Od "Syllabusa" do dialogu* (Warsaw: Odiss, 1972).

74. Kowalczyk, "Klasycy marksizmu a problem ateizmu," in *Chrześcijanin w Świecie*, No. 4 (1973), pp. 11-27.

75. For a complete listing of articles see Kowalczyk, "OHCMDP," p. 178. Text is in *Ateneum Kapłańskie*, Vol. 80 (1973), pp. 187-288 and 337-448.

76. Kuczyński, "The Marxist-Christian Dialogue," *H & D*, Vol. 1, No. 2 (Spring 1974), pp. 117-132.

77. Warsaw, 1971.

78. Kuczyński, "The Marxist-Christian Dialogue," p. 122.

79. *Ibid.*, p. 121.

80. *Ibid.*, p. 123.

81. *Ibid.*, p. 125.

82. As precursors of dialogue he mentioned Lenin and Thorez, but more specifically the Marxist Henryk Dembinski, founder of the Vilnus journal *Po Prostu*, executed by the Nazis, and Emmanuel Mounier after his sojourn in Poland.

83. *Ibid.*, p. 127.

84. *Ibid.*, p. 128.

85. *Ibid.*, p. 130.

86. *Ibid.*, p. 132.

87. *D & H*, Vol. 5, No. 1 (Winter 1978), pp. 97-106 and 107-112 respectively.

88. Zabłocki, "Dreissig Jahre des polnischen Zusammentreffens," in *Der Christ in der Welt*, No. 2 (1974), pp. 1-11.

89. *Ibid.*, p. 10.

90. *Ibid.*, p. 2.

91. *D & H*, Vol. 2, No. 1 (Winter 1975), pp. 133-144.

92. *D & H*, Vol. 2, No. 3 (Summer 1975), pp. 157-69, 170-182 respectively.

93. Kasia, "Catholic Mediocentrism," *D & H*, Vol. 3, No. 1 (Winter 1976), pp. 145-162.

94. *Ibid.*, p. 159.

95. *Ibid.*, pp. 163-200 (articles by Gogacz, Kuksewicz, Kasia, and Kuczyński).

96. Mysłek, "A Turn in the Catholic Interpretation of Work," and Wołkowski, "The Philosophy of Work as an Arena of Christian-Marxist Dialogue," in *D & H*, Vol. 5, No. 1 (Winter 1978), pp. 79-95 and 113-122 respectively. For the ideas expressed in these articles see Chapter 8.

97. *D & H*, Vol. 5, No. 1, pp. 137-149.

98. *Ibid.*, p. 146.

99. *Ibid.*, p. 147.

100. Borgosz, "Toward a Further Concretization of the Christian-Marxist Dialogue," *D & H*, Vol. 5, No. 3 (Summer 1978), p. 125.

101. *Ibid.*, p. 128.

102. *Ibid.*, p. 129.

103. *Ibid.*, p. 131. To my knowledge Borgosz is the only Marxist who has publicly acknowledged this.

104. *Ibid.*, p. 132.

105. *Ibid.*, p. 133.

106. *Ibid.*, p. 135.

107. Garadja, "Transcendentalism and History—A Dialogue Between the Christian Philosophy and the Present Time," in *D & H*, Vol. 5, No. 3 (Fall 1978), pp. 137-144.

108. In *ibid.*, pp. 183-193.

109. *Ibid.*, p. 190.

110. *D & H*, Vol. 6, No. 1, pp. 5-27.

111. *Ibid.*, p. 12.

112. *Ibid.*, p. 25.

113. *Ibid.*, p. 27.

114. Wiesław Gwizdz, "Catholics and the Church in Poland," in *C.S.A. Information Bulletin*, No. 4 (April 1977), p. 25.

115. Letter of Charles Robertson to Mojzes, November 26, 1979, Bloomington, Indiana.
116. Morawski, speech to the general assembly of the C.S.A., in *C.S.A. Information Bulletin*, No. 5 (May 1977), p. 28.
117. Edward Gierek answering workers in a factory, in *C.S.A. Information Bulletin*, Nos. 7-8 (July-August 1976), p. 3.
118. Full speeches of both Gierek and Paul VI published in *C.S.A. Information Bulletin*, No. 12 (December 1977), pp. 25-32.
119. Quoted in *C.S.A. Information Bulletin*, No. 2 (February 1978), p. 30.
120. *Ibid.*
121. Letter of June 10, 1978, in *Religion in Communist Lands*, Vol. 7, No. 2 (Summer 1979), pp. 117-120.
122. *C.S.A. Information Bulletin*, No. 3 (March, 1978), p. 12. All quotes rendered as transl. in Poland.
123. February 12, 1978.
124. Quoted in Mieczysław F. Rakowski, "The Basis of Cooperation and Dialogue," *D & H*, Vol. 5, No. 1, p. 127.
125. This response in *Polityka* (March 25, 1980) is transl. in full in *ibid.*
126. *Ibid.*, p. 113.
127. *Ibid.*, p. 116. Note the doctrinal tone of much of the Polish dialogue.
128. *Ibid.*, p. 121.
129. *Ibid.*, p. 123.
130. Except for the last article, extensive translated excerpts can be found in *C.S.A. Information Bulletin*, No. 5 (May, 1978), pp. 1-22.
131. *Ibid.*, p. 17.
132. *Ibid.*, pp. 19-22.
133. *Spotkania*, No. 5 (January 1979). English version published in *Religion in Communist Lands*, Vol. 7, No. 4 (Winter 1979), pp. 252-257.
134. *Ibid.*, p. 254.
135. *Ibid.*, p. 255.
136. *Ibid.*, p. 256.
137. Quoted in Alexander Tomsky, "John Paul II in Poland: Pilgrim of the Holy Spirit," in *Religion in Communist Lands*, Vol. 7, No. 3 (Fall 1979), p. 164.
138. Hansjakob Stehle, "The *Ostpolitik* of the Vatican and the Polish Pope," *Religion in Communist Lands*, Vol. 8, No. 1 (Spring 1980), p. 20.
139. *Ibid.*
140. Letter of Robertson to Mojzes, Nov. 26, 1979, Bloomington.
141. Paris: Institut Literacki, 1977. Not available to this author.
142. Robertson to Mojzes, Nov. 26, 1979, Bloomington.
143. E.g., Ludwig Wiśniewski, "About the Basis for Dialogue and Cooperation," *Bratniak*, Nos. 12-13 (September-October 1978); Jacek Salij, "Dialogue Between the Church and the 'Left' in Poland," in *Zapis* [*samizdat*], No. 4 (1977), reprinted in *Religion in Communist Lands*, Vol. 7, No. 1 (Spring 1971), pp. 42-46; Ludwig Wiśniewski, "Christians in the Struggle for Justice," *Spotkania* [Catholic samizdat], No. 2 (January 1978).
144. The intellectual dialogue shows no sign of slowing down. Among recent publications not available to this author at the time of this writing are Kowalczyk, *Z problematyki Dialogu Chrześciańsko-Marksistowskiego* (Warsaw: ODISS, 1977), and Kowalczyk, *Podstawy Światopogladu Chrześciańskiego* (Warsaw: ODISS, 1979). Kuczyński, *Christian Marxist*

Dialogue in Poland (Warsaw: Interpress, 1979) is merely a reprint of his articles in *D & H* in honor of the papal visit.

145. The concern of the Polish bishops about the problems of the nation are ably reported in *C.S.A. Information Bulletin*, No. 11-12 (Nov.-Dec., 1980), pp. 2-3, 36-52.

146. Papers of all symposia are being published in English, German, and Russian in *Peace and the Sciences* (Vienna: International Institute for Peace). The collected papers and discussion of the first three symposia were published by Rudolf Weiler and Walter Hollitscher (eds.), *Christen und Marxisten in Friedensgeschpräch* (Vienna, Freiburg, Basel: Herder, 1976). Vol. II under the same title was published by the same publisher in 1979 covering the next three symposia. Hereafter abbreviated *CMF*.

147. Rudolf Weiler, "Der Ausbau des Institutes für Friedensforschung in den Jahren 1972 und 1973," in *Wiener Blätter*, No. 1 (January 1974), p. 6.

148. The German text in *CMF*, Vol. I, pp. 31-43.

149. The list is derived on the basis of having taken part in the discussion. It is impossible to reconstruct the exact list of those in attendance from *CMF*, Vol. 1. *CMF* has only a composite list of all who attended the first three symposia (pp. 315-318).

150. German versions of the two papers are in *CMF*, Vol. 1, pp. 63-90 and 109-131 respectively.

151. Printed text names Vitaliy Borovoy, but an errata sheet states Archbishop Vladimir, which is probably the correct identification.

152. Weiler, "Wiener Universitätsinstitut für Friedensforschung Mitveranstalter eines Symposiums in Moskau: 10.bis 17. September 1973," in *Wiener Blätter*, No. 1, p. 44.

153. *Ibid.*, p. 46. Transl. by Mojzes.

154. On the basis of the published data it is not possible to establish which of the three meetings were attended by Andrzej Wiezorek (Marxist) from Poland, František Cinoldr (Marxist) from Czechoslovakia, Nicolae Ion (Marxist) from Rumania and Leonid Ermenow, Alexander Galkin, Oleg Yanitskiy, Igor Yastrebov, Vsevold Moishaev, Nelli Motroshchilova, Nikolai Polyanov, Antonina Strebalova, and Semyon Tangian, all Marxists from the U.S.S.R. One may surmise, at least in the case of the Soviets, that they attended the Moscow symposium.

155. Maurice Boutin, "Education for Peace and Ideological Debate," in *Varieties*, pp. 197-200.

156. The papers presented by the participants in that symposium are available in English in *Peace and the Sciences*, No. 3 (1978). For a Soviet interpretation see D. Atamali and Yu. Denisov, "Razoruzhenyie: Mnen'ie Marksistov i Hristian," in *Mirovaia ekonomika i mezhdunarodniye otnoshenyiya* (Moscow), No. 12 (1978), pp. 111-113.

157. Interview with Weiler, December 12, 1975.

158. Interview with Silvin Eiletz, S.J., November 30, 1975, at Mondsee.

159. This author's own impression as a participant and cowriter of the communiques.

160. Dorothea Neumärker, *Josef L. Hromádka: Theologie und Politik im Kontext des Zeitgeschehens* (Munich and Mainz: Chr. Kaiser and Matthias Grünewald Verlags, 1974), pp. 73-75. Some Marxists assert that it was always Marxists who initiated the dialogue. At least in Czechoslovakia this was not true. The Christians initiated it and the Marxists did not respond.

161. For a more complete treatment of Hromádka in English see

Charles West, *Communism and the Theologians* (New York: The Macmillan Company, 1963), pp. 51-77. West provided a balanced and accurate analysis of Hromádka's theology and his views toward communism, with which I am fully in agreement.

162. Neumärker, p. 133 and *passim*.

163. Hromádka, *Theology Between Yesterday and Tomorrow* (Philadelphia: Westminster Press, 1957), pp. 47-57.

164. West, p. 63.

165. Hromádka, "The Present Age and the Crisis of Christian Civilization," in *Communio Viatorum* (Prague), Vol. 1, Nos. 2-3 (Summer-Fall 1958), p. 94.

166. West, pp. 58 and 71-73.

167. Hromádka, "Gospel for Atheists," in *Risk* (Geneva), Vol. 1, No. 1 (Spring 1965), p. 34.

168. *Ibid.*

169. West, p. 72. One must observe that such an occasion did take place with the Soviet invasion of Czechoslovakia when Hromádka, just a few months before his death, courageously and with integrity, did say "no" to the Soviet interference.

170. Neumärker, p. 242.

171. Hromádka, "Towards a Dialogue," in *Communio Viatorum*, Vol. 2, No. 4 (Winter 1959), p. 310.

172. Neumärker, p. 245.

173. Hromádka, *Pole je tento svět* (Praha: Kalich, 1964). The most relevant section of the book were published in English in article form, "On the Threshold of a Dialogue," in *Communio Viatorum*, Vol. 7, No. 2 (Summer 1964), pp. 119-146.

174. "On the Threshold of Dialogue," p. 124.

175. *Ibid.*, p. 138. The italics are Hromádka's.

176. *Ibid.*, p. 134.

177. *Ibid.* Italics are Hromádka's.

178. *Ibid.*, pp. 144-145. Italics are Hromádka's.

179. *Smysl lidskeho života* (Prague: Nakladatelství politické literatury, 1965), transl. into German *Vom Sinn des menschlichen Lebens* (Freiburg: Verlag Rombach, 1971).

180. *Vom Sinn des menschlichen Lebens*, p. 215.

181. *Ibid.*, p. 207.

182. *Ibid.*, pp. 207-208.

183. *Ibid.*, pp. 208-209.

184. *Ibid.*, pp. 209-210.

185. *Ibid.*, p. 214. Transl. by Mojzes.

186. *Ibid.*, p. 216. Transl. by Mojzes.

187. In *Club Voltaire, Jahrbuch des deutschen Humanisten-Verbandes*, 1967, as reported by Albert Rasker in a letter to the author from Oestgeest, Holland, August 10, 1979.

188. Milan Opočenský, "Christlich-marxistischer Dialog in Prag," in *Stimmen aus der Kirche der ČSSR*, p. 131.

189. Machovec, "Der Dialog in der Tschechoslowakei," pp. 301-304.

190. *Ibid.*, p. 308.

191. *Ibid.*, p. 309. Transl. by Mojzes.

192. *Ibid.*, p. 311.

193. Opočenský, "A Christian Existence in Czechoslovakia Today," in *Communio Viatorum*, Vol. 7, Nos. 3-4 (Winter 1964), p. 298.

194. *Ibid.*, p. 229.

195. *Ibid.*, p. 300.

196. *Ibid.*, p. 302.

197. Originally published in Czech, *Bůh neni zcela mrtev*, by Československy spisovatel, 1967. In 1968 it was translated into German. The English edition is Harmondsworth, Middlesex, England, and Baltimore, Md.: Penguin Books, 1973.

198. Gardavský, *God Is Not Quite Dead*, p. 15.

199. Josef Smolik, "Respect and Reservations," *Communio Viatorum*, Vol. 12, No. 3 (Fall 1969), pp. 170-172.

200. The first symposium took place in Jena, G.D.R., June 24-26, 1965.

201. Walter Hollitscher, "Marxistische Religionssoziologie," *Internationale Dialog Zeitschrift*, Vol. 1, No. 1 (1968), pp. 89-94 (subsequently abbreviated *IDZ*).

202. With the exception of some scholarly conferences which took place in Yugoslavia, but which had a different character. See below.

203. Hromádka, "Unüberwindlicher Gegensatz oder ausraumbare Missverständnisse," in *Communio Viatorum*, Vol. 10, Nos. 2-3 (Summer-Fall 1967), p. 109.

204. *Ibid.*, pp. 112-114.

205. Bishop Jan Michalko of the Lutheran Church of Slovakia blamed the Paulus-Gesellschaft for subversion of the social order at the Christian Peace Conference meeting in Siófok, Hungary, September 1975.

206. For Czech analyses of the Congress see Erika Kadlecová, "Die Gespräche in Marienbad," in *IDZ*, Vol. I, No. 1 (1968), pp. 101-109, and Lochman, "Creativity and Freedom in a Human Society," in *Communio Viatorum*, Vol. 10, Nos. 2-3 (Summer-Fall 1967), pp. 115-122.

207. The collected papers and discussion make a large volume published under *Schöpfertum und Freiheit* (Munich: Paulus-Gesellschaft, 1968).

208. Lochman, "Creativity and Freedom in Human Society," p. 119.

209. *Ibid.*, p. 120.

210. *Ibid.* See also Lochman, "On Christian-Marxist Dialogue," in *The Christian Century*, January 7, 1970, p. 16.

211. Gardavský, "Die Wege einer Konfrontation," in *IDZ*, Vol. 1, No. 2 (1968), pp. 179-190.

212. Peter Hebblethwaite, "Introduction," in Machovec, *AMLJ*, pp. 12-13.

213. Kadlecová, p. 102.

214. Beeson, p. 216.

215. Machovec, *AMLJ*, p. 70.

216. James Will (an eyewitness of the meeting) to Mojzes, Evanston Ill., May 4, 1976.

217. Former figure given by Will. Latter figure, Beeson, p. 216.

218. Will.

219. Albert Rasker, "Theologie und Revolution," in *Theologie und Revolution* by Rasker and Machovec (Hamburg: Herbert Reich-Evangelischer Verlag, 1969), p. 39.

220. Machovec, "Theologie und Revolution von Prag aus gesehen," in *ibid.*, pp. 61-62. Transl. by Mojzes.

221. Machovec, "Kampf um den Wahren Kommunismus," in *Evolution oder Revolution der Gesellschaft* (Munich: Paulus-Gesellschaft, 1969), p. 188.

222. In January 1973 Radio Prague stated that the dialogue was an attempt to weaken Marxism and strengthen Christianity and the Marxists who participated in dialogue were renegades. See Beeson, p. 222.

223. Machovec, "Vorwort," in Wieland Zademach, *Marxistischer Atheismus und die biblische Botschaft von der Rechtfertigung des Gottlosen* (Düsseldorf: Patmos-Verlag, 1973), p. 12.

224. Gardavský, *Naděje ze skepse* (Prague: Svoboda, 1969), in German, *Hoffnung aus der Skepsis* (Munich: Chr. Kaiser, 1970), p. 73.

225. Machovec, "Atheismus und Christentum—Wechselseitige Herausforderung als Aufgabe," in *IDZ*, Vol. 1, No. 1 (1968), p. 41.

226. Gardavský, "Dialog in Amerika," in *IDZ*, Vol. 2, No. 2 (1969), p. 187.

227. Krejči, "Dialog des Marxismus mit dem Christentum als Friedensbeitrag," in *IDZ*, Vol. 1, No. 1, pp. 43-49; "Ein neues Modell des wissenschaftlichen Atheismus," in *IDZ*, Vol. 1, No. 2, pp. 191-195; and "Der monologische Robot als Gefahr," in *IDZ*, Vol. 3, No. 4 (1970), pp. 380-384.

228. *Jesus für Atheisten* (Stuttgart: Kreuz Verlag, 1972).

229. *A Marxist Looks at Jesus*, p. 34.

230. "Die 'Sache Jesu' und marxistiche Selbstreflexionen," in *Marxisten und die Sache Jesu*, Iring Fetscher and Milan Machovec, eds. (Munich and Mainz: Chr. Kaiser and Matthias Grünewald Verlags, 1974).

231. "Die Gottfrage und der moderne Atheismus," in *Gottfrage und moderner Atheismus* by J. Blank, W. Kasper, M. Machovec, and H. Zahrnt (Regensburg: Verlag Friedrich Pustet, 1972).

232. Czech version published in 1969 not available to this author. German version *Hoffnung aus der Skepsis*. Not published in English.

233. Lochman, "Gardavský's Wandlung von Jakob zu Jeremia," in *Orientierung* (Zurich), Vol. 42 (1978), p. 110.

234. *Ibid.*, p. 111.

235. (New York, Evanston, and London: Harper & Row, Publishers, 1970).

236. *Ibid.*, p. 185.

237. Lochman, "Kirche und Erneuerung der Gesellschaft," in *Communio Viatorum*, Vol. 11, No. 3 (Summer 1968), pp. 121-128.

238. Lochman, "Evangelium für Atheisten," in *IDZ*, Vol. 1, No. 2 (1968), pp. 221-229.

239. Lochman, "Dimensionen Marxscher Religionskritik," in *IDZ*, Vol. 6, No. 4 (1973), pp. 351-360.

240. Lochman, *Encountering Marx: Bonds and Barriers Between Christians and Marxists* (Philadelphia: Fortress Press, 1977). The article of the previous footnote is included in this book.

241. The dates are approximate and not equally applicable to all regions in Yugoslavia. For a different periodization based on the attitudes of the Roman Catholic Church in Yugoslavia toward the government see Zdenko Roter, "Razvoj odnosov med katoliško cerkvijo in deržavo v socialistični Jugoslaviji," in *Teorija in praksa* (Ljubljana), Vol. 7, Nos. 8 and 9 (September 1970), pp. 1280-1282.

242. For a detailed description of the first three periods see Mojzes, "Christian-Marxist Encounter in the Context of a Socialist Society," *Journal of Ecumenical Studies*, Vol. 9, No. 1 (Winter 1972), pp. 1-13. The remainder of that article (pp. 12-27) is used frequently in this segment of the book, sometimes taking considerable portions of the article verbatim. For a comprehensive treatment of the position of churches see Stella Alexander, *Church and State in Yugoslavia Since 1945* (Cambridge: Cambridge University Press, 1979).

243. Partisans were guerilla units organized by the National Libera-

tion Front under Communist guidance fighting the Germans and their allies as well as domestic collaborators.

244. This is not to imply that the Serbian and Macedonian Orthodox Churches have no relations with the government. Among the churches the Orthodox churches have a greater degree of contact and cooperation with the government than the other churches, but these contacts can be classified as church-state relations, which are not the subject matter of this book.

245. Comprising about 35 percent of the population.

246. An example of their writings can be found in Erich Fromm (ed.), *Socialist Humanism* (Garden City, NY: Anchor Books, Doubleday & Co., Inc., 1966). Included are articles by Veljko Korać, Mihailo Marković, Danilo Pejović, Gajo Petrović, Rudi Supek, and Predrag Vranicki.

247. Božidar Jakšić, "Današnji smisao sukoba na književnoj levici," in *Kultura* (Belgrade), Nos. 13-14 (1971), p. 210. Transl. by Mojzes.

248. Bošnjak, *Filozofija i kršćanstvo (Philosophy and Christianity)* (Zagreb: Naprijed, 1966), 625 pp.

249. Ćimić, *Socijalističko društvo i religija (Socialist Society and Religion)* (Sarajevo: Svjetlost, 1966), 339 pp.

250. Bošnjak, *Filozofija i kršćanstvo*, pp. 34-44.

251. *Ibid.*, pp. 450-535.

252. *Ibid.*, pp. 574-575. Transl. by Mojzes.

253. *Ibid.*, p. 576.

254. *Ibid.*, pp. 577ff.

255. His work is a slightly revised doctoral dissertation and contains a large number of charts, results of polls, statistical analyses, etc.

256. Ćimić, *Socijalističko društvo i religija*, pp. 13-48.

257. *Ibid.*, pp. 45-47.

258. Interview with Vjekoslav Bajsić, November 14, 1975, in Zagreb.

259. Interview with an eyewitness, Jure Kristo, O.P., March 2, 1979, at Collegeville, Minn.

260. The stenographic notes were published in paperback form. B. Bošnjak and M. Škvorc, *Marksist i kršćanin* (Zagreb: Praxis, 1969).

261. For identification of Yugoslav participants at these dialogues see below section on Paulus-Gesellschaft Congresses.

262. It appeared originally in *Nova pot* (Ljubljana) in the Slovenian language and was translated into Croatian under the title "Filozofija i kršćanstvo" published in *Crkva u svijetu* (Split), Vol. 3, Nos. 3, 4, and 5, pp. 2-19, 1-19, and 1-18, respectively.

263. *Ibid.*, No. 3, p. 4.

264. Bošnjak, "Kritika religije," in *Religija i društvo (Religion and Society)* (Zagreb: Stvarnost, 1969), p. 26.

265. Bošnjak, "Kritika religije," in *Religija i društvo*, pp. 29-30.

266. Bošnjak, "Pogovor," in *Religija i društvo*, p. 256.

267. Oleg Mandić, "Smisao dijaloga izmedju marksista i kršćana," in *Religija i društvo*, pp. 77, 79.

268. *Ibid.*, p. 78.

269. Ante Fiamengo, "Crkva i politika u samoupravnom društvu," in *Religija i društvo*, pp. 158-159.

270. *Ibid.*, p. 160.

271. *Ibid.*, pp. 161-162.

272. Ćimić, "Političko i idejno suočavanje s religijskim fenomenom," in *Religija i društvo*, p. 186.

273. *Ibid.*, p. 187.

274. Roter, "Politika i religija," in *Religija i društvo*, pp. 123-129.
275. Roter, "Smisao dialoga izmedju marksista i kršćana," in *Vjerske zajednice u Jugoslaviji*, pp. 149-154. A slightly revised translation appeared in English under "A Marxist View of Christianity," in *Journal of Ecumenical Studies*, vol. 9, No. 1 (Winter 1972), pp. 40-50.
276. *Fenomenološka filozofija i religija* (Belgrade: Filozofija, 1967).
277. "Socijalističko društvo in religija," in *Nova pot* (Ljubljana), Nos. 10/12 (1964).
278. "Teologija dijaloga Crkve sa svijetom," in *Bogoslovni vestnik* (Ljubljana), Vol. 25, Nos. 3-4 (1965).
279. Information on this subject was gained from informal conversations with Vjekoslav Bajsić, editor of *Svesci-Kršćanska Sadašnjost* and professor of theology, and Trpimir Stjepan-Grmec, editor of *Aksa-Kršćanska Sadašnjost*, during the summers of 1970 and 1971.
280. *Glas koncila*, X, 6 (March 21, 1971).
281. Vjekoslav Bajsić, "Dijalog kršćana i ateista," *Svesci*, No. 3 (April-May, 1967), pp. 31-35. Tomislav Šagi-Bunić published a number of works including *Ali drugog puta nema* (Zagreb, 1969) and *Nema privatnog Boga* (Zagreb, 1970). His work has been critically evaluated by Esad Ćimić, Marko Oršolić, Boris Vušković, and Ivica Mlivončić in *Pogledi*, Vol. 2, No. 6 (1971), pp. 133-160.
282. Published in English, "The Significance and Problems of Dialogue Today," in *Journal of Ecumenical Studies*, Vol. 9, No. 1 (Winter 1972), pp. 29-39.
283. Tomislav Šagi-Bunić, "Današnji kršćanin kao odgovorni član svoje nacije i svoga društva," in *Glas koncila*, X, 6 (March 21, 1971), p. 7.
284. Antun Ivanov, "Vjernici samoupravljači," *Svesci*, No. 12 (November, 1968), pp. 82-84; Jure Juras, "Vjernici-samoupravljači su samoupravljači," *Svesci*, No. 13 (January-March, 1969), pp. 90-92; and I. Ivković, "Na istu temu," in the same issue, pp. 92-93. A. Ivanov responded in No. 14. Another retort came by Jure Juras, "Kip domovine pred početak ljeta 1970," in No. 15, pp. 85-95.
285. "Neka sporna pitanja marksističke teorije religije," in *Naše teme* (Zagreb), No. 6 (1967), pp. 980-993.
286. Kerševan, "Teoretski model za proučavanje religije kao specifične prakse," in *Naše teme*, No. 5 (1969), pp. 732-757, as summarized by Alessandro Russo and Riccardo Lanzoni, "Marxist Sociology of Religion in Eastern Europe," in *IDOC International-North American Edition*, No. 12 (October 31, 1970), pp. 95-96.
287. Kerševan, "Savremeno hrišćanstvo i ideologija," in *Kultura*, Nos. 13-14 (1971), pp. 78-79.
288. *Ibid.*, pp. 90-93.
289. Edo Marinković, "Marksizam: sistem ili inspiracija?" in *Crkva u svijetu* (Split), Vol. 4, Nos. 5-6 (1969), pp. 406-407. (Edo Marinković is a pseudonym.)
290. *Ibid.*, pp. 416-417.
291. Šagi-Bunić, *Ali drugog puta nema*, pp. 377-396, and Bajsić, "Stavovi kršćana prema dijalogu s marksistima," in *Vjerske zajednice u Jugoslaviji*, pp. 141-148.
292. Bajsić, *Na rubovima crkve i civilizacije* (Zagreb: Kršćanska sadašnjost, 1972), pp. 250-251.
293. *Ibid.*, p. 306.
294. *Ibid.*, p. 309.

295. *Ibid.*, p. 316.
296. (Belgrade: Zavod za izdavanje udžbenika S.R. Srbije, 1970).
297. (Sarajevo: Zavod za izdavanje udžbenika, 1971), 232 pp.
298. *Ibid.*, p. 4. Transl. by Mojzes.
299. *Ibid.*, p. 5. Transl. by Mojzes.
300. *Ibid.*, p. 9. Transl. by Mojzes.
301. *Ibid.*, p. 108.
302. Stanković, "Čovjek i religija," in *Praxis* (Zagreb), Vol. 7, No. 4 (1970), pp. 645-646.
303. E. g. Branko Lukšić, "Drama ateizacije," in *Crkva u svijetu*, Vol. 6, No. 4 (1971), pp. 345-349, and "Religija i savremeno društvo," in *Kultura*, Nos. 13-14 (1971), pp. 258-316.
304. Interview with Vuko Pavičević, Nov. 21, 1975, in Belgrade, and Tomislav Šagi-Bunić, Nov. 16, 1975, in Zagreb.
305. Stenographic text of both meetings is included in "Religija i savremeno društvo," pp. 258-316.
306. Željko Mardešić, "XI kongres medjunarodne konferencije za sociologiju religije," in *Crkva u svijetu*, vol. 6, No. 4 (1971), p. 342.
307. E.g., the TV dialogue of Roger Garaudy and Jean Cardinal Danielou in "Komunist bez partije i biskup bez biskupije," *Glas Koncila*, No. 12 (June 21, 1970), p. 5.
308. "Teologija i revolucija," in Frane Franić, *Putovi dijaloga* (Split: Crkva u svijetu, 1973). This book is a collection of articles written by Franić and contains other writings of his on the theme of Christian-Marxist dialogue.
309. Bošnjak, "Die Idee des Humanismus zwischen dem ideologisierten Marxismus und dem politisierten Christentum," in *IDZ*, Vol. 3, No. 1 (1970), pp. 60-70.
310. Interview with Bošnjak, November 16, 1975, in Zagreb.
311. This view he expressed in an informal lecture to my group of students in August, 1971, in Zagreb. That view, unfortunately, is not reflected in his most recent book, *Grčka filozofska kritika Biblije* (Zagreb: Naprijed, 1971), which surveys the philosophical arguments of ancient Greek pagan philosophers with Christian apologists, and considers that as a form of dialogue.
312. "Okrugli stol" in *Pogledi* (Split), Vol. 2, No. 6 (1971), p. 75.
313. The conference took place February 11-13, 1971. Ćimić's address was entitled "Rehabilitation of Religion as a Cultural Fact"; excerpts were reported in *Glas koncila* (Zagreb), X, 6 (March 21, 1971).
314. Srdjan Vrcan, "Suvremena marksistička misao pred fenomenom religije," in *Crkva u svijetu*, Vol. 6, No. 2 (1971), p. 114. Other works of Vrcan include "Neka pitanja sociološkog istraživanja religije i religioznosti danas" in *Sociologija*, Vol. 9, No. 1 (1969), pp. 39-63; "Religioznost Splitskih srednjoškolaca i studenata" in *Školski vjesnik* (Split), Vol. 19, Nos. 5-6 (May-June 1969), pp. 28-52. Vrcan was the editor of this entire issue of *Školski vjesnik* which dealt with the theme "School, Religion and Church in Self-Managing Society," which contains 14 articles on various aspects of the topic. Also Vušković and Vrcan, *Raspeto katoličanstvo* (Zagreb: Naše teme, 1980).
315. Interview with Branko Lukšić, Nov. 17, 1975, in Split.
316. Excerpts from the writings of Roger Garaudy, Harvey Cox, and Roger Shinn were published. See Aleksa Popović, "Povodom pogleda jednog istaknutog marksiste na razvoj 'od anateme do dijaloga' i o mogućnosti priloga ovom razoju pravoslavnih bogoslova," *Teološki pogledi*

(Beograd), Vol. 2, Nos. 5-6 (September-December, 1969), pp. 370-383. Also note Dimitrije M. Kalezić, "O ateizmu," in *Teološki pogledi*, Vol. 4, No. 1 (January-March, 1971), pp. 43-53, which advocates opposition to atheism without escalating the conflict.

317. Jordan Kuničić, "Marksisti i kršćani prema budućnosti," *Crkva u svijetu*, Vol. 5, No. 4 (last quarter, 1970), pp. 369-378.

318. Roter, "Politika i religija," in *Religija i društvo*, pp. 123-129, and "Začarani krog" in *Teorija in praksa*, Vol. 8, No. 5 (May, 1971), pp. 852-853, which is a reaction to a commentary by the Slovene Christian layman Janez Pogačar, published in *Družina* (Ljubljana), No. 7 (1971), p. 15.

319. Mihailo Marković helpfully pointed out that no significant improvements in the political structure in the democratic direction took place after 1965, but the process of liberalization continued to the early 1970s.

320. E.g. Štefica Bahtijarević, *Religijsko pripadanje* (Zagreb: Političke teme, 1975), Ivan Cvitković, *Marksistička misao i religija* (Sarajevo: Svjetlost, 1980), and Nikola Dugandžija, *Religija u uvjetima potrošačkog društva* (Zagreb: Institut za društvena istraživanja, 1980).

321. Interview with Archbishop Franić, Nov. 17, 1975, in Split.

322. *Ibid.*

323. Franić, *Putovi dijaloga*, p. 179.

324. *Ibid.*, p. 206.

325. *Ibid.*, p. 232.

326. *Ibid.*, p. 239.

327. *Ibid.*, p. 243.

328. Vereš, *Filozofsko-teološki dijalog s Marksom* (Zagreb: Filozofsko-teološki institut Družbe Isusove, 1973), 218 pp.

329. *Ibid.*, p. 168.

330. *Ibid.*, pp. 189-192.

331. (Vicenza, Italy: Libreria Internazionale Edizione Franciscane, 1972).

332. Romić, "Dialogue between Marxists and Christians as a Presupposition of Coexistence in Freedom," in *Varieties*, pp. 114-129. See also Romić, "Predrevolucijski Lenjinovi stavovi prema religiji," in *Jukić* (Sarajevo), Vol. 1, No. 2, pp. 86-91.

333. Šimundža, *Čovjek, društvo i crkva (Man, Society, and the Church)* (Split: Crkva u svijetu, 1979), p. 87.

334. *Ibid.*, pp. 85-88.

335. *Ibid.*, p. 87. Transl. by Mojzes.

336. *Ibid.*, p. 89.

337. Evident from many conversations of this author with Šimundža between 1972 and 1979.

338. *(The Church in Contemporary Society)* (Ljubljana: Cankarjeva založba, 1973), 220 pp.

339. *(The Catholic Church and State in Yugoslavia)* (Ljubljana: Cankarjeva založba, 1976), 311 pp.

340. I suspect that no one in Yugoslavia would dare at this time to write a book which would include everything that transpired, because it would unsettle the present political relations too drastically. But see Alexander for a more complete version of these events.

341. Interview with Roter, November 15, 1975, in Ljubljana.

342. Bošnjak, "Was bedeutet das Dilemma: Jesus-Marx?" in *Marxisten und die Sache Jesu*, pp. 103-114.

343. *Ibid.*

344. Bošnjak, "Reflections on Religion," in *Religion and Atheism in the U.S.S.R. and Eastern Europe*, p. 21.

345. *Ibid.*, p. 30.

346. *(Human Being at Crossroads)* (Sarajevo: Svjetlost, 1975), pp. 103-166.

347. *Ibid.*, p. 105.

348. *Ibid.*, p. 109.

349. *Ibid.*, pp. 146-147.

350. *Ibid.*, p. 117.

351. Kerševan, "Odnos komunista prema religiji," in *Naše teme*, Vol. 19, No. 5 (May, 1975), pp. 887-891. For lengthy English citations of that article see Josip Horak, "Church, State, and Religious Freedom in Yugoslavia: An Ideological and Constitutional Study," in *Journal of Church and State* (Waco, TX), Vol. 19, No. 2 (Spring, 1977), pp. 287-292.

352. Kerševan, "Lenin in religija," in *Teorija in praksa*, Vol. 13, Nos. 1-2 (January-February, 1976), pp. 44-45.

353. Kerševan is not specific as to what these errors are.

354. Bajsić, "Marko Kerševan: Teoretski model za proučavanje religije kao specifične prakse," in *Na rubovima crkve i civilizacije*, pp. 315-324.

355. Stres, "Religija kot družbena praksa," in *Bogoslovni vestnik*, Vol. 35, No. 3 (July-September, 1975), pp. 272-299.

356. Althusser, *For Marx*. Transl. by Ben Brewster (New York: Random House, 1970), pp. 221-241.

357. Ante Fiamengo, "Croyances religieuses et changements technologiques en Yougoslavie," in *Archives de Sociologie de Religions*, No. 15 (1963), pp. 101-111 as cited in Srdjan Vrcan, "Vezanost ljudi za religiju i crkvu u nas," in *Naše teme*, Vol. 19, Nos. 7-8 (July-August, 1975), p. 1121.

358. Vrcan, p. 1237.

359. The implications of the Marxist attitude toward religion and the sociological data on mass religiosity for the church have been explored by Špiro Marasović, "Samoupravljanje i religija," in *Crkva u svijetu*, Vol. 15, No. 3 (1980), pp. 232-247.

360. *(The Kingdom of God and Communism)* (Belgrade: Institut za medjunarodni radnički pokret, 1975), 153 pp. The last chapter of the book under the identical title was published in English translation in *Varieties*, pp. 29-40.

361. Krešić, "The Kingdom of God and Communism," p. 40.

362. *Ibid.*

363. *Ibid.*

364. Romić, "Dijalog kršćana i marksista," in *Glas Koncila*, No. 23 (November 9, 1975), p. 6. For more information see section on Paulus-Gesellschaft activities below.

365. Interview with Bajsić, November 14, 1975, in Zagreb.

366. Interview with Djuro Šušnjić, November 21, 1975, in Belgrade.

367. Jože Pogačnik, "We, Believers, Do Not Want to Be Too Exacting," in *Socialist Thought and Practice* (Belgrade), Vol. 17, No. 4 (1977), pp. 44-51.

368. On the issues revolving around Tito's death, see Mojzes, "Hour-X for Yugoslavia," in *Worldview* (New York), Vol. 20, No. 3 (March, 1977), pp. 4-8.

369. An expression of this attitude can be found in the book by a high party leader, Todo Kurtović, *Crkva i religija u socijalističkom samoupravnom društvu* (Belgrade: Rad, 1978).

370. Interview with Erich Kellner, November 5, 1975 at Mondsee, Austria.

371. Gisela Uellenberg, in *Experiment eines kritischen Christentums* (Mondsee, Austria: Internationale Paulus-Gesellschaft, n.d.), pp. 1-3.

372. Interview with Kellner, November 5, 1975.

373. Proceedings were published under the title *Der Mensch, Geist und Materie* (Munich: Paulus-Gesellschaft, 1965).

374. *Christentum und Marxismus Heute* (Munich: Paulus-Gesellschaft, 1966), contains the proceedings of the conference.

375. The list of participants includes the name of the Marxist sociologist Stanko Saksida from Ljubljana, Yugoslavia. To the best of my knowledge he preregistered but did not attend. The lists of participants in Paulus-Gesellschaft sources are highly unreliable because the registration procedures are loosely organized, and the lists are derived mainly from the announced intentions to attend the meetings.

376. Schaff, "Der Marxistische Begriff des Menschen," in *Christentum und Marxismus Heute*, pp. 28-50 and *passim*.

377. *Christliche und marxistische Zukunft* (Munich: Paulus-Gesellschaft Selbstverlag, 1965).

378. Polikarov, "Religion als Kosmologie," in *ibid.*, pp. 153-162.

379. Pavičević, "Religion und marxistische Toleranz," in *ibid.*, pp. 145-153.

380. Bošnjak, "Der Mensch als Mysterium," in *ibid.*, pp. 138-140.

381. A newspaper account estimated it at 120. None of these estimates are completely reliable. The higher figure was mentioned more frequently by eyewitnesses.

382. *Christliche Humanität und marxistischer Humanismus* (Munich: Paulus-Gesellschaft Selbstverlag, 1966).

383. Bošnjak, "Nur ein Humanismus für Christen und Marxisten," in *ibid.*, pp. 252-254.

384. Fiamengo, "Aspekte zu einem Universalem Humanismus," in *ibid.*, pp. 254-264.

385. Lukács, "Auf der Suche nach dem Gemeinsamen," in *ibid.*, pp. 264-273.

386. József Szigeti, "Marxistische Politik und kommunistischer Humanismus," in *ibid.*, pp. 273-282.

387. Milan Průcha, "Von Sinn des praktischen Humanismus," in *ibid.*, pp. 313-326.

388. *Schöpfertum und Freiheit* (Munich: Paulus Gesellschaft, 1968).

389. With the possible exceptions of dialogues in front of an audience in Czechoslovakia, Yugoslavia, and Italy, where no count was possible.

390. Zdenko Roter, a Marxist from Ljubljana, Yugoslavia, is also listed, but he informed me that something prevented him from attending at the last moment. This is illustrative of the fact that some people named above may not have been in attendance and that others who did attend may have been omitted from the list. A Polish source lists the number of Yugoslavs at 9 ["Symposjum w Marianskich Lazniach," *Za i przeciw* (Warsaw), Vol. 11, No. 21 (530), (May 21, 1967), p. 2.]

391. Judgment shared by Kellner, interview Nov. 6, 1975. Their views on dialogue may be found elsewhere in this book.

392. Lochman, "Diskussion," in *Schöpfertum und Freiheit*, p. 153.

393. *Ibid.*

394. Interview with Kellner, November 5, 1975.

395. *Ibid.* Also *EEKC*, p. 26.

396. Günther Nenning, "Warum der Dialog Starb," in *Neues Forum* (Vienna), March 1972.

397. Jan G. Vogeler, "Unter dem Banner des Hl. Paulus—Dialog oder ideologische Diversion?" in *IDZ*, No. 3 (1971). See also Uellenberg, pp. 4-5.

398. Kellner, p. 31, citing Metropolitan Nikodim of Leningrad and Novgorod.

399. Nenning.

400. Robert Thobaben and Nicholas Piediscalzi, "Salzburg Congress on the Future of Europe," in *Varieties*, pp. 207-210.

401. The English translation of that paper is Bernbach, "Socio-Political Theses for the Christian-Marxist Dialogue," in *Varieties*, pp. 87-99.

402. Figure provided by Albert Rasker in a letter to the author from Oestgeest, August 10, 1979. This is in stark contrast to the figure of 350 which is claimed in a statement by Kellner, "Christentum in der Sozialen Revolution," circulated in February 1980, but not dated. A short account of the proceedings, which mentions "exceptionally well attended meetings" is the *Society for the Philosophical Study of Marxism Newsletter*, No. 11 (Fall-Winter, 1978-1979), pp. 1-4. It mentions the attendance of and presentation by Adam Schaff. That is confirmed by Andrzej Grzegorczyk, "Kongress filozoficzny w Düsseldorfie," *Więź*, Vol. 22, Nos. 2-3 (February-March, 1979), p. 154, stating that Schaff was the sole Pole to attend.

403. Kellner, *EEKC*, p. 22.

404. Interview with Kellner, Nov. 9, 1975.

405. *Ibid.*

4

DIALOGUE ABOUT DIALOGUE

The purpose of this chapter is to present the views of various Eastern European authors on definitions and the methodology of the dialogue. The dialogue about dialogue has been given greater attention than any other theme. The survey of these views will be fairly comprehensive though not exhaustive.[1]

I considered the possibilities and advantages of devising a typology of the methods of dialogue and classifying the various writers under one type or another. Because of the need to preserve the variety of views, even at the risk of boring the readers, and to allow each person to speak in his or her own behalf without imposing the framework of an artificial typology which at the same time tends to express a judgment, I rejected such a typology. The categories employed here are simply definitions of what dialogue is not, what it is, and warnings about the pitfalls of dialogue. The author's own evaluation and further suggestions as to the methodology of dialogue conclude the chapter.

WHAT DIALOGUE IS NOT

Not many Eastern European thinkers have written explicitly on what dialogue is not. But a few have.

Tomislav Šagi-Bunić catalogued some of the approaches that

cannot be considered as dialogue or that destroy dialogue.[2]
Dialogue does not take place when one or both partners employ dishonest methods which lower the dignity and equality
of partners; when the partner's thought is caricatured so it
can be more easily negated; when the partner is being ridi-
culed; when cheap effects are used to attract the listeners or
readers; when quick judgments are made of the partner's
position based on one's own views; when force, craftiness,
insincerity, and prejudice characterize a partner's attitude.[3]
Attempts at indoctrinating, or "disrobing" others of spiritual
clothes and dressing them up in our uniform in order to defeat
them spiritually, no matter how gentle the process, is not dialogue. Nor are irony, rhetorical muddling of the issues, and
sudden tactical switching to areas embarrassing, frightening,
or confusing to the partner.[4] Trying to achieve a consensus at
any price is also not dialogue.[5] Apologetics, confrontation, instruction, or polemics, though they have their place in life, are
also not dialogue.[6] Almost all of the above lead to insincere
maneuvers but not to dialogue.

Vjekoslav Bajsić also pointed to what dialogue is not. Dialogue is not a magical wand which solves all problems without
sacrifice and effort. It is also not a particularly effective means
of politics or propaganda, nor is it "a means of quick compromise where differences are removed in a business-like manner
without entering more deeply into human problems."[7] He
also stated that no real dialogue can take place under conditions of fear, lack of knowledge of the concrete local situation,
inner isolation, feelings of superiority or inferiority of the
partners, distrust toward the more powerful partner, or the
desire to eventually annihilate the other.[8]

In some instances there are denials of the authenticity of
certain kinds of dialogues or expressions of apprehension toward certain processes which may go under the guise of dialogue. Thus, for instance, Milan Machovec expressed apprehension lest the dialogue become Moscow's repetition of the
mistakes of the Roman Catholic Church in the past, in which
its own Catholicism became the expressoin of a narrow par-
ticularism of its own interests instead of an all-inclusiveness.[9]
Moscow's tendency to interpret Marx's internationalism as its
own interest, and its tendency to repudiate those forms of dialogue which do not directly serve that interest are not true
dialogue. Christians must not feel like second-class citizens as
they enter the dialogue, and Marxists should not be backed by
the secret police in their affirmation of atheism.[10]

Encounters for the sake of gaining some political advantage are not dialogue.[11] Negotiation—for instance, between church and state or between hierarchies of political parties and churches—is not dialogue. While negotiations can at times aid dialogue or prepare the right climate for it, they are not dialogue, because in negotiations each partner is trying to get as many concessions from the other as possible and the two often regard themselves as opponents. Similarly, disputation or debate is dialogue. In a disputation it is often possible to assess a winner. In dialogue that is not done. A debater attempts to score points to the detriment of the debating partner and concentrates on the other's weaknesses and avoids discussing the other's strengths. This is not the case in dialogue. Dialogue is not a discussion, academic or other. A discussion is usually limited in subject matter and need not affect life. All too often discussants try to be clever, impressive, shrewd, entertaining, and provocative, but not necessarily profound, helpful, and to the point. Too many discussions are mere quibblings about nonessentials, and dialogue is not. In a discussion points are often raised just to make the discussion livelier, to provoke controversy; this is not done in a dialogue.

Finally an expectation that the partner will accept in advance some of our conclusions or that one or the other, or both, lose integrity in the process is not a dialogical approach.

Christian-Marxist dialogue is not an East-West discussion.[12] East and West are notions too comprehensive to be useful in this context. The dialogue can be between Marxists and Christians, all of whom may be either from the East or the West.

WHAT DIALOGUE IS

The crux of the issue of methodology is a positive delineation of dialogue. Since this is so important, instead of trying to draw a composite definition, it is more desirable to present each thinker's own views in order to allow the reader to draw conclusions as to their similarities and differences. It will be clear that enormous differences, even contradictions, exist in conceptions of the dialogue.

First the thought of Marxist thinkers on dialogue will be described, then that of Christian thinkers.

MARXIST VIEWS

Dialogue as a method is an issue giving considerable difficulty to Marxists. Whether to employ it or not, for what purpose, and how, is the subject of much controversy, especially in the discussion between representatives of doctrinal Marxist-Leninism and humanistic Marxism. The latter, as a rule, favor it more than do the former.

Adam Schaff was one of the earliest Eastern European practitioners of dialogue. He contended that dialogue of life (working together on some project) is the most important kind of dialogue, but that theoretical dialogue, such as the one going on in Poland (according to him Poland is the only Eastern European country where such dialogue takes place and is meaningful) on philosophical issues, makes sense as long as there is common concern among partners.[13] Unfruitful talks on subjects such as God or doctrines should be avoided, but dialogue can take place concerning the cultural history of the country, on the existence and meaning of various schools of thought in the past, on different labels for a new society (e.g., workers' "paradise," or kingdom of God) which is the result of common goals. Especially important is that dialogue should lead to the good of our nations.[14]

Schaff's Polish colleague at the European Coordination Centre in Vienna, Teresa Nowacka, defined dialogue from the perspective of a social scientist as "a discussion of attitudes and behavior related to the great political and social issues which mankind now has to face regardless of its religious, philosophical, political, etc. divisions." [15]

Tadeusz M. Jaroszewski maintained that the dialogue is not to be restricted to purely ideological and philosophical questions or such issues as war, peace, or anticolonialism, but, in Poland, it can spread to the more critical fields of concrete measures toward economic development, scientific and cultural life, and political measures, which sometimes bring heated confrontations.[16] The philosophical dialogue should go on, but not as a substitute for the political and social dialogue. On the philosophical issue of materialism vs. the divine origin and guidance of the universe, there can be only philosophical struggle and dispute. However, that should not prevent the two partners from seeking subject matters in which it is possible to narrow the gap between existing viewpoints. Instances of philosophical ideas on which fruitful dialogue is likely are the vision of the human being and society, and the joint appraisal of present levels of culture and civilization. When one adds to this the joint moral responsibility for historical options undertaken thus far, it is obvious to Jaroszewski that the philosophical dialogue is "no longer in opposition to a social one, and they are now firmly linked up." [17] A whole series of practical moral and social problems needs to evoke joint cooperation which can cement the dialogue of two different partners who seek to contribute to the solution of the problem from their respective views. The dialogue in socialist countries, for Jaroszewski, is likely to go much farther than similar dialogue taking place in capitalist countries, because it is likely to have a more profound impact upon social development.

> Finally, I wish to emphasize that there are tremendous cognitive and social values that can be derived from the dialogue. The leading of a dialogue provides an opportunity to discover new values and questions which in the situation of isolation would have passed unnoticed, an opportunity to undertake by both sides from their own cognitive viewpoints, all those essential problems of man and modern culture that have so far been perceived only by one side.[18]

Jaroszewski rejected syncretism and maintained that the two worldviews must continue their philosophical confrontation, but they should cooperate "in the realization of commonly accepted social aims." [19]

Dialogue between church and state authorities should lead to unifying Poles around constructive aims. Its preconditions are the positive reassessment of socialism by the Vatican and by the Roman Catholic Church authorities in Poland, as well as the abandonment of sectarian antireligiosity by some Marxists, according to Mieczysław F. Rakowski, member of the Central Committee of the Polish United Worker's Party.[20]

Janusz Kuczyński maintained that it is important to define dialogue, because at the present there is

> a variety of definitions leading to unusual ambiguity. This state of affairs reflects upon the intellectual benefits flowing from the dialogue. Sometimes one even gets the impression that this lack of precision in defining notions is convenient to certain circles, that it is only a certain climate, even verbalism, without concrete results that matters.[21]

Kuczyński's claim that definitions of dialogue vary enormously is true, and so do, of course, notions about the methodology of dialogue. His own proposals are concrete and detailed. He stated:

1. Christian and Marxist philosophers ought to consider the current situation and discuss how present developments fit into their own respective theories. Mutual respect should characterize these discussions.[22]

2. One ought to look at the practical implications of the two worldviews and their role in society.

3. The need for practical cooperation is so great that it has almost become the rationale for the existence of the Polish state. "Unite or perish" should be the slogan.

4. "The actual cultural power of Christianity as well as the social impact of Marxism can prove to be of benefit." [23] However they need to relate to one another clearly and purely. Only socialism can provide an environment in which this can take place.

5. Unprincipled and sterile isolation needs to be overcome. The two ideologies cannot continue as if the other, except for some practical cooperation, did not exist. Theoretical discussion should be better and more frequent.

6. Every opportunity should be used by both partners to advance values in society.

7. Traditional Marxists objected to attempts to convince an opponent, especially a class enemy, with arguments that a particular approach or solution is reasonable and good. This needs to be changed now because an increasing number of Christians are not class enemies.[24]

8. Worldwide work for peace and improved societies should be a high priority of dialogue.

9. Petty arguments, animosities, and "pseudo-political struggles" should be avoided.[25]

10. It would be more constructive to value one another, even to the point of idealization, than to deprecate each other.

Eugeniusz Czaplejewicz, basing his work on Russian literary critics M. B. Bakhtin and N. V. Voloshinov (who wrote in the late 1920s and early 1930s and were later nearly forgotten), and using the interdisciplinary approach of dialogues, claimed that human personality, human and social contacts, ideology, and meaning are all based on dialogue.[26] Czaplejewicz contended that dialogics is related to dialectics. Dialogics can improve Marxist dialectics, though, until recently, it was neglected by Marxists. He maintained that dialogue is a dynamic, infinite, bidirectional process. It should be anchored in and harmonious with larger social processes.[27] Among the dimensions of dialogue are its situation or wider setting, its subjective or immediate setting, the lingual dimension, the content, and the direction in which the dialogue develops, the various phases of which are called "dialogems." [28]

In the Czechoslovak context, Machovec considered dialogue an art which can easily be misused for political pragmatism or tactics. It consists in listening to one another and correcting one another. This is done when partners use their methodology and problematics to investigate the classical positions of the other in order to help solve them.[29] Machovec started with the proposition that in dialogue one should not try to convert the partner, but the Marxist ought to become a better Marxist and the Christian a better Christian.[30] While this remains a sound principle, he later stated that he has respect for the partner *only* if the partner attempts to convert him.[31] A half-convinced Christian does not merit the same respect as a fully committed one. A person who is really convinced of the rightness of a position will consider that truth valid also for the partner in the dialogue. Dialogue should be more than passive listening and exchanging information; it is the meeting of two partners who attempt to influence one another and yet respect the one who thinks differently. One ought still to hate erroneous thought but be thoughtful of the partner's sensibilities. Friendly argument may take place as long as one remembers the final goal. Then it is possible to cooperate against all hypocrites in both circles. Today it is recognized that we can benefit from people who think differently. Only those who have no real convictions refuse to dialogue with others.[32] One who does believe in something will be eager to affirm values and, in that process, to correct one's own and the partner's mistakes. As a result of the past ten years of dialogue, those Christians and Marxists who participated have become more self-critical. Dialogue is needed to counter the dangers of fanaticism and of indifference.[33] Partners in dialogue will also often admit to the mistakes which their side has committed, and sometimes the two will even compete in pointing out whose existence has been more absurd.[34]

The ups and downs of dialogue and of his own political and human fortunes convinced Machovec even more of the centrality of dialogue.

> The way to truth takes the form of dialogue, . . . truth itself consists in dialogue. It may be that the metaphysics of human existence can be realistically grasped only when it is expressed in terms of dialogue.[35]

The dialogue of the 1960s was thus not merely an episode of meetings of "naive or idealist outsiders" but "the beginnings of a radically dialogical future." [36]

Without regular dialogue, which is now an existential necessity, we cannot add depth to our own or to other's thoughts. The threat of dehumanization, one-sidedness, and self-aliena-

tion require that we learn the hard task of dialogical living.[37]
Christian-Marxist dialogue, as difficult as it is, is a preparation
for the still harder dialogue of the future with non-Western
worldviews. Since the repudiation of Stalinism, Marxism is
paying increased attention to the anthropological-ethical dimensions of life and has need of the insights of the Judeo-
Christian tradition.

In the dialogue one may indeed emphasize the insights of
one's own tradition, but at the same time one may discover the
strengths and advantages of the other tradition. This pertains
particularly to the question of the meaning of life.[38] Christians
and Marxists may join in the common search for the answer
to this question.

Vitézslav Gardavský, who devoted much of his thinking to
issues related to religion, did not provide definitions of dialogue
but suggested that the dialogue is of paramount importance
for the Marxist in order to dissuade Christians from seeking
power, because power has tended to distort the Christian message. Christians in dialogue are a source of constant encounter
with the original Judeo-Christian message, which, for Marxists, is the most important building block of Western civilization. Since Christianity is part of the Marxist heritage,
Marxists need to recognize and dialogue with Christians.[39]

The world, according to Milan Průcha, is less interested in
philosophical agreements or discrepancies which Christians
and Marxists discover in their dialogue than in their common
actions which the dialogue can accentuate and express.[40] The
same social system can lead either to a conflict of philosophical
opinions or to dialogue; philosophical differences do not necessarily mean ideological struggle. Marxism is not likely to destroy a political community of common practical goals because
of differences in metaphysics.[41] Dialogue raises many hopes.
It likewise brings the partners to the same basic questions,
whether the search is for Marxist or Christian humanism.[42]
Since Christians are able to speak to social issues as Christians
and not necessarily as members of some social order, then it is
not necessary that there be conflict between the two as if they
were some contradictory political or economic concepts. Rather,
the discussion is concerned with the "transcendent in the
worldly and the worldly in the transcendent." [43]

Julius Tomin, who seems to reflect primarily Machovec's
influence in his description of dialogue, came to his defense in
the early debates among Marxists regarding the value of dialogue. He agreed that dialogue is the highest form of human

communication. It requires courage to open up and show weaknesses as well as strengths. It requires exposing one's insights to the partner in the spirit of fair play. And it requires that the partners take a very concrete interest in the partner as an individual.[44] Dialogue is a personal engagement. Though one must use all of one's internal resources when engaging in dialogue one must abdicate the use of force, external pressure, and intrigue. Force and dialogue are mutually exclusive. Tomin rejected suggestions made by some Marxists that Marxism is too weak yet to engage in such dialogue, that greater freedom granted to Christians in Czechoslovakia will endanger Marxist victory, and that only when Marxism is sure of that victory should Marxists dare to engage in dialogue.

Tomin suggested that the external "I-Thou" dialogue (between the two groups) is interdependent on the inner dialogue, which must be consciously nurtured. An inner "I-I" dialogue needs to take place within each of the partners.[45] Tomin stated that Marxism has not developed adequate humanistic models for such a dialogue. Therefore Machovec, Kalivoda, and Kosik are breaking new ground. Tomin regarded this new willingness to dialogue as authentic Marxism.

Jaroslav Krejči from Havirov provided the following reasons for carrying on dialogue:

1. To deal with the great problems of the contemporary world, such as nuclear threats, freedom of the individual in the industrial society, and the threats of isolation of technological and scientific research.

2. To remove antihuman threats such as defining human beings by what they own, not what they are, feelings of impotence in the face of mighty institutions, the loss of security, and the feeling of anxiety due to the many dangers that beset the biological and spiritual life of a person.[46]

3. Years of mutual demonizing and antagonisms between Christianity and Marxism took place after World War II when culture was rent asunder and the touching points between the two were reduced at the expense of human welfare.

Hence the dialogue is a historical necessity. It emerged as a tool to resolve these contradictions and remove or reduce the threats.[47] There is always a certain unity between contradictions, yet dialogue must be nurtured carefully as it is very fragile. Among the concrete causes for the dialogue is the recognition that neither American nor Soviet ideals can ultimately win due to nuclear parity.[48] The deadlock made the dialogue a necessity in order to break through the borders of

ideological systems, which tend to express themselves in monological form. Dialogue is a protest against fanaticism, blind-
ness, narrowmindedness, and impatience; it leads to the cul-
tivation of harmony, which affirms itself in the search for
truth. It is the attempt, jointly, to work for an "open end."
Dialogue is an undogmatic search for truths. Therefore one
must respect the constantly changing patterns and subject
matters of dialogue.[49] All worldviews are incomplete and complement one another, yet, from another perspective, dialogue
is a sharp ideological conflict accompanied by certain feelings
of animosity. Yet dialogue is also the effort to change the
enemy into a friend.

One should remember, stated Krejči, that there are many
Christian-Marxist dialogues because there are many types of
Christians and Marxists. In each group there are people who
are more dangerous, to their own group as well as to the world,
on account of their narrowmindedness. Christians and Marxists can learn a great deal from one another as soon as they
recognize that the common interests are greater than the
differences.[50]

In Hungary, as in the German Democratic Republic, the
accent is on cooperation between Christians and Marxists
rather than on dialogue. On the international scene, however,
József Lukács is well-known for having participated in a
number of dialogues and is recognized as a thoughtful and
tactful contributor to such conversations. He strongly emphasized cooperation; dialogue serves the purpose of clearing the
ground for better cooperation. The problems existing between
Marxists and Christians appear increasingly visible only in
dialogue.[51] While in the future the two will certainly develop
more commonalities, their basic orientation remains different.[52]
Differences in ultimate issues should not hinder cooperation in
such common matters as peace, human liberation, and public
welfare. The philosophical bases for motives may differ, but
the aims are the same. These aims can be promoted through
political agreements which increase the possibility of future
dialogue.[53]

> Thus the dialogue has been transformed into practice, but this
> practice needs discussion again, or it needs a particular type of
> dialogue. Based on agreement on the most decisive questions,
> tolerant and consistent dialogue has been and is always de-
> manded.[54]

Even though Marxism and Christianity deal with the same
questions,

their answers given to this question differ in many important respects. It would be misleading if the dialogue participants were convinced that beyond the ultimate ideological questions there is the promised land of convergent ideas which are directly suitable to be the foundations for cooperation. This is not so, and it could not be so; the Christian view of humanity and society and Christian ethics have different contexts of analysis from those of Marxism.[55]

Finally Lukács defended the dialogue against those who attacked it as hopeless by saying that the influence of religion will continue for a significant historical period. Marxists obviously prefer to interact with Christians who offer a progressive stance. That stance would consist of a protest against capitalism and the separation of Christianity from it. Christianity can also contribute to the understanding of human beings and of ethical actions.[56] The important issue for the Marxist is not the existence or nonexistence of God, but the concrete content of religiosity, how this religiosity manifests itself toward participation in social action. Christians, even those who participate in the dialogue, should refrain from simplistically charging Marxists with the deification of socioeconomic factors.[57] This may be true of vulgar Marxists but not of genuine Marxists.

Professor József Szigeti declared that the source of dialogical preparedness for the Marxists is their humanism.[58] This dialogue has constantly to be widened. However, Marxists must not compromise their participation in the dialogue by pretending to be neutral toward socialism. For their part Christians must stop defending private property and be willing to enter into political and moral action with the Marxists. Then the risks of the dialogue, which do exist, are well worth taking.[59]

When Branko Bošnjak published his major work on philosophy of religion. *Filozofija i kršćanstvo,* he did not define the term dialogue. The last chapter, however, is entitled "An Attempt at a New Dialogue About Theology, Christianity, and Religion in General." In that chapter he not only discussed, with much openness, whether it is possible to talk about God, but also maintained that religion can survive in all socioeconomic orders and that it shall not wither, though it will weaken considerably, in the communism of the future.[60] No victory by either partner is to be expected in a dialogue, though both will do their best to present their views. It should be known what atheism is trying to achieve and what atheism has to offer.[61] The dialogue is about the world of ideas and about life but all questions are legitimate for dialoguing.[62]

The purpose of the dialogue is to see whether there are areas in which the partners can unite despite their varying opinions.[63] Concrete world peace and the various understandings of peace could be such a theme, especially when the partners are critical and principled and show dedication to peace.

Bošnjak analyzed the word *dia-logos (raz-govor)* in Croatian and found it to have the meaning of dividing, development, and branching out. The partners meet to criticize one another, to seek out weaknesses in the other's arguments, to explain one's self—namely, what one thinks of one's self and why one wants to continue to be what one is.[64] The partners have the chance to express their grounding authentically. From there, new opportunities are created which enable them to act most adequately as human beings. The practical advantage is that dialogue provides freedom to express one's convictions. Tolerance and the ability to listen are two other earmarks of dialogue.[65] This means that we must tolerate the view which we do not think correct in order to more easily reach the truth.[66]

Bošnjak considered dialogue as a criterion of democracy in the Yugoslav socialist society. He concluded:

> In our community the problem of the dialogue is a new way of thinking, relating, and of educating the people. Much more can be achieved with an open approach than with an unclear intention. If various opinions face one another in theory and in practice then the historical processes and social reality will discern how good they are.[67]

Thus Bošnjak contributed much by explaining to the common citizens what this new relationship between Christians and Marxists should be.

Esad Ćimić is a Marxist of Muslim origin interested in dialogue with Christians. What would appear to be a double barrier of resistance to good relationships with Christians appears in his case to be no barrier at all. He became the foremost leader in attempts at reconciliation in a geographic area (Bosnia and Herzegovina) which had long been a place of religious contention and intolerance. Ćimić maintained that the two-pronged Marxist attitude toward religion is a constant social critique of religion coupled with strict adherence to the principle of full religious liberties. Religious people, to the degree that they are socially progressive, are not the enemies of a humanistic society, but are its support.[68] The dialogue between all citizens, regardless of whether they are believers or not, ought to be intensified, primarily on the local, self-managerial level, rather than among the heads of church and state.

Marxists cannot expect to have a continuous evolution of thought if they do not enter into dialogue with those who think differently. Freedom means freedom to differ. Those who differ are a correction and a stimulus for critical reexamination of one's own presuppositions, directions, and goals.[69] If dialogue were not merely a *desideratum* but a social reality, it would have enormous consequences on society, provided that some care was given to the selection of people and circumstances for such dialogue. Dialogue between communists and representatives of religious communities should be clearly distinguished from state-church relationships. Both theoretical dialogue and dialogue in life should be carried on concommitantly. Within Yugoslav circumstances, it is important that the conditions for dialogue be rational and involve the explicit and real acceptance of the socialist system.[70]

Zdenko Roter suggested that the necessity for dialogue stems from the level of civilization which no longer allows people to live in a "ghetto" of ideas. It is a great misfortune for the dialogue that a competitive bipolar situation exists in the world. On the one hand, there are Christian countries where the Marxists are in the minority and opposition, and on the other, countries where Christians are marginal groups while the Marxists are in power.[71] Dialogue is a meeting into which one cannot enter as an abstract person meeting with other abstract persons; sociologically it is impossible to be in conversation with whole groups of people with varius life-styles and worldviews. Only concrete people can have dialogue.

Marxists reductionism of religion as the opium of the people is an impoverishment and simplification of Marxism, which makes it impossible to achieve the kind of humanism which is the common bond of Christians and Marxists.[72]

> The point of view of dialogue cannot be something superficial, stylish or institutional. The point of view of dialogue implies a vision of existence, of thought and the totality of the human community. Dialogue involves not only the will, but it calls for structural breadth which involves the whole system of ideas and the method of action. Confronting the pressing and dramatic problems of contemporary humanity, the acceptance or the refusal of dialogue represents an historical decision. That is why dialogue cannot represent a tactical game of individuals or of

political or ecclesiastical institutions in order to attract more easily "the other" to "the one and only truth" which is theirs, and it must not be either a means of political manipulation with the man who wants to seek out common points with his neighbors. And there we are face to face with the big problem: Will dialogue take place between Marxists and Christians on all levels as an active force which transforms the world or indeed will it become a "prisoner" of the narrow interests of political or ecclesiastical institutions which wish to use it solely as a means of keeping their power over man and manipulating him? Dialogue that is directed, supervised and limited by an institution can be nothing but a farce, an anti-dialogue.[73]

The socio-institutional framework does not allow those people who are interested in entering the dialogue to do so freely and when they want to. Neither Marxism nor Christianity is a fully spontaneous phenomenon; they are movements in institutionalized form (e.g., Christian states, church as institution; Communist Party, and socialist state). A crisis takes place in the dialogue because institutions possess a cautionary mechanism so that when they become afraid as to where the dialogue will lead, fearing that it may lead to loss of substance, they employ their hindering mechanisms.[74] This is evident from the official texts of institutions. For politicians, both ecclesiastical and societal, dialogue is treated as an instrument which is to be turned off when those in power perceive that it does not suit what they consider to be the interests of the institution.[75] Politicians do not understand and should not understand the dialogue. It is a creative act and leads to an ever richer growth of a dynamic system, in the sense that it provides constant interaction, complementation, as well as constant change in relationships.

Like Ćimić, Roter pointed out that society must be at a certain level of development in order to make dialogue acceptable to many people. To illustrate this he cited a real event. At one of his popular lectures on religion at Slovenske Bistrice, the hall was almost filled with army officers on one side and nuns on the other. During the question-answer period an officer said: "Why didn't we liquidate religion in 1945 [time of the Communist takeover]? Then we would not need to have a meeting such as this." To this a nun responded: "When we supported the liberation movement, we thought that liberty would include religious liberty as well." To this a second officer replied: "Who started World War II? We, the Communists, or the Pope?" [76] Such ignorance and primitivism is evident in

Marxist as well as in Christian circles. No wonder that there is little understanding for the dialogue.

Roter also suggested that the state should be neutral in its relationship to religion.[77] In addition to a free atmosphere which such a relationship would provide, it is important that the partners go into dialogue with full knowledge of the other, especially their views of dialogue. Roter devoted a great deal of effort to acquaint Marxists with Christian views of dialogue as well as to adequately informing them of the recent advances made in theology and social thought of the churches.[78]

Andrija Krešić has only recently made his contribution to the dialogue. He has expressed this mostly through his writings rather than by attendance at public dialogues. According to him, for a dialogue one must have two different partners, as in love. The analogy between dialogue and love is a most satisfactory one. Monologue, the opposite of dialogue, is like self-love and narcissism, and it cannot bear fruit, just as there is no offspring from a single sex.[79] Dialogue is the proper relationship between Marxism and Christianity.

The conditions of the dialogue are: 1) both must have the same subject (a precondition of the dialogue is that Christians turn their attention to this world's concerns so they can have a common subject); 2) both must be so open that they are willing to accept mutual corrections (if they decide in advance not to do that then there can be only parallel monologues); and 3) both should aim at some agreement regardless how far apart they start.[80]

Apart from the above gnoseological (theory of knowing) definition, Marxism needs dialogue in an ontological sense because it is not a complete system. Rather, it is a changing component of the world, and dialogue is a condition for further Marxist development. Neither Marxism nor Christianity has one single meaning or interpretation. Thus there is Cuban or Chinese Marxism, bureaucratic, dogmatic, or humanistic Marxism, Marxism of György Lukács or Herbert Marcuse, etc. Likewise there is traditionalist, renewal, and radical Christianity. Between dogmatic Marxism and traditionalist Christianity there can be no dialogue because they merely reinforce each other's prejudices.[81] Between Christianity oriented toward renewal and humanistic Marxism there can be dialogue under the following presuppositions: 1) that they show mutual acceptance, 2) that both take part in building the future, 3) that the church pull back from sole endorsement of capitalism, 4) that the church abandon active anticommunism and stop considering atheists as devils, and 5) that they both help the world.[82]

Good will should respond to good will. Communist Party forums should be ready to give Christians guarantees of greater freedom for work within the constitutional framework and to stop pressure and persecutions. While dialogue does not mean ideological compromise, it excludes propagandistic attacks. Marxists must get to know the thought of contemporary theologians (especially the left-wing, humanistic theologians or those of the "theology of revolution," "death-of-God theology," Tillichian, Teilhardian, and other modern theologies). The Christian concept that God is love means harmony in social life, and this is what Communists want as they try to stop conflict and give dignity to humans.[83] "Today there is a new *possibility* of tactical and strategic, practical and doctrinal encounter and growing together of Christianity and communism, which, of course, does not mean that all this will *actually* take place." [84] Christianity which merely attempts to adjust to bourgeois society and Marxism which merely wants to rule people by the old methods and institutions are unable to change fundamentally and cannot bring about a synthesis. "But, though the permanent partnership and merger of Christianity with Communism are not matters 'of this world,' i.e. are not characteristic phenomena of the contemporary world, nevertheless it is a real possibility that it may happen." [85] With the joint activity of those Christian protagonists of a radical renewal who engage in revolutionary struggle with the exploited and those Communist revolutionaries who are inspired by humanism and wish to end the world of small changes and usher in a new, humane world, "the other world" will come, a completely new one. "The human kingdom of freedom will replace the superhuman and inhuman rule of necessity." [86] The Christian concept of the kingdom of God, in the sense of an ideal society, begins to mean a this-worldly condition of realized humanity and thus resembles the ultimate aim of the communists.[87]

Dialogue is not mere coexistence, because coexistence suggests that each side keep its own ideology with the hope that in the end it will be able to proselytize or take over and in the future have no competitor or enemy. Coexistence is thus a tactic, with the ultimate strategy still being contraexistence in regard to the partner.[88] Proexistence means finding common ways to transcend basic social contradictions by forming a true human community of persons regardless of their ideological or religious orientation.[89]

The importance of the dialogical approach to the integrity of one's own position is also affirmed by Arif Tanović.

> Engaging in a dialogue with other opposing theories is not possible unless one stands on the principle of one's own theory; but refusing a dialogue, being impervious to argument, is a sign of impotence, defeatism, or lazy, uncritical thinking.[90]

This attitude, shared by many humanistic Marxists in Yugoslavia, springs from their conviction that communism is a movement of human emancipation rather than a static condition or ideal which is achieved once and for all.[91] It seems apparent that such dynamically conceived Marxism is more congruent to entering into dialogue than the dogmatic form of Marxism.

CHRISTIAN VIEWS

No less abundant and varied are Christian views on dialogue.

Among the Polish Christians it is worthwhile to single out the views of Ketrzynski, Kowalczyk, and Mazowiecki.

For Wojciech Ketrzynski one of the important issues that needs to be resolved is that confrontation on fundamental problems should not be waged in such a manner that it leads to attempts at indoctrination or oversimplification, which would tend to create strife.[92] He differentiated three levels of dialogue: 1) dialogue on the highest institutional level between the Polish episcopate and the high state authorities concerning the most important national issues, 2) participation of all citizens in the general life of the country without creating artificial divisions among them, and 3) the involvement of those Christian social organizations or groups which take an active part in the political and social life of the country.[93]

Kowalczyk considered it important that the partner be acknowledged, analyzed, and perceived as holding some positive elements. One's own outlook, both as to worldview and doctrine, needs to be shared.[94] The partner's philosophical humanistic elements need to be recognized. Structured dialogue is preferable to spontaneity with lack of direction. Both methodology and specific, constructive theoretical and practical content need to be discussed. No cooperation is possible or advisable without theoretical dialogue. Changes in the partner's thinking over the years need to be acknowledged. "A frank dialogue between the believers and the non-believers cannot wholly ignore world outlook questions, i.e. the problems of religion and atheism." [95] Kowalczyk acknowledged that a constructive dialogue between those who are divided by deep ideological differences is, indeed, very difficult, but he saw in both movements willingness and flexibility to do so anyway.[96]

Tadeusz Mazowiecki emphasized the necessity of overcoming intellectual self-sufficiency and isolation in order to enter the dialogue. He favored both formal and informal dialogues.

> Whereas the formal dialogue shapes and stimulates human attitudes, the informal dialogue constitutes, above all, a reality in which these attitudes express themselves. . . . Against this background, the direct function of the intellectual dialogue is a double one: on the one hand, it paves the way—to a certain extent at least—for mutual institutional relations; on the other hand, it leads to setting in order all that was produced by spontaneous interhuman contacts and opens a broader prospect for them.[97]

For Mazowiecki dialogue is never an accomplishment, but always an attempt, a new beginning, a life-style. It is not a compromise, nor does it remove all the tensions and contradictions, but rather discovers a dimension in which a meeting is possible. It enables the exchange of social values within a society.[98]

The late Joseph Hromádka, who may be regarded as the single most meritorious Christian inspiration for the dialogue in Czechoslovakia, advocated cooperation with Marxists from the outset. According to Hromádka, a true dialogue can take place only if it is historically and socially well-prepared. At some point there may be a historical necessity to engage in it. While one may start with different concepts of history and society, continued involvement may later lead to a discussion of ultimate questions.[99] These conversations take place in a world that has already undergone great transformations and that now stands perched between a great catastrophe and unparalleled opportunities. Therefore it is not a pure academic discussion but a vital wrestling with partners on the basis of deepest convictions.[100]

Milan Opočenský saw dialogue as an "encounter between persons across lines of estrangement and/or hostility—encounter which makes it possible not simply for the 'separated' to clear up misunderstandings, but for them really to learn from one another as well." [101] The two closed systems have opened toward each other; this openness is a presupposition of dialogue.

Lochman explained that after a period of rather strained

relations between the two groups there was a need to "de-ideologize the situation," namely to dispense with the almost ingrained prejudicial attitudes toward one another.[102] After a process of reorientation it would be possible for the two complex systems to turn to each other. While the old attitudes still prevail among the vast majority, especially the establishment, an important segment has recognized that "the spirit of authentic Marxism *is* the spirit of dialogue." [103]

It is important to recognize both areas of convergence (areas in which the two have common concerns though not identical positions) and divergence. The common concerns are to be found in the concept of humanization, in the importance of history, and in future-oriented thinking, while the main divergence is the question of God or the question of transcendence.[104] Lochman then provided some specific examples of the way the mutual interaction between Christians and Marxists affected specific thinkers in each group. From this it is obvious that some "important shifts of emphasis and discoveries within both traditions" took place.[105] The dialogue does not aim to produce a mixture of the two views—some hybrid "semi-Marxist Christianity or semi-Christian Marxism"— or an indifference to the two positions, "but, on the contrary, an encounter in difference: an interpellation. . . . To listen carefully to the partner's interpellation does not mean to betray one's own tradition." [106]

An important insight of Lochman's is that

> . . . Christianity and Marxism are not only dialogical but also eccentric ways of thought and life. This means that the very impulse which has led to their new encounter necessarily leads them beyond themselves. They cannot remain just "each other's theme." Their mutual interpellation opens transcending horizons of their common historical, social and spiritual horizon.[107]

For Lochman the dialogue is complemented with the efforts of both partners toward the humanization of society, which, under the conditions in socialist countries, means de-Stalinization and the promotion of democratic socialism. Although democratic socialism in Czechoslovakia has received a shattering blow, it still remains a powerful vision for the future.[108] Both partners need dialogue as they "strive themselves towards a reality which is greater than their system." [109] The path toward dialogue is ardent and presupposes a defusion, de-mythologizing, and de-absolutizing of ideology.[110]

Mutual questioning can lead to meaningful dialogue. The

partners need to take account of their own tradition and of the practical tasks ahead and then engage in an open, critical dialogue which reflects common responsibility.[111]

> Dialogue means challenge. The differences are not ironed out, but much more clearly defined. . . . Listening to critical questions raised by colleagues does not lead to a betrayal of one's own tradition. . . . Under the pressure of dialogue with each other a process of renewal is set in motion by which each studies again its own creative possibilities and makes new discoveries. The living spirit of both traditions can be awakened out of the sleep of dogmatism.[112]

Among Hungarian Christians it was András Szennay who wrote at some length on the nature of the dialogue. He expressed his conviction as to the necessity of the dialogue at this point in history. Christians are dedicated to dialogue not as a tactical step but, as heirs of Christ, out of love and openness.[113] This is because the church came not to rule with Christ but to serve with Christ. Vatican II raised no obstacles to the cooperation of Catholics with Marxists for social benefit. Contemporary pluralistic society demands that each worldview freely present its own values to society. Christians and Marxists have the common task of addressing history by interpreting the past and building a happier future, despite the difficult obstacles in mutual relations.[114] Both partners need to offer their solutions, secure in themselves and in the value of their own contributions.

Szennay defined the dialogue as jointly searching and enlarging truth.[115] The Christian is urged by considerations of love to pay careful attention to what Marxists are saying and doing, because Marxism, too, though it verbally denies God, is God's creation. The dialogue should take place under the watchful eyes of party and church leadership; in fact, it ought to be led by this leadership. Participation in the dialogue is a social duty; asking honest questions of each other is a right. Two principles are essential for dialogue: the spirit of receptiveness and the spirit of freedom.[116] Both Marxists and Christians ought to ask questions, search for the best way, involve themselves in issues, offer answers, and honestly criticize one another. The freedom to be religious or nonreligious is an important precondition. Human rights and liberties must be protected. If they are not, the dialogue becomes meaningless, because dialogue is a dialogue of freethinking people who can make free decisions.[117] The exercise of freedom, of course, always demands courage, wisdom, and foresight.

Although the temptation is great to dismiss one another quickly and stop listening to one another, participants in dialogue must patiently persist. Though participants are likely to continue in sharp contradiction and struggle, as long as that struggle is fair and as long as the participants respect one another, the dialogue will probably be successful. It would also be useful if the partners look at one another's best side and give one another the benefit of the doubt. It would help if Marxists ceased to regard Christians as necessarily being proponents of a bourgeoise ideology, when, in fact, many Christians have tried to free themselves from those ties. Christianity is not tied to a class or to the West, but speaks to all human beings everywhere.[118] Christians also need to know that in respect to their attitudes toward Marxism there is a great range of unexplored relations which lie between anathematizing and silence. In the contemporary world monopolies are as dangerous in thought as in commerce; dialogue can prevent such monopolizing.

The dialogue between Christians and Marxists is future-oriented. In this divided, tense world, it is important that the two movements decisively offer themselves to work for the future. This joint endeavor would provide a great example to the whole world, showing that, despite differences and ideological opposition, two movements can have mutual esteem as a foundation for relating to one another.[119] They can be an example showing that former enemies can turn into mere philosophical opponents after they have reexamined one another's position.

The starting point in the dialogue must always be one's own position. Positions do not change in dialogue, but relationships do.[120] Szennay was of the opinion that a Christian who participates in dialogue should not be more appreciated by the Marxist partner than by other Christians, including the leadership. The same should hold true for Marxists.[121] He also believed that the dialogue is still mainly in its first phase, namely that a dialogue about dialogue is being carried out, one devoted mainly to methodological questions. Among those questions are: What does a Christian want? What does a Marxist want? Are Marxism and atheism identical? Is dialogue a general human task, or does it serve only political, social, and economic goals? Should the partners venture beyond certain themes when they feel secure? Who should represent each side in dialogue? Can the dialogue include philosophical and theological issues? Which themes should be discussed? Should basic truths and postulates come under investigation? Szennay implied that all these issues need to be approached dialogically and suggested that one may entrust to the dialogue even the most difficult problems.

The dialogue will remain in a static phase until the partners dedicate themselves to the future. This will render the dialogue dynamic.[122] This second stage will show the partners spiritually close to one another, but at the same time not shying away from the many contradictions and tensions which beset them and the world. This dynamic phase would, having gone through these theses and antitheses, move to a partial synthesis, which, however, does not end in identity or syncretism. Should the partners wish merely to learn something about one another or make some unanimous pronouncements about certain problems of the world, then the dialogue will stay only in its present, early phase. The tension of differences, which can bring about revolutionary changes, belongs to a second, dynamic phase.[123]

The ultimate goals of the partners may differ as long as the partners pursue humane means toward the achievement of worthy goals for the foreseeable future. Dialogue is so important that it should be carried out even if one of the two parties has primarily political or tactical goals in mind.[124] For Christians, the outpouring of inner power is the most important motive for the dialogue. In order to be successful in dialogue, Christians should simultaneously dialogue with God. They should set their gaze firmly on the future and keep steadfastly open. They should always approach the partner in his concrete humanity and respect his freedom. Ultimately each partner can choose whether to opt for the "absolutely holy" God or, having excluded God, consider immanent values holy. Each partner should muster the courage, frequently lacking in the present context, to keep building bridges between the two sides.[125]

Monsignor József Cserháti, bishop of Pécs, regarded the demands of a changing age as the reason for dialogue. The nature of the church and the moral attitude of Christians make them committed to a happier future for people, hence cooperation with Marxists logically follows the coexistence of the two movements.[126] The purpose of the dialogue is to share values, to promote the happiness of people, and to pay heed to each other.[127] Marxists aim to provide happiness for all people by emancipating them from various alienations. The church goes along with this, as it is "the ardent desire of the church to be in agreement with Marxists in economic and political questions, though they [the Marxists] are opposed to religion and the religious morality." [128] There is a dilemma for the Christian entering into dialogue. Marxists are creating a socialist system which would lead to a materialistic, atheistic state. How can a Christian morally support such socialism? This dilemma cannot be resolved *a priori* but only by working it out under real, historical conditions.[129] The boundary line of dialogue is that no mixing of ideological principles must take place, for this is very damaging. Nor can there be a giving up of principles.[130] Nor can Christians cooperate on matters which are incompatible with Christian moral norms. The prerequisite for dialogue is that Christian principles and the practical requirements of Christian life are secure.[131]

In Yugoslavia Christians made efforts to clarify the concepts and methodology of dialogue as the foundation of a meeting ground with Marxists. Members of the hierarchy, theologians, and lay Christians engaged in the task of clarifying and defending the dialogical method.

Archbishop Frane Franić of Split is, among bishops, the most outstanding protagonist of dialogue with nearly every non-Catholic group, including Marxists. He regarded dialogue as a way of communicating ideas more clearly. Mutual sympathy is needed in order to understand the partner's situation. Surprisingly, Christians and Marxists have many related ideas.[132] The relations between church and state and the Christian-Marxist dialogue are two different issues, yet Marxism is tantamount to the soul of a socialist country. But there is more than one kind of Marxism. There is the Marxism taught by the Central Committee, and there is the Marxism of those who were expelled from the Communist Party. For a bishop, the official Marxism of the Central Committee is the decisive one, because it is the one being implemented, but the others are also important since they too influence the Party.[133]

Franić distinguished three types of dialogue: 1) dialogue between the prevalent culture, the social system, and Christian thought which leads to mutual enrichment of thought and practice; 2) dialogue of martyrdom in which the martyr church witnesses to its commitments; and 3) daily dialogue of common Marxists and Christians within the context of their work, play, family life, and so forth.[134] There are neither biblical nor doctrinal obstacles to stand in the way of a Christian's getting involved in dialogue. Though one may find fanatics among both Christians and Marxists, each side is fundamentally ready to engage in dialogue, despite the fact that the founders of Marxism were not too well disposed toward dialogue with believers.[135] Theologians who engage in dialogue, though they need to remain flexible, must be true to essential Christian teachings.[136]

Franić raised the question as to whether Marxists will come to realize that there are some abiding values in which God is hidden, and whether the time will come when Christians will acknowledge the existence of true values in Marxism, or whether both will continue to ignore and demean one another. While wishing to avoid undue optimism, Franić concluded that

> Marxism and Christianity are both sciences for praxis. If Marxists become better Marxists and Christians become better Christians in practice, i.e., if they both work more selflessly for the people, and live for the other, then there is more hope that some day, which is probably still far off, Marxists and Christians can reach full understanding and agreement.[137]

Tomislav Šagi-Bunić noted that people often misuse the term dialogue. Some think that the word magically opens all doors. Others use it as a decoration. The word is even used to cover up things that are in direct opposition to it.

The conciliar church is a church in dialogue both with those outside and those within it. Four basic notions govern the dialogue.

1. People, rather than systems, are involved in dialogue.[138] Dialogue does not take place between Christianity and Marxism but only between Christians and Marxists. The starting points are personal dignity, equality, freedom, and respect for all. Dialogue does not start with some statement acceptable to all but with the affirmation that our partners have the same rights and dignity as we do. We want to hear what partners, different from us, have to say and think, and we want to tell them of our thoughts, aspirations, and needs. Together we seek the truth. There can be no other way for human growth.[139] We must be able to listen, not merely to talk. We need to understand the partners and what they say, not oversimplify their ideas and laugh at them. One needs to be truthful and honest with the partner. To appeal to the public in ways unavailable to the partner is to deny dialogue.

2. In terms of attitudes, the partners need not be like-minded. In fact, they must be different. There is no need to bother

about dialogue if the partners are totally sure of the truth of their position. Force or cunning may not be used. One's views must be explained clearly in the search for the whole truth. One ought to be ready to complete one's own ideas, perfect them, and even reject them if proven false.[140]

3. Partners must accept truth as soon as they find it and continue to be open to truth. Truth is not private but common property. Thus the emphasis ought to be on the common search. Contradictions will be discovered to be either apparent or excessively sharp and historically conditioned. Differences should be regarded as neither arbitrary nor evil nor stupid. They are merely different approaches to reality, sometimes too quickly systematized or emphasized. The approach to truth should be of a convergent nature, but it is not syncretic or like a mosaic. It should aim at mutual enrichment and at joint effort to put order into our affairs.[141]

4. Dialogue requires courage and personal self-assurance. It is more difficult than polemics. Those used to polemics may have a hard time changing to dialogue. Dialogue is mainly for the younger generation or for those who can reorient themselves.[142] Pluralism needs dialogue, but dialogue presupposes the acceptance of pluralism.[143] True curiosity about the other and willingness to accept what is good from them is important. Dialogue is not restricted to discussion of worldviews but can extend to all questions. It must become the normal way of seeking solutions.[144] It is the earmark of a new epoch. Christians ought to initiate dialogues. Communities within which we live need to be prepared for dialogue. So do those whom we may select to be our representatives. Dialogue means responsibility, maturity, and knowledge, yet all need to enter into it.

There are some people who would misuse dialogue for their own purposes, a Machiavellian use of dialogue. Yet dialogue is the only way. It is the mission of the church, not merely a means of its mission.[145] While aware of its difficulties, we cannot reject it.

Šagi-Bunić recognized three levels of the dialogue.

1. The level of simple human relations in which one departs from isolation, distrust, and belief in mutual evil intentions. One needs to recognize the multidimensionality of most problems and to bring about mutual "taming." [146]

2. The doctrinal level which consists in the search for truth. Partners often have diametrically opposite views about crucial problems. For Christians it sometimes seems problematic to discuss truths with atheists, especially those who know Chris-

tianity only superficially. Many faithful will doubt the possibility of this level. But even this can be dialogically solved. "Dialogue is the beginning of love." [147] It is also the means to truth.[148] The doctrinal dialogue must be about problems that grip the partners rather than on just any topic. Awareness is needed to see the specific conditions and limits from which each person approaches the question.[149]

3. Dialogue on the nondoctrinal level, i.e. on other issues, should be carried out similarly to other levels. New solutions can be found when the matter is pursued jointly.[150]

Vjekoslav Bajsić analyzed the philosophy of dialogue in regard to its synthetic dynamic. He stressed the dialectical significance of dialogue; it can take place only where there is disagreement.[151] The subject matter of the conversation is somehow under question. Without dialogue the tendency is to reduce humanity to oneself, since each is satisfied with one's own insight. Others are generally reduced to objects. It is doubtful whether it is possible to know another person authentically without turning directly to that person.[152]

The basic goal of dialogue is not the attainment of compromise, but the integration of the other person in his or her authenticity. Our view must contain all that is authentically human if it is to be true. "The dialectical moment of dialogue develops from the earlier mutual negation of the partners to an affirmation of the partners on a higher level, complementing the thought and value content of each partner, lifting them to a fuller humanity." [153] Thus dialogue has the power of creating a "we" consciousness, a togetherness. Problems become ours. Community is being created through common action.

Dialogue has a philosophical significance for one's view of the human being. It is a meeting of person with person, not with books or doctrines. One needs to know what the partner actually thinks. Rather than get the information from another person, one needs to get it directly from the partner. Fragmentary information and labels must be avoided, because the partner must reveal himself or herself concretely and in the full spectrum of his or her reality.[154]

The problems of dialogue are simultaneously problems of humanization. A *priori* opposition to dialogue indicates an inadequate concept of human nature. Dialogue is one of the main impulses of humanization, because it presupposes a person who does not adhere to a narrow ideology and is willing to accept the partner in his or her specific, concrete reality.[155]

In a self-managing society, like Yugoslavia's, the individual's contribution cannot be conceived without lively dialogue. Freedom and justice must exist for all partners. Dialogue has the ability to enlarge this freedom and justice. Lack of dialogue is symptomatic of some internal weakness.[156] There are, of course, risks in engaging in dialogue, but since it is a search for meaning, it is a "ceaselessly relevant" and urgent task.[157]

Tomo Vereš, O.P., explored at length the philosophic-theological dialogue. He approached the meaning of the word "dialogue" from its roots in Greek *dia legein*, meaning *two* (but also significantly, *through*) *speaking*. Its Latin equivalent is *con verse*. Two or more speakers say who they are and what they intend to do.[158] Dialogue is both possible and necessary in this new, pluralistic world. It is the only possible form of coexistence.[159] Not only do partners have different views, but no one can know all that his or her partner knows. The difficulty between Christians and Marxists in respect to dialogue is that both are, by intention, comprehensive and proselytizing; they want to include all people.[160] But this all-embracing quality is the final goal of their hope and efforts, not the currently achieved level. Since their efforts are directed toward the future, the present must always be viewed self-critically.[161] Both say that true history starts only after current history ends.

The philosophic-theological dialogue with Marx's thought is possible because his atheism did not confront the Christian God in the biblical-theological sense, but in its metaphysical-historical sense, and because the "divine" which Marx applied to the human actually did represent the result of human objectivization toward the endlessness of nature.[162] Marx's own thought, both in formulation and content, was critical rather than dialogical. But there were elements in it which help the dialogue, such as human alienation past and present, human efforts to emancipate themselves from ownership relations so they can be fully free, the demand that truth not be merely thought but acted upon, and the demand for the hidden future.[163]

Difficulties are not caused by principles but by the concrete confrontation of essential and seemingly contrary views.[164] Dialogue must be comprehensive, both doctrinal and practical. On some concrete items it is possible to cooperate without doctrinal dialogue, but, if the goal is the future, then at a minimum they must make sure they are working toward the same future.[165] One needs to figure out one's own meaning and essence, which cannot be compromised. It is important first to confront those antithetical positions which threaten to make the dialogue meaningless (e.g., atheism vs. theism, Marxist search for meaning vs. the expected *parousia*).[166] These seemingly absolute contradictions must be removed. Then one can proceed to learn from another. Even "unsuccessful dialogue" actually makes sense. Though no concrete fruits may be seen, it still tends to improve relations between partners.[167]

An anonymous Catholic sociologist who writes under the pseudonym Jakov Jukić stated, "Yesterday we hated one another, today we listen, and tomorrow we might even love each other." [168] It is unwise to start a dialogue without knowing with whom we are talking. We also need to know ourselves.[169] Without previous knowledge, dialogue would soon turn into monologue.[170] Jukić approvingly quotes the Polish philosopher Mazowiecki: "Dialogue is not merely an exchange of values which are to be found in different systems, but the creation of completely new values which otherwise would not have been discovered." [171] Often there is passing collaboration, superficial tactics, political opportunism, and ideological syncretism, but there is also a search for common values, a process of opening up, getting acquainted, and understanding one another.

Marxism promises to change and humanize the world. This ambition Christians must support, for change in the world is a constant concern of Christians. At this intersection serious dialogue can take place. [172] In this respect Christians have most seriously deserted their responsibility. If Marxists help clear the world of poverty and injustice, they will have done much. Marxism is not a direct atheism. It says that religion has been created by a bad world. Christians can help change the bad world. It is up to Christians to show that religion does not alienate but saves, even in a this-worldly dimension. God can help us to be Christians facing God if we want to be Christians facing the world.[173]

The late Vladimir Truhlar stated that dialogue makes sense only if the other side is not merely apologetic. One must not abandon one's Christian conviction but must contribute to society that which is specifically Christian. Otherwise it would be merely a repetition of what the Marxists are already saying.[174] Christians committed to dialogue must not merely incorporate themselves passively into the socialist system. The Christian substance must be preserved. As a Christian one develops humanism from one's own sources and contributes it to society. A Christian involved in dialogue should not be solely critical of ecclesiastical institutions, avoiding criticism of socialism. Dialogue should not mean a passive incorporation of oneself and others into the socialist system.[175]

Jakov Romić, O.F.M., considered the dialogical approach of Christians toward Marxists the most realistic one but felt that Marxists must first remove two barriers to the dialogue: the monolithic vision of the future as conceived by the founders of Marxism-Leninism, and the exclusion of Christians by Marxists from equal participation in the processes of social change within socialist societies.[176] Unless Marxists abandon their monolithic approach and reinterpret some of their theories, dialogue cannot take place. Christians, too, must abandon some alienating interpretations of God and religion in order to make dialogue possible.

"Dialogue . . . is not a mere Socratic method of discovering the truth, but the only possible manner of human existence." [177] Only the progressives among Marxists and Christians realize this; the traditionalists in both camps think dialogue is impossible, and they, as the establishment, often punish those who engage in dialogue. Yet, without dialogue it is impossible for the two to coexist and in peace in freedom in either the present or the future society.

VOICES OF CAUTION OR OPPOSITION

Criticism of dialogue ranges from warnings of pitfalls or shortcomings into which concrete forms of dialogue may fall to opposition to dialogue as a means of encounter.

The Hungarian Reformed Bishop Károly Tóth, formerly general secretary of the Christian Peace Conference, and now its president, suggests that the dialogue is "heavily encumbered, or even made almost discreditable, by some phenomena." [178] Among the phenomena, he cited: 1) overt or covert forms of anticommunism which consider Christianity identical to anticommunism and antiprogressivism; 2) interest in dialogue by Christians is in direct ratio to the strength of the Marxist parties, but world wide interdependence should make it otherwise; and 3) the tendency of Marxists who are committed to the dialogue to turn against the programs of their own parties.[179] Tóth intended these comments not to deprecate the significance of theoretical dialogue but to warn against hasty conclusions that this form of dialogue takes precedence over practical cooperation between Christians and Marxists.

Jan Vogeler, professor of philosophy, University of Moscow, espoused the confrontation of ideas in order to cooperate on practical projects, for instance, on how to handle the scientific and technological revolution, the multifaceted improvement of human power, the exchange of experiences about long-range planning and prognosis, and similar matters.[180] Vogeler considered the dialogues organized by the Paulus-Gesellschaft to be ideological diversions.

Another Soviet Marxist philosopher, Lev Mitrokhin, of the editorial staff of *Voprossy Filosofii* (Moscow), was very critical of the type of dialogue in which there is a mixing of the two positions. Dialogue must not aim at "softening" the Marxist-Leninist teachings.[181] The purpose cannot be to achieve an identity of views, or lead to a compromise, or to deny atheism on the part of the Marxist partners. Under the guise of being "humanistic" or "creative," Marxist participants in the dialogue often attempt to attack true Marxist-Leninist positions.[182] But dialogue is helpful when Marxists and progressive Christians can look for ways to cooperate against the reactionary, imperialist forces in the world. Lenin believed that Christians can be involved in the revolutionary class struggle. People of all ideological orientations can work against social injustices in order to solve the social problems of our time, concluded Mitrokhin.

AN EVALUATION AND FURTHER CONTRIBUTION TO THE METHOD OF DIALOGUE

The foregoing views of Eastern European contributors on the concept of dialogue are so varied that they are sometimes contradictory. Some have made no effort to explain what they mean by the word. Some use it vaguely, applying it to almost any meeting between a Christian and a Marxist, regardless of the attitudes and motives brought to the meeting. Thus, for instance, a protocol meeting between a bishop and a government official might be described by them as a dialogue. Some more correctly identify dialogue as a specific type of encounter characterized by the equality and freedom of the participants, by a give-and-take situation, by an attempt to solve common theoretical and practical problems without aiming to misuse the partner or win a victory.

It is evident that there is a good deal of overlapping in the discussion of the purpose, motives, and method of dialogue. It should be thus. Without some commonality no success could be expected, because the notions and expectations would be at complete variance. It is most helpful, however, to see not merely the points of overlapping but also the novel points introduced by one or the other of the contributors. It is, in fact, the composite impact which most enriches our understanding of dialogue. Taking a comprehensive view is most helpful. By applying the principle of coherence, it is possible to utilize the accumulated contributions of authors, leaving out only those that are logically incompatible or deficient, and thus gain a very rich understanding of the purpose and nature of the Christian-Marxist dialogue.

Without reiterating all these combined views, a brief synopsis can be offered. Dialogue is a method, a path, a way, by which one person or group relates to another. Views differ. Differences are not to be removed, but are to serve as mutual enrichment. Both partners must be open to insight gained in the joint endeavor. Tension, dissent, and even conflict are seen as part of the process. No attempt should be made to camouflage differences for the sake of the appearance of a superficial agreement. Partners in dialogue must seek to know one another directly by listening, by speaking, by working together.

The following guidelines might be offered to those seeking to engage in a successful dialogue, without claiming that every specific dialogue must meet all conditions or that the list is comprehensive:

1. Both partners must have a need for dialogue.
2. Have a preliminary knowledge of your partner and the position with which you are going to dialogue.
3. Have a clear understanding of your own position.
4. Be well informed about the topic being discussed and present it clearly.
5. Set concrete areas of discussion ahead of time.
6. It is more promising to discuss specific issues than general, abstract issues.
7. Do not stereotype. Be open to the presentation of your partner's viewpoint.
8. Interpret your partner's view in its best light. Look at the whole picture, and do not try to belittle that view.
9. Look at the weaknesses and strengths of both views.
10. Emphasize things you have in common.
11. Listen to what your partner is saying. Strive for a clearer understanding of his or her position. Be willing continually to revise your understanding of the other's views.
12. There should be no hidden agendas. There should be no tactical or selfish motive initiating the dialogue.
13. Be open to constructive criticism, and avoid destructive criticism. Be aware of your partner's sensitivities.

14. Each member of the dialogue should be self-critical and honest. This should not mean giving up dignity and self-respect.
15. Do not assume that the conclusions reached are final. There will always be a need for continual dialogue regarding these views.
16. Each partner must accept responsibility for the good and bad his or her group has done or is still doing.
17. Both the ideals and the realities of each group should be taken into account.
18. Face issues which cause conflict, but emphasize those things upon which partners agree. Antagonistic relationships may then give way to cooperation.
19. Challenge one another to be faithful to your own search for truth.
20. Soul-searching and mutual enrichment should be part of the dialogue. Neither's truth is absolute. Each partner needs the other in order to get a more complete picture of truth. Monopoly in thought leads to sluggishness in thinking and to the perversion of truth.
21. Dialogue is impossible if either partner claims to have already solved the problem for all time to come.
22. Dialogue should present a new appreciation for the value of both positions.
23. Dialogue occurs between persons or groups of persons, not between disembodied ideas.
24. Do not try to convert your partner, or the dialogue may turn again into a monologue. Differences must be maintained, although they should change from irreconcilable ones to a diversity of approaches for the common good.
25. Dialogue should enable easier cooperation.
26. Work toward accomplishing something for the better. Work at improving the situation.
27. Observe the dialectical nature of the dialogue. Both views should be included in final conclusions, though not necessarily in equal measure. Both partners ought to move to new positions (not necessarily convergent ones) which would not have been possible without the dialogue.
28. Be aware that there are other people involved. The dialogue should be for the benefit of the whole community.[183]

Dialogue should thus be a dialectical engagement rather than a path to convergence. No synthesis is to be expected. While some differences may be reconciled and while the partners may reach agreement, even unanimity, on some issues, the goal is not to create Christian Marxists or Marxist Christians as a hybrid of the future.

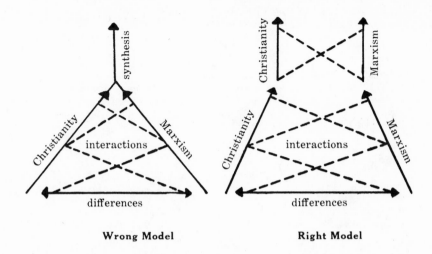

Wrong Model   **Right Model**

At best this model might be called partial convergence with continued dialectical engagement. One should not expect the process to be even and progressively improving. There are likely to be ups and downs, setbacks in some locations, and unexpected gains in others.

In this understanding, dialogue is not a mere prelude to cooperation. Cooperation becomes part of the dialogue, because action can be viewed as the incarnate *logos* (word) of *dia* (two) partners. Hence dialogue should be *the way* of relating Christian and Marxist partners in the present and future. It does not become superfluous after practical cooperation takes place, as asserted by some protagonists from Eastern Europe. Rather it is the constant approach in a pluralistic world to living and finding happiness through struggle. If this be true, one cannot speak of the "death" of the dialogue, unless the partners decide to eliminate the other by warfare, or unless Marxism or Christianity or both should vanish as viable life-styles. While some of these options are not entirely out of the question, one could venture an educated guess that both will survive the foreseeable future and, being unable to ignore one another, must encounter each other in dialogue. The less sophisticated approaches to dialogue will simply be transcended, as the partners seek out those dialogical options which experience proves to be most suitable. Among those suitable alternatives there will likely be many that the Eastern European experience has brought to the surface. These ought to become our common heritage.

Notes

1. Some of the methodological proposals have already been presented in previous chapters and will not be repeated here.
2. At this point the author assumes that the reader is acquainted with the identities of the various persons involved in dialogue as they were described in Chapters 3 and 4. No further identification will be provided.
3. Šagi-Bunić, *Ali drugog puta nema*, p. 378.
4. *Ibid.*, p. 386.
5. *Ibid.*, p. 392.
6. *Ibid.*, p. 387.
7. Bajsić, "Stavovi kršćana prema dijalogu s marksistima," in *Vjerske Zajednice u Jugoslaviji*, ed. by Zlatko Frid (Zagreb: NIP "Binoza," 1970), p. 143. Transl. by Mojzes.
8. *Ibid.*, p. 145.
9. Machovec, "Kampf um den wahren Kommunismus" in *Evolution oder Revolution der Gesellschaft?* (Munich: Paulus-Gesellschaft, 1969), p. 189.
10. *Ibid.*, p. 188.
11. Milan Opočenský, "Christian-Marxist Dialogue in Prague," mimeographed paper in English with no date.
12. Adam Schaff in "Diskussion" in *Christentum und Marxismus Heute*, p. 59.
13. Interview with Adam Schaff in Vienna on Dec. 13, 1975.
14. *Ibid.*
15. Teresa Nowacka, "International Comparative Research Project: The Effect of Information and Dialogue Upon Modification of Attitudes of Roman Catholic and Marxist Youth Toward Social Issues," (Vienna: European Coordination Centre for Research and Documentation of Social Sciences, 1974), p. 1.
16. Excerpts of Jaroszewski's article, "Confrontation, Dialogue, and Cooperation," as reported in *Church Within Socialism*, ed. by Erich Weingartner and Giovanni Barberini (Rome: IDOC International, 1976), p. 188.
17. *Ibid.*, p. 189.
18. *Ibid.*, p. 190.
19. *Ibid.*, p. 191.
20. "Church-State Relations: Debate in the Weekly *Polityka*" in *Christian Social Association Information Bulletin* (Warsaw), No. 5, May 1978, pp. 1-11.
21. Kuczyński, "The Christian-Marxist Dialogue," p. 123.
22. Kuczyński, "To Elevate the World—The Potential of John Paul the Second's Pontificate," p. 23.
23. *Ibid.*
24. *Ibid.*, p. 25.
25. *Ibid.*, p. 26.
26. Czaplejewicz, "Dialogics and the Pragmatic Theory of Dialogue," in *D & H*, Vol. 5, No. 1 (Winter 1978), p. 151.
27. *Ibid.*, p. 155.

28. *Ibid.*, pp. 156-157.
29. Machovec, "Diskussion," in *Schöpfertum und Freiheit*, p. 145. Abbreviated to *S & F.*
30. *Ibid.*
31. Machovec, "Die Gott-Frage und der moderner Atheismus," in J. Blank, W. Kasper, M. Machovec, and H. Zahrnt, *Gottfrage und moderner Atheismus* (Regensburg: Verlag Friedrich Pustet, 1974), p. 68.
32. *Ibid.*, p. 69.
33. *Ibid.*, pp. 70-71.
34. *Ibid.*, pp. 69-70.
35. Machovec, *AMLJ*, p. 38.
36. *Ibid.*
37. Machovec, "Christen und Marxisten auf der Gemeinsamen Such nach dem Sinn des menschlichen Lebens," in *S & H*, pp. 298-299.
38. *Ibid.*, p. 299.
39. Vitézslav Gardávsky, *Hoffnung aus der Skepsis* (Munich: Chr. Kaiser Verlag, 1970), p. 72.
40. Milan Průcha, "Marxismus als Philosophie menschlicher Existenz" in *S & F*, p. 50.
41. *Ibid.*, pp. 60, 57.
42. Průcha, "Vom Sinn des praktischen Humanismus" in *Christliche Humanität und marxistischer Humanismus*, p. 315.
43. *Ibid.*
44. Julius Tomin, "Ist der Dialog dem Marxismus fremd?" in *Stimmen aus der Kirche der ČSSR*, pp. 136-137.
45. *Ibid.*, pp. 139-140.
46. Krejči, "Dialog des Marxismus mit dem Christentum als Friedensbeitrag," *IDZ*, Vol. 1, No. 1 (1968), pp. 48-49.
47. *Ibid.*, p. 43.
48. *Ibid.*, p. 44.
49. *Ibid.*, p. 45.
50. *Ibid.*, pp. 45-47.
51. József Lukácz, "Historisches Bewusstsein und Verantwortung," in *S & F*, p. 97.
52. Lukács in "Diskussion" in *S & F*, p. 154.
53. Lukács, "Cooperation and Dialogue," in *Varieties*, p. 100.
54. *Ibid.*
55. *Ibid.*, p. 105.
56. Lukács, "Auf der Suche nach dem Gemeinsamen" in *Christliche Humanität und Marxistischer Humanismus*, pp. 264-265. Abbr.: *CHMH.*
57. *Ibid.*, pp. 267-268.
58. József Szigeti, "Marxistische Politik und kommunistischer Humanismus" in *CHMH*, p. 274.
59. *Ibid.*, pp. 276-277.
60. Bošnjak, *Filozofija i kršćanstvo*, pp. 562-598.
61. Bošnjak, "Kritika religije," in *Religija i društvo*, edited by Vjekoslav Mikecin (Zagreb: Stvarnost, 1969), p. 29.
62. *Ibid.*, p. 30.
63. *Ibid.*, p. 34.
64. Bošnjak, "Pogovor" in *Religija i društvo*, p. 255.
65. *Ibid.*, p. 256.
66. *Ibid.*, p. 257.
67. *Ibid.*, p. 263. Transl. by Mojzes.

68. Esad Ćimić, "Političko i idejno suočavanje s religijskim fenomenom" in *Religija i društvo*, p. 186.

69. *Ibid.*, p. 187.

70. *Ibid.*

71. Interview with Zdenko Roter, Ljubljana, November 15, 1975.

72. Roter, "Smisao dijaloga izmedju marksista i kršćana," in *Vjerske Zajednice u Jugoslaviji*, pp. 151-152. Also Roter, "A Marxist View of Christianity" in *Journal of Ecumenical Studies*, Vol. 9, No. 1 (Winter 1972), pp. 40-48.

73. Roter, "A Marxist View of Christianity," pp. 48-49.

74. Interview with Roter, Nov. 14, 1975.

75. *Ibid.*

76. *Ibid.* Not verbatim, but Roter's recollection.

77. Roter, *Katoliška cerkev in država v Jugoslaviji, 1945-1973*, pp. 137-154.

78. Roter, *Cerkev in sodobni svet*, pp. 189-204.

79. Andrija Krešić, "Marksizam u dijalogu" in *Marksizam i marksističko obrazovanje danas* (Zagreb: Biblioteka centra, 1973), p. 37.

80. *Ibid.*

81. *Ibid.*, p. 39.

82. *Ibid.*, p. 40.

83. *Ibid.*, p. 42.

84. Krešić, *Kraljevstvo božje i komunizam* (Belgrade: Institut za medjunarodni radnički pokret, 1975), p. 137. Transl. by Mojzes.

85. *Ibid.*

86. *Ibid.*, p. 138.

87. *Ibid.*, p. 144.

88. *Ibid.*, p. 145.

89. *Ibid.*, p. 146.

90. Arif Tanović, "Dogmatism and Contemporary Socialism," *Survey* (Sarajevo), Vol. 2, No. 2 (1975), p. 137.

91. *Ibid.*

92. Ketrzynski, "On Dialogue for Cooperation," in *C.S.A. Information Bulletin*, No. 5 (May 1978), p. 21.

93. *Ibid.*, p. 22.

94. Kowalczyk, "OHCMDP," p. 166.

95. *Ibid.*, p. 178.

96. *Ibid.*, p. 181.

97. Quoted in *ibid.*, p. 174.

98. Winfried Lipscher's book review of Mazowiecki's *Crossroads and Values* in *IDZ*, Vol. 5, No. 2 (1972), p. 184.

99. Hromádka, "Christentum und Geschichtlichkeit," in *S & F*, p. 107.

100. *Ibid.*

101. Opočenský, "Christian-Marxist Dialogue in Prague," a mimeographed paper, n.d., p. 1. The paper is apparently a translation of the author's "Christlich-marxistischer Dialog in Prag" in *Stimmen aus der Kirche der ČSSR*, pp. 125-134.

102. Lochman, *Church in a Marxist Society* (New York, Evanston, and London: Harper & Row Publishers, 1970), pp. 178-179. A slightly modified version of the last chapter of the book ("Christian-Marxist Dialogue") appeared under the title "On the Christian-Marxist Dialogue" in *Christian Century*, January 7, 1970, pp. 11-16.

103. *Ibid.*, p. 172. Emphasis is Lochman's.

104. *Ibid.*, pp. 173-178.

105. *Ibid.*, p. 190.
106. *Ibid.*, p. 191.
107. *Ibid.*, p. 192.
108. *Ibid.*, pp. 196-198.
109. Lochman, *Encountering Marx: Bonds and Barriers Between Christians and Marxists.* Tr. Edwin H. Robertson. (Philadelphia: Fortress Press, 1977), p. 25.
110. *Ibid.*, p. 26.
111. *Ibid.*, p. 37.
112. *Ibid.*, pp. 43-44.
113. Szennay, "Überlegungen zum christlisch-marxistischen Dialog im Geiste des II. Vaticanums," in *IDZ*, Vol. 2, No. 1 (1969), p. 80.
114. *Ibid.*, p. 82.
115. *Ibid.*, p. 83.
116. *Ibid.*, pp. 84-86.
117. *Ibid.*, p. 87.
118. *Ibid.*, pp. 88-89.
119. *Ibid.*, p. 90.
120. Szennay, "Der christlich-marxistische Dialog heute," in *IDZ*, Vol. 3, No. 1 (1970), p. 85.
121. This strikes me as an impossible condition for dialogue, quite impractical or impossible under present circumstances. It presupposes an internal unity in each group which simply does not exist.
122. *Ibid.*, p. 88.
123. *Ibid.*, p. 89.
124. *Ibid.*, p. 91.
125. *Ibid.*, p. 92.
126. József Cserháti, "Open Gates," p. 52.
127. *Ibid.*, p. 49.
128. *Ibid.*, p. 53.
129. *Ibid.*, p. 51.
130. *Ibid.*, p. 52.
131. *Ibid.*, pp. 53, 55.
132. Interview with Franić, November 17, 1975, in Split.
133. *Ibid.*
134. Franić, *Putovi dijaloga*, pp. 127-128.
135. *Ibid.*, p. 132.
136. *Ibid.*, pp. 68-69.
137. *Ibid.*, p. 143. Transl. by Mojzes.
138. Šagi-Bunić, *Ali drugog puta nema*, p. 377.
139. *Ibid.*, pp. 377-378.
140. *Ibid.*, p. 379.
141. *Ibid.*, p. 380.
142. *Ibid.*, p. 381.
143. *Ibid.*, p. 386.
144. *Ibid.*, p. 382.
145. *Ibid.*, p. 383.
146. *Ibid.*, p. 388.
147. *Ibid.*, p. 390.
148. *Ibid.*, p. 393.
149. *Ibid.*, pp. 391-392.
150. *Ibid.*, p. 396.
151. Bajsić, "The Significance and Problems of Dialogue Today," in *Journal of Ecumenical Studies*, Vol. 9, No. 1 (Winter 1972), p. 33.

152. *Ibid.*, p. 34.
153. *Ibid.*
154. *Ibid.*, p. 36.
155. *Ibid.*
156. *Ibid.*, p. 37.
157. *Ibid.*, p. 38.
158. Vereš, *Filozofsko-teološki dijalog s Marxom*, p. 7.
159. *Ibid.*, p. 169.
160. *Ibid.*, p. 171.
161. *Ibid.*, pp. 172-173.
162. *Ibid.*, pp. 18-19.
163. *Ibid.*, p. 161.
164. *Ibid.*, p. 175.
165. *Ibid.*, p. 176.
166. *Ibid.*, pp. 177-178.
167. *Ibid.*, p. 187.
168. Jukić, *Religija u modernom industrijskom društvu*, p. 7. Transl. by Mojzes.
169. *Ibid.*, p. 8.
170. Jukić, "Marksizam u jednoj suvremenoj enciklopediji ateizma," in *Crkva u svijetu* (Split), Vol. 4, Nos. 5-6 (1969), p. 417.
171. *Ibid.*, p. 423.
172. *Ibid.*, p. 428.
173. *Ibid.*
174. Interview with Vladimir Truhlar on November 15, 1975, in Ljubljana, Yugoslavia.
175. *Ibid.*
176. Romić, "Dialogue between Marxists and Christians as a Presupposition of Coexistence in Freedom," in *Varieties*, p. 114.
177. *Ibid.*, p. 123.
178. Károly Tóth, "Report of the General Secretary to the C.P.C. Continuation Committee" (mimeographed report) at Siófok, Hungary, September 17, 1975, p. 19.
179. *Ibid.*
180. Rudolf Weiler and Augustin Wucherer-Huldenfeld, "Bericht über die Forschungsgespräche mit Gastprofessor Jan G. Vogeler, Moskau," *Wiener Blätter zur Friedensforschung* (Vienna), No. 1, January 1974, pp. 30-35.
181. Elisabeth Leska, "Die Dokumentation L. N. Mitrochins über den 'Dialog' der Marxisten und Christen," 1975, p. 12 (mimeographed).
182. *Ibid.*, p. 15.
183. Mojzes, "The Current Status of the Christian-Marxist Dialogue and Suggested Guidelines for Conducting the Dialogue," in *Varieties*, pp. 10-11.

5

CHANGING MARXIST VIEWS ON RELIGION AND CHRISTIANITY

The purpose of this chapter is first to present briefly the conventional interpretation of religion in general and Christianity in particular, and then, at greater length, to point to the changes which took place in Eastern European Marxist scholarship regarding religion and Christianity. Marxist views on religion and Christianity are relevant to the dialogue. Those Marxist views of religion and Christianity which to Christians seemed to be more objective and less antagonistic created a receptive response among Christians, thus facilitating the dialogue. Likewise, participation in dialogue tended to spur Marxists into rethinking their position on religion and Christianty.

In contrast to the previous chapters where the author attempted to be comprehensive, the approach in the next three chapters will be schematic. The aim here will be to present the spectrum of positions on religion and Christianity which was offered by the Marxist thinkers. The purpose is to present the varieties of views which emerged in the Eastern European context and to illustrate them by several representative authors. An evaluation will be made as to whether a particular view advances or retards dialogue.

CONVENTIONAL MARXIST VIEWS ON RELIGION AND CHRISTIANITY

As Marxism developed in the U.S.S.R. and Eastern Europe, a "standard," "conventional," or "vulgar" (in the sense of "most frequently held") view on religion emerged. Its basic postulate is that there is a complete incompatibility between Marxism-Leninism and any form of religion. This was formulated by Lenin, who said, "Marxism as materialism is absolutely atheistic and resolutely hostile to all religion. We must combat religion." [1] Religion is seen as a mystification of natural and social relations, which appears under the conditions of class society. Religion is used by the ruling classes with the aid of the clergy to hold exploited classes in passive subjection. It offers to the suffering an escape into an illusory happiness of an otherworldly salvation, thereby dulling the responses of the exploited classes by lulling them into passivity. Religion is based on superstition and magic. It warps the mind of its adherents, casting them into reactionary political and social positions and cultural backwardness. People with religious convictions can never truly support social progress. It is Marxism's task to actively struggle against religion in order to speed up its inevitable demise. Religion will completely wither in the future communistic society, when all people come to recognize that the highest being for humans is the human being. True happiness can be found only in the creative self-fulfillment through useful work for society. Religion is the product of the imagination rather than a gift of supposed supernatural forces. Human beings are not God's creation. On the contrary, God is a human creation. When humans recognize that they have been worshiping their own best characteristics in the form of God, they will shed this unnecessary apparition and come to glorify their own best achievements. Future human beings will be atheist, anti-God, but prohuman.

Out of this composite picture of the conventional Marxist view of religion we can distinguish three typical responses advocated by Marxists:

First, using the approach of enlightenment and rationalism, the task of Marxism is to show the nonsensical and unscientific character of religious dogmas and superstitions by pointing to how they obstruct human progress.[2] This can be done through atheist education and propaganda. Consequently great efforts were and are being made, particularly in the U.S.S.R. and Albania, but also in other countries, to produce a great variety of atheist propaganda in order to combat religion at this level.

Second, the natural-economic approach stipulates that religion as a false social consciousness is caused by adverse natural circumstances and the class system. As soon as people cease to be terrorized by natural disasters and when the last vestiges of class rule disappear under new socialist economic relations, religion will collapse of itself. Human beings are merely the sum total of social conditions. As soon as the social conditions cease to be enslaving, there will be an automatic change in human social consciousness. It will become nonreligious.

Third, religion can be removed by "administrative measures" against religious people, especially the clergy and institutions. "Administrative measures" is an innocuous term which stands for the not so innocuous physical and psychological persecution and terror, legal restrictions, administrative harassment, job discrimination, vilification in the press, destruction of church edifices, removal of items necessary for the conduct of worship, as well as other repressive measures for the purpose of weakening and finally eliminating religion. Religion will disappear when the religious person finds no support in society and when the institutional conditions for the expression of religiosity are removed.

Most frequently a mixture of two or all three approaches are advocated to increase the efficacy of the opposition to religion. These views about religion were developed first in the Soviet Union and have continued, with little deviation, to be most consistently advanced by Soviet Marxists and those Marxists to whom the Soviet interpretation of Marxism is mandatory if not "sacred."

A sampling of recent Soviet and Soviet-inspired views can be gleaned from the papers delivered in the section on "Philosophy and the Study of Religion" at the Fifteenth World Philosophical Congress in Varna, Bulgaria, September 17-22, 1973.[3]

V. D. Timofeev, of the Soviet Academy of Sciences in Moscow, said that while some believers recently moved to a more progressive consciousness, religion still did not lose its character as "the opium of the people."

I. Slanikov (Bulgaria) stated that religion is the antipode and compensation for the incomplete fulfillment of people. Religion helps to stabilize people but makes it impossible for them to be active in society, to work for change. This causes them physical suffering from which they will be released only by a change in society.

A. F. Okulov, Director of the Institute for Atheism in Moscow, attacked theologians for thinking erroneously that human nature does not change basically and that there is transcendence. Religion will disappear with changes in society.

O. Klohr (G.D.R.) attempted to prove theoretically and statistically that religion is dying out.[4]

A. S. Onishchenko (U.S.S.R.) suggested that there are three types of world views: mythological, religious, and scientific. Today the first two views have been supplanted by the scientific one. Religion cannot save itself either by being open to mergers or by claiming independence.

E. M. Babosov (U.S.S.R.) claimed that the technical revolution weakens religion and strengthens atheism. Yet there are some ambivalent influences of technology on the existence of religious feelings, influences which were also noted by Ya.V. Minkyavichus (U.S.S.R.), as some people are drawn to religion as a refuge against the misuse of science.

I. Loukotka (Czechoslovakia) claimed that science is pushing religion to the outskirts of life and minimizing the influence of the church apparatus, but that Marxists ought to watch out for possible transformations that may take place, instead of the seeming dying out of religion.

D. M. Ugrinovich (U.S.S.R.) and F. Rupprecht (G.D.R.) attacked the "death of God theology" and the "theology of revolution" as attempts to keep modern believers from cooperating with Marxists, as well as a proof of the difficulty of maintaining belief in transcendence.

The claim by some religious people that there is no morality without religion was countered by P. K. Kurochkin (U.S.S.R.) who pointed to the high moral achievements of the Soviet people under the guide of atheism.

The above views show the tenor of the presentations at this congress. A few additional cases ought to suffice to support the contention that the conventional Marxist view of religion is "alive and well" among Marxists who have been labeled by some as "dogmatic" but who designate themselves as "Marxist-Leninist."

D. M. Ugrinovich (U.S.S.R.) wrote that religion is not something which is in a mutual interaction with society. It does not possess its own specific social side, but is, in its very nature, totally socially determined.[5] "The religious view of the world is the illusory reflection of real relations and connections of the existing world in the consciousness of the person," wrote I. G. Ivanov (U.S.S.R.).[6] Attempts by contemporary theologians only serve to further undermine religion and show that "the religious view of the world is in a dead-end street from which there is no exit." [7] Neither attempts to make an alliance with science, nor a flight into irrationality can save religion, which is doomed to extinction.[8]

The conventional Marxist view of Christianity provides no more consolation to a Christian than the Marxist's common view of religion. Marxism generally assumes that a successful attack on Christianity, which is regarded by them to be the most developed form of religion, is simultaneously an adequate invalidation of all religions. For "vulgar Marxism" Christianity is hopelessly compromised through its close association with reactionary governments. The Bolshevik appraisal of the Russian Orthodox Church was that it had completely and irrevocably enmeshed itself with the old tsarist order. Therefore, as a pillar of that society, it must disappear together with the old order. Only occasionally does someone remember that Engels regarded primitive Christianity and Thomas Münster, a radical reformer of the 16th Century, as progressive because they sided with the poor. But the Constantinian pattern of church-state relations drastically changed that association. It was unlikely, if not impossible, that the church would ever extricate itself from its preference for the upper classes until socialism forcibly accomplished this by destroying both the privileged classes and the privileges of the churches.

Christianity is based on dogmas which are irrational and must be accepted on blind faith under the threat of eternal damnation. It is a religion which demands meekness and servility. It dangles the hope of afterlife for those who will accept its dogmas and morality. It worships a nonexistent God. Its religion consists of a series of myths, the greatest of which is the myth of an incarnate God, Jesus Christ. The historicity of Jesus is usually denied. The virgin birth is a biological impossibility, as is the resurrection of the dead. Miracles are contrary to nature and have been created along with elaborate rituals to hold the masses in awe, the more easily to trick them. The churches hold human beings down, denying them any dignity through the doctrines of innate sinfulness, depravity, and corruption. The intense guilt feelings thus created can be forgiven only with the aid of the church, making this a weapon whereby people are kept in perpetual dependence upon the church and its clergy. The Bible is a book of myths, legends, and improbable stories, written by a group of people who consciously wanted to deceive the masses.

It is the task of all Marxists to discredit Christianity in order to liberate the people from it. Marxists must fight clericalism, as well as attempts by religious people to poison the minds of the young with the products of their sick imagination. Young people should, instead, be given a scientific, atheist education. If necessary, Marxism should provide substitute rites of passage (name-giving ceremony instead of baptism, *"Jugendweihe"* instead of confirmation, state weddings and funerals instead of church ceremonies, etc.). Christianity is a moribund religion; the sooner it disappears, the better off humanity will be.

In summary, the common Marxist assumes that Marx, Engels, Kautsky, and Lenin have adequately and scientifically determined the origin, nature, and duration of religion. The "vulgar" Marxist arguments tend to depend on "proof-texting" from some writings of the Marxian canon, feeling that a quote from one of the classic founders clinches the argument. Particularly popular is Marx's statement on religion as the opiate of the people—quoted out of context. Since Christianity is the most advanced religion and the founders proved its untenability, it is not necessary to undertake specific, concrete studies of religion to check whether the conclusions are correct. Those theoretical conclusions were based on the best criticism of religion accomplished in the nineteenth century, culminating in Ludwig Feuerbach and then corrected by Marx. The only task for a contemporary Marxist scholar is to present and explain the views of the founders and to point out how their research supports the complete validity of Marxist-Leninist forecasts. It is also the task of the researcher to point out the continued perfidy and cunning of religion so as to stir up the communist resoluteness to struggle against religion until it is eliminated.[9]

Some of the insights of the founders of Marxism were taken by conventional Marxism not merely as important principles but as absolute truths. Instead of using these principles as theoretical assumptions to guide them in research and action, they were taken as sources for deductive conclusions with no necessity of verification in practice.[10] The vast majority of Marxists in Eastern Europe follow this "vulgar" Marxist approach, which has been unacceptable not only to most Christians, but to those Marxist thinkers who see "vulgar" or dogmatic Marxism as a deformation. And conversely, the view of the critical Marxists is strenuously rejected by the conventional Marxists, who label them "revisionists," which is tantamount to calling them traitorous.

NOVEL MARXIST VIEWS OF RELIGION AND CHRISTIANITY

SCHEMATIC OVERVIEW OF ATTITUDES TOWARD RELIGION

A number of Marxist thinkers believe that Marx's own work, especially his analysis of religion and Christianity, was incomplete, fragmentary, and limited. They see his critique as an oversimplification and the result of mostly pragmatic considerations and historical influences. In the meantime, especially since the establishment of socialism, many new issues have arisen in regard to the relationship of Marxism and Christianity which affect the Marxist notion of religion. Especially significant have been strong evidences of religious flexibility and the ability to adjust to changing conditions.[11]

These Marxists, variously labeled by themselves or their sympathizers as "humanistic," "creative," or "authentic," but by their dogmatic Marxist opponents seen as "revisionists," undertook to restudy Marx's views and elaborate them or rectify them. In their revisiting of the classics of Marxism they came to the conclusion that the "vulgar" Marxist view consisted of a one-sided emphasis on a few of the founders' views, usually their most negative judgments, with little attention to their positive assessments. Hence they started reworking the Marxian theories of religion.

Among the writings of these Marxists we can schematically discern four variants of the Marxist theory of religion.[12]

1. Religion arises out of the specific conditions of class society. It reflects and perpetuates class divisions. The religion of the rulers tries to maintain the given situation. The religion of the ruled mirrors their suffering and expresses, mostly ineffectively and passively, their revolt against misery.

2. Religion is a form of alienation—an erroneous picture of the world, a social anomaly, that came into existence under specific socioeconomic conditions which caused human estrangement. Religion is the incorrect, illusory attempt to overcome this estrangement.

3. Religion is an attempt to cope with some perennial, unresolved human problems. Though it may be an escapist attempt, nevertheless the problems (fear of death, meaning of

life, and personal traumas) persist and may continually give rise to religion.

4. Religion is an ideological, social practice, which is irreducible to and different from all other social practices. The experience of the "holy" is a real experience. Insofar as concrete forms of this experience contribute to the entrenchment of class divisions, it should be fought by Marxists. If it contributes to the class struggle on the progressive side, Marxists should cooperate with it. In and of itself religion is neither good nor bad.

The responses to religion by Marxists can also be presented schematically: [13]

1. Three responses are possible within the first variant.

The first response is that religion will expire with the elimination of class society and exploitation. Struggle against religion is nonsense. Marxists should work only to bring about the classless society and leave religion alone. It will take care of itself, withering when its causes have been removed.

The second response is that the struggle against religion is important because it helps the class struggle since people's consciousness can be changed.

The third alternative is to support those forms of religion which help in the class struggle and attack the other. In the long run religion will wither.

2. Three responses are possible within the second variant.

The first response is that religious alienation is in the sphere of consciousness and is secondary to the more fundamental economic alienation. One need not attack religion until the other, more primary, sources of alienation have been eliminated.

The second response is that religion is a part of total alienation. Religion must be fought by Marxists in order to liberate the whole human being and society.

The third response is a compromise between the other two. Religion is, indeed, a secondary type of alienation which makes it difficult to see one's alienation and to accomplish emancipation. The criticism of religion helps people see their shackles and assists them in freeing themselves.

3. The response to the third alternative can be twofold.

The first response is to try to strengthen human personality so that the perennial human problems can be solved more authentically, without recourse to religion. Some people, however, among them the most sensitive and perceptive, may continue to seek religious solutions, even at advanced stages of a classless society. They will be of no danger to that order.

The second response is that Marxism as a worldview can help shift the focus to problems other than personal problems. People, in preoccupying themselves with social problems, will not dwell excessively with personal ones, and thus religion will lose ground but perhaps never disappear entirely.

4. The response to the fourth alternative is to explore each concrete religion as a form of inescapable ideological grappling with reality. The relationship toward religion should not be based on differences in the religious and Marxist worldviews but only on the evaluation of the concrete religion's role in class struggle. The role of religion is changing. Therefore Marxism needs a flexible response. The Marxist attitude on religion should not depend on the Marxist worldview or on its theories of religion, but on the needs of the class struggle, because Marxism is primarily a theory and strategy for the change of the existing world.

SAMPLES OF NOVEL MARXIST VIEWS ON RELIGION

Individual Marxist scholars who have proposed new Marxist interpretations of religion do not conform precisely to the above scheme. Frequently they mix two or more of those variants or do not cover all aspects of a given variant. Machovec is a good example of one who combines several variants in his synthetic view. In the space of about two pages his statements cover three variants. "From the historical as well as logical perspective the religious answer was the first answer to the question regarding the meaning of human life," he said, pointing to the third variant.[14] Then he maintained that the religious search for the meaning of life developed in those historical periods in which people attempted to explain the presence of so many evils in the world. Religion is the direct attempt to deal with the pressures and enigmas of life, such as sickness, material needs, and political repression.[15] This alludes to the first and the third variant. He concluded that the natural source of religion is in human conditions. "Religion is something typically human, a product of human thought and feeling of a particular period, as people thought about the problems and suffering of their life, but were still not able to control those without illusions."[16] Here we find suggestions of the second variant.

Religion, according to Machovec, is not a barren theory

but a warm promise, appearing in many concrete forms, that the problems of the here and now can be solved in an "other" existence which is worth living for. It satisfies not only the rational needs of humans but all needs, particularly the emotional.[17] It enriched the lives of so many people that one cannot merely dismiss it from the history of the development of consciousness. Religion cannot be replaced by a philosophical or scientific explanation of any of its errors. Faith can be replaced only by another, better faith. The question of our contemporary epoch is whether such a substitute without illusions has been found.[18] The religious illusion is a fairly independent kind of illusion, essentially because it suggests that the problems of this world can be solved in another world by a superior power. But this is simultaneously its weakness, because it develops too much dependence and emphasizes too much limitations, fears, and weaknesses. The perceptive observer will note that the real weakness of religion is that its solution is actually no solution at all but only a deferral. The real problems of hunger, need, death, oppression, illness, and so forth all remain unchanged.[19]

Individuals will continue, according to Machovec, to feel alien in their own life and thus be subject to religion. Only when all of humanity reaches a clear awareness and harmony with the world, an at-homeness in the world, will it be possible to live free of illusions, and thus be free from religion.[20]

While religion caused many evil things, it also contributed much good. So did atheism. A true atheist in search for a constructive, value-oriented life-style has much more in common with a religious person who likewise shows concern for values than with a vulgar atheist who finds satisfaction in the mere negation of the idea of God. The great religious leaders of the past and present have tremendous attraction for people because they are such beacons of moral virtue. They also challenge people to be different than they are, to be more fully human.[21]

From Machovec's example it is clear that the Marxist theoreticians cannot be forced into an iron mold. While it may be justified to say that Machovec's position can be classified as the second variant, he incorporates elements of other variants in his view.

Pavičević attempted to find the root of religion by taking a clue from some of Friedrich Engels' writings. He came to the conclusion that the source of religion is primarily emotional. Surmounting the narrow sociological root of alienation, he sought to establish a wider human, emotional basis of religion.[22] This means that no one has the right to deny a person the right to religiosity because no one has the right to deny a person the right to adjust psychologically to the inevitabilities of life. Just as it is not a rational mistake to hope that one's sick child will get well, so religion is not a rational mistake. Religious feeling is a very special, autochthonous feeling, which cannot be reduced to some other feeling, such as the aesthetic. Yet it is not an extraphysical, historical, or nonsocial phenomenon.[23]

Bošnjak surveyed what the classics of Marxism and the early exponents have said regarding religion.[24] He then proceeded to claim that religion will continue to survive in every social order because its source is not to be found merely in the social conditions, as claimed by the Marxist classics. The disappearance of social sources of religion will indeed reduce religion to a private affair, but will not destroy it because an important function of religion is to deal with the last questions, the *eschaton*.[25] The religious answer to the human limitation of mortality is to transcend it with the hope of an afterlife. The tragic truth for humanity is that this life does not have an inherent, given meaning and that all people, despite yearnings for immortality, simply die. The Marxist answer, according to Bošnjak, is to accept this givenness of human existence heroically, seeking to make this life as meaningful as possible by living for others and by accepting mortality. Religion is a very understandable, even attractive, yet, nevertheless, an erroneous interpretation of life. Marxists must avoid oversimplifying the sources of religion and grasp that this eschatological source of religion is likely to make it into a permanent, though not necessarily widespread, preoccupation. Thus Pošnjak, while not denying entirely the insights of the first and second variant, made a plea for the complexity of religious sources and opted for the third variant.

One of Bošnjak's former students, Djuro Šušnjić, who later became a professor of philosophy at universities of Belgrade and Niš, said that religion continues to live, no matter what Marx or Engels said about it. The survival of religion makes believers joyful and confuses the prophets of its doom, angering atheist activists.[26] Religion and science are relatively independent, closed systems of belief and practice. Each of them attempts an interpretation of reality, adaptation to reality, transformation of reality to human needs, orientation in a reality which is riddled with uncertainty, control of reality, integration of the divided parts of reality, identification of the person in relation to reality, and mobilization of the social powers in order to achieve certain goals.[27] This means that each system has its presuppositions, approaches to reality, logic and methodology, terminology, norms of behavior, rationality, vision of life and death, and criteria of truth and values. Both systems are on an equal level, and neither must be denied its rationality and functionality.

A statement can be gnoseological (a question of truth) or social-psychological. The truth of an idea is not yet sufficient to make it acceptable to all. Some untrue ideas have played at least as great a historical role as true ones. An idea needs to be convincing. From that light one cannot deny the meaningfulness of religious ideas, although they are not scientific. The basic mistake of most critics of religion is that they reduce religion to a system of descriptions of some facts and that they regard empirical facts as the only reality. They fail to understand that those symbols which do not reflect empirical facts may have the same influence on behavior as those that do.[28] Generally their criticism of religion is leveled only against dogmatic theology, whereas religion has emotional, ritual, rational, experiential, moral, and functional dimensions as well.

Most religious statements are nonempirical and can neither be supported nor opposed scientifically. Religion attempts to solve the riddle of life about which science can say little or nothing. Religion does not replace science, but it complements it with values. The consoling power of religion begins where scientific explanation ends.[29] Religion fulfills the need for the complete and the absolute. It changes the hypothetical into the categorical, the uncertain into certainty, the mortal into immortality. It makes virtue out of one of our greatest, last defeats—death. Religion thus accomplishes daily adaptations and transformations of our problems and frustrations, finding some solutions for them.

Humans look for ways to adapt themselves to the unforseen and uncertain, to lack of control, transitoriness, and death. One of the most successful ways of coping with these is religion. Faith is the best sign that a person is not giving in to problems and anxiety.[30] The world is increasingly insecure. Science helps by providing excuses and cover-ups so people do not have to think of ultimate questions. Not to think about oneself is a method used to avoid seeing oneself as someone unique and separate and to analyze oneself apart from one's activity.

Today many people are conscious but not self-conscious. Thus people turn away from the self. Even humans have become objects. Humans immerse themselves in constant activities and social engagements which leave little time to think about truth, about death, about oneself, one's deeds, and one's relationships with others and with nature. Being busy has its positive aspects, but it is also an escape from thinking about ultimate matters and meaning. With the loss of religion, what else may a person be losing? Even death ceases to be upsetting. Death also becomes a way of consuming. Since killing, too, is an action, life seems less worthy. A person who is constantly active cannot be truly critical of others or of himself or herself.[31]

Šušnjić is hard to classify. Obviously he does not regard religion as a disvalue. One could classify him in the third and fourth variant. Obviously he does not gloat over the loss of religion, nor does he regard the advance of secularism as a clear victory for human beings. One gets the impression that Šušnjić values religion rather highly. Šušnjić thinks that Yugoslav Marxism as a whole chose the worst Marxist metaphysics possible, namely that a person is the product of external circumstances. This means that there is no responsibility for one's actions. The consequences in the realm of morality are that people always claim they are not responsible for their acts. Hence a person's deeds cannot be judged, except by history, which is not a relevant judgment. Such an interpretation of Marxism is useful to politicians. This type of Marxism created individuals without personality and integrity, uncertain of their cognitive position. One can manipulate such a person in any direction.[32]

Mladen Stanković, an obscure Marxist from Zagreb, regarded the human condition of incompleteness, partiality, and lack of wholeness as the root of religion. Religion, as Marx said, is the sigh of the oppressed, because to be oppressed is not to be whole. But religion is also the sigh of the oppressor, because in fundamental problems they are in the same position as the oppressed.[33] It is true that religion is the soul of a soulless condition, but religion also exists where social conditions are good, because in essence it is not caused by bad conditions but by the general position of human beings in nature, their limitations which cannot be much improved. Stanković here explicitly rejected the first variant as crucial. He also rejected the second variant, saying that it is illusory to think it is possible to bring about conditions where illusions are unnecessary.[34] No society can be so ideal as to require no illusions. Social conditions have already been changed, yet religion remains, both among the exploited and the exploiters.

Religion does not contradict humanism, since God is the idealized human, or idealized human relations. Thus religion can contribute to the betterment of humanity. The richer the divine-human relationship, the better off humanity is. Human beings looked for a superhuman in the sky because in attempting to find adequate solutions the broken human being was not sufficient. In religion people found an ideal nonalienated person, which was what they wanted to be. They found perfection, completion, and the solution of fundamental contradictions which in reality they were not able to resolve.[35]

Religion is an essential human product. One can better understand human beings by understanding their eternal preoccupation with religion.[36] Religion is the completion of a human's spiritual partiality. Reality is complex but partial. Humans accomplish only a part of their potentiality. People attempt to fulfill themselves with productivity. One of the human limitations is the limitation of the meaning of life. It is impossible to come to grips with limited meaning in this life. Therefore meaning is sought outside and beyond this life. Religion provides such meaning and relates humans to eternity.

Humans are social beings yet are alone. Religion liberates people from such limitations and attempts to provide close interpersonal relations binding them into a community. It also "solves" biological, temporal limitations—death. Thus religion is an idealized spiritual solution to all the problems and limitations of humanity. Religion is the fulfillment of real human partiality. Human beings receive through religion what they do not have. Thus religion is not an alienating factor but an aid to completing oneself. At least in one's consciousness, one becomes more total and fulfilled.[37]

With the new revolutionary changes the church, the association of religious people, seeks new ways to preserve itself. If the church agrees to humanize human relations and give humans the value they ought to have, then there is in principle no problem about the coexistence of socialism and the church. Religion will continue to be needed by many people for a long time.[38] The important thing is not whether one is religious or not but whether one is humane or not. The basic question is what does religion mean to a human being? alienation or fulfillment, ties or liberation, power that demeans a person or power which fulfills so that the person's participation in society increases. If it produces the latter alternatives, religion can become a liberating force within socialism.[39]

Another little known Marxist writer, Zdravko Kučinar, maintained that Marx's criticism of religion was limited and incomplete and that official Marxism approached the matter pragmatically and oversimplified it in the process.[40] The new socialist praxis brought about a changed relationship with religion, since many of the socialist strivings have been experienced within various religions. Marxism forgot Marx's own more complete formulation of the nature of religion when it emphasized only that religion is the reflection of human suffering but neglected to emphasize that religion is also the protest against this suffering. Though perhaps illusory, religion at least contains faith and hope in a better world. It is at this point that it can intersect with revolutionary striving. One of the few Marxists who realized this was the Italian Marxist, Antonio Gramsci, who regarded Christianity as the greatest utopia in history, a utopia which promoted in mythological form the idea of brotherhood, sisterhood, and equality. Kučinar maintained that religion is a form of hope, an expression of human conviction in the possibility of a better and different existence than current suffering. Most of the Marxist "scientific" criticism, such as Engels', Kautsky's, Lenin's, and Bukharin's, is actually primitive and unscientific.

Kučinar then found the study of the Austromarxist, Max Adler, the most satisfactory Marxist view of religion. Kučinar maintained, with Adler, that Marxist criticism tended to center on the mythological aspects of religion but not on its cognitive and critical form. Here Adler and Kučinar sided with Immanuel Kant, saying that religion is a conviction (feeling) which is a necessary transcendental road sign for human behavior.[41] The concept of God is a regulative idea which gives people a sense of unity to their experiences. Only religion seems to care about the destiny of individual human beings. Religion alone, being stimulated by concerns over death and destiny, can tie nature and morality into a whole and give meaning to life. That can be done only by positing the nonempirical notion of God. Religion directs toward wholeness and the meaning of life and the world. It is the experience of that direction. Faith is the form of this religious consciousness.

Since faith is tied to the questions of the purpose and goals of human activity, Marxism itself, then, has a religious element. Without such faith socialism would have never come about.[42] Should Marxism lose this faith, the same economic necessities which can liberate the world could bring even greater enslavement of the proletariat.

Contrary to the conventional Marxist criticism, Kučinar believed that a renaissance, not withering away, of religion will take place. No increase in knowledge can replace religion because religion is an *a priori* given in human consciousness and is thus permanent.[43] Kučinar concluded that Adler's answers are not mandatory for a Marxist, but the questions which Adler raised must be answered by a Marxist. There is indeed a direction, a tendency toward absolute, ideal values, which is a utopian element in all human activity. But Kučinar concluded, departing from Adler, that it is questionable whether this utopian element need be called religion. Its future form may be such that it cannot be labeled *religion* in the classical sense of the word. Religion is not an *a priori* human condition, though it does appear in all historical periods. The utopian faith of the future will not be religious.[44]

For his basic definition of religion Esad Ćimić depends on Glenn M. Vernon's *Sociology of Religion,* saying that religion is the wholehearted faith in the existence of something that can never be reached with human senses.[45] Religion is also a manner by which forms of behavior are accepted or rejected. Those values which help the person or society to relate to the supernatural are considered religious. On the social plane religion is also a dependency upon the personified natural and social forces. Each religion is determined by three factors: 1) dependence upon personified forces, 2) the determination of one's own social function by the type of social structure in which one lives, and 3) by the existential situation of the person, the ultimate source of which is the recognition of human finiteness.[46]

Ćimić basically accepted the second variant (that religion is a form of alienation), but did not consistently maintain this. For instance he said, "Therefore, religion remains today, and will always continue to be, a form of alienation, which witnesses simultaneously to the *potential* power and the *real* powerlessness of the human to be actualized, and who therefore transfers this actualization to the transcendent sphere." [47]

On the other hand:

> But, philosophers did not yet give us a satisfactory answer as to whether religion must always, and in all of its forms be alienating. Marx pointed to religion as alienation and very successfully founded his thesis of the withering away of such reli-

gion. However, if it is probable that religion can exist without alienating, then we have no solid theoretical basis for its disappearance.[48]

Ćimić added that religion as alienation can also appear in the form of atheism. Therefore, he said, "I am for both religion and atheism which are not alienated." [49] The task is to remove "the social and other presuppositions which make authenticity impossible. And whether this authenticity will in the end be impregnated religiously or atheistically, is least important." [50] Should religion remain alive in a society that has otherwise achieved humanism, this would not be a disappointment to a genuine Marxist. This form of religion would probably be rather similar to Marx's atheism.

Ćimić devoted a good deal of attention to those sources of alienation within socialist society which tend to create religion. He identified it primarily with the enormous growth of power of the government and the survival of economic policies in which the worker still continues to hire out for wages. In contemporary socialism many basic features of capitalism have been retained unchanged. It is surprising that the system has not created even more religiosity, according to the Marxian formula, than it has. Religion has, indeed, maintained itself vigorously in the U.S.S.R. and other socialist countries.

Ćimić also emphasized the psychological dimension of religion, which fills the emptiness and senselessness of life.[51] It can free a person from fear and sadness, give strength, and provide meaning in both defeats and successes. The practical, moral, and ethical function of religion has increased in recent years in comparison to the doctrinal and ritual function of religion. It is of the essence to religion that it duplicates reality, adding to this-worldly reality a nonmaterial reality. Thus religion appeared even before the creation of class society. Yet social factors do play a significant role in religion.[52] Ćimić concluded that religion is essentially the struggle for survival projected beyond the grave. Religion is not to be evaluated as an abstraction, but, each concrete form of religion is to be scrutinized by the Marxist criticism of religion.[53]

A colleague of Ćimić from Sarajevo, Fuad Muhić, who is likewise a Marxist of Muslim background, developed Ćimić's theme of socialism as a form of religion. Muhić maintained that religion as alienation did not disappear in the twentieth century but was transformed into a secular form, which fits the fundamental criticism of religion as alienation. Contemporary scientific socialism as an ideology can be criticized by the same method as nineteenth-century religion.[54] The critique of religion ought to become today the critique of politics. Though many Marxists may consider this a "heretical" statement, political alienation took the place of former religious alienation. Socialism attempted to destroy religion administratively but created a new type of alienation.[55] While some people were freed from sacral religion in the process of the "drama of atheization," they also became entwined in the political alienation of contemporary socialism. Scientific socialism is based on the cult of positive science and did not solve the question of alienation.

Socialists tried to fight religion as a form of pure consciousness by means of propaganda, but that did not work. "That was a level of abstract confrontation in which Christian theologians, and even Muslims, became overwhelmingly victorious over Marxists exactly because the so-called 'last questions' cannot be solved on that level." [56] In most instances one form of religion replaced another. Based on the same presupposition on which it tried to negate religion, socialism brought a worldly religion which by its results and consequences is no less an alienation than traditional religion. The problems of human beings have not been resolved. The "cult of personality," the charismatic leadership of one person over a socialist country, is "nothing else but a typical form of worldly secularized religion." [57] In many ways contemporary Marxism followed the path of Christianity, being transformed from its early stages of unity of followers and ideas into an institutionalized form of power of ideas over people. Marxism, as a secularized religion, is less life-giving and less able to survive the more it depends on a few dogmas and the belief that it can solve everything. The best example is the statement, "Marxism is omnipotent because it is true," which differs in no way from Christian assertions that Christianity has the ultimate truth.[58]

Kerševan is probably the best known representative of the fourth variant. He claimed that the Marxist theory of religion is as yet incomplete and that it lends itself to contradictory interpretations.[59] The basic attitude of Marxism toward religion ought to be the relationship of a scientific theory toward one of its objects. Kerševan suggested that there is lack of information as to how the human being and society produced this specific product. The theoretical tool which Kerševan used is the consideration of religion as a social product. The subject of religion is the reaction of the consciousness to those manifestations (natural, social, and psychic powers) which should be, but are not yet, controlled.

Other Marxists have also sought to root religion in dependence, but the novelty of Kerševan is that he suggested that religion is neither competing with nor substituting for some other praxis. Rather it is an addition to other phenomena. Through religion humanity comes to grips with those powers with which it cannot otherwise deal.[60] It is not necessary that the ultimate questions always be the same, but it is necessary that they be ultimate. As soon as some problems cease to be ultimate, they can be dealt with by some other means. Thus religion always deals with human consciousness, and the way it deals with it is through the experience of the holy. With this experience of the "wholly other," religion deals with the unsolvable problems. It is religion's distinguishing mark from all other experiences.[61]

The experience of the holy, however, is the result, rather than the source, of religion. Kerševan rejected the psychological concepts of the origin of religion; there is no pure religiosity. Thus religion is not an essential human need. However, one cannot surmise its duration from this observation. One can neither claim that religion is eternally necessary, nor can one prove that it will die out. It is a relatively autonomous phenomenon which does not depend on alienation, but on an experience of the infinite, absolute, supernatural, holy, mysterious, and radically other power.[62]

The concrete function of religion is ambivalent. Whether it will be reactionary, conservative, progressive, or revolutionary does not depend on religion itself but on its context. Sometimes religion slows down progress; at other times it speeds it up. Sometimes it's an opiate. At other times it is a stimulant. As a rule it tends to be conservative, because it sees the rule of God in the given system. But at other times, it can be revolutionary, because the other world is the "best of possible worlds" and serves as a critique of the present order. Contemporary religion is in a crisis, but it is impossible to determine what new form of religion will follow it.[63] Consequently Kerševan advocated that Marxism as a theory and strategy of revolutionary change should not take an abstract position toward religion but determine which religion aids such social change and in each concrete circumstance aim to work with it. Adjustments in evaluation toward these concrete forms of religion should be made constantly.[64]

Marxism, too, is a worldview and as such offers interpretations different from religious interpretations. It is, however, erroneous to place the emphasis of convincing religious people as to the correctness of the Marxist worldview if this is going to undermine the effectiveness of the class struggle. Marxism, as a scientific analysis, can more effectively change social realities than can Christianity. Christianity could utilize Marxist science. But Marxism cannot always mobilize the masses if the situation is not revolutionary. Here Christianity seems to be more advantageous. The two can complement one another in dialogue because Marxism can ask new questions, while Christianity can raise the old, but still real, questions.[65]

It seems that Kerševan was saying that religion can humanize persons no less than other practices. Marxism and Christianity should attempt to solve the same problems but with different means. Yet they are not necessarily competitors. Competition leads only to enslavement, not to liberation.[66] Cooperation and dialogue are the means of liberation.

This sample of Marxist scholarly views of religion demonstrates that after serious attention was finally given by Marxist thinkers to this subject, a wealth of options has emerged which offers those Christians eager for dialogue more satisfactory alternatives than the conventional ones.

One should not blame Christians for preferring those alternatives that do not predict *a priori* their own demise. Add to this that Marxist scholars have finally acquainted themselves with Christian and other analyses of religion and have started utilizing them in their own theoretical formulation, and it will be clear why the newer options provide more hope for a creative interaction than the former.

MARXIST VIEWS OF CHRISTIANITY

It should be no surprise that Marxist scholars have in mind Christianity when they are discussing religion in general. Much of what has been stated above in the form of generalized notions applies to Christianity. But there are some very specific descriptions and evaluations of Christianity which ought to be added to this account.

Robert Kalivoda, a theoretician from Czechoslovakia, stated that the systematic study of religion was outside the perimeter and competence of the classics of Marxism and the judgment that religion is the opiate of the people is not sufficient as a Marxist teaching on religion. The texts of Engels are more important for the explication of Christianity.[67] His writings do not cover the problems of Christianity, nor are his conclusions acceptable, yet, at least, he clarified the dialectics of early Christianity.

Marxism opposes the notion of "linear opium." This means that due to its monopoly in European history Christianity was not only a weapon in the hands of the ruling classes but also became a weapon for all social opposition. Original Christianity was an expression of resistance to all oppression. Only after a considerable inner struggle did Christianity become an ideology which sanctioned oppression. In the medieval period the death struggle between "orthodoxy" and "heresy" signaled that heresies absorbed the values of early Christianity.[68] In more recent times Christianity has again given support to oppressed people.

No other religion produced such a wealth of ideas as did Christianity. This ability contributed decisively to human emancipation. One can trace lines of development within Christianity, especially those which emphasized the values of the this-worldly, which carried in itself the kernel of atheism. When Christianity today again emphasizes this-worldly values, as did early Christianity, then it becomes again a way for progress.[69] Christianity, wrote Kalivoda, sanctioned restriction of freedom, oppression, and inequality, yet at the same time searched for freedom, equality, and brotherhood/sisterhood. The greatest progress was made when nonconformist Christian thought was united with heterodox institutions. From the Hussite reformation onward, Christians have ceased to await the miraculous intervention of God and attempted to change society themselves. Radical Christian nonconformism gave the world the ideas of emancipation, socialism, and communism and signified a decisive development forward in the two millenia of Christian history.[70] So long as Christians do not realize that antisocialism and anticommunism are contrary to their own development, they will continue to have a false consciousness of themselves which they might be unable to overcome.

According to Machovec, "Christianity has articulated certain important ideas about the human condition," which every Marxist ought to consider seriously.[71] Christian causes are worthy of Marxist adoption. Particularly important are the teachings and actions of Jesus. Insofar as Christianity is the continuation of the work of Jesus Christ it can be a form of humanism and an ideology which Marxists can regard as friendly. Marxists are carrying out scientifically and realistically what Jesus and his heirs aspired to and hoped for but could not carry out because of the primitive means which they had at their disposal.[72] Christian concern, love of neighbor, and mercy are desirable principles, but Christianity embodied these principles primarily in individual acts of almsgiving, which did not change anything in the miserable conditions that evoked these kindly responses. Yet many vulgar Marxists are mistaken in thinking that mere self-identification with Marxism makes them superior to Augustine, Hus, Luther, Barth, or other Christian spiritual giants who waged monumental ethical and existential struggles. The Christian sources, for instance, the Gospels, overshadow all the achievements of Egyptian and Greek antiquity because they are morally penetrating, and have such broad consequences for all those who are searching, suffering, and disquieted.[73] Machovec concluded by saying that the possible passing away of religion would not make a particular impact upon him, but if the heritage of Jesus were completely to be forgotten, he would not wish to live in such a world.[74]

Gardavský saw Christianity as a movement "abounding in ambition which intervenes as much in everyday events as it did a thousand years ago." [75] Christianity aimed to give each person a place in the universal human race and sought to create an institution, the church, which would be a social order worthy of humans. It failed, of course, in this attempt, but it has not given up its search for perfect order. Its great theologians, past and present, wrestled with the most profound human problems.

A Marxist criticism of Christianity should not be grounded on some emotional dislike or abstract anticlericalism.

> Criticism of its [the churches'] policies loses its point and its social justification as soon as Christianity comes to its senses and abandons all its political links with particular classes or reactionary ideas and social schemes; as soon as its theist motivation encourages it to make an effort to solve the current problems threatening mankind; and if it—even if it does this in its own way—makes an effort to eliminate the barriers which separate man from his total dimension and frustrate all attempts to build up a social order in which man could develop himself as a 'commonwealth.' [76]

Marxism needs to critique the Christian tendency to convert most problems into illusory personal consolation without removing the social roots of problems. Yet a Marxist cannot be an anti-Christian or antitheist on principle. Carefully discriminating among the many Christian approaches, a Marxist should seek to engage in dialogue with those who are most supportive of general human welfare, concluded Gardavský.

A number of Yugoslav Marxists attempted to present Christianity not by means of a general overview but by pointing to the recent changes which took place in it. This is particularly true of Roter, Kerševan, and Krešić. Roter carefully recorded the impact of Pope John XXIII and the Second Vatican Council on the Catholic Church.[77] He noted the renewal in liturgical, theological, and social thought. Of particular interest to him is the changed stance toward socialism and communism as socioeconomic systems and toward Marxism and atheism as theoretical postures. The openness of the churches toward dialogue with Marxism received a close scrutiny by Roter, ending in the assessment that contemporary Christianity is indeed able to adjust itself to the requirements of this age.

Kerševan noted that contemporary Christians, especially the left-wing theologians, specify that "the other world" is a world in which the individual is a free and equal person in community and love with others as the cocreators of the development of which God is the course, goal, and guarantee.[78] This notion of personal equality contradicts the class and other inequalities of capitalism. Christianity can provide the motivation but not the means of social change which would bring about its ideals.[79] If it linked itself with socialism and Marxism, it might have a better chance to realize its goals.

Krešić pointed out that communism emerged within the Christian civilization. Communism negates that civilization, but this does not mean that it also negates Christianity.[80] Bourgeois society used Christianity in the form of divine, heavenly transcendence in order to put a stop to this-worldly transcendence, consisting in revolution and human transcendence. Christians, like all humans, desire to raise this concrete life to an ideal level. In this common aim Communists and Christians can find themselves working side by side. On account of their upbringing many are leary of communism and steadfastly remain Christian despite many temptations. Others may become Communists but carry within themselves Christian vestiges which emerge in a time of crisis, resulting in a great spiritual crisis.[81] But these two options are outdated choices forced on people by both crusading atheist Communists and Christians. A *modus vivendi* consisting of proexistence and dialogue can be worked out because Christianity and communism are not necessarily incompatible.

Krešić concluded that contemporary Christianity seriously takes into account the rapid changes in society. Adaptation to these changes in the form of renewal is taking place. While some Christians oppose this renewal, others accept it, and still others vigorously promote change. More and more frequently one discovers Christian indictments of the capitalist order. In most instances the churches ceased to be causes of social and international antagonism, but instead have become proponents of tolerance, cooperation, and dialogue.[82] Renewal manifests itself as a new interpretation of the biblical sources of Christianity, which is actually a way of establishing Christianity in the contemporary world, abandoning outlived styles and approaches which are burdens from which Christianity needs to free itself.

The aforementioned Marxist scholars are not the only ones who find valuable elements in Christianity beyond what the classics of Marxism pointed out. It is not unusual for Polish Marxists to point out that the Catholic Church played a progressive role in Polish history and that, in many respects, the history of the Polish civilization nearly coincides with the history of Christianity in Poland. Christianity caused many evils, yet it did contribute many good things as well. Similar appreciative statements about domestic forms of Christianity can also be discovered in the writings of Marxists from other countries.

EFFECTS ON DIALOGUE

The Christian-Marxist dialogue does not hinge primarily on the Marxist attitudes toward religion. It is possible for Christians to engage in dialogue even with those Marxists who hold conventional views on religion, but this is not easy. The task becomes easier when Marxists involve themselves in a reassessment and in-depth study of religion and Christianity. This has been explicitly stated by Christians.[83] It is, of course, psychologically difficult to be involved in dialogue with a partner who predicts the other partner's demise and has very little positive to say about the other partner. The problem would be greater if conventional Marxist analysis were granted as correct, for this means the Marxist partner in fact would cause Chistian self-destruction, dressed in the guise of cooperative ventures.

The novel variants give more hope to the dialogue. Not all are equally beneficial to Christians. Those that consider religion an aberration, a sort of psychological weakness that will disappear in the process of humanity's maturation, do not inspire lasting trust, though some of them, at least, grant a more permanent root to the religious consciousness.

The view most acceptable from the vantage of dialogue is the one that does not lump all religions together in a derogatory —or even in a praising—manner. Christians themselves know that not all religions are good and that not everything in Christian history is positive. Hence they do not expect full Marxist endorsement. But Marxist critique and evaluation of concrete forms of religion and Christianity, especially when preceded by more objective in-depth study, would inspire Christian confidence. Most Christians are well-satisfied that there is perpetual substance to religion and that Christianity has a survivability if its rightful mission is not thwarted by antagonistic acts of a Marxist government. To Christianity, those Marxist views which encourage Christians to work for human welfare are welcome challenges. Their interface with Marxists who are not malevolent toward Christianity as a matter of principle is likely to be an enriching experience. Many, if not most, Christians would gladly cooperate with Marxists in their effort to better understand and evaluate religion in general and Christianity in particular. Those Marxist institutes which sought some limited Christian cooperation in their scholarly study of religion and Christianity found such cooperation useful. Should this be done on a large scale and should Christian institutions of higher learning seek Marxist input, the Marxist theories and approaches to religion would tend to improve, and with it would improve Christian-Marxist relations. The Marxist search for truth would also be more on target. It is in the Marxist self-interest to have as accurate an understanding of religion and Christianity as possible. No stable view can rest on false premises.

Notes

1. Lenin, "Attitude of the Workers' Party toward Religion," *Selected Works* (New York: International Publishers, 1943), Vol. 11, p. 666.

2. This typology was developed by Ćimić, *Socijalističko društvo i religija*, pp. 13-23. Ćimić surveys these views but rejects them as incorrect Marxist approaches.

3. The summaries of the presented papers were made by Gustav Wetter, S.J., "Die marxistische Religionsphilosophie auf dem XV. Weltkongress der Philosophie," in *Gregorianum*, Vol. 55, No. 1 (1974), pp. 151-160.

4. In his book *Religion und Atheismus Heute* (Berlin, G.D.R., 1966) Klohr provides a conciliatory attitude, saying that an analysis of the so-

cial situation calls for joint thinking and action toward building a new socialist society.

5. According to Pavičević, *Sociologija religije*, p. 63.
6. Ivanov, "Savremena teološka interpretacija religiozne slike sveta," in *Nauka i teologija u XX veku*, p. 126. Transl. by Mojzes.
7. *Ibid.*, p. 139.
8. *Nauka i teologija u XX veku, passim.*
9. William C. Fletcher, *Soviet Believers* (Lawrence: The Regents Press of Kansas, 1981), pp. 15-20, 45-47, 110, and *passim.*
10. Tanović, p. 137.
11. Zdravko Kučinar, "Marksizam i kritički pojam religije," in *Kultura*, Nos. 13-14 (1971), p. 45.
12. The schema (items 1, 2, and 4) is based on Kerševan, "Odnos komunista prema religiji," pp. 887-891, and Stres, "Religija kot družbena praksa," p. 283, but modified and extended by this author.
13. Kerševan, "Odnos komunista prema religiji," pp. 887-891.
14. Machovec, *Vom Sinn des menschlichen Lebens*, p. 31. Transl. by Mojzes.
15. *Ibid.*, p. 32.
16. *Ibid.*, p. 33.
17. *Ibid.*, pp. 34-35.
18. *Ibid.*, p. 35.
19. *Ibid.*, p. 36.
20. *Ibid.*, p. 38.
21. *Ibid.*, p. 42. In 1968 Machovec published a book on Augustine after a visit to Italy to do research on *De Civitate Dei*, the title of which is not available to this author. Machovec's friend Zbynek Fišer wrote a book *Utecha z ontologie* (Prague, 1967) in which he discussed various ontologies including the question of God's existence. Fišer opted for a nonsubstantial ontology, and this preference combined with interest in religion resulted in 1968 in a book on Buddhism, which, in his opinion has a nonsubstantial ontology. Fišer shares Machovec's dedication to rethinking religion and is likewise out of a teaching job, since such views are currently not tolerated in Czechoslovakia.
22. Interview with Pavičević, November 21, 1975, in Belgrade.
23. Pavičević, "Religion und marxistische Toleranz," in *Christliche und marxistische Zukunft*, pp. 146-147.
24. *Filozofija i kršćanstvo*, pp. 450-535.
25. *Ibid.*, p. 574.
26. Šušnjić, "Moć i nemoć nauke u kritici religije," in *Kultura*, Nos. 13-14 (1971), p. 59.
27. *Ibid.*, pp. 59-61.
28. *Ibid.*, p. 64.
29. *Ibid.*, p. 69.
30. *Ibid.*, p. 70.
31. Interview with Šušnjić, November 21, 1975, in Belgrade.
32. Stanković, "Čovjek i religija," p. 650.
33. *Ibid.*, p. 650.
34. *Ibid.*, p. 651.
35. *Ibid.*, p. 652.
36. *Ibid.*, p. 645.
37. *Ibid.*, p. 648.
38. *Ibid.*, p. 553.
39. *Ibid.*, p. 655.

40. Kučinar, "Marksizam i kritički pojam religije," in *Kultura*, Nos. 13-14 (1971), p. 44.
41. *Ibid.*, p. 51.
42. *Ibid.*, p. 54.
43. *Ibid.*, p. 56.
44. *Ibid.*, p. 58. Kučinar is vague at this point. It was impossible to determine exactly what his position is on this issue.
45. Ćimić, *Drama ateizacije*, p. 16.
46. *Ibid.*, p. 17.
47. *Ibid.*, p. 19. Italics are Ćimić's. Transl. by Mojzes.
48. Ćimić's response in "Religija i savremeno društvo," in *Kultura*, Nos. 13-14, p. 283. Transl. by Mojzes.
49. *Ibid.*, pp. 313-314.
50. *Ibid.*, p. 316.
51. Ćimić, *Drama ateizacije*, p. 27.
52. *Ibid.*, pp. 54-55.
53. *Ibid.*, pp. 62-63.
54. Muhić, in "Religija i savremeno društvo," in *Kultura*, Nos. 13-14 (1971), p. 292.
55. *Ibid.*, p. 293.
56. *Ibid.* Transl. by Mojzes.
57. *Ibid.*, p. 294.
58. *Ibid.*
59. Kerševan, "Odnos komunista prema religiji," p. 893.
60. Stres, p. 282.
61. *Ibid.*, p. 285.
62. *Ibid.*, p. 290.
63. *Ibid.*, p. 293.
64. Kerševan, "Odnos komunista prema religiji," p. 894.
65. Stres, p. 296.
66. Bajsić, "Marko Kerševan: teoretski model za proučavanje religije kao specifične prakse," p. 323.
67. Kalivoda, "Christentum in Prozess der menschlichen Emanzipation," in *S & F*, pp. 267-268.
68. *Ibid.*, p. 270.
69. *Ibid.*, p. 274.
70. *Ibid.*, p. 277.
71. Machovec, *AMLJ*, p. 35.
72. Machovec, "Die 'Sache Jesu' und marxistische Selbstreflexionen," p. 85.
73. *Ibid.*, p. 101.
74. *Ibid.*, p. 102.
75. Gardavský, *God Is Not Yet Dead*, p. 14.
76. *Ibid.*, p. 198.
77. Roter, *Cerkev in sodobni svet*, *passim*.
78. Kerševan, "Savremeno hrišćanstvo i ideologija," in *Kultura*, Nos. 13-14 (1971), p. 77.
79. *Ibid.*, p. 84.
80. Krešić, *Kraljevstvo božje i komunizam*, p. 7.
81. *Ibid.*, p. 8.
82. *Ibid.*, p. 23.
83. E.g., Stres, p. 297, and Bajsić, "Marko Kerševan . . . ," p. 315.

6

CHANGING CHRISTIAN PERCEPTIONS OF SOCIALISM AND MARXISM

It is more difficult to find out what the Eastern European Christian views of socialism and Marxism are than the Marxist views of religion and Christianity. This is because the Eastern European Christians have uneven access to the publishing of their ideas. Marxist views can be published in Eastern Europe, though publishing unconventional notions often entails considerable risk to the authors. But Christians have either very limited and circumscribed or no access to the publishing of their views. Christian books are rare, except in East Germany and Poland. Periodical literature is more widely available, especially in Poland, Czechoslovakia, Rumania, and Yugoslavia, but is generally subject either to explicit forms of censorship or to a need to engage in self-censorship. Publishing is not considered a right but a privilege. Privileges can be withdrawn. Therefore most of the Christian literature tends to deal with nonpolitical topics, religious themes designed to bolster the spiritual life of the church. Those articles or books dealing with Christian attitudes toward socialism or Marxism are likely to conform to the official views of the government. The vast majority of Christians are preoccupied with concerns of institutional and personal survival. Little time and psychic energy is left to write on Christian attitudes toward Marxism and socialism beyond general words of praise for government policies, which are endorsed either because of convenience or conviction. Consequently there is a dearth of material on this subject, a dearth which will be reflected in this chapter.

TYPOLOGY OF CHRISTIAN PERCEPTIONS

Five types of perceptions or attitudes toward socialism and Marxism are discernible.

1. All-out rejection of socialism and Marxism.[1]

2. Reluctant acceptance of existence in socialism; little interest in Marxism.

3. Acceptance of Christian existence within socialism; critical engagement with Marxism.

4. Eager acceptance of socialism; minimal criticism of Marxism.

5. Synthesis of Marxism and Christianity.

This spectrum of attitudes is symmetric, but the number of people sharing these types of perceptions is not. The scale is heavily weighted by the preponderate acceptance of the first two options. Extremely few opt for the fifth type. Generally both sides reject this option, but some individuals embrace it. A greater number of Christians can be found in the fourth type than in the third, not only because it is more difficult to practice the third attitude intellectually but because the pressures by the government channels people's thinking in the direction of the fourth type. Type 4 is generally the most favored by the government.

1. ALL-OUT REJECTION OF SOCIALISM AND MARXISM

This was historically the first and for a long time the prevalent approach of Christians. The establishment of socialism was not welcomed. Marxism was anathematized because it was perceived as a system of thought totally contrary to Christianity. Cooperation was considered impossible. Marxism was seen as a diabolical system, usually without examining it beyond the clichés used both by anti-Communists and vulgar Marxists. Marxism was seen as antagonistic to Christian values. Socialism threatened many of the rights and privileges which the churches, especially the large ones, enjoyed in the presocialist systems. Some Christians perceived this as a struggle to the end. One or the other would be destroyed in this monumental struggle between the forces of good and evil. Mutual demonification was the order of the day. Stark conflict characterized this approach. No *modus vivendi* was sought. The pre-Vatican II Roman Catholic Church is the best example of this approach.

No Christian attitudes of this sort surfaced in print because this possibility was withheld by Communists who were unwilling to share their near monopoly over the means of communications which they considered crucial for holding on to power. This attitude is in evidence most clearly in the Christian *émigré* press.[2] This negative attitude toward socialism and Marxism is usually accompanied by attacks on those Christians who have accommodated themselves to the new system. This attitude has been kept aflame by the atrocities committed against Christians, particularly those who were anticommunist, by the communist government. A vigorous anticommunist stand by Christians and a vigorous anti-Christian stand by Marxists keep reinforcing this antagonism. Christian rejection of Marxism generally includes all forms of Marxisms. No differentiation has been attempted between various interpretations of Marxism.

2. RELUCTANT ACCEPTANCE OF EXISTENCE IN SOCIALISM; LITTLE INTEREST IN MARXISM

The Christian attitude consists of regretful acceptance of the churches' continued existence under socialist conditions. Since not much can be done about that fact of life, the adaptation to it consists of attempts to carry on the work of the church as well as possible with little regard for Marxism as a worldview and even less desire to get involved with it beyond the absolutely necessary. The basic pattern is that of two different groups living next to each other with as little interaction as possible.

Three variants of this option are possible. The one, generally characteristic of the Orthodox Churches, consists of the hope that the church will outlive this system as it did so many others. Empires come and go, but the church of Christ keeps going on to the end of history.

The second variant, usually typical of the smaller churches (sociologically more sectarian in attitude), is that no social system is of God. True Christians are pilgrims in a hostile world. Socialism confirms the evils of the world. A Christian needs to live piously and will be given eternal rewards for the suffering in this world.

The third alternative is to attempt to preserve the life of the church as much intact as possible with the hope that some major modifications in the system will occur which will make the existence and mission of the church easier. This variant can be perceived in the Protestant churches in East Germany and more recently among some Roman Catholic hierarchs. These views are not voiced publicly but can be surmised from the general behavior of many Christians, as well as from private conversations. From time to time Christians in this group will point to some Marxist practices which they feel are worthy of supporting. At other times they will resist Marxist policies which they feel are an encroachment on their or other's rights. In general they do not make explicit pronouncements on the value of socialism and do not explore Marxist thought or seek overt contacts with Marxists. For some this means existence in a ghetto; for others it consists of an attitude that having to live in socialism does not mean having to be enthusiastic about it.

3. ACCEPTANCE OF CHRISTIAN EXISTENCE IN SOCIALISM; CRITICAL ENGAGEMENT WITH MARXISM

A growing number of Christians have come to accept that socialism is the system of their country and that it is likely to remain, perhaps with modifications, in the distant future. Some in this group regard socialism as good for their country. Most see some good in it and are not willing to condemn it roundly. They tend to work for the good of the people and are willing to cooperate with Marxists in this task. They realize the interconnectedness of Marxism with the socialist system of their country and have decided to acquaint themselves with Marxist ideology. In Marxism they find some positive and some negative elements. Depending on the political circumstances in their own country, they criticize Marxism, giving support where merited and withholding it where necessary. Usually Christians in this group notice the differences in various interpretations of Marxism and may indicate preferences for the more liberal, humanistic interpretations. Thus "socialism with a human face" is more likely to receive endorsement than Stalinism. In their criticism of Marxism some of this group may be more supportive than others. It is not the degree of support or appreciation of Marxism that distinguishes this group of Christians but their independence in evaluating socialism and Marxism.

Many Marxists are sensitive to criticism and try to discredit this alternative, saying that they are simply different forms of clericalism or anticommunism. Only the humanistic Marxists welcome this Christian stance.

Below are some examples of those whose views can be categorized in this group. Vladimir Truhlar suggested that Christians indeed need to include themselves in the new system, however not as pseudo-Marxists but rather as Christians. They ought to develop humanism from their own sources and contribute to its society, rather than simply follow the Marxist lead in social matters.[3] Some Christians, he thought, had abandoned, for all practical purposes, the distinct Christian contribution. There are many who are tired and resigned. Others follow the path of least resistance. But Christians should make an independent judgment on various social phenomena.

Vereš considers the thought of Marx as the decisive change in modern history, which is one of the sources of the various transitions in the contemporary world and "is a source of hope for an authentically free human future." [4] Therefore Vereš undertook to analyze and evaluate Marx's own thought and its impact on Christian thinking and action.

Archbishop Franić urged young Christians to study the constantly evolving dynamics of Marxism and to enter into a lively exchange on the question of being human.[5] In respect to ways of knowing, Marxists and Christians stand close to one another. Every ideology brings with it some alienations which have to be fought for the sake of the people. But Christian criticism should also take account of the Christian coresponsibility for Marxist failures to implement social justice and equality.[6]

A particularly clear expression of the third option is Jan Lochman, who addressed himself explicitly to this issue:

> But I also find an uncritical acceptance of Marxism without taking into account its variations quite impossible on theological grounds. Certainly, I consider Marxist philosophy to be a relevant and challenging possibility for modern theology, particularly in view of its penetrating and accurate analysis of social conditions. I am also aware of its closeness to the authentic teaching of the Bible. . . . But when I first met this total acceptance of the Marxist position and saw it built into systematic theology in its entirety, I could not accept it. Neither could I accept the Marxist way of thinking, with its unquestioned hypothesis, as suitable for Christian theology.[7]

In his book Lochman proceeded to specify parts of Marxism which he, as a theologian, could not accept uncritically. He mentioned the theory of class struggle, the manipulation of people in Eastern Europe by a ruling elite, the exaggerated expectations regarding the impact of socialization and nationalization of property, and the primacy of economic factors. Lochman considered a meaningful encounter with Marxism impossible if a Christian did not maintain the critical distance, yet appreciated the contribution of Marxism. Lochman, like Vereš, carefully examined Marx's and Marxists' teachings in order to learn from their valid insights and contradict those which he found invalid. This principle he learned from his teacher, Hromádka. Lochman is, however, a bit more clear on saying that it is dangerous for Christianity to relate the gospel too closely to an ideology.[8] A principle of selectivity is needed. In his practical attitude toward socialism Lochman was indeed selective. He supported the "Prague Spring" experiment as a more human and therefore, to a Christian, a more acceptable form of socialism than what preceded it.[9] His decision not to return to Czechoslovakia demonstrated that he was critical of what happened after the events of August 1968. (This is not to imply that those who stayed there might not have been equally critical.)

Hromádka's position was similar in regard to the critical stance toward Marxism where he specified certain Marxist insights in which Christianity challenges communism (e.g. radical historicism, and exclusively social roots of human misery).[10] Yet Hromádka tended to be a more unconditional supporter of the socialist system than most other theologians in this group. He sometimes gave the impression that any socialist order is in the best interest of human beings, regardless of how totalitarian its form may be. In this respect he appears closer to some elements of the fourth Christian perception of socialism.

Another person who seems to straddle the line between the third and fourth variant is the East German Lutheran, Hanspeter Wulff-Woesten. He showed a realistic acceptance of socialism and pointed to some benefits accruing from socialism. The most accepted Christian response to socialism in East Germany, he said, is the one stated by the Federation of Evangelical Churches in the G.D.R.: "We want neither to be a church against nor alongside socialism, but rather a church in the midst of socialism . . . which would accept, with the same freedom of faith, to cooperate fully where in our society human life can be sustained and improved, and also where necessary to help avert danger to human life." [11] This statement, while pledging full support, still leaves room for judgment as to which are the factors sustaining and improving life or averting danger to life. The Federation of Evangelical Churches reserved the right to a critical stance. Wulff-Woesten quietly stated some problems experienced by Christians in socialism but did not criticize Marxist theory.

The degree of enthusiasm in accepting Marxism varies from person to person. The degree of criticism depends both on the amount of leeway available in a particular country and the specific admixture of courage and discretion which the critic displays. Unwillingness to run away from the situation is common to all in this type, as is their willingness to take Marxist theory seriously but critically.

4. EAGER ACCEPTANCE OF SOCIALISM; MINIMAL CRITICISM OF MARXISM

Few Christians started out with a preference for the socialist system. Undoubtedly there were individuals who from the outset had strong antipathies to capitalism and sympathies for socialism. Among the younger Christians there are many who knew no other social system and embraced socialism with little thought as to alternatives. A number of individuals in this group followed the old adage: "If you can't beat them, join them." And, unfortunately, there are some in this group who opted for this type out of opportunism. They sided with the new social system to promote their careers in the church, or even in the government. This group is thus an odd assortment of people with different motivations. It is not always easy to judge the motivations, though, in a few instances, the motives may be clear—and to be regretted.

Two major variants are discernible in this type. One is ideologically motivated; the other is not. In the first variant belong people who have explored Marxist socioeconomic teachings and are enthusiastic about them. Though they do not agree with Marxist metaphysics, they agree with the socialist platform. In their eyes socialism is the best of existing systems. Being the most humane of all systems, it is seen as the most "Christian" of all systems. Christian values are discernible in the system and ought to be selflessly promoted by Christians.

The other variant is somewhat less ideological. On practical grounds, these Christians find many things of value in their socialist country. Whether for reasons of patriotism or for a lack of practical alternatives they have decided to give full support to the building of socialism in their country.

The approach to Marxism also differs according to these two variants. The first finds many positive elements in Marxism and is afraid to criticize the negative elements lest the total Marxist ideology, which they perceive as progressive, suffer rejection. Reactionaries may misuse such criticism. In the name of solidarity disagreements are not made public. This leads to suspension of criticism. Those of the second variant are ideologically more indifferent. They conclude that Marxism and Christianity are totally different worldviews, which cannot be reconciled. But socialism can be supported by people who are not Marxist. For pragmatic reasons of socialist advancement, Marxism is not being criticized by them, though they may vaguely reiterate the incompatibility of Marxism and Christianity.

The term which has become popular in East Germany by proponents of this perception of socialism is *partisanship*. The East German proponents of this type are most eloquent in their view that a Christian cannot remain neutral in the great struggle between social systems. Capitalism is being identified by them with imperialism, warmongering, exploitation, colonialism, racism, inequality, misuse of natural resources, and so forth. Socialism aims to provide humane alternatives to capitalism. These two are locked in mortal combat. No reconciliation can take place; convergence is impossible.[12] The duty of the Christian is to stand against evil, i.e. capitalism. One must not hedge on account of certain imperfections in socialism. If one is for peace, progress, equality, and justice, one must support socialism in the spirit of solidarity. Lukewarm support will not do.

In East Germany the Christian Democratic Union considers its goal the implementation and support of the decisions of the Socialist Unity Party, both in its general direction and in respect to concrete measures. Gerald Götting, leader of the C.D.U., holder of high government positions, and member of the parliament, praised the agrarian reform of 1945 and the Christian support for it. He urged Christians to support the decisions of the Ninth Party Congress of the Socialist Unity Party to intensify farm production and to fulfill, or better yet to overfulfill, the Five Year Plan.[13]

Götz Bickelhaupt, a Lutheran pastor, pointed to the process by which Christians undertook to support socialism.

Many Christians of our country found the way to liberated and liberating actions naturally not on account of theological reflections. They followed the path of active participation in the building and developing of the socialist society, simply because the way was open for them within the realm of this social order. They accepted the alliance with the leading force of socialism, the working class, because it was offered to them, and was shaped through cooperation in the National Front.[14]

Bickelhaupt suggested that this path was much more effective than the "institutionalized continuous reflection," which is his way of criticizing the top church leadership for their reluctance to wholeheartedly accept this fourth variant. Realizing the opposition to this variant, Bickelhaupt proceeded:

The enemies of socialism reproached and continue to reproach those who selected the path of practical engagement by charging them with collaboration. The repetition of this charge does not change things but remains what it always was—a legitimate child of anti-communism. They neglect to see that those who, having come to this position from a non-Marxist position, engaged themselves, having had no other alternative after the experience with Fascism, in order to prove themselves. Their practical pledge was accompanied by spiritual discussions, which represent on the whole an eminent achievement in overcoming the past and directing the future.[15]

Bickelhaupt complained that a great rift appeared between these socially engaged Christians and their churches. These Christians expected to hear a liberating and supportive word from their churches, but those who should have come forth with liberating theological reflections failed to do so. He expressed hope that theological support will be forthcoming.

Peter Weiss, another Lutheran pastor, accused those who advocate greater neutrality rather than partisanship for socialism as being bound to the bourgeois social order in order to hide their motives and to hide class antagonisms.[16] He charged that the churches oppose partisanship only when it is directed toward the left, toward socialism, but not when the sympathies are directed toward the right, the conservative forces. The failure of neutral positions, according to Weiss, can best be attested by the *coup d'etat* in Chile.

A scientifically examined and logically formulated political direction which provides an optimal and reasonable social order for the well being of all who live on this earth, must receive Christian support, even if it is determined by non-Christians. This is especially true when it is evident that the so called

"Christian" politics of the bourgeois social order, having followed unreasonable goals, led to immeasurable suffering and misery for the nations of the world.

With this supposition there can be for Christians and their pastors only an unqualified "yes" for socialism, a "yes" which urges the concrete partisanship for the policy of those states, which are building the future world of tomorrow according to the esteemed principles of the Marxist-Leninist social teachings.[17]

Gottfried Biermann specified what partisanship means in the context of a socialist society.

After the victory of the socialist revolution, partisanship means active participation in the changed form of class struggle during the period of transition from capitalism to socialism. It is struggle against the resisting forces and traditions of the old society and the influence of other capitalist states; and at the same time it is the struggle *for* the unity and strengthening of the socialist community of nations as well as support for the working class and all peace loving forces in capitalist states. On the basis of Leninist principles of peaceful co-existence, socialist states are continually trying to humanize the class struggle.

Lastly, partisanship is shown by recognizing the leadership role of the party of the working class, which is consciously based on scientific communism and has at its disposal the revolutionary theory for carrying out the socialist revolution and creating the developed socialist society.[18]

Biermann asserted that Christians cannot afford anymore to uphold class positions which are unjustified by the gospels. "There is no so called third way." [19] Christianity cannot posit a supposed "Christian social theory" over or against the scientific knowledge of Communists. No distinction must be made by Christians between the support of "the humanist aims of socialism and the ideologically determined partisanship of the class struggle." [20]

A large amount of material was published supporting this variant, because it follows the official communist position of their own countries. Those who support this variant are given the opportunity to disseminate their views, while others who do not share this view are rarely allowed to communicate.

A similar position toward Marxism is evident among Hungarian Protestants. Béla Harmáti, a Lutheran professor of theology from Budapest, wrote, "It is significant for the present Hungarian situation that there are many who agree with Marxism on economic or social questions but who also believe in a Christian way." [21] Harmáti then wrote, "The socialist solution suggested by Marxism (i.e. cooperation instead of competition, political power and control of the means of production by the workers, etc.) is more suitable for the Christian ethic than the capitalist system." [22] "We support socialism not out of 'faith,' but in the perspective of humanism and common sense." [23]

The communiques of the various assemblies and committees of the Christian Peace Conference likewise show a fairly unqualified endorsement of socialist positions on world issues as put forth by the officials of their governments. The decision that socialism is the best of all options underlies these statements. They have been provided with a suitable Christian rationale. Such Christian rationale is one of the legitimate options which Christians have in interpreting their spiritual heritage. What is upsetting to those Christians who do not share this variant is not so much the fact that some Christians take this position, but the vehemence with which it is expressed and the lack of critical distance by its protagonists. The novelty of this option, coupled with the more common Christian antagonism to socialism, perhaps compels representatives of this variant to offer such unqualified support of socialism and to raise only rarely some mild questions regarding the correctness of the Marxist positions. They perceive that the major contemporary rift is not between Christians and non-Christians but between antagonistic classes. Hence a Christian needs to take an antagonistic position toward another Christian who supports the ruling class and side with a Marxist who supports the working class. This group scales down the universal mythical conflict between good and evil to the global conflict between classes and more concretely between socialist countries, representing the interest of the international working class, and the capitalist countries, which incarnate the devilish exploitation over the working class on an international scale.

5. SYNTHESIS OF MARXISM AND CHRISTIANITY

Synthesizing Christianity and Marxism usually means the affirmation of a belief in God and other Christian doctrines (one might call it Christian metaphysics) and the acceptance of the Marxist socioeconomic and related theories and practical strategies. These Christians have concluded that dialectical materialism is not of the essence of Marxism. Hence theism is not seen as contradictory to Marxism. Most people who travel this road will say that their Christian social concern led them to Marxism, in which they recognized the proper, scientifically founded, tool for the achievement of those goals inspired by their Christianity. Some, but not all of these Marxist Christians or Christian Marxists, realize the intellectual difficulty in maintaining this position with integrity. Others come to accept the synthesis rather naively and are adopting it perhaps as only a way station on their road either from Christianity to Marxism or vice versa.

This option is more popular in the West, particularly in Latin America and the Mediterranean area. Giulio Girardi of Italy can be cited as a thoughtful representative. Very few Eastern European Christians favor this option. As noted above, in the section on the dialogue, warnings against synthesizing have been made repeatedly. Harmáti wrote, "We are against any kind of mixtures; 'Christian Marxism' or 'Marxist Christianity' does not exist. . . . The Marxists themselves do not approve of such a mixture." [24] Harmáti pointed out that the various "theologies of liberation" in Latin America which mix theology and Marxism are opposed by Hungarian Lutherans. Pope John Paul II also seems to reject this as a desirable alternative.

Despite the rather categorical rejection of synthesis by most authors, there are some who will at least grant the possibility of such synthesis. Šagi-Bunić, for instance, showed that in the course of church history syntheses took place which were originally unacceptable to Christians. The Cappadocian Fathers said that Aristotle was unsuitable to Christian theology, but Thomas Aquinas showed otherwise. "So, I do not know whether that can happen tomorrow with Marx—as strange as it may sound," concluded Šagi-Bunić. [25] Catholics believe that all which is good comes from God and is somehow connected. Perhaps things will be viewed very differently in the future when Christianity and Marxism cease to be enemies. Šagi-Bunić saw no problem with a Christian's favoring the Yugoslav self-managing type of socialism, but he perceived difficulties with synthesizing Stalinism. [26]

This process of uniting the views has been attempted, at least for a short time, by a few younger Yugoslav Catholics, but they complained that they were consequently mistrusted by both sides. [27] For some of them embracing faith in God in the contemporary world was not an easy task, yet they did it despite their general commitment to socialism. For a while the question surfaced as to whether the Yugoslav Communist party, which consistently banned theists from joining its membership, should start accepting open Christians. This was resolutely rejected, although the influence of this practice in the Italian Communist Party was moderately strong.

The basic question for the synthesizers is whether Marxism is integrally related to atheism. If it is not, their position could be viable. If it is, then their position is not viable. This question has not been decided with finality. The preponderate answer, however, seems to be that Marxism and atheism are inseparable.[28] For the time being this is the prevailing view in Eastern Europe, fairly ruling out this variant.

EFFECT ON DIALOGUE

How a Christian perceives Marxism has a significant influence on that person's participation in dialogue. The all-out rejection of Marxism (Type 1) is clearly not conducive to dialogue. Negotiation may be attempted, but dialogue could not. Neither is the opposite end of the spectrum, the synthesizing of the two (Type 5), particularly conducive to dialogue. Christian Marxists or Marxist Christians may prove to be, in rare instances, a factor in an internal Marxist or internal Christian dialogue and, even more rarely, in a Christian-Marxist dialogue. Currently, however, neither side is comfortable with people opting for this type.

Those reluctantly accepting socialism and showing little interest in Marxist views (Type 2) are also more apt to negotiate than dialogue with Marxists, primarily because of the absence of ideological interest. However, dialogue limited to practical matters may prove to be an option to Christians holding this position. Christians eagerly accepting socialism and minimally critical of Marxism (Type 4) would tend to opt for cooperation rather than dialogue. Limited dialogue on practical matters is an option for them. The lack of critical distance makes these Christians better followers than partners. Leaders and followers do not dialogue, at least not much.

Those Christians who accept their existence in the midst of socialism yet maintain a critical posture toward both socialism and Marxism (Type 3) are the only group which is capable of pursuing a genuine dialogue embracing theory and practice, as defined in Chapter 2. Their acceptance of socialism is often regarded by Marxist partners as a prerequisite for dialogue. However, while Marxists would prefer Christians to make this acceptance a permanent commitment, this preference does not have to be necessarily followed by Christians. Surely Christians must accept the fact of socialism rather than live in a ghetto. But in the long run, Christians ought to be free enough to work for their preference in socioeconomic systems. The particular mode in which socialism is currently practiced may be unacceptable to Christians, without ruling them out as partners in dialogue. An example of this type of posture may be found among the members of the Catholic group Znak in Poland, who have, despite their unwillingness to give unqualified support to socialism, been able and willing to engage in dialogue with Marxists. An interest in Marxist teachings, an appreciation of its content and role and impact on socialism, perhaps even a limited acceptance of some Marxist insights are conditions of a good dialogue, but so is the willingness to differentiate Christianity and Marxism. Otherwise, dialogue will dwindle into monologue. An authentic Marxist will not shy away from a critical Christian; a dogmatic Marxist probably would.

In conclusion, a most useful dialogue can be carried out if the Christian partner holds the position of critical engagement with Marxism, while the Marxist partner abstains from abstract condemnations of religion but makes concrete judgments on the role of religion and Christianity in human progress. These two partners can make the optimal psychological and philosophical-theological and practical space for beneficial dialogue. The mutual perception of the two partners greatly affects the ability of the partners to dialogue about other matters as well as about their mutual relationships. The matters of common concern to Christians and Marxists engaged in dialogue will be discussed in the following chapter.

Notes

1. For the purpose of this presentation socialism is used to designate the socioeconomic system of public ownership of the means of production, while Marxism designates the system of thought undergirding the social system.
2. E.g. *Hungarian Reformed News* (New York), No. 3 (March 1979). *Református Hirek* in Hungarian. Also see writings of Richard Wurmbrand, a Lutheran pastor formerly from Rumania and Haralan Popov, a Pentecostal pastor formerly from Bulgaria.
3. Interview with Truhlar, November 15, 1975 in Ljubljana.
4. Vereš, p. 13. Transl. by Mojzes.
5. Franić, p. 14.
6. *Ibid.*, p. 136.
7. Lochman, *Encountering Marx*, p. 14.
8. *Ibid.*, p. 15.

9. Lochman, "Kirche und Erneuerung der Gesellschaft," p. 122. Also *Church in a Marxist Society*, pp. 105-110.

10. Hromádka, *Theology Between Yesterday and Tomorrow* (Philadelphia: Westminster Press, 1957), pp. 78-87.

11. Wulff-Woesten, "The Mandate of the Christian Community in the Socialist Society of the German Democratic Republic: 'Living Through the Word,' " in *The Encounter of the Church with Movements of Social Change in Various Cultural Contexts* (Geneva: Study Department, Lutheran World Federation, 1977), p. 35. Abbreviated hereafter to *ECMSCVCC*.

12. Gerhard Bassarak, "Konvergenztheorie in der Theologie?" in *Christen und Revolution: Konvergenz und Theologie* (Cologne: Pahl-Rugenstein Verlag, 1971), pp. 15 ff.

13. Götting, "30 Jahre demokratische Bodenreform," in *Blick in unsere Presse* (1975), pp. 14-18.

14. Bickelhaupt, "Zu Freiheit befreit," in *ibid.*, p. 28. Transl. by Mojzes.

15. *Ibid.*

16. Weiss, "Parteinahme für den Sozialismus," in *ibid.*, p. 35.

17. *Ibid.* Transl. by Mojzes.

18. Biermann, "Reconciliation and Partisanship in Class Struggle," in *ECMSCVCC*, p. 26.

19. *Ibid.*, p. 28.

20. *Ibid.*

21. Harmáti, "The Encounter of the Church with Marxism in Hungary," in *ibid.*, p. 75.

22. *Ibid.*, p. 74.

23. *Ibid.*, p. 76.

24. *Ibid.*

25. Šagi-Bunić in "Religija i savremeno društvo," in *Kultura*, Nos. 13-14 (1971), p. 288.

26. *Ibid.*, p. 291.

27. Interview with Branko Lukšić, November 17, 1975, in Split.

28. Stanisław Kowalczyk, "Classical Marxist Philosophers and the Problem of Atheism," in *Bolletino del segretariato per i non credenti* (Vatican), Vol. 10, No. 4 (December 1975), p. 170.

7

MAJOR ISSUES
IN THE DIALOGUE

Almost any topic could become the subject matter of the dialogue. Neither Christians nor Marxists have any "forbidden spheres." This is not to say that all issues are of equal interest or importance. Nor is it to say that all issues can be or have been discussed. Since there has been no sustained, systematically planned dialogue, no single topic has been covered thoroughly. The characteristic of the dialogue is its incompleteness, its sketchy, spontaneous nature. Only in a few instances have partners addressed the same issue at the same time. Hence it is impossible to give a systematic treatment of issues approached.

THE SCOPE OF ISSUES

Homo sum, nihil humani a me alienum puto ("I am a human; nothing human is alien to me"). One might say that this proverb truly signifies the possible scope of the dialogue. But it signifies more than that. It also signifies the basic reason and the basic issue of dialogue.

Many people may expect that the reason for the Christian-Marxist dialogue is that each partner has an ultimate concern or value which propels him or her into interaction with the other. A careful investigation fails to substantiate this expectation, although Jan Lochman maintains that "the very genius of Christianity and Marxism moves toward and inspires dialogue." [1] In view of the long waiting for the dialogue to commence and the general reluctance of both Marxists and Christians to engage in it, Lochman's position is questionable. But were Lochman's proposition stated more negatively, one might agree that nothing in Christianity or Marxism can totally prevent the dialogue.

The reason for the Christian-Marxist dialogue ought to be sought in the practical coexistence of people who designate themselves Christians or Marxists but who are human first, and only secondarily Marxists or Christians. These people, of different convictions, were brought together by history. They inhabit the same land; they dwell next to each other. Their first reaction was antagonism toward each other. Then they sought to cooperate on practical goals. Before too long they realized that they do have a basic common concern—the concern for human beings. Lochman pointed out their commonality in respect to their attempt to humanize, to take history seriously, and to be future-directed." [2]

Recognizing the centrality of one another's humanity prevailed over the artificial imposition of the ideologized human being. Dialogue occurred not in order to find some truths about people but in order to benefit people. Neither did dialogue come into being because of the existence of some common theoretical postulate(though such postulates can be found) but because of life together and because of good will. Dialogue happened because there are differences in theory, but it is actually based on the recognition that neither the designation "Christian" nor the designation "Marxist" is of the essence of humanity. The human quality is joint. It leads to the need to dialogue about differences. Bajsić pointed out that both sides had to develop a more profound consciousness of what it means to be human for the dialogue to take place.[3] Trust in human beings is the fountain of the dialogue.

After the ideology of the other group was initially rejected so emphatically, it was followed by the awareness of the common humanity. Then it was possible to proceed to the next step, which was to see that the other side had some insights worthy of admiration. This level is where the vast majority of Eastern European protagonists of the dialogue find themselves today. It is a very important advance because it presupposes the attempt to familiarize themselves first with the other's tradition before they can sort out those insights which they find most valuable. This process is almost always accompanied with "rethinking and rediscovery of one's own creative possibilities." [4]

These concerns, as well as the contextual adversities which faced those interested in the dialogue, consumed nearly all the energies of the dialogue partners. This meant, however, that no full-fledged dialogue developed on *any* other topic. Often one author worked on one topic but not on others. Most of the partners in dialogue worked on different, sometimes related, sometimes unrelated topics. Almost never was there a case where Christians and Marxists consistently and cumulatively worked on the same topic. Occasionally, for instance at the Paulus-Gesellschaft Congresses and the Peace Symposia, a common topic was addressed from the two perspectives but, even here, the preparations took place in the absence of knowing what the other partners were going to contribute. Almost never was there a follow-up to bring about a progression of ideas based on the previous interplay. Most frequently a Marxist or a Christian thinker approached a given topic dialogically by taking into account the thinking of some people from the other group and emphasizing their positive contributions. (The most comprehensive responses to the themes of the Christian faith was that of Machovec.) Sometimes this type of a gesture would be acknowledged and praised by individuals from the other group.

The conclusion is inescapable that the stage of consistent give-and-take has not been reached in Eastern Europe. But a sense of mutual responsibility to each other and to how one views the other has been developed by many partners in dialogue.

The fundamental and methodological questions which received most clarification are 1) the question of the future of dialogue (covered in Chapter 4), and 2) the reassessment of each other (covered in Chapters 5-6).

SEARCH FOR THEMES

A number of contributors searched for themes for the dialogue that would be most useful for common welfare. Suggestions ranged from very generalized proposals to more detailed enumerations. Tomo Vereš approached the issue of themes from the perspective of what may be the most useful contributions each could make to the other. He thought that the Marxists should remind Christians of the historical dimension and praxis of human beings, while Christians should raise, for the benefit of Marxists, the issues of subjectivity, authentic transcendence, and the fundamental border situations (e.g. the existential difference between ideas and reality, the problems of hurt, death, and fear).[5] Somewhat similar is Jakov Jukić's suggestion that Christianity brings to the dialogue a deep and gentle sensitivity for human suffering, a sense of community, hope against attacks of depression and pessimism, and attitudes of universalism and ecumenism. Marxists should emphasize the virtue of impatience, a sense of dedication to the world and understanding of it, and concentration upon concrete issues.[6] Both should display an optimistic trust in people, attempt to actualize morality in concrete historical and social dimensions, and refuse to accept the balance of fear and the arms race, and stimulate the participation of all in building a more just and humane world.[7]

Archbishop Franić discussed the issue of themes at length. He enumerated the following:

1. the metaphysical structure of being
2. gnoseology (the ways of knowing)
3. the human being or questions of humanism
4. morality and freedom
5. the question of religiosity
6. nationalism and internationalism
7. theology and socialism
8. theology and various types of revolutions, and others.[8]

Franić illustrated the feasibility of these dialogues by pointing out the already existing Yugoslav Marxist inquiries into them.

András Szennay likewise devoted attention to the search for appropriate themes. He emphasized the importance of the philosophical-theological dialogue by saying that the recognition and disclosure of basic truths is a human, and therefore a joint Christian and Marxist, responsibility. To him the existential question of the meaning of life is basic. People have the right to look for truth in this issue.[9] There are many basic truths which need to be explored in the dialogue, e.g., the meaning of good and bad; the "truth" of love, indifference, and hate; the social value of human consolation; joy; suffering; and the problems of family life. No one has the right to neglect those questions or to claim to have the sole answer. Even if validity is claimed for the answers, it is not sure that the answers have been properly expressed and communicated.[10]

Recently, according to Szennay, many people, especially Marxists, have contributed to the study of society and the ways of consciously changing it. But the questions concerning the relationship of the individual to the whole have tended to be neglected. Individuals have been overlooked for the sake of the larger social groups.[11] Szennay considered impatience with theoretical questions in order to proceed with practical issues inadvisable. Both Christians and Marxists consider themselves humanistic, and for humanists there is nothing that is truly human which can be left out. Hence neither basic existential problems nor the exploration of concrete issues can be bypassed. The issue of religious freedom is neither the first nor the central theme from a Christian perspective. Basic human rights, freedoms, and spiritual values are the central concern for Christians in dialogue.[12] A very large number of practical questions can be approached. It is advisable that Christians and Marxists listen to the questions of the younger generation in deciding which of these issues should have priority on their agenda. Dialogue about each other, the recognition of the human being as the center, and everything which gives an inner fulfillment can become the common task and the crucial point of dialogue.[13] The Christian seeks a true faith in God and a life that corresponds to this faith. The Marxist seeks a new social and political order. Such heterogeneous goals need not impede dialogue. The form of the economic and social order are of import but not of primacy for the Christian faith. A believing Christian cares for humans and, through humans, seeks to serve God. In this task the believer finds common concerns with the Marxists.

Machovec observed that politically there are many urgent topics for the dialogue which vary from place to place and time to time. Philosophically the question of theism and atheism is not a great obstacle. He pointed out "how difficult it is in fact to make any real progress without secretly reviving the demons of the 'past' in some new guise." [14] The thinking Marxist can see that Christianity has already confronted some of the issues which face Marxists and that it has something to offer those who attempt to construct a society. Thus dialogue can begin with those experiences. On the other hand, Christians can benefit by seeing not only the failures of Marxism but even more so those successes which caused profound changes in contemporary societies in Eastern Europe.[15]

Other Marxists and Christians have suggested an almost

endless number of themes. Immanence and transcendence, peace, justice, the future, the meaning of history, ethics and morality, property, alienation and sin, God and atheism, revolution and reconciliation, responsibility to one another and to the world, creativity and freedom, Jesus and Marx and other great Christian and Marxist figures, and human crisis situations are among the profusion of themes suggested as suitable for dialogue. The vast majority of these themes, however, have not yet been the subject of dialogue. In fact, only a few of them received even cursory attention. It is evident that Christians and Marxists are not likely ever to exhaust the supply of themes. No absolute contradiction exists which would prevent additional elucidation in dialogue. Partners in dialogue need not depart from their authentic positions by exploring together their basic concerns. As Machovec put it,

> One cannot say that the less someone is a Marxist, the more he will be inclined toward Christianity. The contrary is true. The more deeply and rigorously a Marxist understands himself and the vastness of the tasks which lie ahead and therefore the more he is a Marxist, the more will he be able to learn from the Judeo-Christian tradition and to welcome Christians as potential allies and brothers.[16]

The same remarks can be applied to Christians.

CONCERN FOR THE HUMAN BEING

The theme which received most joint attention is humanism, which is the concern for the well-being of people and the promotion of those values which make a person human. For Marxists the human being is the highest being which needs to be reckoned with. For Christians the human being is not the highest, yet nevertheless human beings and values are upheld as being of utmost importance. Not only do Christians and Marxists share a common concern for human beings, but since Marxism arose out of the Christian context, they even tend to shape their questions and raise their issues in a similar vein. Both seek to respond to dehumanizing factors in order to diminish them or eliminate them. For both of them self-giving love for others is the greatest human excellence.

Not all Marxists will grant that Christianity, despite its theocentrism, represents a form of humanism. The Polish Marxist Dionize Tanalski in his book *Katolicyzm: Problemy filozofii człowieka,* for instance, equated Catholicism with theocentrism and Marxism with anthropocentrism, and concluded that Marxism is humanistic while Catholicism is not.[17] Tanalski represents the conventional Marxist view, which is neither tenable nor followed by all Marxists. This is especially true of the Marxists who have been involved in dialogue, for they have all come to hold that Christians can be humanists though they are theocentric. Naturally these Marxists consider Marxist humanism to be more pure and more excellent, since they regard it to be less burdened with the notion of human dependency than the Christian who regards humanity contingent upon God. The dialogical attitude on the issue of humanism was aptly stated by Bishop József Cserháti:

> Why shouldn't we Christians acknowledge, and add to our image of Christian man, the values found in the Marxist image of man and the structures given in socialism which mean progress and advancement? In the same way, we think, the gospel and its teachings have a lot to say to open-minded Marxists and atheists.[18]

Adam Schaff was one of the first Marxists willingly to share with Christians the Marxist concept of the human being in a dialogical setting. According to Schaff the concept of the human being is the crux of all philosophical studies, but it is the goal rather than the starting point. Only after other problems have been studied can one arrive at a synthetic view of the human being.[19] The ontological status of the human being is clear in Marxism. The human being is part of nature and society. As a natural societal whole the human being needs no additional factors beside the objective reality in order to be understood. The Marxist view of the human being always starts with the concrete human being independent of any other worldly components or influence. The concrete human being is the center of all socialist thought and practice. Each concrete human develops in concrete human surroundings, in specific circumstances of production. The human being is not merely related to society, but is the product of society.[20]

Yet the human being also has an element of autonomy. This autonomy comes from work, from praxis. Through praxis human beings change objective reality and thereby also change the self. Making a thing also involves self-making or self-creation.[21] Thus a human being is the product of his or her own deeds as well.

Schaff maintained that the Marxist view of the human being includes also a theory of personality or a theory of individuality, but this theory is not yet developed.[22] Personality is also socially determined, which means that it is not given but is always becoming, always self-created. This is merely the genesis of personality. In its totality the human being is unique, irreproducible, and incomparable. Marxism implies, but has not claimed explicitly, that the total human being is a value that cannot be repeated and is lost through death.[23] Each person builds a world for herself or himself which is destroyed by death.

Schaff expressed the view that Marxism has an underdeveloped theory of personality because Marxism pushed aside the questions of human individuality in favor of the problems of a mass movement. So far Marxism tended only to criticize idealistic theories of personality, but the positive work is yet to be done. This task is of great importance in order for Marxism to have a more well-rounded view of the human being.[24]

Milan Průcha also attempted to elucidate the Marxist concept of the human being. He stated that the human being is a contradictory being, neither a foreigner to this world nor its supreme purpose. The human being is both rooted in the world and yet distant from it, alienated yet related.[25]

Many discussions outside and within socialism are carried on regarding humanism, but, in fact, the problems of human beings have not been adequately dealt with. The particularly vital question in socialism is how to prevent the neglect of the human dimension, which has taken place thus far in socialism.[26] According to Průcha the crisis of contemporary humanism, both Christian and Marxist, is the "anthropologism," the uncritical acceptance of the human being as the starting point of philosophical inquiry. A human being has the ability to transcend the daily problems by asking about the meaning of his or her life, the meaning of the world, of order and of one's own relationship to that order.[27]

The force which enables people to raise questions about the meaning of life does not merely stem from the subjective human ability to do so, but it is also an element of the totality of concrete existence, an objective quality attached to the relativity of each individual. That transcendent force is an expression of the concrete essence of being, which is tied, inseparably, to the relativity of each individual. The presence and reality of existence which is increasingly accompanied by its partiality and complexity give proof of the real existence of meaning in all its limitation and incompleteness. It also shows the ambivalence of all substances and the lasting absence of a fixed system of order. Therefore the metaphysical is not a secondary and abstract complement of the real world, but is rather the radically real manner in which all substance exists as well as the *milieu* in which it exists.[28] The human is not an abstraction or an essence residing in an individual, but each individual has at her or his disposal many values. The scale by which those values are arranged is influenced by each person. Self-preservation is not necessarily the highest value according to Marxism, stated Průcha.[29] Not only material but intellectual, moral, and aesthetic values are being created in the social context in which the concrete human being lives. Since a human being is a "copious amalgam of specificially human needs," [30] each one needs transcendence, which is the presupposition of knowing an absolute to which all of social life and immanent reality is subordinated.[31] Rather than repeating the standard Marxist request that theologians should eliminate the metaphysical, Průcha concluded with the surprising challenge to theologians not to mask the metaphysical.

Machovec stressed the need for Marxism to take the questions of the meaning of human existence seriously, despite the lack of such attention on the part of Marx. If for no other reason, this would be necessary due to the Marxist atheist abandonment of God concepts, which necessitates coming to grips with the question of human mystery.[32] The postrevolutionary Communist must ask the question of the meaning of life or else communism has no future. The more the material questions of existence are solved, the greater should be the insistence to humanize this life. Thus Marxism needs to consciously appropriate all humanistic values, including those of the Judeo-Christian tradition.[33] There has to be a strong relationship between humanism and a vital social organization; all the rest is either organized egoism or organized barbarism.[34] The crucial question for the dialogue, then, is, What is the human being? and, How can Marxists and Christians really, not just illusorily, help people? Christianity and Marxism share in the wider task of humanization, in the quest of what can become of the human being, what is of help to people.[35]

Hromádka concurred that the question of human beings is the vortex of the dialogue. "Yes, it is man who matters. *But what is man?* Where lies his fundamental nature and destiny? This is where the believing Christian and the convinced communist (or Marxist in general) encounter each other." [36] Hromádka believed that socialism is the endeavor which can best bring about human freedom, equality, dignity, and destiny. Christianity equally aims at benefiting people, since the gospel proclaims that God came to where people are living, struggling, working, suffering, and dying.[37]

> The Gospel reminds us constantly that we cannot believe in God if we do not see man before us, that we cannot love God without loving man and that the actual meaning of faith is the liberation of man from his own Ego, for service, for brotherly love, and for full solidarity with people in their sin and suffering, humility and struggle for a new life. . . . Christians themselves often distorted the true teaching of the Gospel, with their spiritual egoism and false longings for heavenly bliss after death. The real and mighty message about the Kingdom of God and eternal life is a message that God wishes to rule here in this world in truth and justice, in love and forgiveness. Eternal life is the victory of God here among us. Whoever has believed in Jesus of Nazareth has eternal life here, it is here that he is freed, freed from his own ego and from fear of men, it is here that he can, with joy and hope, perform his tasks and fulfill his destiny.[38]

In this dialogue for the sake of humanity both Christians and Marxists need to liberate themselves from stereotypes about each other and from petrified formulas which burden both movements. Christians should long for Communists to be true and enthusiastic creators of their vision, building with passion the new order, which is to be characterized by pure human relationships. Christians likewise ought to intervene in history and stir the conscience of people, which will have revolutionary effects.[39] In dialogue both could understand human beings and give assistance to people to fulfill themselves. Marxists have helped Christians to realize that it is not enough to observe and explain people, but that one must decisively enter into people's practical relationships in order to effect changes for the better.[40] Christians can help Marxists to an understanding of the true depths of human experiences of good and evil, some of which run deeper than socioeconomic conditioning. The new society itself will bring about problems which will need to be dealt with and about which Christians have helpful insights.[41] Christians and Marxists are not to be seen as competitors seeking to weaken one another's witness, nor as copying one another's answers, but as joint seekers to remedy human problems and raise the prospect of a happier future.

Lochman concurred that humanization is a common concern for Christians and Marxists, and that a broad concensus exists between the two. There is agreement 1) that human beings are social creatures, 2) that history is to be taken seriously, and 3) that thinking is to be future-directed.[42] This means that human beings must not be concerned only about themselves but must care for the poor and oppressed and engage in building more just social structures than exist today. Human beings are not what they are but what they are not yet—what they can become. Christians and Marxists are not in agreement as to the future, and there are serious tensions among them, including their differences in regard to the question of God and the transcendence of grace. Christians need to testify to Marxists on their insights into the human conditions and to contribute distinctly to human development.[43]

Lochman maintained that the dialogue between Christians and Marxists became more meaningful after Marxists abandoned their singular preoccupation with structural problems and started paying attention to the meaning of human life. Marxism seeks to abolish the human bonds of estrangement through the abolition of private property in order for work to become again a liberating "creative, spontaneous unfolding of human competence and potential." [44] For Christians the most challenging of Marxist insights are the Marxist initiative to place the problems of human beings into the foreground and its emphasis on the importance of labor, of society, and of history, as well as the seriousness of human alienation in contemporary society. The place of labor in human history could become a particularly fruitful subject for the dialogue. From the Christian perspective, according to Lochman, work is not the justification of being human, though it is a right of each person.[45] Justification by work tends to make idols of human achievements and leads to new forms of alienation in socialism, as it has similarly led to loss of grace in the past.

Emil Fuchs, the late Protestant theologian from Leipzig, East Germany's most notorious fellow traveler and a founder of religious socialism, concluded that Christianity has not really promoted the whole human being, as the encounter with Marxism pointed out. Marxism helps Christianity by showing that there are certain social roots of unholiness which rob people of their creativity.[46] Christianity had exempted certain areas of human life from its area of concern, despite Jesus Christ's concern for the whole person. Christians must answer the issues raised by Karl Marx in the context of work in society. This does not mean that a Christian should appropriate Marxist answers, but it means that a Christian must study and take Marxism seriously. Christians can cooperate with Marxists against all things which deprive people of their complete humanity.[47]

The Catholic theologian Mijo Škvorc pointed out in his public dialogue with Branko Bošnjak in Zagreb, Yugoslavia, that perceptions about the human enigmas constitute the cornerstone of dialogue. If the two do not have some common positions in regard to human interests, there is no sense in dialoguing.[48] Škvorc suggested that the Christian view is that the human being does not suffer the limitations of disappearance into a meaningless nothing after death, but always remains *someone*. Škvorc pointed out that each person is the key to his or her own secret, freedom, thought, responsibility, and happiness. Each person is the carrier of being, infused with the desire to love, to live, and to be eternal.[49] Despite all stumbling, tragedy, betrayal, defeats, and misgivings, there are victories. Life is an incline leading to higher thought and meaning. Humans are, but they are also becoming more than what they are, thereby infinitely surpassing themselves with mind, heart, and willpower. In this life one has to come to grips both with the entrance into life as well as the exit. In this life one searches for values, the only justification for existence.[50] To erase these values is to erase life. Thus people search for the proper hierarchy of values, for truth. Those values that are impermanent and not of service to people are not truly values. Insofar as Marxism defends human values and wants to save human beings from threats to their values, Christians can support Marxist efforts.[51]

It is interesting to note that Bošnjak did not at once reply to Škvorc's comments about human beings but challenged him first on the issue of the meaning of God. Later, in the course of the dialogue, he did turn to the question of human beings and agreed that the dialogue is of meaning only if it is carried out for the purpose of helping human beings, especially in respect to the question of purpose or meaning. While denying the existence of an objective meaning for human being imparted by the cosmos, Bošnjak suggested that meaning is to be found in the development of logos, of humanism, of the development of each person as a true human being.[52] There is no inherent teleology. The tragedy of the human being is the awareness of mortality.

While Bošnjak did not make a significant Marxist contribution to the concept of human being in this particular dialogue setting, he did so in a number of his writings. He contended that by nature people are neither philosophical nor religious beings. Religion cannot discover the meaning of life but can affirm it. Philosophy, on the other hand, explains the tragedy of the human cognizance of mortality, for which religion offers consolation. Those who overcome death with the aid of philosophy do not need religion. The greatest mystery is that human beings do not know why something is and something is not. The human being is alone and remains alone in the universe. The question "why?" can only be answered, "for nothing."[53]

Bošnjak affirmed that human beings come into being, are, and will be. But they do not know from whence they come or where they are going. The human being ultimately has no other reason but to be. From this follows that people are for themselves and must take everything upon themselves.[54] Marxism cannot go beyond the concept of being. Humans are *causa sui* beings out of nature and beings in nature. Nothing else. The Marxist notion of being and the eschatological vision of totality provide the common basis from which Marxists and Christians should seek to answer the question of meaning of existence and activity, the common reality of life.[55] Christian and Marxist humanism differ in respect to the affirmations of the meaning and totality of the human being. Basically the difference is that Marxism cannot follow Christianity in respect to the eschatological vision. That leaves, however, the common ground of regarding people on the level of present reality.[56] They can agree that the human being is never a means but always a goal.

Bočnjak developed the dialogical concern for the human being still further in a lecture to a group of Christians in Heidelberg, West Germany, in spring 1969. He noted that there is a consensus that the idea of humanism means that the person is always evaluated within the scope of history as to how humanely she or he acts toward other people, i.e. how human a person is as a generic being.[57] The problem is that people do not carry out their ideal. Murder has never been, and can never be, proposed as the ideal way of solving arguments, yet, in reality, there are problems along this line. Institutional Christianity is not what the gospel expects to be, and it has not successfully promoted loving one's neighbor as oneself. In politicized Christianity the injunction of Jesus remains an ideal which is not attained. Christianity also has to face the question as to whether the end justifies the means. Bošnjak suggested that such questions should never be decided pragmatically but ethically, and that the truth to such questions cannot be attained collectively but only individually.[58]

Marxist humanism seeks a condition in which each person will be free from exploitation by others and in which, consequently, the realm of freedom will exist. Such an ideal cannot disturb anyone except perhaps the exploiters. This norm could become a common human norm. Marx's concept of human being included liberation from all types of alienations. This state has not yet been attained. As long as the classless society is not a historical reality, the realm of necessity is still in force. In practice the politicized, institutional form of Marxism is often burdened with political interpretations which stand in the way of actualizing the ideal. Political exigencies often seem to require the use of means which compromise the end.[59]

Bošnjak concluded that there are two ideals, the Christian and the Marxist, and, likewise, there are two realities. The fact that in reality the ideals have not been implemented does not mean that there is something wrong with the ideal. On the contrary, it means that something is wrong with reality.[60] The kind of humanism in which every person (regardless of particularities of race, faith, political orientation, and so forth) can be affirmed is able to transform the ideologized type of consciousness. Humanism, then, is the promotion of the human being as the ideal rather than a means to some other end. The imperative of our time, said Bošnjak, is to find criteria which would uphold the equal right of each person, the common right of all people to be human.[61] That striving he called "anthropocracy"—the recognition of humans as humans, and the attempt to liberate them from ideologized forms of life. Only the constant application of humanism can lead to the fullness of anthropocracy.

Bošnjak concluded his report with the following seven theses: [62]

1. Humanism has become the call of our times and represents the most sensible relationship among people as the human "I" is considered to be of value.

2. The meaning and essence of humanism is derived from human rights and can only be an end, never a means.

3. Christian humanism has its purpose *(telos)* in the absolute future; it has a transcendent content.

4. Marxist humanism contains the vision that each person must be free, unexploited. For it, the human being is the

highest being. In praxis Marxist humanism has not been fully implemented.

5. Christian and Marxist humanism differ in respect to the meaning and totality of human beings. Christian humanism sees people as God's creation. Marxist humanism regards them as beings of nature. The difference is not in the material but in the formal object. From the point of formal logic the two do negate one another.

6. The coexistence of Christian and Marxist humanism can take place only in the field of unmediated direct human relationships in the here and now.

7. Humanism is either humanism or it is nothing. In concrete human relationships there can be no difference between Christian and Marxist forms of humanism. There is only one humanism. It leads to a future order which can be called "anthropocracy." Such an order does not exist yet and there is no guarantee that it will ever take place. Only the logos of the future can tell.

Ante Fiamengo, a Marxist sociologist from Zagreb, saw two avenues for the fulfillment of the idea of humanism. One lies in the fulfillment of the social, economic, cultural and political goals of humanism. The other is the rebirth of the human spirit through the ideal of humanness.[63] When pursued separately they result in distortions. Only a combination of both aspects can provide a good basis for humanism. One of the basic characteristics of both Christian and Marxist humanism is the idea of universalism, i.e. the all inclusiveness of both movements. Each movement promotes cosmopolitanism, ecumenism, and internationalism as ways which could truly unite humanity. Fiamengo felt that Marxists are convinced that the true fulfillment of the ideal of humanism cannot be effected by either religion or Marxism alone but only through the principle of mutual tolerance for both types of humanisms.[64]

Marko Kerševan saw the main impact of Marxism in regard to the concern for the human being not in providing new answers to the classical questions but in asking new questions and thereby shifting the attention of people to new experiences. This he considered both the strength and weakness of Marxism as a worldview.[65] The strength consists in that though little is being said about the meaning of life, happiness, and similar human issues, the Marxists spare no efforts "in regard to basic social goals, thereby giving in fact meaning to a larger number of people than any other movement, including religion which continuously talks about meaning." [66] Though Marxism talks relatively little about values, Marxism has inspired more people to sacrifice for the sake of humanistic values than those movements which explicitly propagate humanistic values. The weakness of the Marxist worldview is that it does not compete successfully with religious views, which tend to be turned primarily to private and personal questions as well as to the so called "last questions." There are still people who need such answers. [67]

Archbishop Franić also found some gaps in the Marxist view of human being from the ontological standpoint, especially in regard to the vagueness of the notions of a natural generic and social being, the spirit and body, quality and quantity. [68] He thought that these could provide an interesting theme for dialogue. Marxists aim to bring about a qualitative change in human beings. It is not clear, however, how the structure of the human being is evaluated in Marxism. Who is a true human being? What is a genuine human existence and an authentic human praxis? On some issues Marxism makes its stance on materialistic positivism and sociological economism. For Christians these are unacceptable as satisfactory answers to questions of who and wherefore is the human being. But both Marxism and Christianity aim to remove all obstacles to the infinite development of the human being. [69] While human progress cannot be equated with the coming of God's reign, still there is no total breach between the two. Christians who work to promote both can place the two goals into the same perspective, as noted by Henri de Lubac, concluded Franić. If Marxists become better Marxists and Christians become better Christians, the people will profit from it, and there will be greater hope for the future. [70]

József Szigeti, a Marxist professor from Budapest, pointed out that Marxist humanism concentrates on the removal of class antagonisms through revolutionary praxis. The goal of this revolutionary humanism is to provide the circumstances necessary for the manifold development of human beings. [71] Marxism aims to assist the total human being. Its morality aims to create order out of chaos. It preserves all moral values of the past which are humane but it also creates a new socialist morality and humanity. Christians who are willing to involve themselves in this moral and political endeavor and to abandon their former notions of private property could definitely promote the well being of people. [72]

József Lukács noted among Christians a tendency to oppose exploitation, especially in its capitalist form. Christianity, according to him, can provide a real contribution to human development, especially in its teachings about human beings and ethics. For Marxists, of greatest interest is the quality of human relationships which emerge out of Christian concepts of transcendence. The discussion about humanism is the most important issue of the day.[73]

Marxism postulates that only human beings are responsible for the future. Christianity adds to this creative power a transcendental dimension, making the human being the penultimate goal. Yet according to both, the human being is the goal as well as the cause and means of historical processeses. Contemporary Christians tend to underscore human activity, thereby adding contact points with Marxists. Marxism strives toward disalienation in order to produce harmonious, integrated personalities, without absolutizing either the status of human beings or any structures.[74] Only nature is absolute. Marxism simply wishes to create the harmonious totality of environmental circumstances necessary for human self-development. Neither Christians nor Marxists should think of socialism as the last judgment after which comes paradise. Marxists have noticed the striving among Christians for such human harmony. Christians should likewise notice the Marxist strivings to remove the antagonisms which prevent such harmony. The path to communism simply removes the negative elements characteristic of previous phases of history and preserves those values which help human beings. Among them can be values characteristic of Christian aspirations and efforts. Marxists and Christians should seek common starting points among the factors which influence human growth. Can a Christian afford the luxury to bypass the relative, immanent problems in the name of transcendental longings? Should not both Christians and Marxists appeal to the conscience of humanity to remove such dangers as nuclear warfare so that their descendants may enjoy the future?[75]

Lukács saw the human being as an end. The end is a harmonious personality capable of uniting all strivings in her or his life.[76] Human existence consists in overlapping boundaries. The content of this experience is the fulfillment and development of human abilities and potentialities. Life consists of an unlimited progression, "of an unlimited number of absolute moments which are embodied in a series of relative moments."[77] The human being is not an absolute, completed being. Only the total process of becoming human might perhaps be regarded as absolute.[78]

The fact that Christians and Marxists are both interested in human beings should not mislead one to the conclusion that theoretical agreement on this question is possible. Yet Lukács sees the basis for cooperation in Christian protests against suffering, injustice, inequality, and their striving for a radically changed world. Christians, on the other hand, are likely to welcome Marxist efforts to strike down all idols created by people which obstruct true universalism, idols such as racism, money and private property, aggrandizement of the individual, and satisfaction of selfish interests.[79] Positively, Christians will be interested in the Marxist pursuit of true human wealth, the creation of conditions where morality and human relations will be humanized. Christians are increasingly rejecting those social systems which disallow such humanization of social processes. The answer to these human aspirations can only be sought jointly, concluded Lukács.[80]

ALIENATION AND SIN

Christians and Marxists agree that in concrete practice there are factors which diminish or destroy the essential humanity of persons. Christianity named the inclinations destructive of true human fulfillment as sin. Marx addressed himself to similar factors of dehumanization by means of the concept of alienation. That Christians and Marxists have become interested in discussing these experiences was already evident in the previous section, where reference was repeatedly made to the need of dealing with experiences which demean human dignity. Here we shall briefly report the views of those who explicitly dealt with the issue. The notion of sin has not received much acknowledgement by Marxist authors, though a number of Christians, most notably Hromádka, constantly called attention to the reality of sin and believed that Marxists would profit from the understanding of the persistent and pervasive nature of human evil.

Christians have explored the concept of alienation. Generally they concluded that the Marxists' insights are important, especially as they emphasize aspects of human evil to which Christians have not responded adequately in the past. But Christians regarded the Marxist understanding of alienation as too limited.

Lochman and Vereš both devoted significant portions of

their books to an investigation of Marx's own view of alienation.[81] Vereš classified alienation first in two major groups,
practical and ideological. Then he listed economic, social, and
political alienations under the practical type of alienation,
and religious, philosophical, and artistic alienations under the
theoretical type. An alienated person, for Marx, is the person
who does not bring about his or her own historically available potential in a given sphere of human activity. Economic
alienation is the fundamental alienation as well as the source
of all other alienations. The fundamental phenomenological
characteristic of all alienation is that some inhuman power
rules over the lives of all people who are caught up in an alienating relationship.[82] Thus, for instance, it is not only the exploited who is alienated but also the exploiter. Alienation
perverts the most basic human activity—free and creative
production. It was Marx's conviction that the analysis and
critique of alienation functions similarly to confession, namely
it opens the path for the uncharted new world.[83]

Vereš provided a detailed description of the various types of
alienation as found in Marx's writings, which will not be
summarized here. He also raised some critical questions, mostly of a philosophical nature, which could become a subject of
investigation for Christians as well as Marxists. He pointed
out that it is not clear what is the underlying concept of "human nature" which can be alienated. Granted that Marx did
not postulate an unchanging human nature or essence, he still
must have had a notion of what an unalienated human being
is. Yet there is no clear Marxist formulation of this.[84] Marx
thought that the cause of alienated relationships was the will
for power. He did not elaborate or explore the source of this
propensity for violence. Nor did he carefully explore the relationship between the economic base and the ideological super-
structure and its supposed historical determinant, especially
when applied to religion. Vereš also criticized the dualistic
nature of the concept of class struggle, saying that it fails
when applied to concrete historical changes.[85] Similarly unclear is the way in which Marx pictured the unity of theory
and praxis. He did demonstrate the dialectical tension between
the two throughout history, but the complete unity of the two
has never taken place in historical circumstances, just as the
full absence of alienation has never been attained.

Vereš then pointed out that Marx believed that alienation
can be fully removed. This can be done by the revolutionary
abolition of private property and bringing about communism

via the transitory stage of socialism, culminating in a positive humanism. Positive humanism here means the complete formal independence of the human being from any control from above (natural or supernatural). Marx here proposed the notion of natural and human self-creation, which he argued more from the previous historical development of human beings than from the theoretical negation of a creative God.[86]

Lochman is in agreement with Vereš that the basis of the Marxist notion of alienation is to be found in alienated labor, i.e., in economic alienation.[87] Lochman pointed out that for Marx alienation represented the deprivation of people to become human through their free work. Instead they are being reduced to work on a job in order to survive physically. Both individuals and community are destroyed through alienation. Yet no evil intent can be ascribed to any of the parties. Hence the problem cannot be solved by good intentions. Particularly destructive are the alienating relationships under capitalism, in which money becomes the object of labor, assuming an independence of its own, controlling the lives of people rather than the other way around.[88] When the true enemy, private property, is curtailed, the road will be open for humanizing the process of production and all other processes dependent on it.[89]

Lochman noted that Marx's ideas are somewhat romanticized. In those countries where private property was abolished, the results do not seem to bear out Marx's predictions. Marxism deserves praise for underscoring the importance of human beings and the neglected dimensions of life. Many of the ancient biblical insights about people and society have been re-emphasized by Marxism and are thrust into the arena of Christian concern. However, Lochman criticized the oversimplified economic solutions which, purporting to solve nearly all human problems, neglect to see the full scope of the issues.[90] While Marxism criticizes illusory aspects of life, it has created a "dangerous illusion" by the reductionism displayed in its concept of alienation. The biblical concept of sin is more profound in that it recognizes that the victory over human antagonisms cannot be won by simply expropriating private property. Yet there is place for dialogue on this issue as there is on the question of the place of labor in human self-creation.[91]

Edo Marinković [92] investigated the more recent Marxist thought on alienation, which he considered a major thesis of Marx. He described alienation as denial of the eternal imperative for self-creation which is an almost inescapable perversion of appropriating nature and turning it into property. According to Marinković, contemporary Western Marxists like Domenach, Lefebvre, Alexos, and Fongeyrollas see alienation primarily in the political rather than economic sphere.[93] Alexos, for instance, wrote that Hegel was more realistic than Marx in seeing that alienation would continue even after specific sources of alienation have been removed. It is clear to Marinković that the mechanistic dependence on the economic sphere must be abandoned. There are more basic forms of alienation which do not depend on economic alienation. Yet Marx's richest intuitions retain much validity. Contemporary socio-psychological studies point to the depth of alienation. New forms of alienation appear as some old ones are solved.

Lefebvre pointed to the triangle of alienation-disalienation-new alienation. He also pointed out that socialism does not solve all human problems but it announces a new epoch in which people can state in true terms, without various social impediments, the human problems of knowing, loving, and dying.

Marinković found these recent Marxist explorations helpful. Although he recognized that stating the problem does not solve it, Marinković maintained that these correctives to the concept of alienation are already a step toward a more correct solution of the problem.[94]

The Polish Catholic scholar, Józef Wołkowski pointed out that it is not sufficient to remove private ownership in order to eliminate alienation because Marx himself stated that there are two basic manifestations of alienation, the division of labor and the monetary form of the exchange of goods.[95] The latter two manifestations have not ceased to exist in socialism. Workers lack the feeling that they are comanaging their enterprises. But when work becomes merely a way of making a living while the workers are supposedly to be determiners of the manner of production, it leads to a vivid sense of alienation. Wołkowski cited Marxist Janusz Kuczyński's admission that modern society does not eliminate the division of labor but rather contributes to increasing specialization. Wołkowski opted for the viewpoint which does not fault the division of labor itself, but seeks to free labor from alienation by making it creative under the conditions of division of labor.[96] Wołkowski maintained that the issue of valuation and attitude toward work and the problems of alienation in socialist countries deserve a high priority on the agenda of the Christian-Marxist dialogue.

In my opinion, Christians and Marxists of Eastern Europe stand to gain much by jointly exploring the seriousness of the issues of alienation and sin and in searching for ways to minimize or eliminate their destructive presence in human affairs.

HISTORY

In view of the importance of history for both Christians and Marxists, it is surprising that this subject matter did not receive greater attention.

Hromádka stated that people are rooted in history and that each person works it out in her or his life. Though many Christians live without history by pulling back into their inner faith without recognizing the challenge of human history, Christianity always valued history: the past, present, and future.[97] Hromádka proposed that a Christian does not live out of high spiritual, theoretical, and ethical ideals, but out of the hand of God in history. Revelation is the history between God and the people. History is God's revelation. The believers take history seriously and live it to its fulness. Christians do not think merely about the meaning of history but also about the Lord of history. The Christian is responsible to God for all irresponsibilities, errors, and missed opportunities. But God leads the hopes, achievements, and deeds of the nonbelievers.[98] Christians must not be dogmatic in their interpretation of history and also need to listen to others. The task of a person of deep faith is to criticize oneself while trying to understand the others through the perspective of their best motivation.

The Christian stands in secular history with tasks and responsibilities. Jesus opens the Christian's eyes and saves the Christian from resignation and fatalism enabling him or her to work for the common future. The Christian meets the nonbeliever in history. The difference between them will continue, but in this creative tension they may discover the depth of the meaning of being human.[99] Christian participation in history is accompanied by a feeling of tension with secular life because the Christian sees history in the light of the final goal. A Christian is also part of a society of faith, the church, which is both a human institution and an institution which transcends human structures in becoming a vehicle of revelation. The human being is indeed a product of history and society, but is also much more than that.[100]

Jiří Černý, a Marxist from Czechoslovakia, stated that Marx did not consider history as an unbending, fatalistic destiny.

He made clear the distinction between what results naturally and what are the historical deeds of people. Nature, as a whole, is meaningless. Human beings alone create meaning. Everything receives a sense of purpose through deeds, through history. People have no choice over birth and death but do over other things. Each human being is a product of history but, having stepped into it, changes it.[101] The only meaning of history is the creation and clarification of history for human well-being. In this task it is very important to find the major carrier of history, the proletariat.

Gardavský pointed out that socialism and the revolutionary movement imperils its own existence if it is nurtured merely by its own revolutionary tradition; rather it needs to be constantly exploring all of the historical strata which are capable of nurturing it permanently, or else it will be destroyed. The mistake was made to simplistically divide history into "reactionary" and "progressive." The "reactionary" was dismissed out of hand without deeper analysis and without the chance to consider what nutrients it might have to offer to the revolutionary movement. The "progressive" developments on the other hand were rushed along hastily and were accepted in their entirety, even if they, in fact, may have been devoid of lasting nutrient value. The task of Marxism is to look at all of its roots and to transform as many historical developments as possible into helpful sources of growth. In that respect Marxism must look into the sources of antiquity and such movements as the Renaissance, but, even more importantly, into the sources of the Judeo-Christian tradition. The Judeo-Christian movement, unlike pagan antiquity, is still very much alive, and the creative Marxist must reach into this treasurehouse of experience and integrate it into socialism.[102] This Gardavský proceeded to do in *God Is Not Yet Dead* by exploring such persons as Jacob, Jesus, St. Augustine, St. Thomas Aquinas, and Pascal, and, toward the end of his life, Jeremiah.

Machovec's views on the role of history are similar to those of Gardavský. He too concluded that history makes it possible to realize more adequately who we are. Modern sciences contribute to our self-awareness and well-being, though they also ambiguously create threats to humanity. But without the investigation into past human efforts it is impossible to answer the questions as to who we are, what is our being, what is the meaning of life, and where our personal purpose, happiness, and destiny lies.[103] Flight into the past is of no help. But neither is it possible to understand the present without recourse to the past. History has meaning and value only when we can connect the past with the present, in order to use the accumulated experiences of the centuries.[104]

At a Christian-Marxist symposium at Kazimierz na-Vistuli in June 1978, the Polish historian from Lublin Catholic University, Czesław Bartnik, considered the issue of the meaning of history common to both Marxists and Catholics and thought that it stands out among the humanistic aspirations of both groups.[105] One of the difficulties in dialogue is that unlike Marxism, Christianity possesses a pluralism of philosophies of history. Bartnik, representing the "personalistic" philosophical trend within Polish Catholicism, stated that there are to be discerned many meanings in history and that "meaning" itself is a certain process. Meaning can be found in history, but it can also be projected into it, that is, *created*. He credited Marxism with influencing Christianity both in methodology and in substance. Yet he did not think that Christianity would adopt the Marxist interpretation in its entirety, because he did not consider any of the systems of philosophies perfect. Christianity adopts fully any system only at its own peril.[106] Thus Christianity ought to maintain its pluralism of interpretations of history. Marxism contributes to a fuller appreciation of the wealth of interpretations of the meaning of history, but it also reminds the Christian that human beings constitute the supreme value. Christianity tends to excel in developing the meaning of sacred history but pays little attention to secular history. In contact with Marxists, Christians can develop greater appreciation for the significance of the temporal world, and of human beings as cocreators of that world.[107]

Bartnik concluded by saying that both Christians and Marxists experience the need to discern a meaning in temporal history and to create meaning in history. "Together with Marxists we wish to oppose nihilism, chaos, and pessimism. A struggle for the meaning of life and our history becomes at certain moments more important than material production. Through the creation of meaning for life and history we save ourselves and bring anthropogenesis to fulfillment." [108]

Lukács pointed out the ability of Christianity to inspire anew through its teleologically inspired action. Marxists have the task of uncovering historical processes in the "story of salvation." With a dynamic and open-minded Christianity which leads to responsible human involvement in history, creating a better future, there are many touchstones for a real basis for discussion and common work.[109]

Indeed, it seems to me that Christians and Marxists have much in common in their views on the role of history. It might be that they could assist each other through their respective interpretations of history. But this work seems to be left for some future time. So far too little has been done in this field.

CREATIVITY AND FREEDOM

The topic "Creativity and Freedom" was the subject matter of the Paulus-Gesellschaft dialogue in Marianske Lazňe. Consequently a number of Eastern Europeans addressed themselves to this issue.

Stanko Cajnkar, the late Roman Catholic theologian from Yugoslavia, stated that God lifted the cosmos out of chaos, which means that the world does not have an independent existence. God's creativity is a model for all creativity. All creativity is tied to the triune God, whose revelation is the last qualitative novelty in history.[110] From the outside God's creativity seems like a single act of love, but from the inside it is a triune creation from Father through the Son to the Holy Spirit. An atheist will not be able to understand this without further explanation, stated Cajnkar, for this has its source in the deepest Christian mystery. Marxists likewise must confront their world views with the ultimate truths of their own system, the principle of dialectics. While both are difficult notions, they cannot be given up simply because they are difficult. For the Christian the triune God is the fundamental ground on which everything else, including creativity and freedom, stands.[111]

There is no inner necessity in the Godhead for creativity. It is a free act. Both Marxists and Christians mean by freedom the right to a free life. Catholics defend freedom in theory but not always in practice. Protestants often reverse this. The basis for dialogue is not so much the theory but the practical questions of freedom. Christians and Marxists both ask freedom only for themselves. Creativity depends on freedom, but neither Christians nor Marxists are trusted because of inconsistencies in upholding freedom.[112]

The late Janusz Makowski, a Roman Catholic layman from Poland, member of the Christian Social Association, of the *Sejm*, and former General Secretary of the Christian Peace Conference, stated that creativity is not just God's privilege but also a human duty which the church elevated to the rank of mission. The human being must continue God's work of creation in a world which has its autonomy.[113] Human beings should perform this task well, not only as individuals but so as to transform the whole world into a good place to live. The church has accepted the task to fight for individual development and for social justice for all people.

Freedom and creativity in culture should become a basic theme in Christian-Marxist discussions, concluded Makowski, adding that he did not mean unlimited freedom but a freedom properly placed in a scale of values. True freedom is difficult, but certain Marxists (e.g., Luigi Longo, Lucio Lombardo-Radice, Palmiro Toggliati, and the French Communists) have shown a greater sympathy toward it. Their views have not been actualized widely, but a trend has been set. The basic problem is the conflict between freedom as a right and as a responsibility. How much can the freedom of an individual or a group be restricted in the interest of the larger society? This problem cannot be answered theoretically. For Marxism freedom is the active work for the development of humanity. Catholicism likewise requires that freedom be used for engagement, development, and service of humankind. Both Christianity and Marxism agree that freedom can be changed by human work from antipathy to harmony and that freedom is not merely a spontaneous human reflex but a social stance.[114]

The Czech Marxist Jiří Čvekl pointed out that both Christianity and Marxism aim to instruct the whole person and provide comprehensive worldviews which tend to make them intolerant.[115] Increasingly this absolutism is being perceived as dangerous. Neither is attempting to construct a rational and scientific approach which makes human salvation their goal. Despite their similarities there are contradictions due to their different philosophical bases as well as the type of society which they wish to construct. Without Christianity there would have been no Marxism, yet Marxism arose as an antichurch movement standing in opposition to what the church created. This explains the ambivalence in their mutual relationship.

The Marxist concept of freedom, according to Čvekl, has at least three dimensions:

1. Recognition of the activity and creativity of the person in all aspects of life.

2. Promotion of a universal possession of the world, namely, overcoming alienation and criticism of mythologies, subjectivist projections and personifications of supernatural powers over nature and history.

3. Understanding freedom as a conscious creativity of human beings, which becomes true to the degree that people recognize the laws of development, the necessities which rule their existence, and come to control them.[116]

While Marxism went farther than any other theory of planned emancipation, one can find in it the contradictions between motive and goal, intention and achievement, and means and goal. During the intensified class struggle iron discipline had to be enforced. The result was that the means sometimes became the goal. Some of these were necessities. Others were one-sided excesses. Still others can be regarded as a transitional historical phase.

Čvekl noted that Christians often overlook that the value of Marxism is not in continuation but in surpassing the older forms of materialism. Frequently Christians overlook the necessary concessions which had to be made in adapting Marxism to a mass movement, especially in circumstances of underdevelopment.[117] The third danger is to misunderstand the double character of history, culture, and the human situation as analyzed by Marx. Marx wanted to show how difficult emancipation was and which things were fettering people. One of his main insights was the discovery of historical, social, and individual conditions for community with other people. People must step out of the limits of society where they are objects of manipulation so that they can exercise a direct, personal, and original (thus nonalienating) influence on the world.[118] Marxism opens a new type of authentic relations between the human being and the cosmos. Marxists trust that Christians too will attain these new possibilities. But Christians must grasp their own historicity and preserve those values which will not lose meaning for humanity in the future.[119]

The topic of creativity was discussed not only at the Paulus-Gesellschaft Congress but was also dealt with by Gardavský of Czechoslovakia and Kuczyńsky of Poland.

Vitězslav Gardavský considered the question of creativity from the Greek as well as from the biblical viewpoint. The Greek notion of creativity was dualistic and consisted in subduing the earth, a conflict of the human spirit with the powers of nature. The biblical idea of creativity is monistic; the human being is not separated from nature but immersed in it. Creativity is play, the uninterrupted activity of all human senses, not aimed at controlling the world but rather participating in the "miracle" of creation, increasing options for the future. The new law of Jesus Christ means that freedom did not mean the liberation from natural necessities or pressures, but in the freeing from inner obstacles in order to become what is most essentially human—creative. That means unique, irreplaceable, personal. The meaning of the incarnation is that "a passionate life became a passion for life." [120] The incarnation did not take place because of some outer necessity or goal but out of self-fulfillment; it is its own greatest goal. The law of might has been replaced by the law of love.[121]

Gardavský suggested that the need for work, which did indeed bring civilization to great achievements, pushed creative play to the margins, making it appear childish and silly. But Christianity ought to be thanked for preserving the idea of creative action.[122] Contemporary theology is attempting to remove the layers of Greek dualism in order to restore the more elementary biblical insights of freedom and creativity. Marxism must not let these efforts go unnoticed, because in this respect Christanity and Marxism are heading in the same direction.

Janusz Kuczyński sought Marxist and Christian collaboration in the face of the threat by mass culture, which stifles creativity and prodigiously created mediocre, selfish, nonreflexive individuals who are satisfied with the most trivial values of everyday existence. Neither Christianity nor Marxism condones the shortsighted hedonism and sentimental pragmatism of the mass culture.

Creativity is the production of subjective or objective values which change the meaning of the existence of the individual or the environment. It includes not merely art but scientific discoveries, production of material goods, exploration of social relations, attitudes, and institutions. Because mass culture is the prevalent mode of living today, not only in respect to the majority that succumb to it but also in that it insidiously imposes itself at times on every human being, Kuczyński suggested that Christianity and Marxism have already become allies against egoism, reification, nihilism, and alienation, and seek to transform mass culture into a more creative, constructive world.[123]

The topic of creativity and freedom, in my opinion, offers not merely an interesting theoretical challenge for the Marxists and Christian partners but is of enormous practical implications in a world in which common existence is characterized by routine, unimaginative daily reality, and lacks truly free responses and creativity.

THE FUTURE

Living, working, sacrificing and even dying for the sake of a better future is a common enough attitude in both Marxism and Christianity. Both movements are said to be future-directed or future-oriented. Since present cooperation and dialogue make sense only in view of some future attainment, one would expect that much attention would be given to the vision of that future and the ways of achieving it. In fact, that is not the case. Only a few protagonists of the dialogue have paid explicit attention to this question.

Ivo Stipičić, a Roman Catholic from Yugoslavia, stated that both Christianity and Marxism want to accomplish the "new" and "unseen." They both insist on a permanent revolution and attempt to create the new, just society.[124] The future is for the human being, as Marx saw it so well, the potential for new power and energies which become the source of revolutionary energies in an endangered and exploited world. This is Marxism's latent faith in promise and Christianity's pathos which manifest themselves in revolutionary practice, in the hope for the future, and faith in human beings.

Lochman stressed that the question of the future is a promising theme for the dialogue, especially in view of the grave threats which the future may bring.[125] Lochman pointed to the place of hope in the orientations toward the future which both Marxism and Christianity consciously nurture. The Bible sees history as a journey toward the future. The concept of the coming of the kingdom of God plays a very important role in Christian orientation toward the future. Christian expectations of the future are not as individualistic as some Christians have made it appear. In fact, the message of the prophets and Jesus has definite social implications. "The Christian hope is politically concerned and orientated." [126] While the Marxist notion of future excludes any reference to God, and in this respect the two significantly differ, Marxists should note the similarity of the Christian's political dimensions of the future.

Christian hope, however, is emphatically a hope in the name of God and is not lodged in any particular form of human social arrangement.[127] Marxism frequently criticizes Christianity, with a good deal of justification, because many Christians expect God to do everything while they merely wait for the outcome. These Christians have an erroneous view of the manner of God's intervention. God liberates people for involvement in determining the future. In conversations with Marx-

ists Christians can point out that the future consists of two
dimensions. One is the concrete future or "relative future" of
society and individuals, which is, to a large measure, under
human control. But the other dimension is the "absolute future," which is brought about by God and which is beyond
human manipulations.[128]

While the fate of individuals and groups may be sacrificed
in the name of the "relative future," this is inadmissible from
the perspective of the "absolute future," according to which
each person stands uniquely as part of God's plan. Well-being
is the goal of the "relative future"; salvation is the goal of
the "absolute future." The concept of God as linked to the
future points to its radical openness which proscribes the
sacrifice of basic human values in the interest of any ideology,
or blueprint for the future.[129] This concept of God and "absolute future" is lacking in Marxism, but some of the Marxist
participants in the dialogue have become quite sensitive to
these insights raised by Christians.

An important element of Christian hope deals with the
future of each individual. While Christian hope does not
encourage absorption into one's own problems or magical solutions to them, it does point out that God cares for each individual's problems and offers consolation and deliverance. The
most incredible part of that promise is that even death, the
unavoidable final threatening experience of all people, has been
and will be overcome. Christianity does not deny the reality
of death but does not bestow upon it finality, even in respect
to individual destinies. The proclamation of this hope for the
future must not be abdicated, according to Lochman, even in
a Marxist society.[130] Only a few Marxists have shown appreciation for this role of Christianity, but clearly the contemporary world needs to hear this mesage of hope, and the church
ought to accept the challenge to continue to proclaim it.

Vereš also pointed to God's call to the "absolute future," to
a future which is not merely the evolutionary continuation of
that which is, but to that which has never yet been but can
become any moment the boundless *"novum."* [131] A Christian
need not face the dilemma between the eschatological hope and
the revolutionary transformation of society. Christian expectation is closely related to Christian action in history. True
Christian eschatology is not an "otherworldly" denial of the
values of this world.[132] A Christian must continuously create
circumstances in which the truth can be embodied in the world.

Both Christians and Marxists thus look forward to the "not-yet-become" and "not-yet-conscious." [133]

Gardavský welcomed the reorientation of most of the twentieth-century theologians from preoccupation with the past to that reality which has never yet been with us. The theologian's concern with the future is not theoretical but practical and active. Future for them means a creative breakthrough, which will be the work of humans and which will enable greater human accomplishment in the spiritual sphere.[134] Human beings are not merely creatures but also creators. The specific concrete futures of the world, no matter how much of an improvement they represent over the past, are still equally removed from the perfection of God's reign, or the absolute future, according to Karl Rahner.[135] For the Christian that future is already here as it has already occurred in the meeting of the divine and human in history, in Jesus Christ. Yet from the human perspective everything still needs to be done in the future to achieve the rule of God. Every specific scheme proposed for the future must be contrasted and measured by the criterion of the absolute future, which will make people more radically willing to undertake creative action.[136] Conversely, those social orders in which human beings can more fully realize their creativity are nearer to God's rule of love.

Gardavský found Rahner's views challenging, but primarily as questions rather than answers.[137] Marxism cannot accept God as the absolute answer to Christian questions about the infinite. Marxism admires the asking of questions about infinity. It itself must systematically ask such questions but must not be tempted to give absolute answers. In this respect the Marxist is much more vulnerable than the Christian, yet, if the Marxist were to submit to the temptation, the ability to surpass oneself through one's own actions would be lost to the Marxist.[138] This ability is Marxism's forte.

Marxism does not have an absolute goal for the future. Not even communism is that future, for there is no absolute certainty that it will ever come about, nor that it will be the final phase of history. The Marxist notion of future is an open future which offers human beings an almost limitless range of creative options but which cannot guarantee that it will ever come about or be successful.

> The thought of the future, of socialism, represents for the Marxist the structural principle underlying this conscious creative act. It is a strange principle: it proclaims that it is not

absolutely, and therefore never totally, enforceable, and is also historically not completely secure.[139]

The element of uncertainty about the future can inspire people to change the present inadequate structures in the hope that some future generation may profit by this action. The concept of future has a viable impact on the present in terms of what we make of ourselves and our communities today.

In *A Marxist Looks at Jesus* Machovec devoted many passages to Jesus' and early Christan view regarding the future. He noted that Jesus tied the present and the future into an integral whole by pointing out that the future is the concern of every person in the here and now rather than the passive waiting for what that future may bring.[140] In that respect Jesus recaptured the prophetic vision of the Old Testament at the expense of the contemporaneous apocalyptic preoccupations. Thus early Christians became almost entirely oriented to the future rather than the past.[141] Regretting later Christian developments, Machovec remarked "that the concern for the future—that longing for liberation and radical change once found in Christianity—has been taken over in the modern period almost exclusively by Marxism." [142] Surely Machovec would not deny that contemporary Christianity totally lost that thrust toward the future or else he would not have bothered to devote his career to dialogue at considerable risk to his life and livelihood. But he is rather reminding Christians in the best spirit of dialogue that their task is to recapture that orientation toward the future with both their interior and external actions, an orientation that characterized their Master.

The Marxist project for the future predicts the unpredictable and hopes for the unhoped for, as best pointed out by Ernst Bloch. It is therefore radically critical and revolutionary toward all that exists. While Marxism does not share the Christian hope in the eschatologically unexpected, the two hopes for the future are not absolutely in opposition because the Christian eschatological hope includes the Marxist immanental hope.[143]

To conclude, the common hope makes it possible for Marxists and Christians to meet and agree at least on those issues for which they can hope today. They need to work for the removal of those disagreements which block cooperation for the sake of the future. They can also learn one from another and complement one another in respect to future expectations. Both need to draw upon the experiences of humanity and work for its better future.

IMMANENCE AND TRANSCENDENCE

Traditonally Marxists have fostered an immanentist approach and have spurned transcendence, while Christians have emphasized transcendence and have seemed to eschew immanence. Of course Christian theism generally tends to affirm both the transcendence and immanence of God, holding the two polarities of the paradox together. The Christian-Marxist dialogue has done much to alert Christians to the dangers of letting go of the immanence and drifting off into exclusive concern for transcendence. Many Christians have reaffirmed decisively their interest in the here and now. The neglect of immanence is being corrected by renewed emphasis on the historical and social aspects of life.[144] Christianity cannot be a retreat into pure metaphysics or the private spirituality of a person, but must clearly affirm the social responsibilities of both the individual Christian and the church. Lochman noted that at the Paulus-Gesellschaft Congresses a consensus was reached by theologians that the immanentist aspects of reality must not be a secondary Christian concern.[145]

Unexpectedly a number of Marxist scholars expressed an appreciation for transcendence, showing that they were not immune to Christian influences. Milan Průcha, for instance, refused to reduce the problem of the human being to the historical and social dimensions, for the concept of being transcends the particularities of each concrete person. However, Průcha warned that Christians are misled into quickly robbing transcendence of its power by encasing it into the concept of deity.[146]

Machovec became similarly interested in the transcendent aspects of life. He distinguished three aspects of the problem: 1) the ontological nature of transcendence, 2) transcendence as dialogue, and 3) transcendence and human problems.[147]

1. In respect to the ontological nature of transcendence, Machovec noted simply that "there is something creative outside of atoms and men." [148] Real transcendence goes beyond the duality between traditionally conceived transcendence and immanence, as transcendence includes all of reality. The concept helps see the world as a unity. The difference between the Christian and Marxist concepts of transcendence is that the Christian tends to personalize reality into a God concept, which a Marxist views as too easy an answer since it tries to make every situation meaningful, and this simply is not the case. Marxism wants to affirm that life is more than an absurdity,

yet on the other hand, it cannot affirm that everything has meaning.

2. The life of transcendence cannot be embodied in monologue but only in dialogue. Genuine transcendence means that one person is able to seek out another ("I" seeks the "Thou") in order to listen and be open to that person. Transcendence has the power of changing the present and affirming the limitless possibilities of the future.

3. The idea of transcendence forces Marxists to explore questions which vulgar Marxism neglected. The ultimate questions of the meaning of life and death must also be asked. Christians have been wrestling with those questions longer than Marxists and can be of help to Marxists. Machovec stated that "the idea of transcendence, or the acceptance of transcendence, helps me to be more human." [149] Transcendence also means that no one person, society, or government can succeed in defining truth or reality. It is a protest against reducing life to the tangible, to the conceptually understandable.

Gardavský offered a materialistic and dialectical concept of transcendence. The individual is unwilling to be reduced to a sum total of social relationships because each individual is not only the convergent center of social relations but also alters them. Society, on the other hand, is not merely the sum total of individuals who make up society, but has the power to inspire and instigate changes in individuals as well as in social relations.[150] The individual and society have the power to transcend the many limitations imposed upon them in any specific moment of history.

V. I. Garadja from Poland undertook the task of giving an exposition of Karl Rahner's view on transcendence after pointing out the transition in Catholic thinking from Thomistic "natural theology" to a variety of philosophical and theological influences ranging from subjectivism and existentialism to "political theology." [151] Garadja did not attempt to advance the discussion, though occasionally Rahner's silences on pertinent issues were pointed out. But the importance of Rahner's pioneering work on transcendence and the absolute future was clearly presented. Rahner's views, which were often expressd in the context of dialogues with Marxists, particularly at the Paulus-Gesellschaft Congresses, have had an unusually strong impact. Garadja pointed out that Rahner maintained that Christianity reaches the human being much more profoundly than secular ideologies like Marxism.[152] Despite their other contributions to human future and their adherents being counted among the "anonymous Christians," such ideologies cannot invalidate or make religious truths obsolete. According to Rahner, Christianity stresses both human transcendence and divine transcendence, which reaches "beyond the confines of the natural-historical process of social life." [153] Here is not the place to elaborate on Rahner's views on transcendence, but at least in the philosophical discussions in Poland his views received an airing.

The fact that Marxists have been using the term *transcendence* ought not to lead to the conclusion that both sides are talking about the same thing. As has been stated by numerous observers, Roger Garaudy's and Machovec's and Gardavský's notion of transcendence can be described as "forward or horizontal transcendence" over against "vertical transcendence," which is typical of traditional Christian theology. However, a number of modern theologians have made attempts to rework the concept of transcendence in directions more in line with contemporary experiences, while some Marxists have at least moved in the direction of appreciating the notion of transcendence.

In evaluating the discussion on immanence and transcendence, one can conclude that Christians have probably been more successful in affirming both than have Marxists. This is understandable in view of the rejection of transcendence by conventional Marxists and the novelty of Marxist interest in the idea. It should be clear that Marxists do not equate transcendence with God. So far, it appears that they have not explored this issue sufficiently and that only a few of them affirm the existence of a dimension which goes beyond their more characteristic interest in the concrete and specific.

THEISM AND ATHEISM

At first it may seem curious that there is anything that a Christian and a Marxist can do on this topic except debate one another. No Eastern European Marxist has yet publicly affirmed the existence of God, though a few found some meaning in God-language as a critique of existing circumstances. Some discussions on theism and atheism were in the form of a debate, as for instance the one between Bošnjak and Škvorc.[154] For most Marxists the notion of God is unfounded in reality but is a socially conditioned projection of the human being which robs the believer of the best of human qualities. There is no God; the believer is wrong. On the other hand, Christians consider that the atheism of Marxism is its worst feature and that atheists are missing something so fundamentally important that it renders them evil.

Christians were the first to correct the stereotype. Many came to recognize that atheism did not prevent many Marxists from working for the benefit of humanity and that many of them were not evil persons. They realized that atheism was frequently a rebellion against the misuse of God by Christians, such as God's sanctioning or at least condoning exploitative social orders, human misery, and suffering. Atheism began to be seen as a form of social critique, which, indeed, in many cases it was. It came to be recognized that atheism does not necessarily stand in the way of a person's contribution to human welfare. Theologians such as Hromádka, Lochman, and Franić pointed out that the atheist may be a part of God's plan, doing in fact God's will.[155] Hromádka perceived Marxist atheism as radical humanism and considered its atheism marginal rather than essential.

> The center of gravity of it is not what we call negative godlessness, but an effort to free man and human society of anything that has crippled his understanding and his capacity to master the laws of nature, society, and history. . . .

> The atheism of dialectical materialism is a positive struggle for man, for his adequate self-understanding, for a better order of social and political life, for construction of a society in which all class differences will gradually fade away. . . . If the Christian grasps the meaning of Marxist humanism, and if a communist penetrates beyond all the religious myths and superstitions to the depth of the prophetic struggle for the real God against gods and ideals, then both of them may establish a firm basis of a fertile, creative controversy.[156]

For Gardavský, atheism, however, is of the essence, giving Marxism its radical character. "Without it both Marx's plan for a 'total man' and his concept of Communism are equally inconceivable." [157] But there are many forms of atheism. Some of the forms of atheism which were practiced by Marxists are not Marxist at all. Gardavský provided a thorough history and analysis of atheism, explaining how certain forms of anticlericalism and antitheism can dominate Marxist atheism more than the atheism of Marx.[158] These distortions are almost inevitably connected with the immediate postrevolutionary period and were affected by the churches' stand toward socialism. It was hoped that the vestiges of religion could be removed quickly from people's consciousness. Religiosity was being equated with social and political opposition to science and progress. It provided a great deal of self-satisfaction to those who voluntarily emancipated themselves from God and who were eager to share this elation with the less willing populace.

More recent investigations show that many people who do not formally adhere to a church are not necessarily atheist and that social attitudes are not directly related to theism and atheism.[159] Many of the contemporary developments are creating a primitive godlessness of an apathetic, indifferent sort, which does not inspire positive involvement in social processes. This type of atheism makes the person able to react only to the immediate trivia and worries of life but is incapable of seeing overall patterns or having long-range aspirations. Both capitalism and socialism are capable of producing this type of practical, unreflective atheism. There are also conformist atheists. These people are atheist because of political advantages derived from that position.[160] This position is a position of apathy both toward religion and atheism. It is different from anticlericalism and antitheism, which is virulently opposed to theism but on *a priori* grounds, frequently twisting historical evidence and fitting it into a preconceived mold.[161] The abstract humanistic atheist is also not indifferent to religion. On the contrary, this type of person is appreciative of the value of religion, although she or he gradually regards religion as illusory. Such a person tends to find a humanistic value as a God-substitute but is rather aloof from political engagement.[162]

A Marxist atheist is a critic of the churches and of theism but only insofar as it tends to shore up reactionary ideas and practices. Though not accepting the theist's starting point, the atheist will take the theist seriously and be willing to cooperate and discuss and explore all issues with the theist. Mutual support in initiatives believed to be helping humanity will characterize the relationship of a Marxist atheist with a theist.[163] This Marxist atheist will not always regard all religion as the opiate of the people. While the concept of God may sometimes simply reflect the existing world, a Marxist knows that "God can also represent a direct call for a socially and humanly responsible decision to act. In that case, the concept of God loses its dreamlike quality and challenges men to action in human terms." [164] In this sense a Marxist is interested in the idea of God not so much for what it says about God but what it says about human beings.

Gardavský suggested that Marxists need to construct an atheistic system of metaphysics which would, however, not be a religion or pseudo-religion, but would transcend religious illusions. He did not work out such a system of metaphysics but suggested a few ingredients. It would include the recognition of eternal, constantly recurring, problems which require ever new solutions. It would also recognize the certainty of death and the ability of people to constantly transcend themselves. These two realities are both presupposing one another and are contradictory. Marxism can express optimism in regard to the death of the individual who, having contributed to society, is survived by it. Yet Marxism also realizes that physical and psychological death defeats what each person stands for and represents a discontinuation of relationships which threatens both the individual and the society.

> I myself have no hope of eternity and am at the mercy of death, but I represent hope for others who will outlive me: when my life comes to an end, the sum of what remains is the indispensable precondition of their life. It is true that their lives also end in the same hopelessness. But it is only at this high price, at the price of personal defeat, that hope can be kept alive as one of the unalterable factors of human existence in general, as society's hope for the future.[165]

The most basic ingredient of the metaphysics of atheism operative in life is the human relationship called love. "Genuine love always transcends our present potential." [166] Being a truly human way to interrelate, it is able to overcome the causality of nature. It makes it possible for people to be really creative in the process of self-realization.

> In the end we will not suffer defeat, but we will not rob our survivors of any element which makes the life of a human community a perpetual drama, a struggle, a conflict, not expecting the ultimate defeat.

> We will not lessen their hope for a community offering a life worthy of man. We call this hope Communism.[167]

Esad Ćimić also distinguished several types of atheism. One type is incidental atheism, which attempts to provoke incidents by which the atheist tries to emancipate a theist from her or his religion and substitute it with some other allegiance. The second type is spontaneous atheism, which arises out of the superficial optimism that spontaneous social development will bring about atheism. The third type is Marxist atheism, which consciously aims at social change. This atheism aims to create such humane conditions in which both theists and atheists can truly fulfill themselves.[168]

According to Ćimić, atheism is historically connected with liberation movements and revolts against those factors which oppress people, including oppressive religions. The center of the conflict between atheism and religion is the interest of the human being. The only real task of atheism is the struggle for human freedom. The power of atheism is directly related to the degree of human dependence. Under conditions of dependence religion flourishes. Under contemporary conditions this sometimes takes the form of godless religion. Atheism is the tool whereby people can be liberated from dependence. It is thereby a gage of human liberty. Atheism is related to socialism in such an intimate way because socialism attempts to bring about the complete human being, and atheism can bring about spiritual liberation.[169]

Atheism is very closely related to religion. The form of religion prevalent in a specific place determines the form of atheism. Atheism and religion are correlated, atheism being the shadow of religion, its negation. The two try to destroy one another. The more successful atheism is in destroying religion, the more it, paradoxically but logically, brings about its own demise. When religion is totally negated, the negation itself ceases to be of consequence. When human beings become totally free, there will be neither religion nor atheism.[170]

Lenin's claim that religion and atheism are not truths but postulates made sense to Ćimić. Both can give inspiration for action and provide satisfaction.[171] The dilemma, theism or atheism, can be resolved only in freedom.[172] As people become free, they will not need to postulate either of the two. They will not need the mediation of either of these two worldviews.

Machovec pointed out that Marx rejected the dogma of God as presented by conventional theologians of the nineteenth century. However, when notions of God change, Marxist attitudes toward these notions should change likewise. "Twentieth-century theologians have worked out new models for thinking about God, so that often we Marxists no longer know whether we are still atheists or not in their regard."[173] It may well turn out that as theologians shift to different ways of depicting God, theists and atheists may realize that they have more in common, even on this issue, than they imagined.

Machovec also pointed out the varieties of atheism, including the atheism of the consumer society and of the casual churchgoers, and the negative atheism of persecutors of religions, all of which ignore questions of meaning, evil, guilt, of the absolute.[174] Marxist atheism should be characterized by emphasis on positive values and on raising ultimate questions. Its ideal is the emancipation of human beings and the endowing of them with wholesome personalities by eliminating the causes of alienation. Marxist atheism is not preached but carried out in concrete deeds of destroying evil structures and raising good ones. This atheism is not a negative atheism, despite the fact that in its early stages it did not promote dialogue with Christians but caused sharp antagonisms. It now recognizes that religion is not senseless, because it deals with meaningful issues and sees that they have much in common.[175]

Atheism is in danger of trying to use outdated methods because in the past they were effective. Marxists must be aware that in socialist countries many people became atheists not out of conviction but out of opportunism. They can destroy many atheist achievements. Another danger is the institutionalization of Marxism, in which the organization tends to become the end rather than the means. This produces a sort of scholastic atheism, which does not emancipate, but manipulates the consciences of fellow humans. Modern atheism should be characterized as follows:

1. Although it doubts certain Christian dogmas, it does not set up antidogmas, but nurtures the ability for radical skepticism. Atheism is therefore methodological in approach.

2. It must be related to rational and empirical sciences, not merely to negations of religion.

3. It is not only intellectualistic but attempts to deal with the whole person and all kinds of situations.[176]

Marxist atheism lives for the future and is therefore aware of the need to dialogue with theists because of the common responsibility for fellow human beings. In this process the atheist not only shares his or her world view but is willing to learn and assimilate insights from others. False tolerance and indifference should not mark this dialogue. Marxist atheism must continue to exert its critical influence, although it should be receptive to Christian truths. And it must remain self-critical, not fanatical. Dialogue with believers would aid atheists in maintaining their position more authentically.[177]

On the basis of the contributions of Hromádka, Gardavský, Ćimić, and Machovec, it is possible to conclude that even on an issue such as theism-atheism, which at the outset seems to offer little promise for dialogue, it is possible to have a fruitful interchange which can radically and mutually change perceptions. One might say that if Christians and Marxists are capable of making serious headway on this topic, certainly they are capable of making it on other less controversial ones.

JESUS AND MARX

The traditional views held by Christians and Marxists of the founder of the other movement have not been particularly kind and flattering. Christians often perceive Marx as an evil man who brought about social upheavals, destruction, and persecution of religion. Marxists generally think of Jesus either as a legendary figure or a romantic dreamer who did not effectively bring much good to the world but whose followers perpetrated much evil and suffering.

The changed social situation, wherein Marx is constantly expounded and praised, makes it easier for Eastern European Christians to give a positive appraisal of Marx. Not only is Marx seen as a person passionately devoted to issues of justice and equality and unselfishly promoting the cause of the working class, but his teachings are examined and much good is found in them. This process of seeing Marx and his teachings in a new, more positive light has been accomplished not only by those Christians who are eager to formally dialogue with Marxists but also by Christians who have not been so engaged, for instance, by many Christians in East Germany. It is a rather widespread practice of Christians to quote Marx appreciatively and to accept certain analyses or predictions of Marx.

Not many Christians have written specific articles or books about Marx. One reason is that so much is already published in Eastern Europe that it may seem superfluous. Another reason is that many Eastern European countries have not allowed any public criticism of Marx and therefore a Christian assessment, which could not be in total agreement with Marx or what the official version of Marxism is, would endanger the interests of both the party and the church. It is not surprising then that only in the more liberal Marxist countries are there Christian writers who have examined Marx a bit more thoroughly, and only in Yugoslavia was a book published by a Christian on Marx.[178]

As seen in the above sections on alienation and humanization, the books by Vereš and Lochman deal primarily with these two facets of Marx's thought. Prior to them, Hromádka had incorporated treatments of Marx in various writings of his and he was responsible for the Comenius Theological School in Prague fostering a serious study of the works of Karl Marx.

Nikola Žilić, a Yugoslav Catholic, ascribed great importance to the work of Marx but noted that his work lends itself to many contradictory interpretations. One of the reasons for this is the wealth of Marx's thought as well as the difference in approach to questions between the "young Marx" and "old Marx." In the first period Marx sought to free human beings by radical criticism of all that exists. In the second period he sought to pursue practical and political aims in the struggle against capitalism. The followers of the "old Marx" tended to develop a Marxian dogmatism, which was most clearly manifested in the Soviet Union during Stalinism. Those interested in the "young Marx" tend to develop critical humanism in order to overcome dogmatic aberrations. In Žilić's opinion both the economic determinism and the humanistic liberationism of Marx must be retained. In the structuralist analysis of the French Marxist Louis Althusser, Žilić sees hope for such proper interpretation of Marx, who wanted to free people from all forms of alienation.[179]

The Christian studies of Marx did not surpass in depth the liberal Marxist interpretations. Their main contribution consists in the thoughtful appropriation of Marx's most important contributions which can be of use to a Christian understanding of the world.

Serious Marxist investigations of Jesus are recent and rare. In some Marxist countries no publications of this sort could see the light of day. Most of the contributions of Eastern European Marxists about Jesus were published only in the West with the exception of Gardavský's chapter on Jesus in *God Is Not Yet Dead,* which did appear in Czechoslovakia. In the opinion of many establishment Marxists, a positive rendition of the role of Jesus may be too supportive of Christianity and may give the impression that Marxists favor Jesus far beyond the customary banalities that he was a good man and the first communist. Of course, the views of those Marxists who undertook a serious search of Jesus went far beyond such superfluities.[180]

Lezsek Kołakowski stressed the importance and uniqueness of Jesus, which only Lenin, among the founders of Marxism, did not recognize. Kołakowski attempted to point out Jesus' main contributions to history, without which the contemporary world would have been decisively impoverished.

These consisted of first, lifting the law in favor of love. Marxism took up the motif of voluntary cooperation for the sake of others.

Second, abstaining from force, or the restricted use of violence. Abstaining from violence is neither naive (violence is
not effective) nor does it mean passivity or lack of courage, as
shown in Jesus' own life.

Third, originating the now customary, "Man does not live
by bread alone" statement, which is descriptive of the nature
of human beings.

Fourth, making God available to all, stating that there are
no chosen or privileged people.

Fifth, facing people with the suffering of this world. No
matter how much we succeed in changing the world, we cannot
reach the absolute, for we are mortals.[181]

Kołakowski stated that it is impossible to separate Jesus
from these values without impoverishing them. One cannot
remove Jesus simply because one does not believe in the God
in which he believed. Christianity can exercise self-criticism
only by looking back at Jesus. He taught Christians how to
change the self and the world without violence. He was also an
example of radical authenticity, in which a person takes his or
her own values and makes them real.

Bošnjak ascribed to Jesus an ethic of salvation in the light
of Jesus' eschatological orientation. Jesus made it possible for
his followers to endure all kinds of miseries because, in the
end, God will rescue and save them. For the sake of this salvation, it was worth suffering worldly evil. Jesus' ethics are based
on faith, not on the logic of rationality.[182]

Gardavský, like Bošnjak, shows some ambiguity about (even
disinterest in) the question as to whether Jesus existed, but
proceeds with his inquiry at least from the perspective of what
model of a man Jesus was, and how he figures in the minds of
people.[183] Marxists ought to discover, independently from the
early sources, what kind of model Jesus is. "Christ's challenge
questions our subjectiveness, our plans, our schemes, our practical activity." [184] Jesus was capable of recalling the people of
Israel to their original path and unleashing in them abilities
which were in their power. He located the power of the nation
in the simple people. He demanded that unconditional choices
be made by people, because their future depended on it. But
Jesus was not a social revolutionary standing against the
power of Rome; his influence would not have survived the
times had that been the case. Jesus challenged people to the
more fundamental notion that each person must decide, despite
great inner struggles and personal risks, in order to advance
the community.

The miracles of Jesus are the "kind of subjective action which imprints a new order, a new law on the order of cause and effect, forcing it to aim toward a specific goal and to translate itself into reality along those lines." [185] They show us the essence of action by which a person throws in his or her whole personality and is able to achieve the surprisingly unexpected, the new, which violates the so-called natural order of things. So the law of nature is supplanted by the "law" of love, the act of surpassing oneself. Even death cannot win when confronted with this type of love. Thus the difficult state of love means both "rising from the dead" and living as a human being. By loving, Jesus means that each person enters into a situation wholeheartedly. Then miracles will be possible: "They are nodal points in the web of history, the junctures where something unique takes place, an incident which can never be repeated. And if we look at it this way, love turns out to be the radically subjective element of history." [186] In all the above ways Jesus Christ represents a challenge not only to Marxists but to the world.

Machovec stated that Marxists never denied certain good consequences of Jesus. Marxists themselves are legitimate heirs to Jesus, especially in respect to helping one's neighbor, living out the ideas that one proclaims with integrity, practicing moral self-evaluation (including confession of sins), and the depth of faith.[187] Machovec's book, *A Marxist Looks at Jesus,* is undoubtedly the finest Marxist study of Jesus ever undertaken.[188] In this book Machovec argues that Marxists cannot avoid studying one of the most significant personages of history. Basing his work on advanced biblical scholarship, Machovec discussed the folowing themes: the credibility of sources for the study of Jesus, Judaism before Jesus, the message of Jesus, and the proclamation that Jesus is the Christ. He based his work on some of the best exegetical studies of contemporary biblical scholars but added much of his own personal insight and kept a constant eye on the socioeconomic processes related to Jesus. A Christian can discover meaningful interpretations of Jesus in this book, interpretations useful to the faith, as the book opens another angle of vision on the life and message of Jesus.

Most interesting to a Christian is Machovec's evaluation of Jesus' significance.[189] To him, critics of Christianity cannot blame Christians for following Jesus, but rather for not following him closely enough. His impact is so great that rare are the critics who directly attacked Jesus for who he was and

what he did.[190] The disparity between Jesus and his followers
is usually quite shocking, despite attempts to imitate the Master. The very success of Jesus in solving some tragedies of
Judaism and in making the great insights of Judaism universal
brought about new tragedies. Only recently have Christians
come to see the paradox, for instance, of causing suffering to
Jews in the name of the love and suffering of the Jew, Jesus.[191]
Many of Jesus' demands for a radical return to God and for a
more equitable social arrangement among people by siding
with the weak and the poor were quickly forgotten, though
the ideal still has the power to inspire change. "You can cor-
rupt the heritage, . . . but those who seek it out tomorrow will
find life and new hope beneath the layers of dirt and petrified
outlines—simply because they are attuned to it." [192] People
need to deal with pain, suffering, failure, and death. They also
need to be elevated out of the drudgery, monotony, and humil-
iation of daily life. These two aspects of Jesus attract innumer-
able people despite the layers of dead dogma and the misuse
of Christ by the ruling classes. Jesus' concern for the whole
person, for the past, present, and future, continues to have a
hold not only on those who follow him, but on those who carry
out his injunctions without sharing his religion.[193]

It is interesting that other great figures and interpreters of
Christianity and Marxism generally did not receive much attention. Gardavský wrote brief chapters on Augustine, Thomas
Aquinas, and Pascal.[194] Machovec wrote on Augustine. Jakov
Romić is the only Christian who wrote on Lenin.[195] He examined Lenin's prerevolutionary attitudes toward religion, attitudes which are less well known than his attitudes during and
after the October revolution. He concluded that at that time
Lenin was surprisingly open toward religion, though he was
convinced that religion would soon die out. In this relative
openness of Lenin, Romić sees an inspiration for contemporary
Marxists to reexamine their position toward religion based on
present-day circumstances.

ETHICS

Christians have not written much on Marxist ethics or
morality except for a few very scattered affirmations that a
Marxist can be a moral person or have ethical sensitivity.[196]
Christians have shown awareness that Marxists aim to promote certain ethical values, such as justice, equality, peace, and
liberty, and have praised, on occasion, Marxist successes in this

endeavor. But since Marxists have not published many works on ethics, it is understandable that Christians would not produce reactions to Marxist ethics.

It is a different matter when one turns things the other way. Christianity has devoted an extraordinary amount of attention to matters of ethics and morality. In addition to the many learned treatises on the subject matter, not only has a steady stream of sermons, homilies, and catechetical lessons innundated the Christian consciousness, but it has to be recognized by Marxists that many Christians led exemplary lives and performed well in their place of work, while others, not dedicated to Christianity, violated traditional moral precepts. Hence it is not surprising that many Marxists were willing to admit that Christianity encouraged precepts of behavior advantageous to communal life. It is not surprising that some Marxists have dealt explicitly with the question of Christian and Marxist ethics and morals.

Agnes Heller, a Hungarian Marxist, claimed that Christian and Marxist ethics are based on different ontological principles, namely that Christian ethics is based on the concept of transcendence while Marxist ethics on immanence.[197] She maintained that the claim, "If there is no God all is allowed," is untrue. To the contrary, if there is no God, one's responsibility to other human beings is increased. A Marxist evaluation of an ethical stance should not rely on the issue of ontology but only on whether a particular system of ethics or ethical principle advances or hinders human emancipation.[198] She noted that there has not been a unified system of Christian ethics throughout history and that the same is true of the much shorter history of Marxist ethics; one cannot talk of *the* Christian ethics or *the* Marxist ethics. Hence one cannot consider this question on the theoretical level but only on the level of praxis.[199]

It is apparent that in the contemporary world Marxist and Christian ethics can both be revolutionary (aimed at changing outdated structures) and that they can share a similar stance toward concrete issues. When the complete emancipation is accomplished, there will be no more need for any kind of transcendence or faith. People will directly create and choose values. The question of the existence or nonexistence of God will become irrelevant. This is why it is admirable to see revolutionary Christians struggle for a world in which Christianity or any other religion will become unnecessary.[200] Marxists must admit and respect the fact that Christianity had created ethical values over a period of two thousand years, values which are not merely their values, but universal values.

According to Esad Ćimić, the religious sanction of morality had advanced human beings at a particular stage of historical development, though this is not necessarily the case anymore. However, Christianity has shown a remarkable ability to adapt its moral requirements to contemporary circumstances.[201] Ćimić considered Immanuel Kant as the best representative of the linking of morality and religion. According to Kant, the moral proofs of freedom, immortality, and divinity are postulates of faith. One has to believe in freedom as a precondition for morality. One has to believe in the immortality of the soul in order to enable it to participate in the highest good. God is the absolute guarantee of moral sanctions, forcing people to adhere to them with the threat of punishment.[202]

In a fascinating way Ćimić turned around Kant's arguments by saying that atheism is likewise a fact of the practical mind because it too is ultimately a form of believing, a way of practically living and creating the world without God.[203]

Religion has a greater chance to be useful as it turns from political might to moral might. However, Christian morality ought to be criticized because, with some notable exceptions, it tends merely to advocate *abstinence* from evil rather than an active opposition to evil, the way Marxist morality demands. This is particularly illustrated by the churches' attitude toward private property.

According to Ćimić, a generalized comparison between religious and atheist morality shows that religious morality fosters a feeling of dependence, of passivity, and of the absence of a direct affirmation of humanism. Atheist morality produces the opposite results. But this is only an analytical model. In real life, Ćimić argues, one can approach people—atheists and Christians—only as individuals. Some religious people do not follow religious morality, and some atheists do not abide by atheist morality.[204] No one has a monopoly on moral behavior under contemporary circumstances. Particularly problematic for the world today is the widespread moral indifference.

For Ćimić the basis of Marxist morality is to be found in the human being's ability for direct compassion without self-interest and in the instinct for the preservation of the species.[205] Human conscience is a dependable indicator of the gap between what we want to do and what we ought to do. Our responsibility toward others, the love of other people, is the basis of atheist morality. Society ought to stimulate the moral behavior of individuals by providing the best environment for moral activity, but not to demand moral behavior. People are inherently neither good nor bad. Only society fosters good or bad behavior. The task of morality is to uphold certain norms, which are often outdated, and sanction unequal relations among people. The true task is to create a society which will obviate the need for either religious or atheist morality. The ideal is the human being as a being of possibilities living freely in a free humane society in which old forms of Christian or atheist morality will be transcended and left behind.[206]

Andrija Krešić concentrated on the question of the morality of private property, which he, as a Marxist, considers an obstacle to the free development of people. He presented the revolt against class privileges in the primitive apostolic church in Jerusalem and suggested that this church practiced a community of property or a communism of distribution and consumption. It did not, however, practice a communism of production and was therefore unable to survive. The practice of the monastic communities was too restricted and too tainted with forms of private property to have made a big impact. He expressed the conviction that Christians do not have any *a priori* objections against the sharing of all property because they realize the destructive power of mammon, the idolatry of money, and they strive to enter the kingdom of God. He, too, agrees, that it is impossible to generalize in one's judgment of Christian moral practices. Rather he proposed the practice of proexistence between Christians and Marxists, in the building of a future which can accommodate both in a society of free persons.[207]

It is evident that thus far Eastern European Christians have only scratched the surface of an issue which could be of enormous benefit to humanity.

SEARCH FOR PEACE

Given the great emphasis on peace in Marxist propaganda in the post-World War II setting and the traditional lip service the Christians have paid to peace, it is not surprising that dialogue in search for peace has preeminence in some circles of Christians and Marxists, even to the exclusion of other subjects for dialogue. Peace is the one value to which the two can subscribe at little cost to their reputation and ideological posture. The circumstances of tensions of the Cold War, of great power rivalry, of the nuclear age, of the arms race, and

of the ideological conflicts of the present era provide the sufficient causes for anxiety on the part of thoughtful and less
thoughtful Marxists and Christians, leading to the conviction
that something needs to be done to avoid the annihilation of
the human race. The oft-repeated argument is that without
peace all other values will be destroyed; hence the primary
need is to establish a lasting peace under which all other human
strivings can have a chance.

Christians and Marxists have cooperated in their work for
peace in many international and local forums. The Prague
Christian Peace Conference is an instance of Christian efforts,
primarily those of Eastern European Christians, to make a
contribution to this cause with the blessings of their governments. These efforts are worthy of an analysis, but not in this
book, because no explicit Christian-Marxist dialogues took
place at these conferences (although Marxists have occasionally addressed Christians at these meetings, and Christians
have often communicated their concerns and resolutions to
Marxist leaders). A local dialogue on peace took place in Poland in 1973 [208] and one may expect that the Warsaw European
Christian Forum, created in September, 1979, will likewise involve instances of cooperation between Christians and Marxists on peace questions. But the only sustained theoretical
dialogues on peace have been carried out at the International
Peace Symposia, described in Chapter 3. Since details about
the meetings and the Eastern European speakers and participants were provided in that chapter, only a digest of the Eastern European Marxists and Christian views will be presented
here.[209]

Differences between Christian and Marxist positions on
peace were manifested at these symposia only when the views
of all participants of these symposia were included. But these
differences vanish when one singles out the Eastern European
participants for analysis. Here near unanimity prevails, the
exception being that Rumanian and Yugoslav participants
showed a distinct distrust of the prevalent Eastern European
pro-Soviet position. It should be remembered that this dialogue
for peace is the only Christian-Marxist dialogue which has the
explicit support of the Soviet government. The Marxists and
Christians of Eastern Europe tend to show near unanimity on
concrete issues of peace, though their theoretical underpinnings
differ.

The Marxist position expounded in the major Marxist papers was entrusted only to Soviet scholars. These were deliv-

ered by Nikolai Kowalski, Yuri Zamoshkin, Alexander Galkin, Oleg Bykov, Vladimir Gantman, and Mihail Mtschedlov. The actual topics of the conferences varied, but the main Marxist message is consistent.

According to that message, socialism means peace; capitalism causes wars. The ruling classes in capitalism gain economic advantage from waging war and producing arms. Consequently they push the world into war. Under socialism no one benefits from the arms race or war; therefore socialist countries do not cause war. Only capitalist threats force socialist countries to arm themselves for defensive purposes. Socialist countries also aid wars of national liberation, which are a historical necessity and which are fought to rectify unjust structures under which no lasting peace is possible. Peaceful coexistence between countries of various social systems and détente are espoused, coupled with a struggle of ideologies. However, true peace will come only after socialism prevails world wide. Solidarity with the oppressed colonial or neocolonial people is declared, but only solutions to conflicts around the globe which are promoted by the Soviet Union have been promptly and uncritically endorsed by Eastern European Marxist and Christian participants in these symposia. To them it appears self-evident that the peace proposals of the Soviet Union are the only sincere and constructive solutions to world problems.

No possibility of inconsistencies in socialist policies from 1917 onward is ever admitted. Great stress is placed on the unity and like-mindedness of all people in socialist countries, whose leadership is seen as faithfully reflecting the will of the people and the historical destiny of socialism. Socialism is on a victorious march which nothing but a nuclear holocaust can stop. Capitalists are tempted to employ war as a last resort against socialism. Promoting peace and promoting socialism are seen as synonymous. But military preparedness of socialist countries is seen as the guarantee against capitalist military adventures. Alternate Marxist views on world peace, e.g., those of China or Yugoslavia, are condemned as revisionist and usually totally neglected, except for an occasional swipe of condemnation.

Christians are being perceived by Marxists as slowly coming around to accepting the socialist view on war and peace. A reluctant transition from opposing socialism to the realization of the correctness of the socialist theory and practice is posited by the Marxist spokesmen (the term is used advisedly since no women ever presented the Marxist position at these meetings). It is the hope of the Marxists that the "progressive" and "moderate" Christians will become allies of the Marxists, who are in the vanguard on this issue, as they are on others. With the collaboration of all "peace-loving forces," it is hoped that peace will be preserved.

Eastern European Christians have not presented as systematic an assessment of war and peace as the Marxists because they have not been asked to do so at these meetings. Christians present at these symposia range from those who are enthusiastic supporters of their governments' position to those who tend to be low-key at official meetings and show a more discriminating attitude in private conversations. In public statements the Christians either give vague, generalized endorsements of peace among people of goodwill or they provide very specific endorsement of whatever is high on the agenda of the Soviet policy-makers, regardless of whether or not it fits the conference theme. For instance, if the opposition is to the United States introducing the neutron bomb, all will condemn it. When the introduction of medium-range U.S. missiles in Europe is singled out for criticism, that will be attacked. If the Brezhnev-Carter SALT II meeting is being hailed, that gets the wholehearted Christian support. No public criticism of the Eastern European peace record has yet been in evidence. Soviet interventions in Eastern Europe and Afghanistan and Vietnam's military activities is Southeast Asia are glossed over, while Western military moves are loudly condemned.

In short, Marxist leadership in finding solutions for conflicts is explicitly affirmed by Christians. Christians admit to co-responsibility for peace but not in suggesting concrete measures leading to peace. In this respect the official representatives of the two movements show such an identity of views that no dialogue is necessary. It remains the task of Christians from outside of Eastern Europe to provide whatever difference there is likely to be in order to effect a dialogue.

The urgency of working for peace is undoubtedly great, I believe, since the threat of wars—especially of all-out, apocalyptic conflagration which would denude the planet of human life—is very real. The search for peace should, indeed, be one of the highest priorities of Christians and Marxists. There are still many in both camps who are not doing enough for that cause. There will never be enough dialogue and cooperation on this subject.

The danger in these dialogues is that they might be used

primarily for manipulative purposes by one or the other side. At this moment uncritical pro-Soviet propagandizing appears to be the gravest manipulative threat. Christians participating in these dialogues must recognize this threat, though it ought not discourage them to the point of withdrawal. A mixture of people with diplomatic skill, courage, honesty, knowledge of Marxist tactics, and patience will be needed to continue such dialogues. Over the years a process of maturation and change might take place, making these symposia and similar endeavors true and effective forums of promoting peace.

EVOLUTION OR REVOLUTION OF SOCIETY

The question of the evolution or revolution of society may seem to be one to which a good deal of attention would have been given, but, in fact, this was not the case. The only setting in which a discussion on "The Evolution or Revolution of Society" took place was at a Paulus-Gesellschaft Congress in Bonn, in the fall of 1968. A number of Eastern European Marxists shared their views on that issue at the meeting, but no Eastern European Christians did. The congress itself was planned as a meeting of the Western European "new left" with some Eastern European Marxists and with some of the West European constituency of the Paulus-Gesellschaft. Hence there was no Eastern European dialogue on this issue, but only a few Eastern European Marxist contributions, overshadowed, however, by the Soviet invasion of Czechoslovakia, which occurred a few months earlier.

Machovec stated that the Czechoslovak students selected the nonviolent method of revolutionary change even when beaten by the police. The "Prague Spring" was an attempt to bring about the second stage of the socialist revolution, namely to extend the benefits and responsibilities of communism to all working people, including Christians. The first stage of the revolution, the dictatorship of the proletariat, must not mean the monopolizing of power by the bureaucracy and its subsequent unwillingness to relinquish this power.[210] To freeze the development at this stage is to be untrue to Marx. If the postrevolutionary communist does not raise the question of the meaning of life, then communism has no future. Communism must be willing to take over the entire humanistic heritage from Judaism to the Renaissance. The moral renewal of the Communist Party and the further democratization and humanization of socialism are the only ways of rehabilitating communism.

Progressive Western humanistic practices should be critically adopted in the second revolutionary stage, which has been attempted in Czechoslovakia. The battle was lost, but the Czechoslovak people will carry on the struggle for both renewal and revolution.[211]

Milan Průcha likewise rejected the simple alternative: evolution or revolution. He contended that attempts to bring about changes in socialist countries, though superficially similar to evolution in the West, are not the same. It is a protest against the degeneration of socialism into a bureaucratic machine which reduced all of the components of socialism into a single revolutionary principle of holding the monopoly of power.[212] It is because of this that democracy and humanism have become the watchwords of a permanent revolution in Eastern Europe.

In Czechoslovakia, according to Průcha, the claims to personal liberty and freedom of information were seen as fundamental means for revolutionary social changes. They were ways to criticize the industrial concept of socialism in which all human needs are being subjected to industrialization with the concomitant establishment of bureaucratic centralism.[213] Workers need to be freed from control by technology and technocracy. This is why it is important to renew Marxism, which can assist in giving power to the powerless workers. But freedom is needed for such renewal. The great difficulty of the contemporary situation is that the desire for such changes is usually squelched by the rivalry between the U.S.A. and the Soviet Union, in which these two powers want all the others to take sides. A third way is needed. The Czechoslovak tragedy was that this alternative was not allowed.[214]

Jiřína Siklová compared the East and West European student movements. She pointed out that the radical left of Western Europe evoked only amused curiosity from students in Czechoslovakia. Rejection of being manipulated by the press was the only area of agreement. The revolutionary posture of Western European students was not appreciated, and conversations between these two groups of students usually ended in a lack of understanding.[215] After the Soviet invasion the Czechoslovak students became completely demoralized and unwilling to participate in social processes. Their disillusionment made them skeptical of all politics. They see only the contrast between the high ideals of Marxism and the manipulations of state Marxism. Because of this state monopoly, Marx and Marxism became unattractive to students.

Smiljko Sokol of Yugoslavia presented the Yugoslav model of social self-management as the appropriate revolutionary development from the stage of administrative socialism to the stage of democratic, participatory socialism. While the administrative stage of monopolizing power in order to industrialize and avoid counter-revolution was necessary, it is just as necessary to continue the revolutionary process by bringing about a new synthesis of political and economic democracy in the form of workers' self-management.[216]

As I see it, many if not most Eastern European Christians welcomed and supported the Marxist efforts to humanize, liberalize, decentralize, and democratize the socialist revolution. Whether these steps are perceived as the evolving or the revolutionizing of society, they would not greatly animate Christian thinkers. But there is a Christian consensus that such change should take place.

MEANING OF WORK

The philosophy of labor, the discussion of the role of work in human development, plays an important role in the Marxist notion of human origin, identity, and the future. For Christians, work did not assume a concomitant role, yet both in the biblical sources as well as in later theological tradition, for instance in Calvinism, work played an important role. Here, too, is an area of possibly useful interface, which, in fact, has not yet taken place, except to a limited degree in Poland. Two writers in Poland have addressed themselves to the philosophy of work from the perspective of the dialogue. One is the left-wing Roman Catholic Wiesław Mysłek and the other is Józef Wołkowski.[217]

Mysłek observed a transformation of Catholic attitudes or interpretation of work both internationally and in Poland, where already in 1946 Stefan Wyszyński wrote *Duch pracy ludskiej (The Spirit of Human Work)*. Mysłek noted that during the Patristic period Christian writers had a well-balanced view of mental and manual labor, but that during the Scholastic period Thomas Aquinas introduced the notion that manual labor is a means of penance while leisure means happiness. In the recent period the church's doctrine of labor justified capitalism by not perceiving the antagonism between, but only the solidarity of, classes in work and by seeing work as punishment for original sin.[218]

Since the pontificate of John XXIII, a reevaluation of the

doctrine of work has taken place in the context of the total reevaluation of the sociopolitical doctrines of the church. The accuracy of the Marxist analysis of social relations and their concept of work had a great impact on Catholic thinkers. It is Marxism and not other contemporary philosophies which has provided the most important impetus to modern Catholic social thought, according to Mysłek. However, one must cross some psychological barriers to admit to this fact.

The nature and value of work is the foundation of Marxism and can be, as Mysłek saw it, "christened" and adopted by Christianity.[219] Writers such as the Frenchman M. D. Chenu showed respect for the entire Marxist analysis of the role and function of work, as well as the alienation of labor and the reality of class struggle. Chenu's work helps lay the foundation of the Christian-Marxist dialogue on work, and so does Teilhard's and Mounier's. Even papal encyclicals reflect a change in the doctrine of work, although Mysłek did not think that the popes moved sufficiently far in adopting the Marxist theoretical framework for emancipation from exploitation of work. The popes are still too optimistic and solidaristic.[220] Their statements offer a basis for Christian-Marxist dialogue under socialist conditions, but under conditions of capitalism it promotes the church's support of the ruling class.

The main cause of the increased Catholic interest in Marxist-Leninist theory and socialist practice is the Marxist striving for the ennoblement of work. In Polish Catholicism too little attention was given to that aspect until recently.

Wyszyński's *Duch pracy ludskiej* (1946) was ahead of its time in extolling labor as cocreativity with God and using appropriate biblical passages as proof texts of that. He stated that work improves the worker. Yet Wyszyński had too solidaristic and agrarian notions of work which were theologically surpassed by later Polish writers. Rev. J. Kondziela is among those who stress, according to Mysłek, the leading position of the working class and maintains that socialism is a qualitatively different society.[221] Mysłek classified all Catholic writers on that subject into conservatives and realists. The realists are the ones trying to bring the church into line with socioeconomic progress. The church's adaptation to new conditions and its embracing the value of work proved to be helpful in tying it to the Polish working class and in making dialogue with nonbelievers possible.

The vanguard role of the Marxist interpretation of labor must be admitted by Catholics. Detailed analysis will, indeed, show that Catholics borrowed much from Marxists. Catholics must admit to the correctness of the role of work in anthropogenesis, in self-creation, in the depersonalizing or personalizing character of work depending on the context of social relations in which work takes place, and in the liberation of labor by social change.[222] The only critique by Catholics of Marxism is that Marxism may impoverish the personality by negating transcendence.

Thus the polemic with Marxism, according to Mysłek, has shifted entirely to eschatological matters, but in regard to worldly matters there is no room for debate but only a broad dialogue on this issue. Too little has been made of this opportunity. Even within the church the differences in this respect are minor. Kowalczyk, in *Z problematyki dialogu chrześcijańskomarksistowskiego,* pointed out a convergence between Christians and Marxists in regard to the philosophy of work. Both recognize work as essential, recognize its dignity, and oppose alienation of labor.[223] C. S. Bartnik of the Catholic University of Lublin in his work *Teologia pracy ludzkiej (Theology of Human Labor)* also pointed out the dependence of Catholicism upon Marxist insight in respect to alienation of labor and urged mutual enrichment. Mysłek concurred with this direction of the Christian-Marxist dialogue.[224]

Wołkowski pointed out that originally the Marxist and Christian views of labor emerged in totally different philosophical contexts. The former emerged in a dynamic, evolutionary worldview based on nature's and human activity, and the latter in a static worldview based on God's creation. But Christians are increasingly perceiving the anthropogenic role of work which they adopted from Marxism. Humans continue the act of creation through work (self-creation), a view common to both. Christian philosophy still tends to be a philosophy of the contemplating person rather than of the working person who is transforming the world and himself or herself. Here Marxism has more to offer. On the other hand, Marxism tends to be satisfied in raising questions about the already existing nature, while Christianity persistently raises questions about the deepest sources of human beings, even beyond nature. That is Christianity's *forte.*[225]

Wołkowski then analyzed the struggle against alienation of labor especially under socialist circumstances. Even after the liquidation of private property there are still sources of alienation through division of labor and the exchange of goods based on money. These tend to produce a lingering alienation of labor, even in socialism, so that "the basic gain of socialism may sometimes be subjectively unfelt at the place of work." [226]

The division of labor need not be demonized, maintained Wołkowski. Every sort of work can be converted into creative work, work which brings fulfillment of one's own plans. But it is important that a person feel in charge of her or his own destiny. This is why in socialist enterprises it is important to promote coresponsibility in decision making, to welcome initiatives, and in general to promote fulfillment of personal goals, as this will bring about an internalization of labor ethics.

Among Marxists there is discussion about whether work is the supreme human value or whether work is to be subordinated to the needs of fuller human development. Christians, who have persistently promoted the infinite value of personhood, ought to side with those Marxists who see work as a means of personal fulfillment.[227] Christians likewise need to support those Marxists who are trying to invoke social justice against the vestiges of exploitation which continues to exist in socialist societies resulting from the need to improve the level of productivity. The burden of social growth should be equally distributed. Those who are most painfully affected ought to be given recognition for their discomforts. The Christian valuation of each individual is consistent with this goal.

Humanistic values need to be inculcated into people in order to effectively implement the relationship between work and personal development. Here is a distinct possibility and need for Christian-Marxist cooperation. Inducement for work should be humanistic, not egoistic or detrimental to human dignity.[228] Positive attitudes toward work ought to be shaped, consistent with the Christian or Marxist worldview. Dishonesty and unconscientiousness and other negative attitudes toward work ought to be combated by jointly creating a humanistic framework within which individual and societal worth will be related to work.

It seems to me that this instance of the Polish dialogue is a good beginning to a useful interchange which other groups of Marxists and Christians ought to follow up.

Notes

1. Lochman, *Church in a Marxist Society*, p. 172.
2. *Ibid.*, pp. 174-175.

3. Bajsić, Na rubovima crkve i civilizacije, p. 274.

4. Lochman, "On Christian-Marxist Dialogue," in The Christian Century (January 7, 1970), p. 16. The article can be recommended for its perceptive tracing of the processes of dialogue in Czechoslovakia.

5. Vereš, p. 187.

6. Jukić, "Marksizam u jednoj suvremenoj enciklopediji ateizma," in Crkva u svijetu, Vol. 4, Nos. 5-6 (1969), p. 423.

7. Ibid.

8. Franić, pp. 133-144.

9. Szennay, "Der christlich-marxistische Dialog Heute," in IDZ, Vol. 3, No. 1 (1970), p. 87.

10. Ibid., p. 88.

11. Ibid.

12. Ibid., p. 90.

13. Ibid., p. 91.

14. Machovec, AMLJ, p. 27.

15. Ibid.

16. Ibid., p. 31.

17. (Warsaw: PWN, 1977) as reported by H. K. "Humanizm katolicki w oczach marksisty," in Więź (Warsaw), Vol. 21, No. 6 (242) (1978), pp. 112-114.

18. Cserháti, p. 61.

19. Schaff, "Der marxistische Begriff des Menschen," in Christentum und Marxismus Heute, p. 47. Schaff's view of human beings expressed in his book Marksizm a jednostka ludzka will not be discussed here. They predate the dialogue, and are not a conscious attempt to come to grips with Christianity on this issue, as are the views reported here.

20. Ibid., pp. 30-34. It seems that this claim could be one of the useful subjects for dialogue.

21. Ibid., p. 38.

22. Ibid., p. 41. This would seem to be another place for a useful Christian-Marxist interface.

23. Ibid., p. 46.

24. Ibid.

25. Průcha, "Marxismus als Philosophie menschlicher Existenz," in S & F, p. 44.

26. Průcha, "Vom Sinn des praktischen Humanismus," in CHMH, p. 314.

27. Ibid., pp. 315-316.

28. Ibid., p. 325.

29. Průcha, "Marxism as a Philosophy of Human Existence," in The Christian-Marxist Dialogue (ed. by Paul Oestreicher), p. 250.

30. Ibid.

31. Ibid., p. 254.

32. Machovec in "Diskussion," in S & F, p. 146.

33. Machovec, "Kampf um dem wahren Kommunismus," in Evolution oder Revolution der Gesellschaft, p. 187.

34. Ibid., p. 190.

35. Machovec, "Atheismus und Christentum—wechselseitige Herausforderung als Aufgabe," in IDZ, Vol. 1, No. 1 (1968), p. 42.

36. Hromádka, "On the Threshold of a Dialogue," p. 130. Italics are Hromádka's.

37. Ibid.

38. Ibid., p. 131.

39. *Ibid.*, p. 134.
40. *Ibid.*, p. 139.
41. *Ibid.*, pp. 142-143.
42. Lochman, *Church in a Marxist Society*, pp. 174-175.
43. *Ibid.*, p. 178.
44. Lochman, *Encountering Marx*, p. 65.
45. *Ibid.*, p. 74.
46. Fuchs, "Christlicher Glaube—wissenschaftliches Denken—Gesellschaftliche Zielsetzungen," in *Communio Viatorum*, Vol. 2, No. 1 (Spring 1959), pp. 12-13.
47. *Ibid.*, p. 16.
48. Bošnjak and Škvorc, *Marxist i kršćanin*, p. 25.
49. *Ibid.*, p. 27.
50. *Ibid.*, pp. 27-29.
51. *Ibid.*, pp. 35-36.
52. *Ibid.*, p. 101.
53. Bošnjak, "Der Mensch als Mysterium," in *Christliche und marxistische Zukunft*, pp. 138-139.
54. Bošnjak, "Was bedeutet das Dilemma: Jesus—Marx?" p. 105.
55. *Ibid.*, pp. 106-107.
56. Bošnjak, "Nur ein Humanismus für Christen und Marxisten," in *CHMH*, p. 253.
57. Bošnjak, "Die Idee des Humanismus zwischen dem ideologisierten Marxismus und dem politisierten Christentum," in *IDZ*, Vol. 3, No. 1 (1970), pp. 60-61.
58. *Ibid.*, p. 63.
59. *Ibid.*, p. 64.
60. *Ibid.*
61. *Ibid.*, p. 67.
62. *Ibid.*, pp. 68-70.
63. Fiamengo, "Aspekte zu einem universalem Humanismus," in *CHMH*, p. 254.
64. *Ibid.*, p. 263.
65. Kerševan, "Odnos komunista prema religiji," p. 897.
66. *Ibid.*
67. *Ibid.*
68. Franić, p. 240.
69. *Ibid.*, p. 242.
70. *Ibid.*, p. 243.
71. Szigeti, "Marxistische Politik und kommunistischer Humanismus," in *CHMH*, pp. 273-274.
72. *Ibid.*, pp. 276-277.
73. Lukács, "Auf der Suche nach dem Gemeinsamen," in *CHMH*, pp. 265-266.
74. *Ibid.*, p. 268.
75. *Ibid.*, pp. 270-272.
76. Lukács, "Historisches Bewusstsein und Verantwortung," in *S & F*, p. 99.
77. *Ibid.*, transl. by Mojzes.
78. *Ibid.*, p. 100.
79. *Ibid.*, p. 107.
80. *Ibid.*, pp. 107-108.
81. Lochman, *Encountering Marx*, pp. 48-75, and Vereš, pp. 44-144.
82. Vereš, p. 46.

83. *Ibid.*, p. 48.
84. *Ibid.*, p. 78.
85. *Ibid.*, p. 80.
86. *Ibid.*, p. 143.
87. Lochman, *Encountering Marx*, p. 55.
88. *Ibid.*, pp. 56-61.
89. *Ibid.*, p. 64.
90. *Ibid.*, p. 71.
91. *Ibid.*, p. 73.
92. A pseudonym of a Roman Catholic author from Split, Yugoslavia.
93. Marinković, "Marksizam: sistem ili inspiracija?" pp. 406-407.
94. *Ibid.*, pp. 409-411.
95. Wołkowski, "The Philosophy of Work as an Area of Christian-Marxist Dialogue," in *D & H*, Vol. 5, No. 1 (1978), p. 116.
96. *Ibid.*, p. 118.
97. Hromádka, "Christentum und Geschichtlichkeit," in *S & F*, p. 106.
98. *Ibid.*, p. 108.
99. *Ibid.*, p. 109.
100. *Ibid.*, p. 110.
101. Černý, "Der Mensch und die Geschichte," in *S & F*, pp. 73-78.
102. Gardavský, *God Is Not Yet Dead*, pp. 11-14.
103. Machovec, *Vom Sinn des menschlichen Lebens*, p. 28.
104. *Ibid.*, pp. 29 and 27.
105. Bartnik, "Prolegomena to a Discussion on the Meaning of History," in *D & H*, Vol. 6, No. 1 (1979), p. 33.
106. *Ibid.*, pp. 34-35.
107. *Ibid.*, p. 35.
108. *Ibid.*, p. 37.
109. Lukács, "Historisches Bewusstsein und Verantwortung," in *S & F*, pp. 97-98.
110. Cajnkar, "Schöpfertum und Freiheit," in *S & F*, p. 168.
111. *Ibid.*, p. 179.
112. *Ibid.*, p. 171.
113. Makowski, "Kirche und Autonomie der Kultur," in *S & F*, pp. 278-279.
114. *Ibid.*, pp. 282-283.
115. Čvekl, "Marxismus und Freiheit," in *S & F*, p. 284.
116. *Ibid.*, p. 286.
117. *Ibid.*, p. 287.
118. *Ibid.*, pp. 288-289.
119. *Ibid.*, p. 290.
120. Gardavský, *Hoffnung aus der Skepsis*, p. 62.
121. *Ibid.*
122. *Ibid.*, p. 65.
123. Kuczyński, "The Sense of Existence: Creativity and Community," in *D & H*, Vol. 5, No. 3 (1978), pp. 190-193.
124. Stipičić, "Povijesnost kršćanske misli," in *Svesci* (Zagreb), No. 13 (January-March 1969).
125. Lochman, *Encountering Marx*, p. 117.
126. *Ibid.*, p. 122.
127. *Ibid.*, p. 123.
128. *Ibid.*, p. 125.
129. *Ibid.*, p. 128.
130. *Ibid.*, pp. 129-132.

131. Vereš, p. 182.
132. *Ibid.*, p. 184.
133. *Ibid.*, pp. 185-186.
134. Gardavský, *God Is Not Yet Dead*, p. 132.
135. *Ibid.*, p. 135.
136. *Ibid.*, p. 136.
137. Here Gardavský responded to the views of Karl Rahner, S.J., expressed at the 1964 Paulus-Gesellschaft meeting at Salzburg, Austria. The gist of Rahner's views on the future in the context of the Christian-Marxist dialogue can be found in his "Christian Humanism," in *Journal of Ecumenical Studies*, Vol. 4, No. 3 (1967), pp. 369-405.
138. Gardavský, *God Is Not Yet Dead*, p. 145.
139. *Ibid.*, p. 208.
140. Machovec, *AMLJ*, p. 88.
141. *Ibid.*, p. 42.
142. *Ibid.*, p. 193.
143. Vereš, p. 186.
144. Lochman, "On Christian-Marxist Dialogue," pp. 14-15.
145. *Ibid.*, p. 15.
146. *Ibid.*
147. This treatment of Machovec's view on transcendence is based on an unpublished paper by James Stillman, "Milan Machovec: Transcendence as the Life of Dialogue," based mainly on Stillman's interview of Machovec in Prague, June 1972.
148. *Ibid.*
149. *Ibid.*, p. 17.
150. Gardavský, *God Is Not Yet Dead*, p. 210.
151. Garadja, "Transcendentalism and History—A Dialogue Between the Christian Philosophy and the Present Time," in *D & H*, Vol. 5, No. 3 (1978), pp. 137-144.
152. *Ibid.*, p. 141.
153. *Ibid.*, p. 140.
154. Bošnjak and Škvorc, *Marxist i kršćanin*, pp. 39-58.
155. See particularly Hromádka's *The Gospel for Atheists*.
156. Hromádka, *Theology Between Yesterday and Tomorrow*, pp. 82-84.
157. Gardavský, *God Is Not Yet Dead*, p. 157.
158. *Ibid.*, pp. 149-218.
159. *Ibid.*, p. 181.
160. *Ibid.*, p. 191.
161. *Ibid.*, p. 194.
162. *Ibid.*, p. 197.
163. *Ibid.*, pp. 198-199.
164. *Ibid.*, p. 200.
165. *Ibid.*, p. 212.
166. *Ibid.*, p. 217.
167. *Ibid.*
168. Ćimić, *Drama ateizacije*, pp. 197-200.
169. *Ibid.*, pp. 64-67.
170. *Ibid.*, pp. 69-70.
171. *Ibid.*, p. 70.
172. Ćimić, *Čovjek na raskršću*, p. 116.
173. Machovec, *AMLJ*, p. 21.
174. Machovec, "Die Gott-Frage und der moderne Atheismus," in *Gottfrage und moderner Atheismus*, pp. 51-53.

175. *Ibid.*, pp. 58-59.
176. *Ibid.*, pp. 64-65.
177. *Ibid.*, pp. 70-71.
178. Vereš, *Filozofsko-teološki dijalog s Marxom*. Lochman's book *Encountering Marx* was published only in the West.
179. Žilić, "Sukobi u interpretaciji Marxa," in *Jukić*, pp. 79-85.
180. For a first-rate summary of the views of Kołakowski, Gardavský, and Machovec on Jesus, see Thomas Pröpper, *Der Jesus der Philosophen und der Jesus des Glaubens* (Mainz: Matthias-Grünewald-Verlag, 1976), pp. 39-57.
181. Kołakowski, "Jesus Christus—Prophet und Reformator," in *Marxisten und die Sache Jesu*, pp. 67-84.
182. Bošnjak, "Was bedeutet das Dilemma: Jesus-Marx?" in *ibid.*, pp. 103-115.
183. Gardavský, *God Is Not Yet Dead*, p. 36.
184. *Ibid.*, p. 39.
185. *Ibid.*, p. 47.
186. *Ibid.*, p. 49.
187. Machovec, "Die 'Sache' Jesu und marxistische Selbstreflexion," in *Marxisten und die Sache Jesu*, pp. 85-102.
188. According to Pröpper, Machovec's book belongs among the truly creative studies of Jesus regardless of the orientation of the author. Due to its scope *AMLJ* cannot be adequately summarized here. Pröpper, p. 48.
189. Chapter 6 of *AMLJ*, pp. 192-204.
190. *Ibid.*, p. 194.
191. *Ibid.*, p. 199.
192. *Ibid.*, p. 203.
193. *Ibid.*, p. 193.
194. *God Is Not Yet Dead*, pp. 53-99.
195. Both in his aforementioned book *De Dialogo inter Marxistas et Christianos* and "Predrevolucijski Lenjinovi stavovi prema religiji," in *Jukić*, Vol. 1, No. 2, pp. 86-91.
196. An exception to this is the East German theologian Emil Fuchs, *Christliche und marxistische Ethik*, 2 vols. published in 1957 and 1959, but not available to this author.
197. Heller, "Marxistiche Ethik, christliche und gesellschaftliche Revolution," in *IDZ*, Vol. 5, No. 1 (1972), p. 70.
198. *Ibid.*, p. 71.
199. *Ibid.*, p. 73.
200. *Ibid.*, p. 78.
201. Ćimić, *Čovjek na raskršću*, pp. 121, 123.
202. *Ibid.*, p. 123.
203. *Ibid.*, p. 122.
204. *Ibid.*, pp. 129-130.
205. *Ibid.*, p. 127.
206. *Ibid.*, pp. 132-133.
207. Krešić, "The Kingdom of God and Communism," pp. 39-40.
208. *D & H*, Vol. 1, No. 1 (Winter 1974). See also Chapter 3.
209. The extensive personal experience of the author in these symposia made it possible to summarize and evaluate the dialogue on peace directly. The bibliographical information is contained in Chapter 3 under "International Peace Symposia." The speeches upon which this analysis was made are to be found in *Christen und Marxisten im Friedensgespräch* and certain issues of *Peace and the Sciences*.

210. Machovec, "Kampf um den wahren Kommunismus," in *Evolution oder Revolution der Gesellschaft*, p. 186.

211. *Ibid.*, p. 190.

212. Průcha, "Die dritte Alternative," in *ibid.*, p. 179.

213. *Ibid.*, p. 180.

214. *Ibid.*, p. 184.

215. Siklová, " 'Neue Linke' im Osten?" in *ibid.*, p. 130.

216. Sokol, "Die soziale Selbstverwaltung," in *ibid.*, pp. 167-173.

217. Mysłek, "A Turn in the Catholic Interpretation of Work," in *D & H*, Vol. 5, No. 1 (Winter 1978), pp. 79-95.

Wołkowski, "The Philosophy of Work as an Area of Christian-Marxist Dialogue," in *ibid.*, pp. 113-122. No explicit identification and very little internal evidence exist about Wołkowski's orientation. On the basis of internal evidence, it appears that Wołkowski is a Catholic.

218. Mysłek, p. 80.

219. *Ibid.*, p. 83.

220. *Ibid.*, p. 87.

221. *Ibid.*, p. 91.

222. *Ibid.*, p. 94.

223. *Ibid.*

224. *Ibid.*, p. 95.

225. Wołkowski, p. 113.

226. *Ibid.*, pp. 115, 116.

227. *Ibid.*, p. 122.

228. *Ibid.*

8

CONCLUDING REFLECTIONS

Eastern European Christianity and Marxism are full of ambiguities and complexities. Even when taken separately, they are complex movements. Their mutual relationship is likewise so complex that very few generalizations can be made. Even if dialogue is singled out for analysis, as it has been in this book, it is evident that it is not a single relationship, *the* Christian-Marxist dialogue, but rather *many* Christian-Marxist dialogues.

Both Christianity and Marxism are flexible, elastic movements which are able to absorb much that is old and much that is new in the world. This ability to appropriate the best in other traditions (unfortunately, however, not only the best, but sometimes even what is worst) brought forth the dialogue between the two, despite considerable resistance by the exclusivistic, dogmatic power-centers in both movements. For the most part the churches and the Marxist parties in Eastern Europe practice *democratic centralism,* in which the *centralism* is usually more heavily underscored than the *democratic* tendencies. The dialogue itself is an expression of the democratic strivings in both camps and is one of the most democratizing forces at play in the current phase of history. It is not surprising that when the centers feel threatened by too many unsettling, creative, autonomous currents of change, they tend to suppress the dialogue. Hence the dialogue has had a very uneven course since its emergence, experiencing both progress and frustration, affirmation and defeat, growth and hibernation. Despite setbacks, especially in some countries, the dialogue has shown a tenacious ability to be sustained in new forms and even embraced by some who bitterly opposed it. Unfortunately, one has to admit that there are those who formerly practiced and praised dialogue but later saw fit to denounce it.

The dialogue in Eastern Europe has been carried out primarily by intellectuals. That is both its weakness and its strength.

It is a weakness because many prominent people in the party and the church who are not intellectuals in the narrow sense should have been included. And while the few public dialogues showed the enormous interest in this dialogue, it has been artificially prevented from becoming a grassroots movement, mostly due to restrictions by the ruling political party.

It is its strength because intellectuals in Eastern Europe are in a unique situation of responsibility unparalleled by the status of intellectuals in the West, especially in the United States. In the West, partners in dialogue are hardly noticed by the media or general public because Western societies have ceased to fear the power of ideas and, by their indifference, have rendered many ideas powerless. In Eastern Europe top political leaders, sometimes inspired by pathological fear, pay attention to what the intellectuals are saying. Since they have aimed to control ideas fully, they are watchful for any statement that may deviate from their concept of truth. When Marxist and Christian protagonists, after years of dogmatic repression of all intellectual dissent, come with novel interpretations and attitudes, their ideas receive attention far out of proportion to the number of such thinkers. Hence it comes about that dialogue, though promoted by relatively few people (as is evident from the foregoing account), has a significant effect, measurable by the officials' fear that these ideas will have a chance to become even more widely embraced.

Dialogue is a novel relationship between Christians and Marxists, which at this point is not firmly accepted as the preferable mode for dealing with one another, despite the fact that the overall world wide popularity of dialogue has made it mandatory to pay lip service to it even at the highest levels, such as at meetings of the European Communist Parties. With all the advances that dialogues have brought with them, the two communities, by and large, are still not prepared or willing to enter fully into dialogue. Future historians may describe the dialogues to date as tentative probings of new avenues of approach. Perhaps future historians will also be able to say that these probings made it possible for a more massive dialogical encounter between Marxists and Christians. This, at least, is the hope of many who are involved in dialogue. Machovec, for instance, said that the dialogues up till now may be regarded "as the modest beginnings of a radically dialogical future."[1] Genuine widespread dialogue and true pluralism have not yet become reality.

The reason for the emergence of the dialogue is that Christianity and Marxism have some common foes and common tasks. The common foes or common challenges are the widespread indifference, disengagement, fatalism, amorality, social injustices, poverty, suffering, and threats to human survival in the contemporary world. These challenge representatives of both movements to rethink some of the traditional postulates which seem not to have been adequate in dealing with problems. Mutual antagonism has been overshadowed by the more profound antagonisms of the world. It is not surprising that some Marxists and Christians conclude that they can deal with these challenges more effectively when they are joined in dialogue rather than joined in combat with one another.

Among the common tasks are the creation of optimal conditions for the development of individuals and society, conditions characterized by peace, justice, liberty, growth of wholesome personality and human relations, and the ability to deal constructively with those crises that threaten to tear both the social fabric and personal identity. The dialogue in Eastern Europe has touched on nearly all the common human tasks, yet, on the whole, it has not yet reached desirable levels. In that respect we can agree with András Szennay, that the dialogue is still in a beginning phase in which the partners are still primarily interested in exploring one another's ideas and discussing whether and under what conditions they can enter into dialogue.[2]

The more dynamic processes of dialoguing for the sake of the world in pursuit of common tasks have not yet taken place. Whether it is lack of courage, as Szennay suggested,[3] or lack of proper social conditions, or both, is hard to say.

Great strides, however, have been made in the reappraisal of views about each other. The dialogue has produced, as seen in Chapters 5 and 6, very creative reinterpretations of religion and Christianity by leading Marxists and of socialism and Marxism by leading Christians. To this we ought to add the staggering number of interesting explorations of the concept of dialogue which were recorded in Chapters 1 and 4. These will turn out to be among the lasting contributions of the Eastern European dialogue. The issues which were covered in Chapter 7 are of great significance, but, as yet do not equal in scope or depth the aforementioned topics.

Eastern European dialogue is so riddled with problems that one is easily tempted to say that the problems often obscure the achievements. These problems are so great that they tend to dominate the Western observers' perception. In order to neutralize preoccupation with the problems alone, this study has attempted to emphasize the positive achievements and minimize, though not totally neglect, the negative aspects of Eastern European reality which impinge on Christian-Marxist relations. The problems, however, are there.

One problem is that Marxists often claim that they alone, through the insights of Marx, have the correct way of promoting human well-being, while non-Marxists, including Christians, cannot effectively contribute to changing and humanizing society. Christians have a reciprocal tendency to appropriate certain virtues, such as love, forgiveness, mercy, and hope, as if only Christians were capable of experiencing them.

Another difficulty is the unsettled question of authority. The teaching and administrative authority of the church or the Communist Party at this point is capable of countering the faith and convictions of partners in dialogue, proclaiming the views of those in dialogue ungenuine, and punishing them for their statemets and actions.

A third is that the Eastern Europeans, due to historical and political differences, tend not to learn much from one another. An investigation of the source of inspiration of any individual participant in dialogue shows that they get their knowledge and inspiration either from other thinkers in their own country or from the West, but very rarely from another Eastern European source. Westerners know more about dialogue over the whole territory of Eastern Europe, and vice versa, than protagonists from one Eastern European country tend to know about another.

A fourth is the temptation to abandon dialogue in favor of

a policy of concordats, negotiation, and practical cooperation, agreeing to leave theoretical questions aside. The Vatican's East European policy is merely one illustration of this temptation, which abounds and actually dominates in many Eastern European countries.

Perhaps the most staggering and unexpected conclusion which was reached was the impact of nationalism on the Christian-Marxist dialogue. Both Christianity and Marxism claim universality and internationalism, but in practice they have not yet resolved their relationship with nationalism. My assumption before undertaking this research was that the primary stimuli for dialogue were factors inherent in each of these two universal movements as well as the historical fact of existing in the same territory. But again and again representatives of Marxism and Christianity turned primarily, and sometimes exclusively, to their counterparts belonging to the *same* nation.

Even more significantly, the appeal or the motive for dialogues and cooperation was the well-being, not of humanity, but of the nation: Polish Marxists appeal to Polish Christians to dialogue for the sake of Poland. Hungarian Christians sought dialogue with Hungarian Marxists for the sake of the Hungarian nation. Czechs, who made up the preponderate element in dialogue (Slovaks were rarely prominent in it) underlined the specificates of the Czech national and religious heritage, and this element strongly colored their approach to one another. One of the reasons that dialogue in Yugoslavia became muffled after 1972 was that many perceived it as a strengthening of Croatian nationalism, as it was mostly Croatian Catholics and Croatian Marxists who figured prominently in those exchanges. The Russian Orthodox Christians invoke the love of motherland as a rationale for cooperation with Marxists. And so forth. Thus it is obvious that nationalism, especially threatened nationalism, is conducive to dialogue between Christians and Marxists of the same nation despite their bitter animosities.

A disturbing question is thus raised for both Christians and Marxists as to whether nationalism may not be a stronger divisive force or bond between people than either Marxism or Christianity. Eastern European religious life was organized primarily along national lines, even in the case of such universalistic churches as the Roman Catholic. Polycentrism among European Communists similarly shows the power of nationalism in interpretations of Marxism. A disturbing question arises: is the ultimate allegiance of many Eastern Europeans to their nation rather than to their God or to their ideology? This is something Eastern European Marxists and Christians may do well to ponder. These two are the largest and most influential groups with specific commitments. If they cannot impose limits on national chauvinism, it is likely that no one can.

Marxists in Eastern Europe have relatively clearly delineated tasks. Since the Marxists are in power, they have the urgent task of actualizing Marxist theories under less than perfect circumstances. The Christians in Eastern Europe, apart from the instinct for survival, do not have as clear a task. They are aware that they have much to offer to solve the world's problems, perhaps as much as the Marxists, though they do not have the same prestigious position in society. They need to escape the Scylla of dogma and outlived responses and the Charybdis of aping Marxist solutions. Christians need to seek their own unique, creative approaches to problems. Since salvation and God's reign are to take place even now (though more fully beyond history), the Christian faith demands that love, righteousness, and peace are to be the social practice of today. Salvation does have a sociopolitical dimension. Christians do not agree in their assessment as to what is necessary and where it is to be applied. Christians come from different strata of the population, from different nations. Yet somehow in God's providential care the whole process, including conflicts among Christians as to how to proceed, is leading to a fuller oneness with God. Out of that conviction Christians should not absolutize antagonisms (including class, national, and racial antagonisms) but keep paving the way for reconciliation. In this effort they are duty bound to share concerns and actions with all those who share their humanistic concerns. Among those are the humanistically oriented Marxists.

The path may be the same. We may even walk it together. But each person walks it in her or his own way. The mutual encouragement in the long and arduous path makes the task more pleasant and more endurable. It may well be the only way that either will reach the destination. It is clear that both Christians and Marxists feel that they can walk it alone and that they can reach their destination. But under present circumstances to walk it alone would mean that the two are walking alongside but unwilling to talk to each other. Silence of this kind should not prevail. The impulse to communicate, which is so typical of the human species, will undoubtedly carry the victory. Christians and Marxists have been, are, and will be in dialogue.

Notes

1. Machovec, *AMLJ*, p. 38.
2. Szennay, "Der christlich-marxistische Dialog heute," pp. 84-86.
3. *Ibid.*, p. 92.

Index